BEYOND THE ALGORITHM

In *Beyond the Algorithm: Qualitative Insights for Gig Work Regulation,* Deepa Das Acevedo and a collection of scholars and experts show why government actors must go beyond mass surveys and data-scrubbing in order to truly understand the realities of gig work. The contributors draw on qualitative empirical research to reveal the narratives and real-life experiences that define gig work, and they connect these insights to policy debates being fought out in courts, town halls, and even in Congress itself. The book also bridges academic and nonacademic worlds by drawing on the experiences of drivers, journalists, and workers' advocates who were among the first people to study gig work from the bottom up. This book is a must-read for anyone interested in gig work, the legal infrastructure surrounding it, and how that infrastructure can and must be improved.

Deepa Das Acevedo is a legal anthropologist and an assistant professor of law at the University of Alabama. Her scholarship draws on original fieldwork among gig workers, policymakers, and workers' advocates, and has been published in several law reviews. She cochairs the Collaborative Research Network on Labor Rights of the Law and Society Association and chairs the Section on Law and Anthropology of the American Association of Law Schools.

Beyond the Algorithm

QUALITATIVE INSIGHTS FOR GIG WORK REGULATION

Edited by

DEEPA DAS ACEVEDO

University of Alabama School of Law

CAMBRIDGE
UNIVERSITY PRESS

CAMBRIDGE
UNIVERSITY PRESS

University Printing House, Cambridge CB2 8BS United Kingdom

One Liberty Plaza, 20th Floor, New York, NY 10006, USA

477 Williamstown Road, Port Melbourne, VIC 3207, Australia

314–321, 3rd Floor, Plot 3, Splendor Forum, Jasola District Centre, New Delhi – 110025, India

79 Anson Road, #06–04/06, Singapore 079906

Cambridge University Press is part of the University of Cambridge.

It furthers the University's mission by disseminating knowledge in the pursuit of education, learning, and research at the highest international levels of excellence.

www.cambridge.org
Information on this title: www.cambridge.org/9781108487764
DOI: 10.1017/9781108767910

First published 2021

A catalogue record for this publication is available from the British Library.

Library of Congress Cataloging-in-Publication Data
NAMES: Acevedo, Deepa das, 1984– editor.
TITLE: Beyond the algorithm : qualitative insights for gig work regulation/ edited by Deepa das Acevedo, University of Alabama School of Law.
DESCRIPTION: Cambridge, United Kingdom ; New York, NY : Cambridge University Press, 2020. | Includes index.
IDENTIFIERS: LCCN 2020021128 (print) | LCCN 2020021129 (ebook) | ISBN 9781108487764 (hardback) | ISBN 9781108767910 (ebook)
SUBJECTS: LCSH: Labor laws and legislation. | Precarious employment – Law and legislation. | Temporary employment – Law and legislation. | Independent contractors – Legal status, laws, etc. | Self-employed – Legal status, laws, etc. | Sharing – Economic aspects.
CLASSIFICATION: LCC K1816 .B49 2020 (print) | LCC K1816 (ebook) | DDC 344.01/25729–dc23
LC record available at https://lccn.loc.gov/2020021128
LC ebook record available at https://lccn.loc.gov/2020021129

ISBN 978-1-108-48776-4 Hardback

Contents

Figures

Tables

Foreword

Catherine L. Fisk

"Gig work" and the "gig economy" are among the most overused terms and the least understood phenomena in the contemporary policy landscape. And, as one chapter in this book astutely observes, they are among the most hyped, in ways that have influenced the development of the industry and policymaking about it. Beyond the well-known app-based or web-based markets for services like Uber, Lyft, Taskrabbit, and so forth, there lies a huge, ill-defined, and (to some) confusing welter of companies that provide services to consumers through the labor of people who contract with the company on terms that have become quite controversial. And even as to the most familiar of the companies – the ride-hailing and delivery service companies like Uber, Lyft, and Postmates – there is an interesting combination of familiarity (many love the convenience of summoning a ride or food delivery with a few taps on a smartphone) and mystery (do the drivers earn a fair or adequate income? If not, what can be done?). This timely, creative, and ambitious book aims to shed light on the work of the gig economy, on what we know and don't know about the work, and about how law does and should regulate working conditions in this segment of the economy.

The question of whether or which minimum labor standards laws should govern gig economy work has been controversial for years, and especially since California adopted the so-called ABC test for distinguishing employees, who are entitled to the protections of minimum labor standards laws, from independent contractors, who are not.[1] California companies must comply with all minimum labor standards laws unless their workers are (1) free from the company's control in performing the work; (2) the work is outside the usual course of the company's business; and (3) the worker is customarily engaged in an independent occupation of the same nature as that involved in the work performed.[2] Litigation and the media frenzy surrounding the new law portray sharp differences of opinion – and no agreement on the facts –

[1] California first adopted the ABC test in a 2018 court decision Dynamex Operations West, Inc. v. Superior Court, 4 Cal. 5th 903 (2018), and then codified and extended it through legislation effective January 1, 2020, Cal. Lab. Code § 2750.3.

[2] Cal. Lab. Code § 2750.3.

regarding whether workers and companies benefit from treating workers as employees. Will the new law eliminate the schedule flexibility that workers desire? Will it destroy the app-based business model? Into this fog of partisan rancor and disagreement about the facts, the chapters of this book shine clear light.

As the California legislature debated the legislation adopting the ABC test, unions, worker advocates, and some large app-based service companies negotiated behind the scenes to carve out a partial exemption from the new law for companies that recognized a union for their workers.[3] Among the questions in those negotiations were fundamental issues of worker preference and policy design. Do app-based drivers want a union? What should a union bargain over, and how would it get leverage to improve wages, benefits, and other working conditions through negotiation? What legal protections should or can a state grant to a union for independent contractors, given that business groups have staunchly insisted in litigation elsewhere that collective bargaining by independent contractors violates antitrust law? This book provides creative, rigorous, valuable empirical research to address these questions.

The issues discussed in this book are both new and old. They are new in the sense that technology has enabled companies to coordinate (or, as critics might say, control) a vast workforce with great ease, and to ensure good customer service while paying the lowest wages necessary to induce workers to work. Thus the "gig economy" has the veneer of innovation and disruption (as Silicon Valley boosters love to say). But short-term or episodic work is as old as modern capitalism. In the early twentieth century, when labor had pushed states to adopt laws providing for minimum wages and social welfare protections funded by payroll taxes, companies figured out that they could lower wages and avoid payroll taxes by treating their workers as independent contractors (or, as they were called in those days, peddlers). So bakeries, dairies, and other companies fired all the drivers they had employed to deliver their goods to stores and sold their fleets of trucks to the drivers who then set themselves up as peddlers.[4] Something similar happened in the entertainment industry in the late 1940s, when movie studios, faced with declining movie attendance, revamped their business model to transform their stables of writers, directors, actors, and tech people into short-term contractors.[5]

Whether in trucking, entertainment, construction, or many other sectors, the workers who fared best in gig work were those who figured out how to negotiate

[3] Kate Conger & Noam Scheiber, *California Labor Bill, Near Passage, Is Blow to Uber and Lyft*, N.Y. Times (Sept. 9, 2019).

[4] *See Bakery Drivers Local 802 v. Wohl*, 315 U.S. 769, 770 (1942) (accepting trial court finding that after the Social Security Act and New York unemployment compensation act imposed payroll taxes, the number of independent contractors among bakery delivery drivers in New York City increased from less than 50 to over 500 as bakeries fired drivers and sold their trucks to them for nominal amounts and continued to contract with them to deliver goods).

[5] Catherine L. Fisk, *Hollywood Writers and the Gig Economy*, 2017 U. Chi. Leg. F. 177.

collectively for pay and benefits. Hollywood, for example, has been a gig economy for half a century, and the guilds and unions that represent workers negotiate on a sectoral basis for pay and portable benefits to enable workers to survive (and, in some cases, to thrive) in an industry characterized by unpredictable short-term employment punctuated by periods of unemployment.[6] The employee–independent contractor distinction for truckers did not matter (much) when the Teamsters Union was strong.[7] Unionized construction work has enabled workers to control the job-matching process (through hiring halls), to train new workers (though apprenticeship programs), to monitor safety (through union trainings and contractual protections), and to have portable benefits. Scholars and journalists have documented the strengths and weaknesses of these regimes and, especially, the extent of, the reasons for, and the impact of their decline.[8] What policymakers, scholars, students, and activists need to know, however, is how to build something new in gig work as it exists today. The need for a new approach has become even more acute as the coronavirus pandemic and unemployment levels reaching levels not seen since the Great Depression have revealed the devastating economic and health consequences of the gig economy's massive shift of risk from enterprises to workers.

This book provides important insights into that question through its thought-provoking combination of empirical and legal analyses by academics and observers or participants in the gig economy. It provides a window into what Uber drivers think about their working conditions, what they want from law and from a union, and how Uber's End User License Agreement (the contract between drivers and the company) in combination with Uber's algorithmic management undermines driver independence. It fills a huge gap in the literature about how care workers find jobs on technology platforms. It provides data and analysis to inform tax policy for gig work, transportation planning for local governments, and to explain why workers get (and feel) "stuck" in app-based gig work even though they started it only as a stopgap. As Harry Campbell (an Uber driver, former aerospace engineer, and author) observes in his chapter, it is extremely "important for regulators to listen to, and understand the lives of the rideshare drivers they are trying to regulate." Indeed it is. This book does a huge service by helping all of us who read it to understand a bit about the work lives of the people who comprise the gig economy.

6 *See id.*

7 Steve Viscelli, The Big Rig: Trucking and the Decline of the American Dream (2016).

8 *See, e.g.*, Jake Rosenfeld, What Unions No Longer Do (2014).

Acknowledgments

This book, like the genre of labor exchange it explores, came into being in remarkably little time. The original invitations were sent out around October 2018, the publication agreement was signed in January 2019, draft chapters were circulated in July, and the final manuscript was assembled in November of that year. While that pace certainly indicates the pent up need for this type of interdisciplinary conversation about gig work regulation, it also reflects the combined efforts and enthusiasm of many individuals.

The project would not have gotten off the ground without the encouragement of my colleague at Alabama Law, Ron Krotoszynski. Ron was willing to entertain my spur-of-the-moment thinking about how to bridge disciplinary divides in the study of gig work, he was a fantastic resource throughout the publication process, and – perhaps most importantly – he introduced me to Matt Gallaway at Cambridge University Press. Matt, in turn, was willing to engage with a nontraditional book proposal from a junior scholar, and to move the project through the review process in an admirably timely way. He, along with a fantastic editing and production team, made it possible for this project to continue on schedule despite the complications of the COVID-19 pandemic. At Alabama Law, I also benefited from Dan Joyner's careful advice, Gabriell Jeffrey's superb research assistance, library help from Penny Gibson, and all-round administrative and technical support from Erica Nicholson, who made it possible for me to finish this project while on maternity leave.

Most of all, of course, I am grateful to the contributors themselves. I am thrilled to be able to include each one of them in this volume because, collectively, they represent almost the entire corpus of qualitative research on gig work. Moreover, participating in this project was an intellectually demanding exercise: it required the social scientists to address themselves to a normatively inclined audience, asked the legal scholars to think creatively about the nature and value of qualitative research, and pushed nonacademics to view their everyday activities as a kind of "research" and to translate them accordingly. Each of the contributors also read and commented on someone else's chapter in order to facilitate the volume's goal of being intelligible across disciplinary and professional boundaries, and they had to do all this – write, read, comment, and revise – in less than ten months. As if all of this were not enough, three of the contributors gave birth in that ten-month period. I am not sure I can adequately thank all of them for including this project in their already busy schedules.

Lastly, as always, I owe thanks to my family for their support: to my husband, John, who did not flinch at the onset of yet another project; to my mother, Mallika, who kept me fed and happy as I wrote parts of it; and to my son, Ananth, who made his appearance while this volume was being assembled and who consequently spent his first few weeks competing with it for my attention.

Introduction

Deepa Das Acevedo

This book, although it may appear to be a single book, is in fact two. On the one hand, this is a book about labor exchange in the gig economy masquerading as a book about the value of qualitative empirical data for law and policy development. On the other hand, this is also a book about the value of qualitative empirical data masquerading as a book about the buying, selling, and performance of labor via gig companies like Uber and Airbnb. Since a reader may find it difficult to tell which of these two she is reading at any given moment this introduction will sketch the contours and purpose of each book.

GIG WORK

As a book about labor exchange in the gig economy this volume dives deeply into what is, in many ways, *the* hot-button work law issue of the day. The gig economy has generated immense popular interest in labor conditions – no mean feat in an era of decreasing unionization and growing corporate power – as much as it has commanded attention from policymakers and scholars. In many ways this appeal is unsurprising given the aura of innovation and entrepreneurship that surrounds the gig economy, the way it reflects broader trends toward micro- and on-demand transactions, and its incorporation of widely accessible technology. Within weeks of the 2020 shutdowns triggered by the COVID-19 pandemic, it became clear that the simple acts of providing transportation or delivering meals had become "essential labor" in most countries, and that these tasks were largely undertaken by gig workers. At the same time, many commentators are arguing that key aspects of the gig business model simply replicate strategies used by a variety of employers well before Uber became a household name. The empirical insights contained in this volume speak to both this sense of newness and this sense of familiarity in the course of serving three broad purposes.

Most obviously – but perhaps also most importantly – this volume provides substantive empirical information about gig work across multiple industries. What are the conditions under which gig workers work? How exactly does the tripartite relationship between consumer, provider, and company operate? While such foundational information is in far greater supply today than it was just a few years ago when many of the contributors to this volume first began studying gig work, the gig economy is still new enough, and *secretive* enough, that answers to these kinds of questions are still well worth gathering. This is all the more true given the rapid pace at which the companies themselves have evolved and the worries they generate have changed. In the "early" days of the gig economy, one of the most common concerns voiced with regard to transportation companies like Uber was that they compromised consumer safety, while one of Uber's most widely criticized practices was its refusal to facilitate a tipping mechanism within its smartphone app. Today, the overwhelming worry associated with transportation companies (as with the gig economy more broadly) is worker welfare. Similarly, tipping is no longer a dominant concern since Lyft has allowed it since 2012 and Uber has allowed it since 2017.[1] Gig worker concerns, as the coronavirus pandemic made clear, are worker concerns – even if the mechanisms and dynamics under which they operate are somewhat different.

Secondly, this volume provides insights as to how gig workers experience, engage with, or think about the regulatory infrastructures that apply to them. This type of insight matters inasmuch as labor and employment law is concerned with creating conduct rules for lay actors – yet, remarkably, there is little empirical information about how the realities of gig work intersect with the legal rules meant to govern it. The same type of insight also serves to bridge two immensely interesting and quickly expanding literatures that, as yet, have had unfortunately little crossover impact. Over the last few years, scholars in anthropology, sociology, communication studies, and information technology have conducted a wide range of qualitative empirical studies on gig labor that do not address law and policy concerns despite widespread interest and the relatively urgent need for regulatory action. Meanwhile, legal scholars interested in devising better oversight mechanisms for gig work have accessed comparatively little of the qualitative research that is currently available in these social science literatures and that could provide valuable insights for normative scholarship. The chapters that follow bridge these two literatures both directly, in that they bring the contributors' own qualitative research to bear on gig work regulation, and indirectly, by drawing on and combining the insights of the contributors' disciplines.

Finally, this volume offers decisionmakers who are interested in learning more about gig work a sense of what information to look for and where to look for it. The state legislators, municipal officials, judges, and labor board members who, in the absence of any federal legislation, must devise regulations for gig work are left to do

[1] Kari Paul, *Uber Allows Tipping in 121 Cities – Here's How Much You Should Tip Your Driver*, MarketWatch, July 8, 2017, www.marketwatch.com/story/this-is-exactly-how-much-you-should-tip-your-uber-driver-2017–04-18.

so without much empirical knowledge to draw on.[2] What information they do have largely comes from the experiences of peer regulators elsewhere (who are necessarily facing *other* circumstances), from journalistic accounts (operating under *other* incentives), from scholarship (frequently facing the *same* limitations), and from their own intuition about how things ought to be. Confusion and dissatisfaction have been the overwhelming result of this makeshift approach. In contrast, the kind of granular empirical information produced by the contributors to this volume can help regulators understand the mechanics and the dynamics of the relationships they are trying to govern.

This is perhaps the ideal time to empirically study the relationship between gig work and regulatory practices. Many jurisdictions now feature some legal infrastructure, whether judicial or administrative, that gig companies and workers must engage with. Influential states like California and New York are beginning to develop more substantive legislation to address labor exchange in the gig economy – legislation that is likely to inspire or simply be duplicated by regulations elsewhere.[3] The COVID-19 pandemic will arguably have accelerated this process, inasmuch as, for the first time, many categories of gig workers were included alongside conventional workers in legislation providing job-related benefits or defining "essential labor." Nevertheless, even in those jurisdictions that feature the thickest web of regulations, there is hardly anything amounting to consensus or stability regarding how gig work ought to be governed. In other words, we are now at that rare moment where it is both possible and useful to improve our understanding about how law and society – in this case, work law and gig workers – interact.

QUALITATIVE RESEARCH

As promised, this is also a book about highlighting the value of qualitative empirical data for law and policy development. Thanks in part to the rise of law and economics, interdisciplinary legal conversations have been largely dominated by quantitative research methods. Qualitative research – the kind of research that involves interviews, informal conversations, and participant observation, usually as part of a mixed-methods approach along with other techniques like archival research or content analysis – has been significantly less prominent. This book is not concerned with changing that. What it is concerned with, however, is showcasing the types of insights that are uniquely accessible to individuals using qualitative research techniques, as well as demonstrating why those insights, like the insights produced by quantitative studies, can be useful to legal scholars and decisionmakers.

[2] As Chapter 1 recounts, there have been some efforts to regulate gig work at the federal level, most notably separate bills developed by Senator John Thune and Senator Mark Warner, but these have not progressed beyond the committee level.

[3] *See* Chapter 1 (discussing AB5 in California and the Dependent Workers Act in New York).

To begin with, qualitative research can produce extremely granular information. Quantitative sources like data sets and mass surveys, on the other hand, give sky view insights. Put differently, the one more reliably offers depth over breadth while the other more reliably offers breadth over depth. While the generalizable conclusions usually enabled by quantitative research are both valuable and appealing in a law and policy context (since regulations are developed for the many rather than for the few), it would nonetheless be a mistake to conclude that granular qualitative insights are of no use to legal scholars and decisionmakers. One of the earliest studies of Uber and Lyft explained the mechanics of surge pricing from the drivers' perspective using largely qualitative methods and by reproducing individual smartphone screenshots showing the companies' efforts to shape driver behavior.[4] Neither of these types of information would surface in large-scale quantitative studies, yet both have been instrumental in shaping scholars' and decisionmakers' thinking about how much control these transportation companies exert over drivers and, consequently, whether they should be treated as the drivers' employers.

Second, qualitative research can more easily allow researchers to explore how people make sense of the world around them – and, which is more immediately relevant for law and policy folk – how they make sense of the legal infrastructures with which they are constantly interacting. This is perhaps best understood as the ability to answer the "why" question: *why* do people think as they do, *why* do they behave in ways that do not reflect what they consciously think, *why* do they seem to think and behave differently than we, as outsiders, might expect, and so on.[5] Quantitative research can sometimes capture parts of this puzzle because it can, in select instances, tell us whether there is a distinction between what people do or say and what they *say* they do or say; for instance, it can reveal whether Airbnb hosts discriminate against Black customers despite claiming to do otherwise.[6] But in circumstances where there is no alternate source against which peoples' statements can be measured – that is, where there is no data set to analyze and no website to mine – then even this cannot be done through purely quantitative methods. Municipal officials, for example, are unlikely to admit that their gig work policies are based more on journalistic accounts than on locally relevant data, but this is

4 Alex Rosenblat & Luke Stark, *Algorithmic Labor and Information Asymmetries: A Case Study of Uber's Drivers*, 10 Int'l J. Comm. 3758 (2016).

5 For examples of relevant ethnographically informed scholarship answering these kinds of questions, see Deepa Das Acevedo, *Unbundling Freedom in the Sharing Economy*, 91 S. Cal. L. Rev. 793 (2018) (exploring why the "control test" has proven both appealing and dissatisfying to scholars, decisionmakers, and even workers themselves) and V. B. Dubal, *Wage Slave or Entrepreneur? Contesting the Dualism of Legal Worker Identities*, 105 Cal. L. Rev. 65 (2017)(exploring why Bay Area taxi drivers disagreed on the value of employee classification).

6 Benjamin Edelman, Michael Luca, Dan Svirsky, *Racial Discrimination in the Sharing Economy: Evidence from a Field Experiment*, 9 Am. Econ. J. Applied Econ. 1 (2017). There is also an earlier study suggesting that non-Black hosts charge a higher amount for equivalent rentals. Benjamin Edelman & Michael Luca, *Digital Discrimination: The Case of Airbnb.com* (Harv. Bus. Sch., Working Paper No. 14–054, 2014).

nonetheless true in many cases simply because data on gig work is notoriously difficult and expensive to come by.[7] Not only is it difficult to prove, quantitatively, that officials do not rely on data in formulating their policies, it is virtually impossible to explain *why* – or, for that matter, to understand how they *actually* go about creating policy – without the participant observation and repeated conversations that are the stock-in-trade of qualitative research.

All of this is to say that qualitative research can often reveal substantive insights about the everyday workings of the law that are *inherently invisible* to quantitative methods. Moreover, while these substantive insights are valuable in themselves, they can also give rise to theoretical and doctrinal advancements that would not otherwise be possible. It is no coincidence that "invisible work" and "emotional labor," qualitatively derived concepts that add nuance and accuracy to our understanding of the phenomena being regulated by law, were developed by sociologists.[8]

However, in addition to shedding light on practices and dynamics that are *inherently* invisible to quantitative forms of data collection, qualitative research can also help open up spaces that are *temporarily* beyond the reach of quantitative study. Again, the gig economy is an excellent example: corporate secrecy and isolating working conditions mean that large-scale, data-set driven information about gig work has been hard to gather. This is slowly starting to change as companies create measurable impacts on third parties (like banks),[9] as they become publicly traded (and make necessary disclosures), and as researchers become more adept at extracting information from platforms and websites. But for several years, individuals who wanted to study gig work were obliged to rely on company-packaged information, independently collected qualitative information (usually compiled by journalists), or little empirical information altogether.[10] Interest in and concern about the gig economy, though, waited for no one.

Now is an especially good time to reevaluate and reiterate the value of qualitative empirical research to law and policy conversations. The recent reemergence of sociological ethnography within interdisciplinary legal scholarship has meant that

7 See Chapters 7 and 8 of this volume.

8 Arlene Kaplan Daniels, *Invisible Work.*, 34 Soc. Problems 403 (1987); Arlie Russell Hochschild, The Managed Heart: Commercialization of Human Feeling (3rd ed. 2012) (developing the concept of "emotional labor").

9 *See, e.g.*, J. P. Morgan Chase, Paychecks, Paydays, and the Online Platform Economy: Big Data on Income Volatility (Feb. 2016) (on file with author).

10 Perhaps the most well-known example of gig work researchers using company-packaged information is a 2018 paper by Hall and Krueger. Jonathan V. Hall & Alan B. Krueger, *An Analysis of the Labor Market for Uber's Driver-Partners in the United States*, 71 Indus. Labor Relations Rev. 705 (2018) (describing the results of a study conducted by an employee of Uber and an academic economist who was employed as a consultant for Uber at the time of the study, using information obtained from Uber). *See also* Janine Berg and Hannah Johnston, *Too Good to Be True? A Comment on Hall and Kruger's Analysis of the Labor Market for Uber's Driver-Partners*, 72 Indus. Labor Relations Rev. 39 (2019) (critiquing the underlying data used by Hall and Krueger as well as their interpretation of that data).

there is both greater interest in and confusion about what good qualitative research is *and* what good qualitative research can do for law.[11] On the former point, contributors to this volume demonstrate that innovative and insightful qualitative research takes diverse methodological and theoretical forms. On the latter, this volume offers a range of examples, from critiques of how work law imagines worker subjectivities to proposals for regulatory reform, in the hope that legal scholars and decisionmakers can see for themselves how qualitatively grounded insights can contribute to the task of regulating gig work.

CROSSING THE ACADEMIC BRIDGE

This book has a third goal, one born of necessity as much as design, and that is linking academic experts who have used qualitative methods to learn about gig work regulation with nonacademic researchers who have done likewise. Much of the earliest empirical information about the gig economy came from journalists and policy analysts who did the difficult and time-consuming labor of conducting interviews and engaging in participant observation before qualitatively minded academics joined in the effort.[12] Consequently, many of the legal and policy positions that scholars and decisionmakers have developed over the last decade, as well as many of the arguments they continue to make, are built on these foundational studies by various nonacademic industry experts. Although every edited volume is only a partial reflection of its topic, to exclude industry experts altogether from a book about qualitative insights for gig work regulation would be to grossly misrepresent the range and origins of those insights.

This is not to say that there are *no* differences between the approaches taken by academic contributors and those taken by industry experts. Qualitative empirical research done within a university context is almost always preplanned, financially funded, and subject to highly formalized disciplinary practices as well as ethics constraints that are overseen by institutional review boards. By contrast, the information collected by this volume's nonacademic contributors is largely acquired in the course of performing other tasks – developing policy reports, advising gig workers, or

[11] For just one example of sociological research that has inspired both great interest and critical debate among legal scholars, *see* ALICE GOFFMAN, ON THE RUN: FUGITIVE LIFE IN AN AMERICAN CITY (2014) (based on the author's six year study of policing in an African-American neighborhood of Philadelphia). See also STEVEN LUBET, INTERROGATING ETHNOGRAPHY: WHY EVIDENCE MATTERS (2017) (critiquing certain practices in sociological ethnography).

[12] The following is a decidedly incomplete list of these early journalistic studies: Josh Dzieza, *The Rating Game: How Uber and Its Peers Turned Us into Horrible Bosses*, THE VERGE, Oct. 28, 2015, www.theverge.com/2015/10/28/9625968/rating-system-on-demand-economy-uber-olive-garden; Emily Guendelsberger, *I Was an Undercover Uber Driver*, CITYPAPER, May 7, 2015 (on file with author); Sarah Kessler, *Pixel and Dimed: On (Not) Getting By in the Gig Economy*, FAST COMPANY, Mar. 18, 2014, www.fastcompany.com/3027355/pixel-and-dimed-on-not-getting-by-in-the-gig-economy.

reporting on the gig economy for the news media. As such, it is subject to different and more varied imperatives.

Likewise, nonacademic writers are rarely bound by the conventions that govern scholarly writing – the citations, literature reviews, methods sections, and prose styles that, although they vary considerably from discipline to discipline, are still commonly and recognizably "academic." As a result, nonacademic writing is often remarkable for its liveliness, brevity, and skill at translating unfamiliar concepts to lay readers. The industry experts who have contributed to this volume take an intermediate approach by retaining the style and concision of their usual writing but including some citations for facts not established by their own work as well as some methodological explanation as to how they arrived by their insights. In order to acknowledge these differences, their chapters appear together, as Part II of the volume, following the chapters written by academic contributors.

SCOPE AND TERMINOLOGY

Nearly ten years in, two boundary-drawing challenges underlie virtually all commentary on the gig economy: determining what exactly is meant by the "gig economy" and identifying the proper terminology with which to reference it. Some of the earliest scholarship in this area was specifically concerned with establishing the field of debate by developing taxonomies and terms, but these efforts appear to have been more successful at identifying gig work than at naming it.[13] Now, many participants in this conversation operate on a shared sense that, when it comes to gig work, they too "know it when [they] see it"[14] – and, for the most part, their approach has worked well enough. Like the contributors to this volume, who did not explicitly agree on a definition or a term, most commentators have focused their attention on companies that share two characteristics: they *participate* in the transactions they give rise to between third parties, and they (albeit to varying degrees) *substitute* themselves for governmental safeguards that would otherwise apply to those transactions.[15] (To be sure, gig companies contest both these descriptions of what they do.) Additionally, most gig companies use some forms of advanced technology – "algorithmic management"[16] mechanisms and smartphone applications are the most common – to facilitate the transactions they generate.

[13] *See, e.g.*, Deepa Das Acevedo, *Regulating Employment Relationships in the Sharing Economy*, 20 Emp. Rts & Emp. Pol'y J. 1 (2016); Valerio De Stefano, *The Rise of the "Just-in-Time Workforce": On-Demand Work, Crowdwork, and Labor Protection in the "Gig-Economy,"* 37 Comp. Lab. L. & Pol'y 471 (2015–16); Orly Lobel, *The Law of the Platform*, 101 Minn. L. Rev. 87 (2016–17).

[14] The original phrase – "I know it when I see it" – was written by Justice Potter Stewart with reference to pornography in 1964. Jacobellis v. Ohio, 378 U.S. 184, 197 (1964).

[15] This definition is taken from Das Acevedo, *supra* note 13, at 9–11.

[16] Min Kyung Lee et al., *Working with Machines: The Impact of Algorithmic and Data-Driven Management on Human Workers*, Proc. 33rd Ann. ACM Conf. Human Factors Comput. Sys. 1603–1612 (2015).

Not all companies that seem to use technology to change the means or ends of consumer behavior meet these criteria.[17] Some of the more well-known entities that might appear to belong in any discussion of gig work do not generate financial transactions at all; rather, the exchanges they give rise to are merely swapping exercises in which the company (often a nonprofit) acts as an online bulletin board. Couchsurfer, for instance, does not shape interactions between individuals wanting a place to stay during their travels and individuals wanting to host travelers. Similarly, not all companies that promote on-demand, micro-consumption actually generate "peer to peer" transactions between two third parties – many are business-to -consumer entities much like conventional brick-and-mortar stores. ZipCar, which rents cars in increments of thirty minutes or more (and is in fact owned by the legacy rental company, Avis), exemplifies this type.

In contrast, companies like Uber, Airbnb, Feastly, and Handy generate financial transactions between third parties – usually, an individual consumer and an individual service provider. The same companies participate in those transactions by means of ratings systems, vetting and termination standards, real-time tracking practices, and by enforcing brand management techniques, among other strategies.[18] And, in the process, these companies often substitute themselves for governmental safeguards that would otherwise apply to those transactions – either industry safeguards (like licensing or hygiene requirements) or labor safeguards (like unionization and minimum wage rights) or both. Industry safeguards and consumer protection concerns dominated earlier phases of the debate on gig work, but the conversation has overwhelmingly shifted to labor and employment safeguards and the extent to which gig companies ought to provide for them.[19] As Chapter 1 explains, that conversation is rooted in the American system of worker classification, which allocates most work-related benefits and protections to individuals classified as *employees* while excluding those classified as *independent contractors*. And, as many of the chapters in this volume demonstrate, any attempt to fairly and effectively classify gig workers has to be grounded in an empirically based awareness of their conditions of work and the way in which those conditions are impacted by regulations.

Even if there is tacit agreement as to which companies' practices present common regulatory challenges and should thus be grouped together, there is little consensus as to how to reference those companies and the workers whose services they sell. The most popular term in the earliest days of this conversation was the *sharing economy*. That phrase, which was quickly and easily lampooned for the aura of altruistic,

[17] For further discussion of these close-but-not-quite examples, *see* Das Acevedo, *supra* note 13, at 3–9.

[18] Deepa Das Acevedo, *Invisible Bosses for Invisible Workers, or Why the Sharing Economy Is Actually Minimally Disruptive*, 2017 U. Chi. Legal Forum 35 (2018).

[19] For examples of the earlier focus on consumer protection, see Christopher Koopman et al., *The Sharing Economy and Consumer Protection Regulation: The Case for Policy Change* 2 (Mercatus Working Paper, May 2015) (on file with author); Nancy Leong, *New Economy, Old Biases*, 100 Minn. L. Rev. 2153 (2016).

noncommercialized exchange it inaccurately bestowed upon the sale of goods or labor for money, proved to have considerable lasting power simply because it was widely recognizable. Indeed, critics and admirers alike continued to use *sharing economy* even as they agreed it was a less than ideal label.[20]

Today, the comparable term – both with regard to recognition and criticism – is the *gig economy*. As contributors to this very volume argue here and elsewhere, this new term is no more neutral than its predecessor: it advances the idea that the workers in question are entrepreneurs engaging in discrete (and consequently nonemployee-like) tasks that have little to do with the companies who market their services.[21] That said, and despite the periodic surfacing of other terms – economies variously described as peer-to-peer, on-demand, platform, and 1099 – the *gig economy* remains the most efficient way to reference the forms of labor exchange with which this volume is concerned. For this reason, and because there is as yet no preferable alternative in circulation, contributors to the volume have largely retained this terminology or used it alongside other terms.[22]

Just as the substantive scope of this volume is restricted to companies that engage in the kind of technologically mediated participation and substitution described above, the volume's geographic scope is limited to the United States. This is emphatically *not* because the gig economy or the regulations circumscribing it are at their thickest here, nor is it because scholarship on gig work – empirical or otherwise – is more developed in the United States than elsewhere. Rather, the volume's geographic focus is at once an attempt to foreground the value of qualitative insights for gig work regulation against a common legal landscape and an admission that no one volume can do justice to the topic on a global scale.

CHAPTER OVERVIEW

The two parts to this volume reflect different styles of empirical engagement with gig work that, together, underscore just how much there is to learn from qualitatively informed analysis. In Part I, six chapters by academic authors (or coauthored by academic authors working with policy analysts) draw on a range of methodological and analytical approaches to offer regulatory insights about gig work. The academic contributors include two sociologists, one of whom writes with a policy analyst trained as an anthropologist, two legal scholars, and three law professors who also hold doctorates in social science disciplines. Part II features slightly shorter chapters

20 For a positive account that uses the term *sharing economy*, *see* Arun Sundararajan, The Sharing Economy: The End of Employment and the Rise of Crowd-based Capitalism (2016). For a negative account that also uses the term, *see* Tom Slee, What's Yours is Mine: Against the Sharing Economy (2015).

21 *See, e.g.*, the criticism of "gig economy" and "gig work" in Chapters 4 and 5.

22 For instance, Chapter 1 uses both "gig" and "platform," with the latter most often being used synonymously with "company" – as in, "Uber is a *transportation platform*" (it is also a *transportation company* but so is the long-haul trucking giant Schneider National).

by nonacademic industry experts – a reporter, a policy analyst, two staff members from the National Employment Law Project, and the founder of one of the oldest online resources for drivers in the gig economy. Like their co-contributors based at academic institutions, these authors also draw on information gained through qualitative empirical means – observations, conversations, firsthand participation – but in their case, the information may or may not have been acquired for the express purpose of informing regulatory strategy.

Part I

Chapter 1 lays the groundwork for the empirically informed contributions that follow by describing the current landscape of gig work regulation. Deepa Das Acevedo constructs a brief tour of legislative, judicial, and administrative developments ranging from municipal ordinances to federal appellate court opinions with the goal of offering "something of a refresher for readers who are familiar with the topic and provid[ing] some basic information for those who are not."[23] As the chapter demonstrates, regardless of who undertakes the regulatory action or at which level of government it occurs, the central concern remains determining whether gig workers are employees who receive a moderate range of benefits and protections or independent contractors who do not. This question of worker classification also surfaces repeatedly throughout the volume as contributors demonstrate the different and often surprising ways in which it impacts the incentives and conditions of work for individuals in the gig economy.

Following this opening chapter, V. B. Dubal draws on her ethnographic work among Uber drivers to argue that the question of worker classification is, for the drivers themselves, much more complicated than widespread scholarly, activist, and political opinion would have it. Although most survey research reports that Uber drivers prefer being independent contractors because of the autonomy it affords them, drivers in Dubal's research express ambivalence toward this outcome in direct conversation. Perhaps more relevantly, many drivers have pushed for legislation that would grant them employee status. At the same time, drivers do not act out of a conviction that being an employee is unequivocally superior to being an independent contractor. Rather, Dubal's interviews and long-term engagement with drivers reveal that they are less invested in classification per se and more in particular benefits associated with one worker status or the other. Commentators – and perhaps especially regulators – who interpret either survey results or a willingness to rally around concrete legislative goals as definitive proof of what drivers want (and what might achieve basic labor regulation goals) do so at their own risk.

In Chapter 3, Alexandra Mateescu and Julia Ticona use content analysis and interviews to explore the sociological concept of "invisibility" as it applies to

[23] Das Acevedo, Chapter 1.

carework platforms like Care.com, UrbanSitter, and SitterCity. Since it was coined in 1987, "invisible work" has come to have a range of meanings, from referencing work that is decommodified and unpaid (like household tasks) to work that is performed in isolation and thus free from critical and particularly *regulatory* observation (like domestic work) to describing unpaid tasks that are a required part of paid work (like emotional labor). Gig workers who perform carework are invisible in all these senses.[24] The dominant scholarly response to invisibility has been what Mateescu and Ticona call a "visibility as inclusion" approach that views "regulation [and] more visibility as a solution."[25] However, based on their research, the authors argue that the mechanics of platform- and algorithm-mediated gig work mean that greater visibility is in fact not always beneficial for workers and may even prove detrimental.

In the next chapter, two tax law scholars discuss various approaches to studying how gig workers learn about their tax obligations and tax compliance in the gig economy more generally. Shu-Yi Oei and Diane Ring argue that the inadequacies of existing administrative data (such as information collected via the IRS) necessitate the use of alternate qualitative data collection methods. Not only is administrative data unable to answer all the relevant questions one might ask about tax law and gig work, it is also subject to severe path dependencies inasmuch as the companies' threshold decision to classify workers as independent contractors predetermined what kinds of administrative data would later be available to study. As an example of the kind of alternative approach that is needed, Oei and Ring offer their own 2015 study of tax awareness and compliance among Uber drivers; their study relied on a content analysis of statements scrubbed from three online discussion forums frequented by Uber drivers: Reddit.com, Uberpeople.net, and Turbotax's Intuit AnswerXchange.[26] Oei and Ring argue that while such qualitative methods are subject to their own limitations, they offer valuable insights into how workers understand and experience tax laws that would be otherwise inaccessible.

Chapter 5 closely interrogates one of the most widespread assumptions about gig work: that it is a convenient, low-risk way to build supplementary income. Alexandrea Ravenelle draws on longitudinal interviews conducted in 2015 and 2019 with workers from TaskRabbit, an odd job platform. She notes that, far from finding their ability to work via the platform as a liberating experience, workers engaging in these activities often find their work stigmatizing and damaging to their personal well-being while they perform it. They also find it hard to escape, since the need to constantly "hustle" in order to make a livable wage from their gig work precludes them from being able to pursue more lucrative and satisfying long-term positions. Put differently, gig work may be *intended* to be temporary, but the dynamics of engaging in it effectively ensure that it is *not*.

24 Mateescu and Ticona, Chapter 3.
25 *Id.*
26 Oei and Ring, Chapter 4.

Ravenelle's insights complicate the argument often made by gig companies that, since this work is inherently and intentionally temporary, it should not come with the broad suite of employment protections and benefits associated with full time work.

The final chapter in Part I, by Julia Tomassetti, takes a different approach by relying on a close reading of contract language in the "end user license agreements" (EULAs) that currently govern relationships between gig companies and gig workers. EULAs are more commonly associated with producer-consumer relationships (like when an individual downloads a smartphone app or joins a social media platform) than with employer-employee or even client-independent contractor relationships. Tomassetti notes that EULAs, like traditional employment contracts, attempt to "project autonomous, agentic selves across un-assented to commands" so that gig companies – again, like many conventional employers – can claim that they do not meet one of the central characteristics of employer status: telling workers *how* to do their work.[27] However, unlike traditional employment contracts, EULAs are markedly aided in this task by the digital algorithms that constrain worker behavior long after the initial point of agreement, and that do so in a manner that appears to lack all human authorship. Tomassetti blends her own contractual analysis with the qualitative work undertaken by other scholars to argue that "the partial automation of managerial authority should not matter legally."[28]

Part II

Part II opens with a chapter that underscores the importance of early and adequate data collection for long-term regulatory planning. Zak Accuardi, who was formerly Senior Program Associate at the TransitCenter, an independent research and advocacy foundation, draws on his experiences studying, advising, and collaborating with local government officials and transportation agencies. He notes that transportation companies like Uber and Lyft heavily impact urban infrastructure – for instance, they affect traffic patterns and congestion, public transit needs, and parking revenues – but that local governments rarely have any information about the *how* and *how much* of that impact. Without this information, public officials are not only left ill-equipped to respond to new challenges raised by gig companies themselves, they are also unprepared to deal with routine infrastructure tasks. Accuardi tells the story of how the San Francisco County Transportation Authority (SFCTA) managed to resolve some of this "data deficit" through a partnership with researchers from Northeastern University.[29] Based on interviews with SFCTA staff and the Northeastern researchers, as well as on extensive knowledge derived from similar

[27] Tomassetti, Chapter 6.
[28] *Id.*
[29] The term "data deficit" comes from Deepa Das Acevedo, *Data Deficits in Municipal Rideshare Collaborations*, 63 St. Louis *U. L. J.* 69 (2019) (discussing public-private contracts between municipal

engagement with transit agencies around the country, Accuardi identifies aspects of the partnership that helped to make it successful at resolving a pressing regulatory need and offers guidance for similar collaborations elsewhere.

In the next chapter, Sam Harnett, a reporter at KQED who covers technology and capitalism, offers an eye-opening journey into the development and dynamics of "tech journalism." Relying on his own background and expertise as well as on an analysis of prominent moments and articles in gig economy reporting, Harnett explains how media coverage has been shaped by market constraints and professional trends that are internal to journalism. More significantly, he argues that the resultant lopsided reporting has shaped public and governmental opinion while leaving regulators with the impression that they are simply acting on unvarnished facts about gig work. Harnett's chapter at once highlights the need for empirically derived information on gig work and dispels any illusion that the journalistic coverage most often relied on by regulators can, by itself, fulfill that need.

Chapter 9 comes from two researchers at the National Employment Law Project (NELP), a nonprofit organization dedicated to advancing worker welfare via research, advocacy, and collaboration with community partners. Rebecca Smith and Maya Pinto show how gig companies and their workers have been engaged in battles over the meaning of the employment relationship and what work ought to provide. They provide an account of the tactics and arguments companies have used to maintain an independent contractor workforce despite contestations on multiple fronts – and, importantly, they also provide an account of workers' efforts to resist them. To do so, Smith and Pinto draw on NELP's longstanding law and policy expertise as well as the many conversations and interviews NELP researchers regularly conduct with workers' advocates across geographic and industry contexts.

In the final chapter of the volume, Harry Campbell draws on five years of engagement with transportation companies like Uber and Lyft to specify why regulators stand to benefit from listening to gig workers' perspectives. Campbell, who writes from the vantage point of a driver, a driver-educator, and an industry observer, argues that many regulators incorrectly assume that the interests of companies and workers are aligned – for instance, that both parties want fewer barriers to entry in the form of licensing and safety requirements. In fact, Campbell's interactions with thousands of drivers have led him to believe that gig drivers often want greater oversight, and for mixed reasons: because it may help attract safety-conscious consumers, and in order to discourage new entrants into the market. Although he is deeply aware of and sympathetic to the constraints under which drivers operate, Campbell resists the idea that driver preferences ought to dictate regulatory strategy any more than company preferences. Instead, he advocates for a better understanding of the incentives and power dynamics operating behind the scenes in gig work –

actors and transportation companies like Uber in which the municipal actors struggle to access basic data regarding the services they are purchasing).

the kind of understanding achieved via the qualitatively derived insights contained in his own chapter and in the volume at large.

CONCLUSION

As this introduction shows, the contributions to this volume encompass a remarkable diversity of authors, methodologies, industries, thematic concerns, and lessons for regulatory actors. Together, they present a strong case for the value of qualitative insight in developing law and policy: qualitatively derived information can help answer "why" and "how" questions that are often inherently invisible to quantitative methods, provide preliminary data on issues that fall temporarily outside the reach of other research methods, and provide granular information about the mechanics of work in this still-new area of labor exchange.

What the volume does *not* include is the firsthand perspective of gig workers themselves – those individuals whose energies and enthusiasm for a new way to work are at the heart of the discussion here and in classrooms and city halls across the country. In honor of their work, and in the hopes that more information can help inspire regulation that is both compassionate and efficacious, we offer our own.

1

The Rise and Scope of Gig Work Regulation

Deepa Das Acevedo

This chapter provides some background information about legal responses to gig work in the United States, but it does so subject to an important qualification: there is less volume than one might imagine, and even less coherence. This is in large part because of the frequently forgotten newness of the gig economy. However ubiquitous and powerful some platforms may now appear to be, the precursor to Airbnb only appeared in 2007 and the first transportation platform, Sidecar, was only founded in 2011.[1] There is litigation to be sure, and some rulemaking as well, but there can only be so much within this limited time frame.

Secondly, the relative lack of gig work regulation is also due to the fact that much of the rulemaking that has occurred with respect to gig companies pertains to industry practices and consumer protection – in other words, the universe of gig *economy* regulation is far broader than that of gig *work* regulation. Zoning, driver qualifications in the context of for-hire transportation, building codes, and food and safety requirements are just some of the nonwork concerns that gig companies raise and that states and municipalities have been at pains to address. Moreover, state and local governments' eagerness to tackle these issues is understandable: the average taxpayer is much more likely to care about the gig economy because of how specific industries impact her everyday life (e.g., via traffic congestion and housing shortages) than because of the labor conditions of gig workers whose services she may or may not use.[2]

1 Deepa Das Acevedo, *Data Deficits in Municipal Rideshare Collaborations*, 63 St. Louis L.J. 69, 69 n. 1 (2019); Biz Carson, *How 3 Guys Turned Renting an Air Mattress in Their Apartment into a $25 Billion Company*, Bus. Insider (Feb. 23, 2016, 11:22 AM), www.businessinsider.com/how-airbnb-was-founded-a-visual-history-2016-2. Throughout this chapter, I will alternate between "gig" and "platform," with the latter most often being used synonymously with "company." For more on terminology and the use of platform over company, see the Scope and Terminology section in the Introduction.

2 Taxpayer priorities may also help explain why state and local governments seem to be more willing to overcome Uber's instrumental power and structural power when it comes to issues of safety and infrastructure than in matters of labor regulation. Tasha Fairfield, *Structural Power in Comparative Political Economy: Perspectives from Policy Formulation in Latin America*, 17 Bus. Pol. 411, 412 (2015) (stating that "instrumental power relates to business actors' deliberate political engagement, whereas structural power stems from investors' profit-maximizing responses to market signals"); Ruth

Finally, gig work regulation is limited because there are limitations on who can meaningfully regulate work. Labor and employment law – the mixed body of statutory, administrative, and judicially created law that impacts everything from wages to workplace behavior – is significantly controlled by state and federal actors. In some areas, as with the rules governing employer-sponsored retirement plans, *only* the federal government and federal courts are empowered to establish and interpret rules. In others, as in wage and hour regulation or antidiscrimination measures, states are able to enact rules that are *more* protective than an established federal floor – but no more. Municipalities, whose governance powers in all areas are granted by states and may be reduced or revoked, face even more challenges in their efforts to regulate work, as exemplified by the long-running battle between Seattle and national actors like the Chamber of Commerce discussed at various points throughout this chapter. New York City's successful efforts to legislatively protect gig workers is the exception rather than the rule.[3] In truth, because companies are increasingly (and successfully) lobbying state governments to revoke local rulemaking authority, municipalities also face considerable resistance in their efforts to regulate the gig economy on matters that would ordinarily be well within their authority and that are only indirectly related to work.[4]

For all these reasons – newness, incentives, and regulatory authority – there are fewer laws and precedents governing the labor conditions of gig workers than we might expect given widespread media coverage. This chapter will survey some key elements in the rise and scope of gig work regulation, broken into four broad categories: federal case law, state level adjudication (including decisions by courts, labor boards, and unemployment boards), federal legislative and administrative developments, and state and local ordinances. The goal is *not* to sketch a comprehensive or even representative landscape of legal engagements with gig work because, although there is not as much of this as one might expect, there is still more than can be exhaustively considered here. Instead, the chapter constitutes something of a refresher for readers who are familiar with the topic and provides some basic information for those who are not.

Two final notes: the chapter does not address the full range of legislative and regulatory actions taken in response to the COVID-19 pandemic that affect gig workers, nor does it discuss the many legal developments involving gig work that have been taking place outside the United States.[5] Labor and employment law

Berins Collier, V.B. Dubal & Christopher L. Carter, *Disrupting Regulation, Regulating Disruption: The Politics of Uber in the United States*, 16 PERSPECTIVES ON POLITICS 919, 923–25 (2018).

3 *See* the discussion in Section 1.4 below.

4 Rebecca Smith et al., *Uber State Interference: How TNC's Buy, Bully, and Bamboozle Their Way to Deregulation*, NAT'L EMP. L. PROJECT (Jan. 2018), www.nelp.org/publication/uber-state-interference/.

5 Aslam v. Uber, [2015] No 2202550/2015 (London Emp't Trib., Oct. 28, 2015); European Parliament Press Release, MEPs Approve Boost to Workers' Rights in the Gig Economy (Apr. 16, 2019)(available at www.europarl.europa.eu/news/en/press-room/20190410IPR37562/meps-approve-boost-to-workers-rights-in-the-gig-economy); Helen Coffey, *Strict New Rules Imposed on Airbnb Rentals in Paris,*

developments associated with COVID-19 merit independent study because of their complexity and rapidly evolving nature. Additionally, this chapter is meant to construct a unifying legal background for the qualitatively informed chapters that follow, all of which focus on the United States. Although the content of specific state and local regulations (as well as whether any such regulations even exist) will naturally vary across chapters, they all draw on the legal landscape set out below to a greater or lesser extent. Readers who are interested in regulatory developments outside the United States may want to consider some of the materials that are freely available at https://gigeconomyresources.com.

1.1 FEDERAL CASE LAW

Until quite recently, the two most famous legal developments regarding gig work – whether judicial *or* statutory – were a pair of opinions by the United States District Court for the Northern District of California. *Cotter v. Lyft*[6] and *O'Connor v. Uber*[7] were issued on the same day in 2015, albeit by different judges. The two disputes as well as the two opinions are substantially identical: in both cases, plaintiffs were current or former platform drivers who argued that they had been wrongly classified as independent contractors rather than employees, and in both cases the Northern District declared that worker classification was a mixed issue of fact and law that must be decided by a jury.

Cotter and *O'Connor* have been widely influential. Judge Chhabria's closing remarks in *Cotter* – that "the jury in this case will be handed a square peg and asked to choose between two round holes" – snappily summarized a long-standing theme in labor and employment law scholarship about the shortcomings of American classification doctrine and consequently generated countless references in popular and scholarly writing.[8] Similarly, the latest edition of a prominent employment law casebook excerpts *O'Connor* within its first fifty pages to help illustrate the nature and importance of worker classification doctrine.[9]

To a degree, the classification question remains preeminent in conversations about gig work regulation because it singlehandedly determines whether gig workers may access a broad suite of benefits and protections that are available to employees but not to independent contractors.[10] Some of the protections reserved for employees include protections against antidiscrimination and harassment based on

INDEPENDENT (Nov. 14, 2017, 6:08 PM), www.independent.co.uk/travel/news-and-advice/airbnb-paris-rules-new-rental-limit-bookings-stay-nights-latest-a8054771.html; Dani Deahl, *Airbnb Cancels Bookings Under New Japan Law*, THE VERGE (Jun. 8, 2018, 2:03 PM), www.theverge.com/2018/6/8/17442230/airbnb-cancels-bookings-under-new-japan-law.

6 Cotter v. Lyft, Inc., 60 F. Supp. 3d 1067 (N.D. Cal. 2015).

7 O'Connor v. Uber Tech., Inc., 82 F. Supp. 3d 1133 (N.D. Cal. 2015).

8 Deepa Das Acevedo, *Unbundling Freedom in the Sharing Economy*, 91 S. CAL. L. REV. 793, 798 nn. 14–15 (2018).

9 STEVEN L. WILLBORN ET AL., EMPLOYMENT LAW: CASES AND MATERIALS (6th ed. 2017).

10 Again, some of these caveats do not apply to COVID-19 legislation, which sometimes treated gig workers and other independent contractors on par with employees.

characteristics like race, religion, sex, national origin, disability, and age;[11] equal pay guarantees as between men and women;[12] minimum pay guarantees and rules about when workers are eligible for overtime pay;[13] fiduciary standards that apply to employer-provided health and retirement benefits;[14] workplace health and safety protections;[15] job protections for family and medical leave;[16] and, of course, protections for workers who engage in collective activity.[17] With all of these protections dependent on "employee" status, it is no surprise that the two of the earliest and most prominent legal treatments of gig work revolved around worker classification or that a substantial portion of legal engagements with gig work since then have had a similar focus.[18]

Nevertheless, federal case law on gig work has not been solely concerned with determining whether platform providers are employees or independent contractors. Antitrust violations have emerged as another important issue, especially with regard to platform drivers. In 2016, the Southern District of New York refused to dismiss an Uber passenger's complaint that the platform and its then-CEO, Travis Kalanick, had engaged in an illegal price-fixing conspiracy with Uber drivers against passengers.[19] In contrast, in 2017, the Western District of Washington dismissed a complaint by the United States Chamber of Commerce arguing that, by passing an ordinance that enabled Uber drivers to bargain collectively, Seattle had engaged in illegal price-fixing by conspiring with drivers as against Uber itself.[20] However, the district court opinions were overturned in part or in whole on appeal – in *Meyer v. Kalanick* as to the enforceability of Uber's arbitration provision, and in *Chamber of Commerce v. Seattle* on the merits of the dispute.[21]

Another emerging area of gig work-related federal litigation is one we might broadly call "consumer welfare." Disputes in this area range from consumer safety (such as the sexual assault and harassment complaint in *Doe v. Uber*)[22] to antidiscrimination (*Selden v. Airbnb*,[23] on race), and they usually involve the claim that

11 Civil Rights Act of 1964, 42 U.S.C. §§ 2000e (2012). Note that the Civil Rights Act does not limit itself to employees, but rather applies to all contracts (including all employment contracts).

12 Equal Pay Act of 1963, 29 U.S.C. § 206(d) (2012).

13 Fair Labor Standards Act of 1938, 29 U.S.C. § 201, §§ 203(d)–(e) (2012).

14 Employee Retirement Income Security Act of 1974, 29 U.S.C. § 1002 (2012).

15 Occupational Safety and Health Act of 1970, 29 U.S.C. §§ 651–52 (2012).

16 Family and Medical Leave Act of 1993, 29 U.S.C. § 2611(4) (2012).

17 National Labor Relations Act of 1935, 29 U.S.C. § 157 (2012).

18 For instance, another high profile (and still ongoing) federal case dealing with classification and the bread-and-butter benefits it controls is Razak v. Uber Tech., No. 16–573, 2016 WL 3960556 (E.D. Pa. Apr. 11, 2018). Razak was vacated and remanded by the Third Circuit in March, 2020.

19 Meyer v. Kalanick, 174 F.Supp.3d 817, 820 (S.D.N.Y. 2016).

20 Chamber of Commerce v. City of Seattle, 274 F.Supp.3d 1155, 1169 (W.D. Wash. 2017).

21 Meyer v. Uber Tech., Inc., 868 F.3d 66 (2d Cir. 2017); Chamber of Commerce v. City of Seattle, 890 F.3d 769 (9th Cir. 2018). For a discussion of the antitrust issues at play in both cases, see Sanjukta Paul, *Uber as For-Profit Hiring Hall: A Price-Fixing Paradox and Its Implications*, 38 Berkeley J. Emp. & Lab. L. 233 (2017).

22 Doe v. Uber Tech., Inc., 184 F. Supp. 3d 774 (N.D. Cal. 2016).

23 Selden v. Airbnb, Inc., No. 16-cv-00933, 2016 WL 6476934 (D.D.C. 2016).

platforms should be held responsible for the bad acts of their service providers. (Scholars have also suggested that consumer protection law might be a productive way to address the information asymmetries inherent in platform-mediated transactions, but a quick search of databases like WestLaw and Lexis does not reveal much litigation in this area.[24]) Importantly, consumer welfare disputes hinge heavily on the existence of an employment relationship between the platform and the service provider; consequently, plaintiffs in these cases must both establish the baseline question of worker classification and also prove the degree of employer liability necessary to win on their specific claim. Moreover, in all claims brought against gig companies, consumers and providers alike must overcome the agreement to arbitrate all disputes that are ubiquitous in modern contracts.[25] Because of these logistical hurdles and because of the fact that legal actors are still struggling with broad issues like how to think about the nature of gig work and of platform-mediated transactions, the original decisions in *O'Connor* and *Cotter* remain among the most prominent legal developments of any kind that relate to gig work.[26]

1.2 STATE ADJUDICATION

Since *O'Connor* and *Cotter*, few judicial developments have made as much of a splash among observers of the gig economy as the 2018 California Supreme Court decision in *Dynamex v. Superior Court*.[27] The primary issue in *Dynamex* was whether delivery drivers shared a sufficient "commonality of interest" to proceed with a class action suit alleging that they were employees who had suffered harms under one of California's wage orders. That the drivers won permission to proceed as a class was itself a striking outcome, but what really made *Dynamex* a watershed event was the Supreme Court's decision to switch to a test (called the "ABC test")[28] for determining employee status for wage order claims. The ABC test is widely considered to be more worker-protective than the one previously in use in California.

24 Ryan Calo & Alex Rosenblat, *The Taking Economy: Uber, Information, and Power*, 117 COLUM. L. REV. 1623, 1686 (2017).

25 *See, e.g.*, Bekele v. Lyft, Inc., 918 F.3d 181 (1st Cir. 2019) (affirming the District Court's grant of Defendant's motion to dismiss in favor of arbitration); Mohammed v. Uber Tech., Inc., 848 F.3d 1201 (9th Cir. 2016) (reversing the District Court's denial of Uber's motion to compel arbitration). Plaintiff-workers, whether inside or outside the gig economy, find it very difficult to avoid mandatory arbitration clauses, but it *does* sometimes happen. Cullinane v. Uber Tech., Inc., No. 16–2023 (1st Cir. 2018) (reversing the District Court because the hyperlink leading to Uber's terms and conditions of service, including the arbitration clause, was not conspicuous enough).

26 Many other federal gig work cases have died quiet deaths, such as Teague v. Lyft, Inc., No. 3:16-cv-01768 (S.D. Cal. 2016) (voluntarily dismissed); Agruss v. Homejoy, No. 1:15-cv-00767 (N.D. Ill. 2015) (terminated within six months).

27 Dynamex Operations W. v. Superior Court, 416 P.3d 1 (Cal. 2018).

28 *Id.* at 48.

Properly speaking, *Dynamex* has little to do with the gig economy, at least as that term is now commonly understood.[29] Users do not access the delivery service via a smartphone app or a website and, although the company does offer on-demand services, individual consumers do not make delivery requests to Dynamex the way, for instance, an Instacart customer asks Instacart to have bananas delivered. Nevertheless, it is hard to read the opinion's description of Dynamex's operations and *not* imagine that the California Supreme Court is actually talking about Uber, Lyft, or one of the many delivery platforms that exist today:

> Dynamex obtains its own customers ... [on-demand] drivers are generally paid either a percentage of the delivery fee ... or a flat fee basis per item delivered ... Drivers are generally free to set their own schedule but must notify Dynamex of the days they intend to work for Dynamex. Drivers performing on-demand work are required to obtain and pay for a Nextel cellular telephone through which the drivers maintain contact with Dynamex ... Although drivers are not required to make all of the deliveries they are assigned, they must promptly notify Dynamex if they intend to reject an offered delivery ... Drivers make pickups and deliveries using their own vehicles, but are generally expected to wear Dynamex shirts and badges ... [and] are sometimes required to attach Dynamex and/or the customer's decals to their vehicles ... when they are not making pickups or deliveries for Dynamex, drivers are permitted to make deliveries for another delivery company ... Drivers are ordinarily hired for an indefinite period of time but Dynamex retains the authority to terminate its agreement with any driver ...[30]

In 2019, the California Legislature Assembly passed a bill that effectively codified *Dynamex* into state law and the bill was signed by Governor Newsom.[31] Uber, Lyft, and DoorDash have together pledged $90 million in support of a referendum to overturn the measure, which itself indicates the seriousness of the threat.[32] Given California's economic clout and the concentration of gig companies as well as other technology industries within the state, a worker-protective and Supreme Court-immune classification test can be reasonably expected to have severe implications well outside the state's borders.[33]

[29] As many of this volume's contributors would – and sometimes do – argue, "gig" work need have nothing to do with smartphones or algorithms since it has long been used to describe work that is discrete and temporary. *See, e.g.*, Ravenelle, this volume.

[30] *Dynamex*, *supra* note 27.

[31] Andrew J. Hawkins, *California Just Dropped a Bomb on the Gig Economy – What's Next?*, The Verge (Sept. 18, 2019), www.theverge.com/2019/9/11/20860578/california-ab5-bill-passage-uber-lyft-drivers-union-techlash.

[32] Nicholas Iovino, *Gig-Economy Giants Will Back $90M Ballot Measure to Stop California Labor Bill*, Courthouse News Service (Aug. 29, 2019), www.courthousenews.com/gig-economy-giants-will-back-90m-ballot-measure-to-stop-california-labor-bill/.

[33] At the time of writing, an amendment narrowing the scope of AB 5 had passed the Assembly Labor and Employment Committee, an important first step toward becoming law. However, the amendment, AB 1850, was authored by Lorena Gonzalez, the same legislator who had authored AB 5. Gonzalez

Other California decisions have also been important milestones in the development of gig work regulation. In 2015, the California Labor Commission held that Barbara Berwick was an employee of Uber and that, consequently, Uber had to reimburse her for costs incurred during her work as a driver.[34] Berwick won $3,878.08 in mileage and toll charges as well as $274.12 in interest on that amount.[35] In 2018, the California Court of Appeal held in *Smythe* that Uber's arbitration agreement did not apply when a plaintiff who drove for both Uber and Lyft mounted a complaint against Uber in his capacity as a Lyft driver.[36] In that case, the plaintiff argued that Uber engaged in unfair business practices and intentionally interfered with his economic prospects as a Lyft driver when it required drivers (including himself) to generate phantom ride requests on Lyft. Given the premium that transportation platforms (and platforms more generally) have placed on the argument that workers are not employees because they can simultaneously provide services via competitor platforms, practices like the one at issue in *Smythe* are bound to raise interesting legal consequences.

While California undoubtedly sees a large proportion of gig work-related litigation, there have also been important legal developments elsewhere, especially centered on unemployment benefits. In Pennsylvania, for instance, *Lowman v. UCBR* was heard by the state Supreme Court, which decided in 2020 that an individual who drives for UberX is not disqualified from receiving unemployment benefits because he is "self-employed."[37] Conversely, in *McGillis v. Department of Economic Opportunity*, a 2017 case from the Florida District Court of Appeal, an Uber driver was held to be an independent contractor and consequently ineligible for unemployment compensation.[38] For its part, New York has seen conflicting outcomes regarding gig workers' eligibility for unemployment compensation: in 2018, an appellate court held that delivery persons for Postmates are *not* eligible while the state's Unemployment Insurance Appeal Board found that Uber drivers *are* eligible.[39] In light of the coronavirus pandemic, to say that unemployment compensation is likely to continue being an important source of state-level litigation

was reported to have planned amending AB 5 even before Governor Newsom signed it into law. Hannah Wiley, *Musicians, Freelancers and Coaches Could Soon Be Free of California's Landmark Labor Law*, Sacramento Bee (May 20, 2020), www.sacbee.com/news/politics-government/capitol-alert/article242869871.html.

34 It is worth noting that Berwick is far from a unique dispute or outcome with respect to transportation platforms – what makes it unusual is the publicity surrounding the dispute and Uber's decision to appeal the Commission's ruling.

35 Berwick v. Uber, No. 11-46739EK, 2015 WL 4153765, at 10 (Ca. Dept. Lab. 2015).

36 Smythe v. Uber Tech., Inc., 24 Cal. App. 5th 327, 333 (Cal. Ct. App. 2018).

37 Lowman v. Unemployment Comp. Bd. of Review, 178 A.3d 896 (Pa. Commw. Ct. 2018), appeal docketed, No. 41 EAP 2018 (Pa. Jul. 24, 2020). The Pennsylvania Supreme Court heard oral arguments in September, 2019; as of this writing, however, the court had yet to issue an opinion.

38 McGillis v. Dep't of Econ. Opportunity, 210 So.3d 220, 226 (Fla. Dist. Ct. App. 2017).

39 Matter of Vega (Postmates Inc. – Commissioner of Labor), 162 A.D.3d 1337, 1339 (N.Y. App. Div. 2018); Uber Tech., Inc., A.L.J. Case No. 016–23494 (July 12, 2018), available at www.nyctaxinews.com /Uber%20AB%20Decision-redacted.pdf.

over gig work is to understate the issue in the extreme. As of 2018, Uber claimed that drivers were ineligible for such benefits in six states (Florida, Arizona, Georgia, Kansas, Massachusetts, and Minnesota).[40] Whether – or perhaps how much – that changes in response to the widespread economic destruction caused by COVID-19 will affect the lives of millions of Americans who depend on gig work to provide or supplement their incomes.

1.3 FEDERAL LEGISLATIVE AND ADMINISTRATIVE DEVELOPMENTS

Federal legislative and administrative activity regarding gig work has been minimal. While Congress has not yet passed any gig work-specific legislation, it did include gig workers and other independent contractors under the expanded unemployment insurance provisions of the Coronavirus Aid, Relief, and Economic Security (CARES) Act of 2020.[41] In early 2019, Senator John Thune (R-S.D.) reintroduced the New Economy Works to Guarantee Independence and Growth Act, or NEW GIG Act.[42] Thune first introduced the NEW GIG Act in 2017 during President Trump's tax reform effort but the proposal generated considerable criticism and was eventually removed from the committee-reported tax bill.[43] Both the 2017 and 2019 versions of the NEW GIG Act construct a "safe harbor" with respect to worker classification: gig companies that meet certain requirements may classify their workers as independent contractors for income and employment tax purposes. Both versions also determine eligibility for the safe harbor using the same three criteria:

1. the relationship between the parties . . .
2. the location of the services or the means by which the services are provided . . .
3. a written contract with specific requirements (e.g., stating the independent-contractor relationship, acknowledging that the service provider is responsible for his or her own taxes, providing the service recipient's reporting and withholding obligations).[44]

[40] Liz Carey, NY: *Ruling That Uber Drivers Are Employees Could Impact "Gig Economy,"* Workers' Compensation Inst., www.wci360.com/ny-ruling-that-uber-drivers-are-employees-could-impact-gig-economy/.

[41] Pub. L. 116–136.

[42] NEW GIG Act, S.700, 116th Cong. (2003).

[43] Press Release, John Thune U.S. Senator for South Dakota, Thune Reintroduces Bill to Add Certainty to Worker Classification Rules (Mar. 7, 2019), www.thune.senate.gov/public/index.cfm/2019/3/thune-reintroduces-bill-to-add-certainty-to-worker-classification-rules (discussing removal from the committee-reported tax bill); Shu-Yi Oei & Diane M. Ring, *The Senate Tax Bill and the Battles Over Worker Classification*, TaxProf Blog (Nov. 11, 2017), https://taxprof.typepad.com/taxprof_blog/2017/11/the-senate-tax-bill-and-worker-classification.html (critiquing the bill's language).

[44] Press Release, *supra* note 43; Press Release, John Thune U.S. Senator for South Dakota, Thune Introduces Bill to Add Certainty to Worker Classification Rules (July 13, 2017), www.thune.senate.gov/public/index.cfm/2017/7/thune-introduces-bill-to-add-certainty-to-worker-classification-rules.

Because these factors emphasize the disaggregated, lopsided nature of platform-worker relationships – for instance "the location of the services" is unlikely to ever be the platform's own property – Thune's bills largely resolve the important threshold issue of classification by finding most gig workers to be independent contractors.

Even though it did not incorporate the NEW GIG Act, one of the provisions of the Tax Cuts and Jobs Act of 2017 generated considerable debate among observers of the gig economy because of the effect it might have on gig workers. The Act's 20 percent deduction for pass-through income, meaning business income that is taxed at the personal income rate rather than the corporate rate, is potentially applicable to gig workers who function as sole proprietorships.[45] Commentators disagree on the extent to which the deduction is helpful. The center-left OnLabor blog estimated that the effect would be minimal because "a childless, full-time gig worker earning $25,000 a year would save about $450."[46] Conversely, the right-leaning *National Review* declared that the tax reforms were "a boon for freelancers, contractors, and the 24 million American workers who participate in the 'gig economy'" and that a "single freelance photographer in Seattle making $60,000 a year, for example, will save roughly $4,000 next year."[47]

Finally, Senator Mark Warner (D-VA) has also been developing a range of bills in this area. To date, Warner has introduced at least four bills that either explicitly target gig workers or are designed to include them: the Investing in American Workers Act, the Lifelong Learning and Training Account Act, the Self-Employed Mortgage Access Act, and the Portable Benefits for Independent Workers Pilot Program Act.[48] The issue of portable benefits for gig workers has received more media and policy coverage than many other challenges, in part because of the state-level activity discussed later on in this chapter in Section 1.4. Senator Warner's Portable Benefits Act – which would have provided $20 million in funding to states that developed pilot programs – received support from both the nonpartisan Freelancer's Union and several prominent gig companies.[49] However, the bill (as well as a similar bill introduced in the House) ultimately died in committee.[50]

45 Maddy Joseph, *Can We Fix Gig Workers' Taxes*, OnLabor (Mar. 27, 2018), https://onlabor.org/can-we-fix-gig-workers-taxes/.

46 *Id.*

47 Christopher Rufo, *The GOP's Tax Reform Is Great for Gig-Economy Workers*, Nat'l Rev. (Jan. 5, 2018, 9:00 AM), www.nationalreview.com/2018/01/tax-reform-helps-gig-economy-workers/.

48 Ruth Reader, *Senator Mark Warner Has a New Plan to Protect Gig Economy Workers*, Fast Company (Feb. 26, 2019), www.fastcompany.com/90312184/senator-mark-warner-has-a-new-plan-to-protect-gig-economy-workers.

49 Press Release, Mark R. Warner U.S. Senator from the Commonwealth of Virginia, Legislation to Test-Drive Portable Benefit Models Introduced in the House and Senate (May 25, 2017), www.warner.senate.gov/public/index.cfm/2017/5/legislation-to-test-drive-portable-benefit-models-introduced-in-the-house-and-senate (on support from the Freelancer's Union and gig companies).

50 Robert Maxim & Mark Muro, *Rethinking Worker Benefits for an Economy in Flux*, Brookings (Mar. 20, 2018), www.brookings.edu/blog/the-avenue/2018/03/29/rethinking-worker-benefits-for-an-economy-in-flux/ (stating the bill died in committee).

In 2019, gig worker advocates were unpleasantly surprised by two almost back-to-back developments involving federal administrative actors: a Department of Labor (DOL) opinion letter concerning an unnamed gig company and an advice memorandum concerning Uber from the National Labor Relations Board (NLRB).[51] The DOL opinion letter was issued in response to an inquiry from the representative of a "virtual marketplace company (VMC)" as to whether or not the VMC's workers qualify as employees and are thus eligible for wage and hour protections under the Fair Labor Standards Act (FLSA).

Rather than the default common law-inspired "control test," the FLSA uses a distinct classification test to distinguish between employees and independent contractors. Whereas the control test only measures the putative employer's control over how the worker performs her task, the FLSA's "economic realities" test considers multiple – usually seven – factors to determine whether, as a matter of economic reality, the worker is dependent on the alleged employer. The economic realities test is no easier to apply than the control test but, in keeping with the FLSA's broadly protective mission, it is generally considered to be more worker-friendly.[52] Nevertheless, the DOL held that workers who provided services via the unnamed VMC's platform do not qualify as employees under the statute because "as a matter of economic reality, they are working for the consumer, not [the VMC]."[53]

The NLRB's advice memorandum, written just two weeks before the DOL letter, concerns another bedrock issue of work regulation: protections for collective activity. As with the DOL letter, the advice memo was issued in response to a specific request for clarification. Unlike the DOL letter, however, the memo names the company at issue and its delayed release raised suspicions that the timing was calculated to boost Uber's fortunes after its disappointing stock market debut just two business days earlier.[54]

The memo advises regional NLRB directors to dismiss three active unfair labor practices charges against Uber on the grounds that drivers for both UberX and UberBLACK are independent contractors under the control test and are consequently unprotected by the National Labor Relations Act. In practical terms, the NLRB memo means that Uber drivers, and by extension other platform drivers, can be subjected to discriminatory treatment if they engage in collective activity such as

51 U.S. Dep't of Labor, Wage and Hour Div., Opinion Letter (Apr. 29, 2019); U.S. National Labor Relations Board, Advice Memorandum (Apr. 16, 2019). Note that although the DOL letter does not name the gig company in question, the following language in the letter suggests that the company is likely either a TNC or a delivery company: "Service providers may consider a variety of factors when determining whether to accept work – such as, for example, fee amount, expected time, dynamic pricing in effect, location, availability of parking, traffic, and access to additional consecutive service opportunities – in order to maximize their profit or fit their work into their individual schedules."

52 Sec'y of Labor v. Lauritzen, 835 F.2d 1529, 1534 (7th Cir. 1987).

53 U.S. Dep't of Labor, Wage and Hour Div., Opinion Letter (Apr. 29, 2019).

54 Vanessa Romo, *Uber Drivers Are Not Employees, National Relations Board Rules. Drivers Saw It Coming*, NPR (May 15, 2019, 8:25 PM), www.npr.org/2019/05/15/723768986/uber-drivers-are-not-employees-national-relations-board-rules-drivers-saw-it-com.

strikes, pickets, and other types of workers' rights campaigns. It also means that transportation platforms may form their own company-sponsored workers' organizations and that they may refuse to bargain with any such organizations that workers themselves have formed.

The New York Taxi Workers Alliance, a "21,000-member strong union of yellow taxi, green cab, App-based, livery, and corporate black car drivers," called the NLRB memo "political football."[55] Similarly, Sharon Block, a DOL official during the Obama Administration who is currently affiliated with Harvard Law School's Labor and Worklife Program, called the DOL opinion letter "a get-out-of-jail free card."[56] While neither the NLRB memo nor the DOL opinion letter are dispositive with respect to gig workers as a whole, they do provide clear indications of the current administration's approach to gig work regulation – and they do limit the protections that are even *potentially* available to some gig workers.

A final type of activity at the federal level constitutes neither legislative nor administrative rulemaking but it is nonetheless worth noting. National lobbying groups for state and local governments have been trying to understand the governance implications of the gig economy for some time now. As the introduction to this chapter suggested, most of their attention is focused on the infrastructural challenges raised by short-term rental platforms like Airbnb and the traffic and safety challenges raised by transportation platforms like Uber and Lyft. Nevertheless, state and local actors are hardly unaware of the ways in which gig work may complicate existing problems in work regulation or generate new ones. The National Association of Counties, for instance, hosted a workshop on gig work at its 2017 annual conference;[57] the National League of Cities has developed several reports on how cities can and should be interacting with the gig economy;[58] and the National Conference of State Legislatures has started collecting information and featuring some presentations at its meetings regarding gig work. Indeed, the November/

55 *Historical Affiliations*, www.nytwa.org/historic-affiliations; Bhairavi Desai, *NYTWA Statement on NLRB Legal Memo on Uber Drivers*, N.Y. Taxi Workers Alliance (May 14, 2019), www.nytwa.org/statements/2019/5/14/nytwa-statement-on-nlrb-legal-memo-on-uber-drivers.

56 Sharon Block, *Questionable Opinion About the Gig Economy*, OnLabor (May 8, 2019), https://onlabor.org/questionable-opinion-about-the-gig-economy/ (explaining that "parties who receive an opinion letter and follow the advice contained therein are shielded from liability if their conduct is challenged in court, even if the court disagrees with WHD's conclusions contained in the letter . . . as long as none of the facts provided by the requester are inaccurate").

57 Emilia Istrate & Jonathan Harris, *The Future of Work: The Rise of the Gig Economy*, Nat'l Ass'n Counties (Nov. 2017), www.naco.org/featured-resources/future-work-rise-gig-economy (noting that "counties need to be prepared to adapt to the changing labor arrangements . . . a growing gig economy may result in higher economic activity and spending . . . [but since gig workers] are freelancers without the benefits provided by traditional work arrangements . . . they may end up consuming more county social services" and suggesting various ways that counties could better prepare themselves).

58 *Sharing Economy*, Nat'l League Cities, www.nlc.org/topics/economic-development/sharing-economy.

December 2018 issue of the NCSL's internal magazine even features an article about the ethics of state legislators moonlighting in the gig economy.[59]

These kinds of developments are even less dispositive with regard to gig work regulation than the NLRB and DOL statements. Nevertheless, they demonstrate that state and local actors are starting to think about gig work seriously, on its own terms (not just as it impacts housing or traffic patterns), and across jurisdictions. The final section of this chapter dives deeper into how these public officials have been trying to engage with the gig economy, sometimes in ways that have explicit implications for labor and employment law.

1.4 STATE AND LOCAL REGULATION

Relative to their state and federal counterparts, municipal governments have probably been the most immediately impacted by the rise of the gig economy. The growth of gig platforms has affected local housing stock and traffic patterns, created new sources of tax revenue without making them easily accessible to municipal coffers, forced a reconsideration of eligibility for local safety net resources, and prompted discussions over how those resources are best packaged. Most of these changes are due to the fact that gig platforms reconfigure resources and practices in new ways rather than because they create genuinely new practices posing novel problems.[60] Still, municipal actors have had to develop a range of policies in response to these challenges.

One of the first and most prominent local rules to explicitly target the conditions of gig work was a 2015 Seattle ordinance enabling platform drivers to collectively bargain with their companies. The ordinance allowed drivers to elect "exclusive driver representatives" and required platforms to bargain with those representatives.[61] Transportation platforms, along with the United States Chamber of Commerce, filed suit to prevent enforcement of the ordinance on two grounds: that the ordinance violated antitrust law by permitting drivers to form price-fixing cartels, and that the ordinance violated labor law by regulating an activity that was preemptively governed by federal statute.[62] (Interestingly, some legal scholarship has argued that it is the *platforms* who are violating antitrust law by enabling – or requiring – independent contractors to agree to fixed prices.[63]) While the District

[59] Mary A. Burke, Senior Economist, Fed. Res. Bank Bos. New England Economic Outlook, Address at NCSL Atlantic States Fiscal Leaders Meeting (Feb. 24, 2017), www.ncsl.org/Portals/1/Documents/fiscal/Mary_Burke_Presentation.pdf (analyzing gig work in the Atlantic states region); Savannah Gilmore & Erica Mackellar, *Back from the Brink*, St. Legislatures, Mar./Apr. 2019, 8; Nicolas Birdsong, *What About That Second Job?*, St. Legislatures, Nov./Dec. 2018, 45 (discussing legislators working gig jobs).

[60] Lee Anne Fennel, Slices & Lumps: Division and Aggregation in Law and Life (2019); Das Acevedo, *supra* note 8.

[61] Seattle, Wash., Ordinance 124968 (Dec. 23, 2015).

[62] Ryan Wheeler, *Ninth Circuit Puts the Brakes on Uber Unionization*, OnLabor (May 23, 2018), https://onlabor.org/ninth-circuit-puts-the-brakes-on-uber-unionization/.

[63] Paul, *supra* note 21.

Court agreed with Seattle on both counts, the Ninth Circuit issued a split opinion in which it agreed with Uber on the antitrust claim and Seattle on the labor law claim.[64] Seattle amended the ordinance to address the antitrust argument but, in 2020, all parties walked away from the litigation and instead agreed to cooperate on a "Fare Share Program" that would bring drivers within Seattle's minimum wage, and on a Driver Resolution Center to arbitrate disputes between drivers and transportation platforms.[65]

New York City – though it has clearly been influenced by Seattle's efforts regarding collective bargaining[66] – has so far taken a different approach by choosing to first address, for at least some gig workers, the problems of benefits and inadequate earnings.[67] In 2018, Mayor de Blasio signed Intro-890 into law (along with four other pieces of legislation affecting platform drivers), making New York City the first jurisdiction within the United States to offer a minimum wage for any kind of gig worker.[68] The new rule guarantees platform drivers an hourly wage of $17.22 – a number that is "designed to cover the drivers' expenses and still provide the equivalent of $15 hourly pay."[69] The Council Member who sponsored Intro-890, Bill Lander, is also working with a fellow Council Member to create a surcharge-funded health benefits system for platform drivers.[70]

Indeed, municipal politicians from across the country are now working together outside of their associations (like the National League of Cities) in order to develop

64 Wheeler, *supra* note 62.

65 Monica Nickelsburg, *Uber, Seattle and U.S. Chamber End Dispute over Union Law as City Plans Minimum Wage for Drivers*, Geek Wire (Apr. 13, 2020), www.geekwire.com/2020/uber-seattle-u-s-chamber-end-legal-dispute-union-law-city-plans-minimum-wage-drivers/.

66 Samar Khurshid, *City Council Developing New Protections for Workers in Gig Economy*, Gotham Gazette www.gothamgazette.com/?id=5971:city-council-developing-new-protections-for-workers-in-gig-economy (discussing Lander & Johnson's work with NYTWA on establishing a health benefits fund).

67 *Id.* It may be worth noting that New York City has also been at the forefront of another fight involving the gig economy, this time with the short-term rental platform Airbnb. Although the city's efforts to force data-sharing and minimal regulations on Airbnb and similar platforms have drawn interest from labor – the Hotel Trades Council, a union for hotel workers, strongly backed New York – the battle has largely been waged on housing, safety, and other non-work-related grounds. Benjamin Weiser & J. David Goodman, *Judge Blocks New York City Law Aimed at Curbing Airbnb Rentals*, New York Times (Jan. 3, 2019), www.nytimes.com/2019/01/03/nyregion/nyc-airbnb-rentals.html (describing the regulation passed by New York City and recently overturned by a United States District Court).

68 Press Release, Mayor Bill de Blasio of New York City, Mayor de Blasio Signs For-Hire Vehicles Legislation (Aug. 14, 2018) (available at www1.nyc.gov/office-of-the-mayor/news/409–18/mayor-de-blasio-signs-for-hire-vehicles-legislation) (discussing new legislation to provide minimum wage for TNC drivers); Jared Odessky, *Today's News & Commentary*, OnLabor (Dec. 6, 2018), https://onlabor.org/todays-news-commentary-december-6–2018/ (stating that the NYC rule is the first of its kind).

69 Statement from NYC Council Member Brad Lander on New Report Proposing an Earnings Standard for App-Based For-Hire Vehicle Drivers (Jul. 2, 2018) (available at https://council.nyc.gov/brad-lander/2018/07/02/statement-from-nyc-council-member-brad-lander-on-new-report-proposing-an-earnings-standard-for-app-based-for-hire-vehicle-drivers/).

70 Khurshid, *supra* note 66.

policies that target the challenges of the gig economy, among other things. Bill Lander is a member of a group, called Local Progress, that is comprised of over 400 elected officials from 40 states.[71] Lander describes efforts by Local Progress members that include establishing city-level offices of labor standards to ensure companies are not misclassifying workers as independent contractors when they should be considered employees, and to verify that service providers on gig platforms carry any required licensing and follow safety standards.[72] Both of these tasks have traditionally been undertaken by state and federal actors – for instance, the Department of Labor has a longstanding practice of cooperating with state agencies to identify and correct instances of worker misclassification. The fact that municipal officials are also focusing on these issues underscores the extent to which labor and employment problems emerging from the gig economy are similar in kind, if different in scale and scope, to longstanding challenges in the conventional labor force.

Beyond rules or practices that explicitly target gig work, municipal actors are also experimenting with new initiatives that have indirect consequences for gig workers. A prime example is the slowly but definitively growing trend toward public-private contracts for subsidized services. To date, all of these contracts have been with transportation companies for the provision of subsidized public transport,[73] but contracts with short-term rental platforms for affordable housing are likely to follow soon.[74] Existing transportation agreements cover a range of services – everything from traditional "first/last mile" programs (in which the municipality subsidizes a certain amount of taxi fare in order to connect residents with available public transportation systems) to "safe ride" services (which are broadly similar to first/last mile programs except that they operate at nights and on weekends and usually within a more flexible geographic zone) to para-transit programs.[75]

At present, observers of public-private contracts with platform companies are more often concerned with municipalities' ability to collect data regarding the services they are paying for than with the work law implications of gig workers providing public services. After all, gig workers who provide public services via these types of contracts are no more employees of the municipal agency in question than they are, under current law, employees of the platforms through which they work.[76] At the same time, the labor performed by these workers is partly paid for by public funds, is largely required to adhere to public standards, and is meant to improve the

71 John Avalos, et al., *How to Build the Movement for Progressive Power, the Urban Way*, THE NATION (Oct. 27, 2015), www.thenation.com/article/how-to-build-the-movement-for-progressive-power-the-urban-way/.

72 *Id.*

73 Das Acevedo, *supra* note 1.

74 See a version of this involving Boston and Nesterly, Age Strong Commission, *City Launches Intergenerational Homeshare Pilot Program*, CITY OF BOS. (Sept. 28, 2017), www.boston.gov/news/city-launches-intergenerational-homeshare-pilot-program.

75 Das Acevedo, *supra* note 1.

76 *Id.*

overall functionality of public actors. As municipal contracts with gig companies proliferate, labor-related concerns – as to both performance standards and the conditions of work – are likely to command more attention from city officials. Perhaps more importantly, increased attention to labor concerns may very well invite involvement from the state governments that traditionally regulate such matters.

Austin, Texas experienced precisely this kind of state involvement when it attempted to institute local regulations for platform drivers. As with public-private contracts for municipal services, the Austin regulations were not developed with labor and employment concerns specifically in mind, but they did significantly impact the working conditions of platform drivers. In 2015, Austin enacted Ordinance No. 20151217–075, which amended a section of the City Code to require (among other things) that platform drivers be fingerprinted.[77] Uber and Lyft immediately organized a petition supporting a more lenient policy and forcing Austin to either adopt the petition-led policy or to call a referendum on the matter.[78] Austin opted to call a referendum; in response, Uber and Lyft poured approximately eight million dollars into a campaign supporting their preferred policy and vowed to leave the city if the results were unfavorable.[79] When the results of the May 7, 2016, referendum unambiguously supported Austin's original ordinance, both platforms immediately ceased operations within city limits.[80]

For approximately one year afterwards, Austin saw a rise in experimentation as new transportation platforms – and some true "ridesharing" systems – tried to meet market demand while simultaneously offering new opportunities for drivers who found themselves out of work.[81] Although predictions regarding the new companies were initially positive, with both drivers and newly minted CEOs declaring that "there is life after Uber," that optimism was severely moderated after the Texas Legislature passed a bill in 2017 to override the Austin ordinance.[82] Uber and Lyft returned to Austin while

77 Austin, Tex., ch. 13–2, art. 4 (2015). The ordinance also imposed requirements: TNCs had to "have permits from the city, pay annual fees, limit driver hours, and use geo-fenced pickup and dropoff areas during special events." S.F. Cty. Transp. Auth., The TNC Regulatory Landscape 13 (2017). However, fingerprinting was the most controversial element of the new rules.

78 Madlin Mekelburg, *Austin's Proposition 1 Defeated*, Tex. Trib. (May 7, 2016), www.texastribune.org/2016/05/07/early-voting-austin-proposition-against/.

79 Kriston Capps, *Austin's Uber War Is the Dumbest One Yet*, CityLab (May 2, 2016), www.citylab.com/transportation/2016/05/uber-and-lyft-bluff-all-of-austin-with-proposition-1-ballot-measure/480837/.

80 *Id.*

81 Sam Levin, *'There Is Life After Uber': What Happens When Cities Ban the Service*, The Guardian (Sep. 23, 2017, 12:01 PM), www.theguardian.com/technology/2017/sep/23/uber-london-ban-austin.

82 *Id.*; David Lumb, *Texas Legislature Overrules Austin, Allows Uber and Lyft to Return*, Engadget (May 25, 2017), www.engadget.com/2017/05/25/texas-legislature-overrules-austin-allows-uber-and-lyft-to-retu/?guce_referrer=aHR0cHM6Ly93d3cuZ29vZ2xlLmNvbS8&guce_referrer_sig=AQAAAEPrEjVD0RLZ2w1k9lII3dV9k2yY8s0OIOgejUR8_YDfFek0W1NSmq3ni88nRDlSNvDFNZGxIJ3wJ5Wz2Fror05lJNuHB9jJ3ZdpreGcwR5_-b4BGUO0A_YmW1taSFzf32-pSEfatC8k-vuolYZB0d3BDw9gZigYG1ljN5wJXGMm&guccounter=2 (describing HB-100).

RideAustin, a nonprofit that launched approximately one month after the gig giants left, soon saw its demand drop more than 70 percent.[83] Other platforms, including Fare, GetMe, and Wingz, stopped operating in Austin altogether.[84] The Mayor of Austin issued a statement announcing his disappointment "that the legislature chose to nullify the bedrock principles of self-governance and limited government by imposing regulations on our city over the objection of Austin voters."[85]

State involvement in gig economy regulation has tended to favor platform interests, much as it did in Austin. So far, at least fifteen states have considered "carve-out" rules that would codify gig workers' status as independent contractors; as of March 2019, the carve-outs were pending in two states and had passed in eight.[86] Nevertheless, matters are not wholly one-sided. A number of states are working on developing portable benefit schemes in order to provide gig workers with something approximating the social safety net available to employees as far as health and disability insurance, unemployment compensation, and employer-sponsored retirement savings plans are concerned.[87] Moreover, several gig companies have supported these efforts: many signed onto a widely circulated 2015 manifesto praising portable benefits and declaring that "society and the economy are served best when workers have both stability and flexibility."[88] However, these declarations often demand that state officials agree to classify gig workers as independent contractors in return for monetary contributions from the companies.[89] Indeed, even during the

83 Sebastian Herrera, *RideAustin Battles to Survive in Space Dominated by Uber, Lyft*, STATESMAN (May 3, 2018, 12:01 AM), www.statesman.com/news/20180503/rideaustin-battles-to-survive-in-space-dominated-by-uber-lyft.

84 *Id.*

85 Statement by Mayor Adler on Passage of HB 100 (May 17, 2017) (available at www.mayoradler.com/statement-by-mayor-adler-on-passage-of-hb-100/).

86 Carve-outs have passed in Arizona, Florida, Indiana, Iowa, Kentucky, Tennessee, Texas, and Utah, and are pending in Missouri and West Virginia. MAYA PINTO, REBECCA SMITH, IRENE TUNG , RIGHTS AT RISK: GIG COMPANIES' CAMPAIGN TO UPEND EMPLOYMENT AS WE KNOW IT, NAT'L EMP. L. PROJ. (Mar. 25, 2019) (available at www.nelp.org/publication/rights-at-risk-gig-companies-campaign-to-upend-employment-as-we-know-it/).

87 Robert Maxim & Mark Muro, *Rethinking Worker Benefits for an Economy in Flux*, BROOKINGS (Mar. 30, 2018), www.brookings.edu/blog/the-avenue/2018/03/29/rethinking-worker-benefits-for-an-economy-in-flux/ (naming Washington, California, New York, and New Jersey as states developing or experimenting with portable benefits systems). Some portable benefits systems that rely on forced-savings from workers have also emerged from the private market, like the app Even, and from the advocacy realm, like the app Alia that is being tested by the National Domestic Workers Alliance and Trupo, which was launched by the Freelancers Union. Miranda Katz, *How an App Could Give Some Gig Workers a Safety Net*, WIRED (Jul. 9, 2018, 7:00 AM), www.wired.com/story/how-an-app-could-give-some-gig-workers-a-safety-net/ (Alia); EVEN, https://even.com/about (last visited Aug. 7, 2019) (Even); Lydia DePillis, *Gig Economy Workers Need Benefits. These Companies Are Popping Up to Help*, CNN BUS. (Aug. 23, 2018), https://money.cnn.com/2018/08/23/technology/gig-economy-worker-benefits/index.html (Trupo).

88 *Portable Benefits, Common Ground for Independent Workers*, WTF ECON. (Nov. 9, 2015), https://wtfeconomy.com/common-ground-for-independent-workers-83f3fbcf548f.

89 Benjamin Sachs, *Regressive Federalism*, ONLABOR (Jan. 11, 2017), https://onlabor.org/regressive-federalism/.

initial weeks of the COVID-19 pandemic, Uber's CEO Dara Khosrowshahi asked President Trump to include Uber drivers in any pandemic-related federal assistance and, in the very same letter, reiterated that drivers should not be considered employees and that the current binary system of worker classification could not adequately accommodate gig platforms like Uber.[90]

Even where states have not acceded to platforms' demands regarding classification, their efforts have not been met with unqualified approval. For example, the Dependent Workers Act introduced in the New York State Legislature in June 2019 gave certain workers collective bargaining rights but little in the way of substantive benefits associated with employee status. As a result – and because of the Legislature's attempt to rush it through without any public input – the Act has been criticized by a range of workers' advocates.[91] Some of these critics have pointed approvingly to California's efforts, via AB 5 and the codification of *Dynamex*, to simply change the way workers are sorted into employee and independent contractor categories rather than to address the specific circumstances of gig workers: if an Uber driver is reclassified as an employee, there is no longer any need to develop a special and selectively applicable portable benefits system.[92]

1.5 CONCLUSION

In a little over ten years, the gig economy has drawn significant public and political attention to the problems in America's labor and employment regulation system. To be sure, not all gig companies pose similar – or similarly pressing – challenges to existing work law. Similarly, not all state actors have been equally interested in responding to the rise of gig work nor have the responses undertaken so far necessarily been made by the state actor conventionally responsible for regularly labor conditions. Courts have been heavily involved because of the foundational nature of worker classification doctrine, while local governments have attempted to extend their influence into areas traditionally governed by state or federal lawmakers because localities are the most immediately impacted by the rise of gig work. At this point, it is difficult to tell whether decisive policy change will be spurred by the

[90] Dave Lee, *Uber Calls on Trump to Extend Economic Safety Net to Its Drivers*, FINANCIAL TIMES (Mar. 23, 2020), www.ft.com/content/f15d595c-942a-46e9-aad0-a039028f75aa.

[91] S.B. 6538, 2019-2020 Gen. Assemb., Reg. Sess. (N.Y. 2019) (stating in §§9ii–iii that the labor commissioner should consider to what extent and what kinds of benefits would be appropriate for dependent workers); Rebecca Smith, *New York State's Dependent Worker Act Falls Short for Gig Workers*, NAT'L EMP. L. PROJECT (Jun. 17, 2019), www.nelp.org/news-releases/new-york-states-dependent-worker-act-falls-short-for-gig-workers/ (providing a statement on behalf of NELP regarding the Dependent Worker Act); Hector Figueroa & Bhairavi Desai, op-ed, *Throwing Drivers Under the Bus: Albany Is Poised to Rush Through a Bill That Purports to Protect Gig Economy Workers; It Would Do Nothing of the Sort*, DAILY NEWS (Jun. 18, 2019), www.nydailynews.com/opinion/ny-oped-throwing-drivers-under-the-bus-20190618-iy2ad63sf5fujhicmu7knisfnu-story.html (criticizing the Dependent Worker Act).

[92] Figueroa and Desai, *supra* note 91.

actions of a few influential states and cities, or whether it is likely to come from federal legislative and administrative actions that constrain other government actors.

The chapters that follow engage with the legal developments discussed here to varying degrees: some chapters explore gig work challenges that arise in the shadow of the law while others explicitly consider the nature and impact of specific regulations. All of them, however, address ground realities faced by workers who are operating in a legal environment characterized by uncertainty and unevenness because of complex interactions across vertical and horizontal levels of government.

2

An Uber Ambivalence

Employee Status, Worker Perspectives, and Regulation in the Gig Economy

V. B. Dubal

Before beginning to work for Lyft in 2013, Kevin Banks[1] spent twenty-five years as a unionized carpenter in Northern California. He made "pretty dang good money"[2] working in construction, especially after his promotion to general foreman. But Kevin was badly injured on the job, and the timing of the injury coincided with the Great Recession. A white, native-born American who came from a union family, Kevin had never performed nonunion, low-wage work, but by 2009, his job choices were limited. With a trace of resigned shame in his voice, he disclosed in one of our conversations over coffee,

> My old man was a union painter ... my wife is a fourth generation Longshoreman. There was no me not being in the union, period. I used to – honestly, I used to make fun of Walmart workers and all that ... until the Recession hit. And then I couldn't find a job anywhere, doing anything. I went back to school, I got my construction management degree ... It was like alright, let's move it up. Nothing. Still isn't any [work].[3]

After the stint in school, Kevin turned to truck driving, working as a putative independent contractor for the first time in his life. He purchased a semi-truck and drove all over the country for a company whose business model was analogous to the one later used by labor platform companies Uber and Lyft; he bore all the risk and costs traditionally associated with running a business. The money was low and unpredictable. Sometimes, Kevin told me, after expenses, he would end a haul with just $100, not enough to justify being away from his wife and small daughter for long periods of time. After several unhappy years driving cross country, years that took a toll on his body and on his family, a friend told Kevin about Lyft. Kevin and his wife researched the company, which had been around for roughly one year, and based on Lyft's advertised wages, they determined that he should sell his truck, lease

[1] Pseudonyms are used in the place of real names to protect the identity of interview subjects.
[2] Banks, Kevin. Interview by V. B. Dubal, May 10, 2016.
[3] Ibid.

a sedan, and switch jobs. As a Lyft driver, he could make more money, have a flexible schedule, and be a more present parent and husband.

At first, Kevin said, things were good; he enjoyed being able to spend more time with his child and only drove while his daughter was at school. For several months, he made enough to meet his expenses. But as Uber and Lyft recruited more drivers, thereby increasing supply, the companies also dropped driver commissions. Kevin was getting fewer fares and earning less for each one. Almost overnight, his income became unpredictable and insufficient. Kevin described a few weeks in late 2015 – one and a half years into working for Lyft – when the insecurities of his work made him think drivers needed to organize to form collective power.

> So, when they [Uber and Lyft] started dropping the prices in this price war, and I just kept working more and more and more to where I'm going, I'm working 60, 70 hours a week. You know, over Christmas, I worked what, 60 hours every week. But the last week of December, and by the time all my expenses were done, I had $200 leftover. So, my family for Christmas presents got to go to Star Wars, that's it. No popcorn, you know, because it's $30 to get into the movies ... It was the rate cuts. That's how I realized we needed to get together as drivers.[4]

In his quest to organize Uber and Lyft drivers who could collectively demand that the companies raise and stabilize their wages, Kevin reached out to the Teamsters. Like other unions in early 2016, the Teamsters Joint Council 7 in Northern California was hesitant to invest in the organization of gig workers without a legal decision on their worker status.[5] If drivers were found to be independent contractors, a union helping to organize them might run afoul of antitrust laws and could be held liable for price-fixing, a huge legal and financial risk.[6]

Unwilling to support Kevin's vision of collective driver power with sustained organizing resources, the Teamsters asked if he wanted to be involved in a lawsuit against Lyft. Kevin agreed to file an official objection in a proposed settlement to *Cotter v. Lyft*,[7] a major wage and hour class action filed in the federal district of Northern California. Nationally, at this early stage in the tech-enabled gig economy, the labor community had looked to a decision in *Cotter* (and a sister lawsuit filed against Uber, *O'Connor v. Uber*)[8] to settle the matter of how workers in the gig economy should be classified. Many saw a legal decision in favor of employee status as not only providing a safety net for workers in the ride-hailing industry, but also as a way to slow the expansion of the app-based, contractor business model into other sectors of the service economy.[9]

4 Banks, Kevin. Interview by V. B. Dubal, April 4, 2016.
5 Bloch, Doug, Political Director, Teamsters Joint Council 7. Interview by V. B. Dubal, Sept. 3, 2016.
6 Paul, Sanjukta M. "The Enduring Ambiguities of Antitrust Liability for Worker Collective Action." *Loy. U. Chi. LJ* 47 (2015): 969.
7 Cotter v. Lyft, 176 F.Supp.3d 930 (2016).
8 O'Connor v. Uber, 201 F.Supp.3d 1110 (2016).
9 Later, Kevin also supported the Teamsters in their attempted intervention in *Cotter*. Rather than allow the case to settle, the Teamsters wanted to litigate the case and get a decision on the status of drivers so as to undermine Lyft's business model. *Teamsters, Lyft Drivers to File Objections in Class Action*

Kevin said that like the Teamsters, he wanted a decision in *Cotter*, and not a settlement: "The settlement money isn't that big of a deal ... it's not going to help in the long run."[10]

"You think employee status *will* help you in the long run?" I asked.

> "Oh, I don't want to be an employee," Kevin answered.
> "Really?!" I gasped, "Then why did you object to the settlement?"[11]

Kevin explained that he appreciated why others wanted employee status; he, too, wanted many of the benefits associated with employment including a wage floor, reimbursement for his vehicle expenses, and the right to unionize. He had objected to the settlement in *Cotter* because he was furious at the company for "robbing him."[12] It was an act of resistance and rebellion. But Kevin also wanted the "freedom and flexibility" that he associated with being a "real" independent contractor, "I want to be able to go, you know, take my daughter fishing on Wednesday in the summer instead of going to work if I want."[13] He was worried about the kinds of rules Lyft might impose if they thought of themselves as his employer. Would he get fired for taking the day off? Would he be forced to work in the afternoon after his daughter came home from school?

According to survey-based research, the majority of drivers for labor platforms Uber and Lyft share Kevin's stated preference for independent contractor status. Many gig companies have leveraged these findings to justify their opposition to both employment regulations and their fierce defense of lawsuits alleging misclassification. For example, in an opinion piece in *USA Today* timed to oppose AB5, an internationally heralded 2019 California bill crafted to deter misclassification of workers in the gig economy, Uber's general counsel wrote, "[D]rivers tell us in focus groups and surveys [that] they don't want to be employees."[14] In another major class action lawsuit against Uber, *O'Connor v. Uber*, the company submitted to the record 400 sworn statements from drivers saying that they did not want to be employees.[15] To date, these findings and assertions have played a powerful role in averting the regulation of gig work as employment.[16]

Lawsuit Settlement, March 15, 2016. https://teamster.org/news/2016/03/teamsters-lyft-drivers-file-objections-class-action-lawsuit-settlement.

10 Banks, Kevin. Interview by V. B. Dubal, May 10, 2016.

11 Ibid.

12 Ibid.

13 Ibid.

14 Tony West. "Uber: Drivers Tell Us Through Focus Groups and Surveys They Don't Want to Be Employees." *USA Today*, Sept. 16, 2019. www.usatoday.com/story/opinion/2019/09/16/uber-drivers-tell-us-they-dont-want-employees-editorials-debates/2346851001/.

15 "Uber in Legal Battle Over Drivers' Employment." *ABC 7 News*, Aug. 6, 2015. https://abc7news.com/business/uber-in-legal-battle-over-drivers-employment/909341/.

16 Janine Berg and Hannah Johnston. "Too Good to Be True? A Comment on Hall and Krueger's Analysis of the Labor Market for Uber's Driver-Partners." *ILR Review* 72, no. 1 (2019): 39–40.

The results of my survey research on Uber drivers who work in San Francisco, conducted between February 2016 and August 2016, affirmed this data and the gig companies' assertions about driver preference. Regardless of gender, immigration status, and whether Uber driving was their only, primary, or supplemental job, a majority of Uber drivers stated they preferred to be independent contractors. Despite this, grassroots ride-hailing drivers' groups in California supported and even advocated for the passage of AB5, affirming driver commitment to employee status as a path to economic security and resistance.

How can we explain this discrepancy between drivers' stated preferences and their advocacy? What do perspectives like Kevin's tell us about how drivers make sense of employee status in relationship to their lives and visions for the future of their work? And how might understanding these perspectives impact how regulators approach worker status in the tech-enabled gig economy? Consistent with the complexity of Kevin's relationship to employee status, my extensive qualitative investigations troubled the survey data. Over fifty in-depth, semi-structured interviews with Uber drivers and three years of ethnographic engagement with drivers' advocacy groups in the San Francisco Bay Area revealed that gig workers were not of one mind about employment.[17] Drivers understood employee status simultaneously as a potential source of stability and resistance *and* a source of fear and subjection.

To make sense of the contradictory findings between driver narratives and survey data, I draw on the social psychology and sociology literature on cognitive conflict.[18] Rather than approach driver perspectives toward employment as bidimensional, as existing survey research has done, my ethnographic data uncover the complexity of drivers' views on the concept in an antecedent context – that is, before employee status has been enforced and experienced. I argue that the paradoxes embodied in the perspectives of workers like Kevin can be theorized as attitudinal *ambivalence*. This ambivalence toward employee status was informed both by their relative powerlessness in relation to gig companies and

[17] The ethnographic research included hundreds of hours of participant observation and action at drivers' meetings, protests, in meetings with regulators, on group phone calls and texts, in government hearings, and one-on-one conversations. With some drivers, who I got to know over a period of time, my ethnography continued into social spaces. All workers in the drivers' groups were Uber or Lyft drivers, and many worked for other gig platforms as well, including Wonolo, Doordash, and Postmates. This research gave me insight into the complex and unpredictable links between law, work, and everyday life. Rather than claim generalizability or static sociological ascription, my multifarious findings problematize overbroad claims to knowledge about workers.

[18] See generally, Margo Buchanan-Oliver and Angela Cruz. "Discourses of Technology Consumption: Ambivalence, Fear, and Liminality." *ACR North American Advances* (2011); Mark Conner and Christopher J. Armitage. "Attitudinal Ambivalence." *Attitudes and Attitude Change* (2008): 261–286; S. Craig and M. Martinez, eds. *Ambivalence, Politics and Public Policy*. Springer, 2016; Alice H. Eagly and Shelly Chaiken. *The Psychology of Attitudes*. Harcourt Brace Jovanovich College Publishers, 1993.

by the uncertainties and insecurities specific to app-based gig work. Overwhelmingly, drivers both wanted employee benefits and feared how the companies might behave as an employer. This attitudinal ambivalence of drivers toward employment holds implications for both organizing in the gig economy and for the future regulation of work.

This chapter proceeds in three parts. Section 2.1 provides an overview of the existing definitional debates in legal scholarship on the legal identities of gig workers. I argue that scholarship proposing refinements on the prevailing legal tests for employee status generally fail to account for the legally inscribed ability of businesses to reshape their business models and evade employment obligations. They also reflect an understanding of employment as a natural fact, rather than a historically contingent phenomenon. In contrast, the ABC test – codified in California employment laws in 2019 by a bill referred to as AB5 – shifts the focus of the legal inquiry to enforcement, thereby confronting the ability of businesses to avoid liability to and for their workers.

With the legal debates as backdrop, Sections 2.2 and 2.3 analyze select empirical findings from multimethod research on Uber drivers in San Francisco between 2016 and 2019. In Section 2.2, I situate my survey data amidst the existing research on driver preference and then contrast these findings with worker narratives. Drivers in my ethnographic research took seriously their subjection to and by gig companies, but they also imagined and aspired to the possibility of better and more stable work lives, often through the medium of employee benefits. Section 2.3 also draws on deep qualitative investigation, including participant observation, to consider how driver ambivalence toward employee status was managed by California drivers' groups who advocated for employment status in the context of AB5. Specifically, I examine how a membership-based, driver-led group of gig workers, Rideshare Drivers United, engaged worker ambivalence about employee status and mobilized support for the bill.

Finally, the Conclusion (Section 2.4) considers implications of these empirical findings for regulators. Given the complicated ambivalence of gig workers toward employee status, this research suggests that the bidimensional inquiry on gig worker preference for employee or independent contractor status is the wrong question. Gig workers in the app-based ride-hailing industry uniformly desire the benefits traditionally associated with employment, but the subjection associated with employee status has produced anxieties. Rather than reshape employment laws and restrict worker benefits to accommodate the policy prescriptions of app-enabled gig companies, regulators may use these research findings to expand the benefits available through the traditional employment regime. For example, in attending to the need that many workers have for time flexibility, regulators could inscribe scheduling autonomy into the panoply of benefits available to labor platform workers.

2.1 LEGAL TESTS FOR EMPLOYEE STATUS: SUBJECTIVITY, POWER, AND ENFORCEMENT

The legal test for employee status has been a subject of increasing debate since the New Deal when safety net protections were inscribed through employment, significantly increasing the costs of doing business in the US.[19] Not until the late 1940s, however, did Congress, by statute, carve "independent contractors" out of the protections afforded by employment and labor laws.[20] By the late 1970s, the independent contractor carve-out in work laws began to incentivize changes in business models in many industries, including the taxi and trucking trades.[21] In 2012, labor platform companies Uber and Lyft built upon and expanded these business models.[22] Using app technologies, they grew the number of people working as independent contractors.[23] The rapid, high growth of these companies and the number of workers laboring without employment protections in turn spawned an entire genre of scholarship on the legal test to determine employee status.

Much recent scholarship focused on finding the "correct" test for employee status refines or builds upon the major tests that have been developed in courts and legislatures over the past forty years.[24] The two tests (and versions thereof) currently used for federal employment protections attempt to capture some essential "truth" about employment with little regard to the legislative purpose of the work protections. The root of most legal tests for employee status – the common law of agency test – examines the putative employer's right to control the "means and manner" of a worker's performance.[25] The more a putative employer controls or retains the right to control how workers conduct their work, the more likely a decision-maker is to find that the worker is an employee.[26] The majority of federal and state employment

19 Estimates put the additional costs of employment benefits at roughly one third of the employee's compensation. See, for example, the Bureau of Labor Statistics breakdown for the average costs of employment compensation. "Employer Costs for Employee Compensation." *Bureau of Labor Statistics, Department of Labor*, June 2019. www.bls.gov/news.release/pdf/ecec.pdf.

20 V. B. Dubal. "Wage Slave or Entrepreneur: Contesting the Dualism of Legal Worker Identities." *Calif. L. Rev.* 105 (2017): 86–88.

21 As I have shown in previous work, the taxi industry was one of the first places to shift to lower costs and risks by shifting to an independent contractor model. Taxi companies toyed with "leasing models" to lower both the overhead associated with employment and to de-unionize the industry. Rather than pay drivers by commission with an underlying guaranteed wage, the companies leased cars to drivers by the shift. Drivers paid for gas and the lease and kept the remaining earnings from his shift. V. B. Dubal. "The Drive to Precarity: A Political History of Work, Regulation, & Labor Advocacy in San Francisco's Taxi & Uber Economics." *Berkeley J. Emp. & Lab. L.* 38 (2017): 100–109.

22 Ibid., 120–129.

23 Ibid.

24 See, for example, Keith Cunningham-Parmeter. "From Amazon to Uber: Defining Employment in the Modern Economy." *BUL Rev.* 96 (2016): 1725–1727; Nicholas L. DeBruyne, "Uber Drivers: A Disputed Employment Relationship in Light of the Sharing Economy." *Chi.-Kent L. Rev.* 92 (2017): 315; Jillian Kaltner. "Employment Status of Uber and Lyft Drivers: Unsettlingly Settled." *Hastings Women's LJ* 29 (2018): 44.

25 Dubal, "Wage Slave or Entrepreneur," 72–75.

26 I use the plural "they" as a singular, gender-neutral pronoun.

laws currently reflect some version of this test. Another, more recent test, is the "entrepreneurial potential" test which was articulated in 2009 by the DC Circuit in *FedEx Home Delivery v. NLRB*,[27] and in 2019, by the NLRB in *Supershuttle DFW, Inc.*[28] In this test, used to decide whether or not workers have the rights ascribed to employees under the National Labor Relations Act (including the right to collective organizing and bargaining), the more "entrepreneurial opportunity" workers have for financial gains and losses – even if the opportunity is never realized – the more likely the worker is to be an independent contractor.

Courts and legal decision-makers who have applied these tests to determine employee status have alluded to how they capture an underlying "truth" about employment. For example, in *Estrada v. FedEx*,[29] an appellate court decision holding that FedEx drivers were employees, the decision included a now famous line: "The drivers look like FedEx employees, act like FedEx employees, are paid like FedEx employees, and receive many employee benefits . . . if it looks like a duck, walks like a duck, swims like a duck, and quacks like a duck, it is a duck."[30] But years of inconsistent legal outcomes expose how the application of such tests reflect the subjectivity of decisionmakers.[31] Indeed, Julia Tomassetti has shown through empirical research, whether a worker is determined to be an employee by the NLRB has depended on whether the administration is Democratic or Republican.[32] Thus, even when factors to be considered in analyzing control are clearly delineated, application of the prevailing legal tests has not resulted in consistent outcomes. As Deepa Das Acevedo has argued, sometimes and for some people "control" is interpreted as noninterference at work, and in other moments, that noninterference is more accurately about nondomination.[33] In both instances, perceptions of employee status hinge on subjective ideas and experiences of freedom.

Another reason that tests for employee status have frequently failed to protect workers is because of their post-hoc approach. The means and manner of control test is sometimes useful in capturing violations where employers attempt to "fly under the radar." However, historically, a number of employers have attempted to "fly over" enforcement. By this I mean that employers have used their power – both structural and instrumental – to either create statutory exceptions for themselves in the law or to change their business models to conform to the tests, even after being found in violation of the law. With this in mind, Noah Zatz has argued that the legal

27 FedEx Home Delivery v. NLRB, 563 F.3d 492 (D.C. Cir. 2009).

28 SuperShuttle DFW, Inc. and Amalgamated Transit Union Local 1338. Case 16–RC–010963, Jan. 25, 2019.

29 Estrada v. FedEx, 64 Cal. Rptr. 3d 327 (Ct. App. 2007).

30 Ibid. at 9.

31 Dubal, "Wage Slave or Entrepreneur," 70.

32 Julia Tomassetti. "Who Is a Worker? Partisanship, the National Labor Relations Board, and the Social Content of Employment." *Law & Social Inquiry* 37, no. 4 (2012): 815–847.

33 Deepa Das Acevedo. "Unbundling Freedom in the Sharing Economy." *S. Cal. L. Rev.* 91 (2017): 793.

root of the misclassification problem is not in the application of these tests, but in the fact that the tests and refinements to them "fail to confront employers' power to shape their business practices to substitute contracting for employment . . . ."[34] As I have shown elsewhere, even in cases where employers were found in violation of employment laws through misclassification of their workers, those employers used the court's legal decision as a roadmap to "more accurately" define their workers as independent contractors.[35] In some instances, this has increased the precarity of workers' lives instead of providing them with employment protections.[36]

Yet another test for employee status – the ABC test – attempts to account both for the subjective application of other employee status tests and for the power of companies to rewrite their business models to evade enforcement. Although different versions of the test exist, the ABC test as articulated by the California Supreme Court and later codified into California employment laws by AB5 creates a presumption of employment and puts forth a conjunctive three-part test for hiring entities who wish to classify their workers as independent contractors.[37] In order to get out from under the employee presumption, the hiring entity must prove that the workers are (1) free from control, (2) performing work that is outside the usual course of the hiring entity's business, and (3) engaged in an independently established trade of the same nature as the work performed.[38] The most exacting aspect of the ABC test is, of course, prong B. Whether or not this test will prevent gig companies from remaking themselves to get out from under the law remains to be seen.

2.2 THEORIZING AMBIVALENCE: DESIRES AND FEARS ABOUT EMPLOYEE STATUS

In this section, I turn to empirical data on driver perspectives on employee status. For context, I begin with a short discussion of my previous ethnographic study of workers in the San Francisco taxi industry. In comparison to Uber drivers between 2016 and 2019, taxi workers in San Francisco in the years immediately preceding the advent of Uber and Lyft harbored fairly consistent feelings about employee status. This comparison is useful because it underscores the degree to which worker preference for or against employee status is situationally variable and may be contingent upon any number of job-specific factors including economic uncertainty and lack of access to transparent decision-making structures.

34 Noah D Zatz. "Beyond Misclassification: Tackling the Independent Contractor Problem without Redefining Employment." *ABA Journal of Labor & Employment Law* (2011): 280.

35 See generally, V. B. Dubal. "Winning the Battle, Losing the War: Assessing the Impact of Misclassification Litigation on Workers in the Gig Economy." *Wis. L. Rev.* (2017): 739–802.

36 Ibid. at 780–791.

37 The California ABC test was articulated in Dynamex Operations West, Inc. v. Superior Court of Los Angeles, No. S222732 (Cal. Sup. Ct. Apr. 30, 2018).

38 Ibid.

Following this discussion of worker preference in the antecedent gig economy, I examine both existing survey data on Uber driver preferences for and against employee status and my own survey data, gathered among San Francisco Uber drivers in 2016. A majority of drivers in all survey studies – including my own – stated a preference for independent contractor status. But I argue that as an empirical instrument, the survey – for a number of reasons discussed herein – cannot capture the complex desires, fears, and visions of workers on this issue.

Narratives derived from three years of ethnographic research among Uber drivers and driver groups and over fifty semi-structured qualitative interviews reinforce this critique. Using worker voices and life stories, I argue that Uber drivers do not have a unidimensional, but rather complex, ambivalent relationship to employee status. This ambivalence, I show, arises from the conflict between their need for the stability offered by employment benefits and protections, and their fears about their perceived powerlessness in relationship to gig companies.

2.2.1 *The Taxi Gig Economy*

In a series of articles stemming from an earlier ethnographic and historical project on the San Francisco taxi industry in the decades preceding the advent of ride-hailing apps Uber and Lyft, I revealed how the employee and independent contractor categories for taxi workers were "meaningful not just for employment regulation, but also for worker identities and collectivities on the ground."[39] After taxi companies shifted from an employee-based business model to independent contracting, forcing the de-unionization of the taxi industry in the late 1970s, San Francisco taxi drivers formed worker groups to protect their interests.[40] For decades, a central locus of debate among drivers in these groups was whether or not to fight for reclassification as employees.[41]

Through an extensive examination of historical documents and interviews, I showed how this issue was divisive among taxi drivers. Many immigrant and racial minority drivers, in particular, valued their independent contractor status and the practice of long-term leasing because of the structural control and scheduling freedom it permitted. These drivers sometimes relished "the promises of social mobility engendered by the 'entrepreneur' identity" that they associated with being an independent contractor.[42] In contrast, nonmigrant white taxi drivers – especially those of an older generation – longed for and fought for employee status, believing that employment would bring stability, professionalism, and dignity back to their work.[43] This divisive approach to worker status among a diverse workforce frequently fractured attempts at building collective worker power.

39 Dubal, "Wage Slave or Entrepreneur," 71.
40 Dubal, "Drive to Precarity," 111–115.
41 Ibid.
42 Dubal, "Wage Slave or Entrepreneur," 105.
43 Ibid. at 107–109.

In making sense of the steadfastness of individual workers in their perspectives on worker status in this antecedent gig economy, the regulatory framework in the taxi industry is an important backdrop. Until the advent of Uber and Lyft, San Francisco taxi drivers, though treated as independent contractors for most employment protections, benefited from relative economic stability and predictability.[44] Due to municipally controlled vehicle caps and regulated fares, which were enacted in response to union advocacy during the Great Depression, drivers in the post-union taxi economy had low but predictable incomes.[45] Since the taxi industry was locally regulated as a semipublic utility, drivers had regular access to city regulators and the ability to shape the rules governing their work.[46] The Police Commission and later the Taxi Commission oversaw the rules governing the industry, met weekly, and made decisions in transparent public fora, always with input and advocacy from the driver community.[47]

In contrast to other gig workers, San Francisco taxi drivers had an unusual degree of involvement in the industry regulations that shaped their everyday work lives, some safety net protections, and a degree of economic security. During economic downturns, taxi drivers lobbied the city to recalibrate taxi supply and fares so as to increase driver income. Although cab companies could terminate workers "at will," drivers could appeal any decision to take away their occupational license. And while drivers did not have access to the minimum wage or the right to unionize, they could, as a result of a 1996 lawsuit, file for unemployment insurance if laid off and workers' compensation if injured on the job.[48]

In sharp contrast to this earlier moment in the ride-hailing industry, Uber and Lyft drivers in my research had very limited access to state regulators, endured high on-the-job risk, and suffered with an unpredictable income. They experienced plummeting wages and an ever-fluctuating supply of competing vehicles on the road. Long-term drivers in my research said that from 2014 to 2019, their incomes dropped by roughly 60 percent. Drivers also reported being unfairly terminated – or deactivated – sometimes permanently. Unlike taxi drivers, Uber and Lyft drivers absorbed the erratic costs and risks of driving all the time – including hybrid insurance, wear and tear on their vehicle, and the costs and income loss associated with accidents. This comparison helps to explain why driver preferences for independent contractor status were relatively stable in the taxi industry, and why that changed so dramatically in the app-based gig economy.

44 Dubal, "Drive to Precarity," 116–120.
45 Ibid.
46 Ibid.
47 The Taxi commission even had a voting driver representative. This changed in 2009 when the SFMTA took over regulation of the taxi industry. Ibid. at 123.
48 Tracy v. Yellow Cab Coop., No. 938786 at 10–11 (Super. Ct. Cal. Oct. 22, 1996). For a longer discussion of this case, see Dubal, "Winning the Battle, Losing the War," 758–769.

2.2.2 *Survey Data on Gig Driver Preferences for Worker Status*

Given the backdrop of sometimes extreme Uber driver insecurity, observers – both scholars and regulators – have been surprised by survey data suggesting that drivers are satisfied with their relationship to Uber as independent contractors. In this section, I appraise the existing scholarly research on the issue and also present data from my own survey of Uber drivers in San Francisco.

2.2.2.1 Literature Review of Survey Research on Uber Drivers' Classification Preferences

The most influential scholarship to date on Uber driver preference is a piece written by economists Jonathan Hall and Alan Krueger.[49] Hall and Krueger concluded based on survey research conducted in 2015 and paid for by Uber that roughly 79 percent of US Uber drivers preferred independent contractor status to employee status.[50] The data has been cited in a variety of regulatory contexts to deter employment regulations.[51] The specific survey question was as follows,

> Which of the following would you most prefer regarding your driving with Uber: being classified as an employee of Uber so you could be eligible for a minimum wage, health care and other benefits, but you would not have the flexibility to set your own schedule; or being classified as an independent contractor for Uber so you would have the flexibility to set your own schedule, but you are not eligible for a minimum wage, health care or other benefits?

The outsized role this data has had on policy discussions on the rights of gig workers prompted two academics employed at the ILO – Janine Berg, an economist, and Hannah Johnston, a geographer – to probe the survey. In a peer-reviewed comment, Berg and Johnston concluded that the Hall and Krueger article is "fraught with methodological problems including sample bias, leading questions, and selective reporting findings."[52] The question on worker status preference, Berg and Johnston point out, is double-barreled, "forcing respondents to answer two questions at once when their opinions about the two may diverge."[53] Indeed, drawing on this critique, I argue that the question also obfuscates the law and communicates a falsehood to survey participants. Although many employees in the US have an

49 Jonathan V. Hall and Alan B. Krueger. "An Analysis of the Labor Market for Uber's Driver-Partners in the United States." *ILR Review* 71, no. 3 (2018): 705–732.

50 Although this article was ultimately published in 2018, the 2015 working paper version was highly cited.

51 For example, it was quoted in testimony given to the House Small Business Committee Hearing, United States House of Representatives on May 24, 2016. Berg and Johnston, "Too Good to Be True?,"40.

52 Ibid. at 39.

53 Ibid. at 43.

inflexible schedule, employee status is not fundamentally incompatible with scheduling flexibility, as the question appears to claim.

A more recent peer-reviewed study conducted, in part, by two economists employed by Uber, found that only a minority of Uber drivers in the United Kingdom surveyed in 2018 desire employee status.[54] The economists found correlations between flexibility, self-employed status and subjective well-being that they suggested meant that "[m]ost individuals selecting into such arrangements – at least on the Uber platform – seemingly have strong preferences for autonomy and scheduling flexibility."[55] Like the Hall and Krueger study, this analysis made deceiving and legally erroneous associations between scheduling flexibility and independent contractor status. Rather than probing the presumptions that workers might have about employee status and disaggregating these associations in relationship to what the law does and does not require, both of these studies do the cultural work of entrenching misconceptions about the law. Scheduling flexibility and on-the-job autonomy arise from business practices.[56] Although time flexibility is *sometimes* one of many factors considered for determining worker status, it is also commensurate with employment.

2.2.2.2 Survey of Uber Drivers in San Francisco and Findings on Classification Preferences

To get a broader descriptive view of the Uber drivers who work in San Francisco – where I conducted an ethnographic study of Uber worker collectivities – I, too, developed a survey project.[57] In capturing preference for an employee or independent contractor classification, the survey instrument avoided the double-barrel problem in Hall and Krueger's question. Subjects were asked in binary terms whether they preferred to be an employee or independent contractor, and they were not given any information on what those statuses meant or entailed. To gauge what informed their preferences, subjects were then asked an open-ended question: "Why?" Findings from the binary question were similar to those in other research studies: most drivers preferred the independent contractor classification. This was true for immigrant drivers, nonimmigrant drivers, women, and men. It was also true regardless of whether subjects reported that they were engaged in Uber driving as

54 Thor Berger, Carl Benedikt Frey, Guy Levin, and Santosh Rao Danda. "Uber Happy? Work and Well-being in the 'Gig Economy.'" *Economic Policy* (2018).

55 Ibid. I might argue that most people – not just those on the Uber platform – have strong preferences for autonomy and scheduling flexibility.

56 See generally, Luc Boltanski and Eve Chiapello. *The New Spirit of Capitalism*. Verso, 2005; Benjamin H. Snyder, *The Disrupted Workplace: Time and the Moral Order of Flexible Capitalism*. Oxford University Press, 2016.

57 The survey instrument was designed in collaboration with political scientists at the University of California at Berkeley, Professor Ruth Collier and graduate student Christopher Carter. It was completed with funding from the Chip Robertson Fund.

their primary work, supplemental work, or only work. Answers to the open-ended question of why drivers favored one or the other identity suggested that workers took an instrumentalist approach to answering this question; almost invariably, they associated each status with features of work they wanted or needed, for example, health insurance, vehicle reimbursements, flexibility, autonomy. Answers also revealed that many Uber drivers – like the economists in the two studies discussed above – incorrectly conflated employee status with a mandate against scheduling flexibility.

Surveys of Uber drivers in San Francisco were conducted in-person between February and August 2016. Surveys were administered in Uber rides taken by researchers from different locations and at different times of the day (to capture as much driver variability as possible).[58] Each survey took approximately twenty minutes, and drivers were not otherwise incentivized.[59] The sole purpose of each Uber ride was to complete a survey. Of the total 218 surveys attempted, 214 were administered, and 13 were discarded for lack of completion. The collected sample was not intended to be representative of the larger San Francisco driver population, but to offer descriptive insight. The relevant demographics of the driver population were as follows: immigrant drivers made up 71 percent of total respondents; women constituted only 8 percent of respondents; 58 percent of drivers worked as a ride-hail driver as their only job; 15 percent of the sample worked as a ride-hail driver as their primary job but also had other work; and 27 percent drove as a supplement to another primary job.

Overall, 47 percent of survey subjects reported that they preferred employee status. Of the nonimmigrant respondents, the percentage difference was greater; only 32 percent stated they preferred employee status. In the small sample of women, 31 percent preferred employee status. I initially hypothesized that workers for whom Uber was their primary or only work would be more likely to prefer employee status. However, the number of workers across the three categories with this preference – whether Uber driving was their only, primary, or supplemental work – was fairly consistent. For the majority of drivers working in San Francisco who answered this survey, driving for Uber is their only work, and of these, 45 percent preferred to be employees. The number of drivers who had other jobs but for whom Uber is still their primary work was the smallest, and of these, 40 percent wanted to be employees. For those who drive for Uber as supplemental work, 38 percent wanted to be employees. These percentages are reflected below in Figure 2.1.

If regulators take the position that driver preference matters – that the law should to some extent reflect the desires and perspectives of those it is intended to serve – then all the survey data across studies seem to indicate that labor platform companies like Uber and Lyft should be allowed to continue to treat their workers as

58 Neither the timing nor the location of rides was systematized to capture optimal variability.

59 Researchers informed the drivers upon beginning the ride that they were conducting research and that no matter whether the driver took the survey, the researcher would give them a five-star rating.

FIGURE 2.1 SF Uber driver stated preference for worker status, by identity variable (2016 survey data)

independent contractors, and that employment and labor laws should accommodate this. Indeed, in several states, it already has.[60] But a survey question that conceptualizes driver perspectives as either positive or negative oversimplifies the complexity of workers' fears, needs, and perceptions about employment. Hence, after this binary query, drivers were asked to answer *why* they preferred one or the other.

Unsurprisingly, a majority of drivers who indicated a preference for employee status – 79 percent – stated that they wanted the security and/or benefits that come with employment. Of those who preferred to be treated as independent contractors, 67 percent stated that this answer was informed by a need or desire for scheduling flexibility and/or autonomy on the job. Flexibility may roughly corelate to real life experiences with independent contractor status, but by law, employee status does not mandate inflexible work or shift scheduling. Other survey answers explaining a preference for independent contractor classification included 5 percent of drivers who indicated that they did not know the difference between the two statuses; 4 percent of drivers who said that they did not deserve employee benefits because they worked part-time (also a legal misperception); and 6 percent who were expressly ambivalent – either would be fine. Hence, 15 percent of drivers who indicated a preference for independent contractor status in the previous question subsequently stated that they did not understand, had a misconception of what the law mandated of employment, or did not care. Accordingly, even the short open-ended follow up question of "why" drivers had a preference for one or the other status complicated the initial survey question's findings. These percentages are reflected in Figure 2.2.

My ethnographic research further unsettled both the survey numbers and the practice of determining complicated preferences through an efficient survey

60 Ruth Berins Collier, V. B. Dubal, and Christopher L. Carter. "Disrupting Regulation, Regulating Disruption: The Politics of Uber in the United States." *Perspectives on Politics* 16, no. 4 (2018): 930.

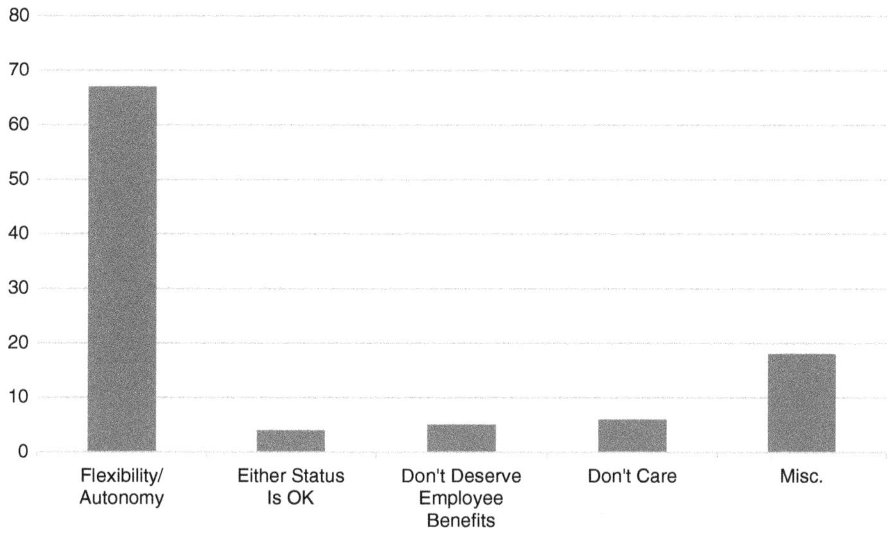

FIGURE 2.2 Explanation for independent contractor preference (2016 survey data)

medium. Below, based on driver narratives drawn from interviews and ethnographic data, I argue that the survey findings capture not attitudinal realities or desires, but in many cases, driver perceptions rooted in fear.

2.2.3 *Ethnographic Findings on Driver Perspectives on Employee Status*

In over fifty several-hours-long, semi-structured interviews and innumerable unstructured conversations with drivers in driver organizing meetings and social settings, I probed the question of employee and independent contractor status. How did workers' think about these classification categories? In the context of their relative powerlessness and economic reliance on Uber, employee status was subjectively constructed through duality. It was both a desirable way to fight back against the company and a status that came with its own undesirable uncertainties, including, most critically, the potential loss of schedule flexibility. Worker narratives overwhelmingly suggested that drivers had an *ambivalent* relationship to the employee identity.

2.2.3.1 Ambivalence and Powerlessness

In making sense of these legal categories, which have been perplexing even for law professors and judges to parse, Uber drivers' said they unequivocally needed and wanted the protections and benefits that employment status offered, but many were afraid of what a company like Uber would do if they embraced their role as "employer." Drivers, in conceptualizing their fears, had a strong sense of the structural and instrumental power of the company.[61] Their ambivalence was fueled by what a terrible employer Uber could be, how Uber would never agree to an employment model, and fears that the company would take away their flexibility – not because employee status necessitates a shift schedule – but just because they could.[62]

Nina's perspectives on employee status embodied all of these concerns. A fifty-year-old immigrant from Venezuela, Nina began driving for Uber and Lyft in March 2015. She had previously co-owned a small company with her ex-husband. After the divorce, she was out of work and without an income. She could not hold a steady job because of a medical need to take frequent and unpredictable rest breaks. Nina was involved in a driver-led organization when I met her, and she had officially objected to a proposed settlement in a class action against Uber. Like Kevin, she told me that she didn't want settlement money from Uber; unlike him, she wanted to be an employee. But every now and again, Nina would divulge her fears about the employee classification she was fighting for. In one conversation, she told me,

> Of course, I want to be an employee, but on the other hand, I think, how would I be treated by Travis Kalanick, as him being my employer? He would have a whip on us. What is he going to do to me as an employee? I know he is capable of many things. This man is an awful man, awful to the point that I think he is a sociopath. And to have so many people feeding families in the hands of a sociopath is bad. Uber is so ruthless to these software engineers. Imagine what they would do to us [drivers].[63]

On the one hand, all of Nina's organizing efforts were oriented toward achieving employee status. On the other, she was plagued by concerns about what working conditions she would have to endure if Uber became her employer. She already felt exploited by Uber and disrespected by company executives' attitudes toward drivers. But without access to company managers, a human relations department, or even accountable regulators, Nina funneled her fury to Uber's legal Achilles' heel – how they classified their drivers. Her quest for employee status was fueled by a desire for employee benefits and by a need to resist.

Like other drivers in my ethnography, Nina also frequently alluded to the company's structural power: the amount of venture capital money behind Uber and the company's influential political connections. My interlocutors regularly sent individual and group emails and texts with links to articles discussing investments in

61 For a discussion of structural and instrumental power of US businesses, see Jacob S. Hacker and Paul Pierson. "Business Power and Social Policy: Employers and the Formation of the American Welfare State." *Politics & Society* 30, no. 2 (2002): 277–325.

62 Workers perceived Uber as setting the tone and practices for other companies; hence, in these narratives, Uber served as a symbolic stand-in for gig companies more generally.

63 Hernandez, Nina. Interview by V. B. Dubal, Sept. 20, 2016.

Uber and other gig companies or comments by prominent politicians supporting the companies for their "innovation" and "job creation." For the senders, these articles were evidence that companies were engaged in unscrupulous graft. "They are lining lawmaker's pockets," was a sentiment that I heard often, from Nina and others. Many believed that the companies were actually involved in illegal bribes, but most were alluding to the instrumental power of Uber and other gig companies in their deliberate and successful political engagements.[64] The companies, they believed, had so much power in the regulatory arena, that no matter what, they could not be forced to recognize their drivers as employees.

For example, Rusty, a Filipino-American immigrant driver, felt there was no way Uber would give him basic employee benefits, no matter what the law and regulators said. Like many migrant drivers in California, Rusty drove from his home in Orange County to San Francisco for work because the rates were higher than in Southern California. In the context of how much he could benefit from employee benefits, he described his migrant work life to me,

> [For] most of the day, I stay in my car, living in my car . . . I'll have a curtain that I'll use to [sleep] . . . and then there are days that I would be able to get a bath, but there are times when I'm not going to be able to take a bath for two or three days. Then you sleep in your car and as soon as you get up then you start driving. It's really – it's terrible. I'm far from my family.[65]

Rusty wanted the benefits associated with employment, but he chose "independent contractor" status on the survey. In one of my discussions with him, he explained that his preference was based on what he thought was most realistic. Over the phone, after returning home, he further discussed his thoughts on employment,

> It will be great if they make us employees, but I don't think that Uber will. They're very smart and they're very shrewd and very greedy. They're not going to go for it ever because they make money out of this kind of system that they have right now. Where I have to sleep in my car. Why would they change? The law bends for them.[66]

Rusty's assessment and his reason for stating a preference for independent contractor status were well-informed. But they did not reflect a rejection of employment benefits – only a realistic assessment of the company's power. "Why fight for this? We will never win," he told me. Eventually, Rusty stopped driving for Uber because of the toll it was taking on his mental and physical health and on his relationship with his family.

64 For more on the structural and instrumental power of Uber in the regulatory arena in the US, see generally, Collier, Dubal, and Carter, "Disrupting Regulation," 919–937.

65 Cruz, Rusty. Interview by V. B. Dubal, May 4, 2017.

66 Cruz, Rusty. Interview by V. B. Dubal, Aug. 19, 2017.

Rather than being clear-cut, Nina and Rusty's perspectives on employee status were fueled by an ambivalence generated from a fear that the company could act with impunity. Unlike judges applying a legal test, drivers took into account the external influences that might impact their lives beyond the obvious benefits of the status. Their knowledge of the amount of capital that the gig companies spent lobbying to get laws written in their favor, of the companies' political connections, and of their ruthless litigation tactics left workers with little faith in the law's ability to address their on-the-job problems.

2.2.3.2 Ambivalence and Schedule Flexibility

In addition to their feelings of powerlessness in relationship to Uber, the ambivalence that a majority of drivers harbored toward employee status also stemmed from the necessity of scheduling flexibility in their lives. When drivers who said they wanted to be either an employee or independent contractor said what they wanted most, benefits like health insurance and a wage floor loomed large, but flexibility was omnipresent. Whether they led transnational lives, endured disabilities that made a shift schedule impossible, or were responsible to and for young children, flexibility for work was not just a desire, it was a necessity. Contextualizing the need for scheduling flexibility and the ways in which it is conflated in driver narratives with the independent contractor classification also helps to explain – and undermine – the survey data.

For example, Paul, a white, twenty-five-year-old internal migrant from Pikeville, a poor mining town in Kentucky, had indicated in the survey that he didn't want to be an employee of Uber. When, over coffee, I asked him, again, why, he answered,

> Well, maybe not me personally because eventually I would like to move on to another job. But it would be nice to have like paid time off though. But at the same rate, Uber's a horrible company. If they did have us as employees, they may be a lot more strict in terms of customer feedback. Maybe if a customer gave really bad feedback, they may fire us.[67]

Paul's answer was much more complicated than represented in the survey. On the one hand, Paul wanted the protections associated with employee status; specifically, he wanted to be able to take paid-time-off.[68] Our conversation troubled popular assumptions of what workers meant when they said they wanted to be independent contractors because of the "flexibility." Paul did not mean that he wanted the privilege to work whenever he felt like it; he meant that he wanted to work whenever he *could*. Suffering from a mental illness that presents sporadically, Paul was, on unpredictable days, incapable of working. He wanted income protection during

67 Jefferson, Paul. Interview by V. B. Dubal, April 25, 2016.
68 Paid-time-off is provided under California law.

those times. That, he noted, would be one positive aspect of being an employee. But, like Nina and Rusty, he was afraid that if Uber were his employer, he would be even more at the whim and whimsy of the company, who might fire him based on a single customer's feedback.

Another Uber driver, Ashraf, echoed the sentiments of many other workers in my ethnography when I asked them why they preferred the independent contractor classification, "Flexibility. Nothing else. If I get someone to hire me for flexibility; I will work for them."[69] A Sudanese-American refugee who came to the US in 1999, Ashraf had three small children. His wife, a health care worker, had a shift schedule – and health insurance. Soon after I got to know him, Ashraf had a kidney transplant. When I visited him in the hospital, he emphasized to me how much he needed flexibility in his work. With three children and living in one of the most expensive areas in the world, he needed to start working again soon.

> "You know, if you were an employee for Uber, they would have to cover your gas and car expenses," I explained as a nurse came in to check on him.
>
> "Okay. Then it's okay with me. Then it's okay," he trailed off exhausted. "I have been an employee. But I need the flexibility. For now, my situation is . . . I need the flexibility."[70]

Ashraf needed to rest, so I didn't want to belabor the point or force him to think about how he needed to start driving again – perhaps before he was physically ready. But I wanted to tell him – as I had to so many others – that in spite of what the gig companies told him, employee status did not mandate a shift schedule. And conversely, schedule discipline did not necessarily lead to the economic security of regulated work.

As discussed in Section 2.1, legal analysis of employee status, by law, has mostly focused on how much control a hiring entity exerts over a putative employee. But the eight to ten hour shift is a relic of factory work and the result – not of employer control – but of massive, labor-driven reform movements that sought to exert worker control over the rhythm of work.[71] If we conceptualize time discipline in the service economy not by the existence of a shift schedule but by how long one has to work to eke out a living, then gig work is fairly inflexible. Because Uber controls how much drivers earn per fare, what fares the drivers receive, how many fares the drivers receive, and how drivers conduct themselves in the context of the fare, drivers must work long, unpredictable hours and are subject to all kinds of control while at work. As one astute driver told me, "What flexibility? I sleep in my car; I eat in my car; I work in my car. That is not freedom."[72]

69 Saad, Ashraf. Interview by V. B. Dubal, May 8, 2017.
70 Ibid.
71 Snyder, *The Disrupted Workplace*, 36.
72 Younan, Tony. Interview by V. B. Dubal, Mar. 4, 2017.

Despite the overwhelming ambivalence toward employee status captured in my qualitative interviews and ethnographic fieldnotes, Uber, Lyft, and other app-based service workers rallied behind a California law, AB5, which aimed to stop the misclassification of workers. In the next section, I examine how and why drivers supported the regulation despite their deeply complicated and contested feelings about employment.

2.3 ORGANIZING AMBIVALENCE: WORKER MOBILIZATION FOR EMPLOYMENT STATUS IN CALIFORNIA

A bill widely referenced as AB5 was signed into California law in September 2019, standardizing the test for employee status across the state's laws, including those embodied in the wage orders, the labor code, and the unemployment insurance code. In contrast to the prevailing test for employee status with its subjective focus on the putative employer's right to control how work was conducted, AB5 created a presumption of employee status and codified the ABC test to determine who is excluded from California employment protections (discussed in Section 2.1). As a result of its potential impact on clarifying the employee status (under state laws) of workers in the platform-enabled gig economy, AB5 was heralded as "set[ting] the tone for the future of work."[73] The general secretary of the International Transportation Federation, went so far as to state, "[AB5] is nothing short of historic and must be the beginning of something big. Global unions see this as a source of inspiration in our fight for an international governance framework for 'gig economy' workers . . . ."[74]

The law's passage was attributable in no small part to the impassioned advocacy of gig drivers and drivers' groups. In the face of aggressive campaigning against the bill by gig companies,[75] drivers' groups engaged in near constant organizing and lobbying. Drivers from the three major gig workers' groups in California – Rideshare Drivers United (RDU), Gig Workers Rising, and Mobile Workers Alliance – met with state representatives to discuss the precariousness of gig work and their need for basic benefits. They participated in group caravans from San Diego to Sacramento to rally in favor of the bill. Some protested in front of Uber headquarters, and others

[73] Kate Conger and Noam Scheiber. "California Bill Makes App-Based Companies Treat Workers as Employees." *New York Times*, Sept, 11, 2019. www.nytimes.com/2019/09/11/technology/california-gig-economy-bill.html.

[74] "CA AB5 Law: Now We Need a Global Law for 'Gig' Workers." Sept. 12, 2019. www.itfglobal.org/en/news/california-ab-5-law-now-we-need-global-law-gig-workers

[75] Major gig companies headquartered in California, including Uber and Lyft, engaged in aggressive organizing and lobbying to defeat the bill. They flooded workers with in-app messages stating that the bill threatened their flexibility, lobbied legislators to vote against it, and even cosponsored an astroturf campaign alongside the Chamber of Commerce entitled "The I'm Independent Coalition." The I'm Independent Coalition paid gig workers up to $100 to appear at a rally opposing AB5. And citing the survey research discussed in Section 2.2, the companies repeatedly told regulators and journalists that workers want to be independent contractors, and not employees.

came to every legislative hearing on the bill. In speaking to lawmakers and journalists covering the issue, workers conveyed the urgency of basic protections and the perils of algorithmic management.

Given the uncertainty about employee status felt by many drivers, the passionate support among drivers' groups for AB5 defied predictability. Why were workers who felt ambivalence about employment fighting so hard to become employees? Through participant observation and ethnographic engagement with workers in RDU – the only grassroots, worker-led association of Uber/Lyft drivers in California with significant membership (in May 2019, the group had over 5000 driver members; by May 2020, they had grown to 17,000)[76] – I found that the drivers' embrace of the law was rooted most fundamentally in fury at the gig companies. For many, AB5 represented a way to assert power over intransigent corporations who were otherwise unaccountable to and for their workers. Drivers had endured wage cuts for many years, protested in front of the company headquarters, delivered petitions to executives, and tried to garner media advocacy around their plight. But despite all this activism, nothing in their work lives or about the companies' behavior had changed. Getting AB5 passed was a form of resistance that the companies could not ignore. As, Mike, a long-time Uber driver and RDU driver organizer, commented,

> Three to four years ago, there is no way anyone would have been for employment. People were getting what they needed, and they felt loyalty to the company. So, if the company said come to Sacramento [to defeat this bill], they would have come. That didn't happen this time [with the astroturf campaign]. Instead, drivers went to Sacramento to fight the companies. We are fed up.[77]

Mike and other RDU driver organizers also reflected on how empowered drivers felt when they heard regulators openly side with workers. "Did you hear what [Speaker of the California State Assembly] Anthony Rendon said [at the rally]?" Shaheen asked me at one organizing meeting, "he said 'this is fucking feudalism.' He actually said that. And the press quoted him on it. Can you believe it?" After spending years hearing how politicians supported gig companies, to finally have their working conditions recognized and condemned by state representatives was galvanizing.

In addition to mobilizing driver frustration and fury, driver advocates were also strategic in approaching the ambivalent attitude toward employee status among the gig workforce. Before the introduction of AB5, core RDU driver organizers "were not sure if employment was going to fly" among their membership base. When I asked Nicole Moore, a Lyft driver and one of the lead organizers, precisely how RDU rallied drivers in favor of employment, she explained that it happened organically and was a collaborative process.[78] The driver organizers started by asking drivers

76 The other two organizations have been formed and sponsored by unions.
77 Smith, Mike. Interview by V. B. Dubal, March 29, 2019.
78 Moore, Nicole. Interview by V. B. Dubal, May 30, 2019. Nicole Moore is the only driver whose real name I use in this article because she has taken on the public face of RDU.

about their priorities. Using their own app-based technology, they sent questions to their members on what they most wanted to prioritize to change about their working conditions. From those responses and after thousands of conversations, members democratically voted on a Drivers' Bill of Rights. "It just happened," Nicole said, "that what a lot of what drivers wanted mapped to [benefits provided by] employee status, including a fair wage and a union." When I pointed out that AB5 did not give them union rights, Nicole told me, "It's a first step. This is just the first step. We *are* a union, and with fair wages and basic protections, we can grow and become stronger."[79]

Still, in the height of the AB5 campaign, drivers and driver organizers expressed occasional fears that they would lose their flexibility because of the law. "Even though we know employee status doesn't mean we have to work shifts. We're worried they'll do it anyway. Just because it's easier, and maybe to punish us," said Chris, a driver I talked to at an RDU meeting. But among the core RDU organizers, the need for basic benefits and their anger at the gig companies trumped these lingering anxieties about what would happen to their schedule flexibility. "That's our next fight," Nicole disclosed. "First, we get this bill passed, and then we raise hell when they say we can't have flexibility. We are going to have to fight for that, too. But right now, we are just fighting for our freedom. Our freedom to put food on the table and pay our rent."[80]

2.4 CONCLUSION

In resisting labor regulations, platform gig companies have tried to frame the debate around research findings suggesting workers prefer the independent contractor status. In this article, I have destabilized the basis for this assertion. Not only is the research methodologically flawed, but the desires and needs of gig workers on the subject of employee status are much more complex than can be adequately represented in survey research. My deep ethnographic engagement, participant observation, and qualitative interviews underscore that gig workers are ambivalent about employee status. While they need and want protections, many recognize the immense structural and instrumental powers of the corporations, and they fear what kinds of control gig companies might exert if they feel authorized to behave as employers. Workers are particularly worried about losing on-the-job scheduling flexibility. Nevertheless, both because of their precarious work lives and because they had been ignored, for years, by both gig companies and regulators, gig workers in California mobilized in favor of employee status and rallied to pass AB5.

Based on these findings, I conclude that for the purposes of workplace regulations, the question of whether gig workers want to be employees is fundamentally the

79 Moore, Nicole. Interview by V. B. Dubal, Aug. 8, 2019.
80 Ibid.

wrong one. For lawmakers seeking to stabilize worker incomes and extend safety net protections to gig workers, the better inquiry is what kinds of protections do workers in the platform-based service economy need. Many of the answers to this question are embodied in the existing panoply of work protections accorded to employees. Among other things, gig workers need wage guarantees, workers' compensation if they are injured on the job, unemployment insurance if they are terminated through no fault of their own, freedom from discrimination at work, healthy and safe workplaces, and the rights to engage in organizing and to form a union.

Instead of limiting the protections that gig workers have access to – as the gig companies have suggested in their own legislative proposals – lawmakers may approach the regulation of gig work by *growing* employment protections. For example, based on the professed needs of gig workers like Paul, Nina, Kevin, and Ashraf, regulators could append the right to set one's own time schedule into state labor codes. Ironically, in their attempt to undermine AB5, Uber and Lyft penned alternative legislation in which they expressed a willingness to commit to exactly this in exchange for other basic employment protections.[81] But gig workers need both. As Nicole from RDU said passionately at an AB5 organizing meeting, "Regulators cannot improve this work without engaging the people that do it. Ask us and we'll tell you . . . we need healthcare, we need fair wages, and we need flexibility. And together, we are going to fight like hell for those things . . . All of those things, and more."

BIBLIOGRAPHY

Acevedo, Deepa Das. "Unbundling Freedom in the Sharing Economy." *S. Cal. L. Rev.* 91 (2017): 793.

Berg, Janine, and Hannah Johnston. "Too Good to Be True? A Comment on Hall and Krueger's Analysis of the Labor Market for Uber's Driver-Partners." *ILR Review* 72, no. 1 (2019): 39–68.

Berger, Thor, Carl Benedikt Frey, Guy Levin, and Santosh Rao Danda. "Uber Happy? Work and Well-being in the 'Gig Economy.'" *Economic Policy* (2018).

Boltanski, Luc, and Eve Chiapello. *The New Spirit of Capitalism*. Verso, 2005.

Buchanan-Oliver, Margo, and Angela Cruz. "Discourses of Technology Consumption: Ambivalence, Fear, and Liminality." *ACR North American Advances* (2011).

Collier, Ruth Berins, V. B. Dubal, and Christopher L. Carter. "Disrupting Regulation, Regulating Disruption: The Politics of Uber in the United States." *Perspectives on Politics* 16, no. 4 (2018): 919–937.

Conger, Kate, and Noam Scheiber. "California Bill Makes App-Based Companies Treat Workers as Employees." *New York Times*, Sept, 11, 2019. www.nytimes.com/2019/09/11/technology/california-gig-economy-bill.html.

[81] This legislation is embedded in a San Francisco Chronicle article for reference. See Carolyn Said. "Uber Circulates New Gig Bill as Alternative to AB5." *San Francisco Chronicle*. Sept. 20, 2019. www.sfchronicle.com/business/article/Uber-circulates-new-gig-work-bill-as-alternative-14426247.php.

"CA AB5 Law: Now We Need a Global Law for 'Gig' Workers." Sept. 12, 2019. www.itfglobal.org/en/news/california-ab-5-law-now-we-need-global-law-gig-workers.

Conner, Mark, and Christopher J. Armitage. "Attitudinal Ambivalence." *Attitudes and Attitude Change* (2008): 261–286.

Craig, S., and M. Martinez, eds. *Ambivalence, Politics and Public Policy*. Springer, 2016.

Cunningham-Parmeter, Keith. "From Amazon to Uber: Defining Employment in the Modern Economy." *BUL Rev.* 96 (2016): 1673–1728.

DeBruyne, Nicholas L. "Uber Drivers: A Disputed Employment Relationship in Light of the Sharing Economy." *Chi.-Kent L. Rev.* 92 (2017): 289–315.

Dubal, V. B. "Wage Slave or Entrepreneur: Contesting the Dualism of Legal Worker Identities." *Calif. L. Rev.* 105 (2017): 65–123.

Dubal, V. B. "Winning the Battle, Losing the War: Assessing the Impact of Misclassification Litigation on Workers in the Gig Economy." *Wis. L. Rev.* (2017): 739–802.

Dubal, V. B. "The Drive to Precarity: A Political History of Work, Regulation, & Labor Advocacy in San Francisco's Taxi & Uber Economics." *Berkeley J. Emp. & Lab. L.* 38 (2017): 73–136.

Eagly, Alice H., and Shelly Chaiken. *The Psychology of Attitudes*. Harcourt Brace Jovanovich College Publishers, 1993.

"Employer Costs for Employee Compensation." *Bureau of Labor Statistics, Department of Labor*, June 2019. www.bls.gov/news.release/pdf/ecec.pdf.

Hacker, Jacob S., and Paul Pierson. "Business Power and Social Policy: Employers and the Formation of the American Welfare State." *Politics & Society* 30, no. 2 (2002): 277–325.

Hall, Jonathan V., and Alan B. Krueger. "An Analysis of the Labor Market for Uber's Driver-Partners in the United States." *ILR Review* 71, no. 3 (2018): 705–732.

Kaltner, Jillian. "Employment Status of Uber and Lyft Drivers: Unsettlingly Settled." *Hastings Women's LJ* 29 (2018): 29–54.

Paul, Sanjukta M. "The Enduring Ambiguities of Antitrust Liability for Worker Collective Action." *Loy. U. Chi. LJ* 47 (2015): 969–1048.

Said, Carolyn. "Uber Circulates New Gig Bill as Alternative to AB5." *San Francisco Chronicle*. Sept. 20, 2019. www.sfchronicle.com/business/article/Uber-circulates-new-gig-work-bill-as-alternative-14426247.php.

Snyder, Benjamin H. *The Disrupted Workplace: Time and the Moral Order of Flexible Capitalism*. Oxford University Press, 2016.

Teamsters, Lyft Drivers to File Objections in Class Action Lawsuit Settlement, March 15, 2016. https://teamster.org/news/2016/03/teamsters-lyft-drivers-file-objections-class-action-lawsuit-settlement.

Tomassetti, Julia. "Who Is a Worker? Partisanship, the National Labor Relations Board, and the Social Content of Employment." *Law & Social Inquiry* 37, no. 4 (2012): 815–847.

"Uber in Legal Battle Over Drivers' Employment." *ABC 7 News*, Aug. 6, 2015. https://abc7news.com/business/uber-in-legal-battle-over-drivers-employment/909341/.

West, Tony. "Uber: Drivers Tell Us Through Focus Groups and Surveys They Don't Want to Be Employees." *USA Today*, Sept. 16, 2019. www.usatoday.com/story/opinion/2019/09/16/uber-drivers-tell-us-they-dont-want-employees-editorials-debates/2346851001/.

Zatz, Noah. "Beyond Misclassification: Tackling the Independent Contractor Problem without Redefining Employment." *ABA Journal of Labor & Employment Law* (2011): 279–294.

3

Invisible Work, Visible Workers

Visibility Regimes in Online Platforms for Domestic Work

Alexandra Mateescu and Julia Ticona

Care work is often described as the last bastion of "human" work – work that still evades the grasp of technological optimization, while remaining forever in demand. Yet domestic work is a part of the platform economy. Nannies, housecleaners, and eldercare workers are increasingly logging in to digital platforms on their smartphones and desktops to find work. These shifts are happening as direct care is one of the fastest growing jobs in the US.[1] Over the past forty-five years, the US and other postindustrial nations have faced care crises that have created a rising demand for care workers and health paraprofessionals such as personal care and home health aides. A combination of factors have spurred high demand for direct care services at a greater scale than smaller agencies and informal networks have been able to provide; such as women's entrance into the formal paid labor market, longer lifespans among older Americans, and preferences for remaining at home instead of living in nursing homes. This confluence of forces have made for an attractive market for "disruption" by technology companies. Within a patchwork environment of staffing agencies, informal networks, and online classified boards like Craigslist, online care platforms aggregate care workers available in local areas at a significantly greater scale than other options. Described as an "Amazon.com for caregivers," Care.com launched in 2007, and has more than 13.4 million registered worker profiles worldwide (11.5 million in the US) and $192 million in annual revenue.[2] On Care.com and platforms like it, employers place job listings and members contact each other and negotiate the terms of employment. They are more than simple job boards or classified ads, however, as they have embraced features now

[1] Bureau of Labor Statistics. "Fastest Growing Occupations: Occupational Outlook Handbook: U.S. Bureau of Labor Statistics." www.bls.gov/ooh/fastest-growing.htm.

[2] Farrell, Michael. "Care.com, the Big Business of Babysitting." *BostonGlobe.com*, August 14, 2014. www.bostonglobe.com/magazine/2014/08/14/care-com-big-business-babysitting/4Fjpf5q3YUSw3rMn9GraOM/story.html; Care.com, "Care.Com CRCM Investor Presentation." May 2019. https://s22.q4cdn.com/780994659/files/doc_financials/2019/q1/FirstQuarter2019 InvestorPresentation_FNL.pdf.

ubiquitous across gig economy platforms, such as rating systems, metrics, and marketing rhetorics that frame workers as entrepreneurial agents.[3]

At the same time, there is remarkably little scholarship about the role of technology in care work.[4] These platforms are often on the periphery of current policy debates about the gig economy, as are the complicated politics of visibility specific to these forms of work. Domestic workers are often cited as "invisible" workers – because they work behind the doors of people's private homes, and are invisible in many ways to policymakers. In turn, policy prescriptions often focus on increased visibility as a solution for issues of invisible or undervalued work, generating enthusiasm that labor platforms are generating digital trails for an otherwise "off the grid" informal economy. While many scholarly critiques of platform labor have focused on platform infrastructures that render workers *invisible*,[5] another strand sees it as an opportunity to make workers *visible*, by generating data and thus making actionable policy possible. In an article discussing the lack of reliable data on sexual harassment in the freelancing sector, journalist Nathan Heller notes a potentially positive role to be played by platform companies that collect data about their workforces: "We can't fix what we don't see, and we can't protect what we do not see whole."[6] By both aggregating a disaggregated workforce onto a platform, and making their experiences' visible through data, systemic issues that these workers face could be better understood and addressed.

Indeed, certain avenues of visibility into the informal employment relationships of domestic work are opened up through platforms. In 2016, for instance, the public policy think tank New America collaborated with labor platform Care.com to produce a Care Index that provided insights into contemporary cost, quality, and availability of care services across the US based on the company's user data.[7] While these collaborations are illustrative of one promising trajectory for the uses of data, not all visibilities are the same. Lines of visibility into unfair or discriminatory

[3] Ticona, Julia, and Alexandra Mateescu. "Trusted Strangers: Carework Platforms' Cultural Entrepreneurship in the On-Demand Economy." *New Media & Society* 20, no. 11 (November 2018): 4384–4404. doi:10.1177/1461444818773727.

[4] Ticona and Mateescu. "Trusted Strangers"; Flanagan, Frances. "Theorising the Gig Economy and Home-Based Service Work." *Journal of Industrial Relations* 61, no. 1 (February 2019): 57–78. doi:10.1177/0022185618800518; Hunt, Abigail, and Emma Samman. "Gender and the Gig Economy: Critical Steps for Evidence-Based Policy." Working paper. London, UK: Overseas Development Institute, 2019. https://apo.org.au/sites/default/files/resource-files/2019/01/apo-nid217091-1279081.pdf.

[5] Roberts, Sarah T. *Behind the Screen: Content Moderation in the Shadows of Social Media*. Yale University Press, 2019; Gray, Mary L., and Siddharth Suri. *Ghost Work: How to Stop Silicon Valley from Building a New Global Underclass*. Eamon Dolan Books, 2019; Van Doorn, Niels. "Platform Labor: on the Gendered and Racialized Exploitation of Low-Income Service Work in the 'On-Demand' Economy." *Information, Communication & Society* 20, no. 6 (2017): 898–914.

[6] Heller, Nathan. "The Gig Economy Is Especially Susceptible to Sexual Harassment." *The New Yorker*, January 25, 2018. www.newyorker.com/culture/cultural-comment/the-gig-economy-is-especially-susceptible-to-sexual-harassment.

[7] Schulte, Brigid and Alieza Durana. "The Care Report," *New America*, 2016, www.newamerica.org/in-depth/care-report/.

employment practices do not inevitably mobilize action. Indeed, as one recent study analyzing Craigslist ads for nanny jobs found, it is common for employers to openly advertise unreasonable and/or illegal working conditions in their online listings.[8]

We argue that visibility on these labor platforms needs to be conceived as multiple "visibility regimes" that are felt, grappled with, and leveraged in context. Various stakeholders have differently aligned or even conflicting interests over the multiple ways that digitized job markets render workers visible – to clients, to platform companies, or to regulatory actors. To families hiring a care worker, platform companies promise a vast database of online worker profiles as a solution to the struggles of selecting the perfect and trustworthy employee. But for workers on the ground, this new competitive landscape can feel unnerving. The pressures to self-brand, attune themselves to metrics, and put themselves "out there" can be alternately challenging or opportune depending on the kinds of visibility regimes at work in each situation. Through interviews with child and eldercare workers and a content analysis of company-produced materials, we discuss how online labor platforms for domestic care work make workers visible in order to facilitate trust with clients. We then illustrate the ways that this kind of visibility comes into tension with other types of "visibility regimes" that workers must navigate.

The power that care work platforms wield in the job market is often overlooked because these platforms are themselves difficult to categorize; on the one hand, they do not fit neatly into current legal debates around worker misclassification because they leave users to self-regulate around hiring decisions and negotiating terms of employment. Yet they still shape the landscape and conditions of the job market through design decisions that affect workers unevenly. Consequently, it is important that policymakers grasp the complicated politics of visibility for this labor market, so as to not exacerbate harms for vulnerable workers.

3.1 VISIBILITY AS INCLUSION

Domestic care work is considered a paradigmatic example of "invisible" work. This term, coined by Arlene Daniels, originally referred to unpaid household labor, and was meant to highlight the ways that the value of unpaid domestic work was hidden because of the prevailing understanding of the home as a gendered and decommodified space, away from the market.[9] Since then, the term has been expanded to describe activities within the context of paid work that go unmarked, unnoticed, and uncompensated – like emotional labor, or racial tasks.[10] The invisibility of domestic

8 Lair, Craig D., Chad MacLeod, and Ethan Budgar. "Advertising Unreasonable Expectations: Nanny Ads on Craigslist." *Sociological Spectrum* 36, no. 5 (2016): 286–302.

9 Daniels, Arlene Kaplan. "Invisible Work." *Social Problems* 34, no. 5 (1987): 403–415.

10 Hochschild, Arlie Russell. *The Managed Heart: Commercialization of Human Feeling*. University of California Press, 2012; Wingfield, Adia Harvey and Renee Skeete, "Maintaining Hierarchies in Predominantly White Organizations: a Theory of Racial Tasks As Invisible Labor," In

care work usually falls under the former definition of invisible work, because workers are working inside of their employers' homes, and therefore out of the public eye, but also because labor conditions are frequently informal and unregulated.

Importantly, care work platforms have inherited the deeply entrenched inequalities and historical struggles for recognition that have long defined domestic work. The history of domestic workers in the US begins with enslaved and indentured workers in colonial America. Throughout the nineteenth century, it was one of the only occupations available for women of ethnic and racial minority groups. In the early-twentieth century, Black women fled the violence and segregation of Reconstruction and the Jim Crow era and migrated from the South to Northern cities like New York where they worked as domestics.[11] Now, as employment opportunities have broadened for these women, new migrants are being drawn into domestic work. The American Community Survey found that 46 percent of domestic workers report being born outside of the US,[12] while other studies estimate that between 35 percent and 47 percent of immigrant domestic workers are undocumented.[13] Domestic workers are overwhelmingly female, and the majority (54 percent) are women of color.[14] The oppressive history of domestic work has left contemporary workers and platforms to navigate a legacy of institutionalized racism that is compounded by the devaluation of women's work, and work in the home generally.

Scholars of "invisible work" point out that work that falls into this category, because of racialized or gendered stigmatization, or many other reasons, is often characterized by poor conditions because it's not acknowledged or seen by regulators, policymakers, and employers, and therefore not valued. As Poster, Crain and Cherry explain:

> work that is not seen is not valued, either symbolically or materially ... the invisibility of ... work – and in many cases, of the workers themselves – may make it difficult for them to gain political traction or support from consumers. Finally, and most crucially, if the state and legal systems do not acknowledge the labor, it will not be addressed in policy and law.[15]

Crain, Marion, Winifred Poster, and Miriam Cherry. *Invisible Labor: Hidden Work in the Contemporary World*. University of California Press, 2016.

[11] Burnham, Linda, and Nik Theodore. "Home Economics: The Invisible and Unregulated World of Domestic Work." 2012. www.2016.domesticworkers.org/homeeconomics/; Glenn, Evelyn Nakano. "From Servitude to Service Work: Historical Continuities in the Racial Division of Paid Reproductive Labor." *Signs* 18, no. 1 (1992): 1–43; Ehrenreich, Barbara, and Arlie Russell Hochschild. *Global Woman: Nannies, Maids, and Sex Workers in the New Economy*. Macmillan, 2004.

[12] Based on the National Domestic Workers Alliance's analysis of data from the American Community Survey, 2004–2010. Burnham and Theodore. "Home Economics."

[13] Burnham and Theodore. "Home Economics," 12, 41.

[14] Burnham and Theodore. "Home Economics." Although this article focuses on domestic care work, these statistics include domestic care and cleaning work, as it is not possible to distinguish between domestic care work and other kinds of domestic work in these surveys.

[15] Crain, Marion, Winifred Poster, and Miriam Cherry. *Invisible Labor: Hidden Work in the Contemporary World*. University of California Press, 2016, 5.

We refer to this as the "visibility as inclusion" approach. Domestic workers were intentionally excluded from New Deal era labor protections, and despite legislative victories to include them under the Fair Labor Standards Act, are in practice often excluded from many labor market protections, because they apply to businesses with more than one employee.[16] Informal employment conditions also predominate, where employers do not offer contracts, pay employee taxes, or offer standard benefits like health insurance. The "visibility as inclusion" perspective sees regulation as a solution to invisibility. We argue that the role played by online labor platforms complicates this presumed relationship between increased visibility, accountability, and social value, illustrating the ways that data aggregation can create forms of visibility that are not always in workers' best interests.

3.2 VISIBILITY AS DISCIPLINE

The issue of data and visibility at work is usually understood in relation to surveillance and labor control. Compared to the "inclusion" approach described above, this approach examines a narrower set of relationships, focusing on the visibility of workers to managers. It originates in the work of Michel Foucault, who observed that powerful institutions, such as prisons, schools, and hospitals, used visibility as a mechanism to induce subjects to behave according to institutional expectations.[17] Scholars of labor drawing on this perspective understand visibility as a means of control exercised by a powerful employer over less powerful workers, and sometimes see workers' efforts at securing privacy as a form of individual resistance.[18] This literature opens questions about different types of visibility, and under whose gaze, will be beneficial for workers. For instance, Otis and Zhao point out that visibility is a form of labor control, and systems of surveillance can prompt workers to seek out invisibility in order to regain control of their time and bodies at work.[19] However, for workers using care work platforms, visibility occurs in

[16] Perea, Juan. "The Echoes of Slavery: Recognizing the Racist Origins of the Agricultural and Domestic Worker Exclusion from the National Labor Relations Act." *Faculty Publications & Other Works*, January 1, 2011. https://lawecommons.luc.edu/facpubs/151.

[17] Foucault, Michel. *Discipline and Punish: The Birth of the Prison*. Vintage Books, 1995.

[18] Lyon, David. *Surveillance Society: Monitoring Everyday Life*. First Edition. Open University Press, 2001. Zuboff, Shoshana. *In the Age of the Smart Machine: The Future of Work and Power*. Reprint Edition. Basic Books, 1989.

[19] Otis, Eileen M. and Zheng Zhao, "Producing Invisibility: Surveillance, Hunger, and Work in the Produce Aisles of Wal-Mart, China." In Crain, Marion, Winifred Poster, and Miriam Cherry. *Invisible Labor: Hidden Work in the Contemporary World*. University of California Press, 2016. See also, Ajunwa, Ifeoma, Kate Crawford, and Jason Schultz. "Limitless Worker Surveillance." *California Law Review* 105, no. 3 (2017): 735–776; Brown, Kenneth, and Marek Korczynski. "When Caring and Surveillance Technology Meet: Organizational Commitment and Discretionary Effort in Home Care Work." *Work and Occupations* 37, no. 3 (2010): 404–432; Van Oort, Madison. "The Emotional Labor of Surveillance: Digital Control in Fast Fashion Retail." *Critical Sociology*, July 13, 2018, 0896920518778087. https://doi.org/10.1177/0896920518778087.

networked online spaces, and does not stay within the boundaries of a single employer or workplace.

Recently, Adler-Bell and Miller pointed out a new twist in this long-standing use of visibility as workplace discipline, arguing that practices of data tracking and targeting have migrated from consumer services like information searching and retail, to workplace contexts.[20] Individualized data "footprints" are starting to be used in ways that determine who gets hired and who doesn't, in ways that could harden existing disadvantages.[21] As Zuboff argues, the rollout of new data collection systems within workplaces can be seen as a tactical maneuver by companies like Google to "habituate" new users to increasingly invasive surveillance.[22] This perspective sees the solution to the injustices of surveillance as less visibility, or privacy for individual workers. However, as this literature points out, the effects of surveillance are not uniform across different types of workplaces, or even across different workers within the same workplace. Additionally, surveillance may not always feel like discipline, but like empowerment and choice. This chapter illustrates that care work platforms create a form of visibility that has contradictory effects for individual workers, with some seeing it as an energizing challenge, and others experiencing it as alienating and degrading.

Other scholars have taken a different approach, suggesting relational or spectrum-based approaches to understanding visibility and invisibility at work. Hatton points out that the invisibility of work is produced by intersecting "cultural, legal, and spatial mechanisms of invisibility" that act together to hide certain types of work.[23] Poster proposed a "multi-surveillance" approach that illuminates the diverse actors, motives, and alliances possible across a spectrum of power in global networks of technologically mediated work.[24] However, these approaches were designed to explain the visibility of the labor process, or the things that workers do as they go about their daily tasks. How do we think about cases where visibility acts as a gatekeeper to employment? What are the stakes when workers must navigate visibility, not only in the context of their daily work tasks, but to get a job in the first place?

[20] Adler-Bell, Sam and Michelle Miller. "The Datafication of Employment." *The Century Foundation*, December 19, 2018. https://tcf.org/content/report/datafication-employment-surveillance-capitalism-shaping-workers-futures-without-knowledge/.

[21] Adler-Bell and Miller. "The Datafication of Employment"; Ajunwa, Crawford, and Schultz. "Limitless Worker Surveillance"; Ajunwa, Ifeoma, and Daniel Greene. "Platforms at Work: Automated Hiring Platforms and Other New Intermediaries in the Organization of Work." In Vallas, Steven P., and Anne Kovalainen. *Work and Labor in the Digital Age*. Emerald Group Publishing, 2019: 61–91.

[22] Zuboff, Shoshana. *The Age of Surveillance Capitalism: The Fight for a Human Future at the New Frontier of Power*. First Edition. PublicAffairs, 2019: 157–158.

[23] Hatton, Erin. "Mechanisms of Invisibility: Rethinking the Concept of Invisible Work." *Work, Employment and Society* 31, no. 2 (April 2017): 337.

[24] Poster, Winifred R. "Emotion Detectors, Answering Machines, and E-Unions: Multi-Surveillances in the Global Interactive Service Industry." *American Behavioral Scientist* 55, no. 7 (July 1, 2011): 868.

3.3 VISIBILITY REGIMES IN NETWORKED MARKETS

Care work platforms are only one part of larger shifts that are occurring across many different fields that blur the lines between social media and work. Cultural "influencers" who use social media to build personal brands and earn money through brand sponsorships similarly face pressures surrounding visibility. As Duffy and Hund have observed, these digital laborers face a "visibility mandate" to make themselves legible through data-driven metrics to advertisers and audiences in order to make a living, all while navigating the trade-offs for their own privacy.[25] While social media sites and online labor platforms are not typically understood as sharing many similarities, the convergence of labor and online spaces of communication have created similar pressures for these dissimilar kinds of workers.

Care work platforms have borrowed this "visibility mandate" from social media platforms, and facilitate a form of visibility that uses technology to "focus an increasingly bright light on the activities of some populations in ways that amplify disadvantage for them while shielding themselves from risk."[26] This kind of "individualized visibility" is "aimed at maximizing the extent to which careworkers can be seen by potential clients, displaying specific qualities of workers in standardized and comparable ways."[27] Care work platforms encourage clients to investigate workers' online identities (through searches of social media) as part of their hiring processes, as well as require background checks. Workers are encouraged to post photos and videos of themselves, write extensive personal biographical descriptions, solicit reviews from former clients, and put their weekly schedules online. The assumption is that transparency on the part of workers is necessary to facilitate trust with prospective clients.

Care work platforms make this kind of individualized visibility a precondition for getting access to jobs. This means that rather than being a mechanism to control and surveil workers during their daily work, care work platforms encourage workers to actively cultivate visibility to clients. Configured as "entrepreneurial" workers, domestic workers are presented by networked digital media with challenges of "visibility management," or decisions about what and to whom information should be disclosed, that are similar to the pressures faced by social media influencers.[28] However, online visibility is an ambiguous condition for social media "influencers" and domestic workers alike. As Duffy and Hund point out, women in publicly visible professions face gendered harassment and threats, creating a "bind" between the professional and economic benefits of

[25] Duffy, Brooke Erin, and Emily Hund. "Gendered Visibility on Social Media: Navigating Instagram's Authenticity Bind." *International Journal of Communication* 13 (2019): 4984.

[26] Ticona and Mateescu. "Trusted Strangers" 4388.

[27] Ibid., 4394.

[28] Flyverbom, Mikkel, Paul M. Leonardi, Cynthia Stohl, and Michael Stohl. "The Management of Visibilities in the Digital Age." *International Journal of Communication* 10 (2016): 98–109.

visibility and risks of vulnerability that are unequally distributed between men and women in creative online professions.[29]

For domestic workers, this ambiguity extends in different directions, as marginalized people live in contexts defined by the extreme poles of visibility and surveillance. As Gilman and Green point out, undocumented workers are simultaneously invisible to public and nonprofit institutions that could help them, and highly visible to employers, criminal justice, immigration and customs enforcement, among others, who seek to control, and often exploit their vulnerability. Marginalized populations experience "privacy extremes" on the one hand, being seen too much, and on the other hand too little.[30] In this way, care workers may experience overlapping and conflicting "visibility regimes," as we call them in this chapter. We use the term to refer to institutionally defined norms, mandates, expectations, or policies regarding the extent to which an individual should be seen by specific audiences in order to access institutional resources. Institutions, from social media platforms, to workers' rights organizations, construct visibility regimes through policies, design choices, and organizational cultures, that individuals must navigate in order to safeguard resources.

Scholars often use the term "regime" in connection with surveillance, for example, to specify how people experience and resist particular kinds of institutional surveillance.[31] However, by calling these "visibility regimes," we hope to distinguish our use of the term along two lines. First, workers may face multiple visibility regimes that exist in tension with one another. This is perhaps especially important in the context of work obtained in networked online spaces, where friends, family, and potential employers collide in the same social spaces. Second, while surveillance often connotes a loss of agency, as explained above, "visibility" remains more agnostic about the ends of these different regimes, and their effects on workers' lived experiences.

This more relational and intersectional view of visibility helps transcend dichotomous or additive models about who stands to benefit and who faces risks in the face of pressures toward being seen in networked public spaces.[32] For example, a workers' rights organization may encourage supporters to attend a workshop where photos will be taken and posted to the group's Facebook page in order to learn about their rights to safety on the job, and a platform may encourage workers to post photos of themselves to communicate with potential clients. Both of these visibility regimes require workers to navigate trade-offs between visibility and privacy in order to access

29 Duffy and Hund. "Gendered Visibility on Social Media."

30 Gilman, Michele, and Rebecca Green. "The Surveillance Gap: The Harms of Extreme Privacy and Data Marginalization." *NYU Rev. L. & Soc. Change* 42 (2018): 255.

31 Gilliom, John. "Struggling with Surveillance: Resistance, Consciousness, and Identity." In *The New Politics of Surveillance and Visibility*, edited by Kevin D. Haggerty and Richard Victor Ericson, 111–129. University of Toronto Press, 2006.

32 Collins, Patricia Hill. "Toward a New Vision: Race, Class, and Gender as Categories of Analysis and Connection." *Race, Sex & Class* 1, no. 1 (1993): 25–45.

resources, but an undocumented worker with a set of steady clients and a US-born worker who just lost her full-time position will experience these trade-offs in ways that are obscured by dichotomous distinctions between vulnerable and privileged workers. Instead, it offers a way to see how different identities can become salient in different circumstances without losing sight of the ways that race, ethnicity, and immigration status continue to pattern the opportunities within domestic labor markets to the disadvantage of women of color.[33]

3.4 DATA AND METHODS

This research is based on a combination of qualitative methods, utilizing both content analysis and ethnographic interviews with care workers. We analyzed materials from care work platforms, including marketing and recruitment materials, app- and web-based platforms, public statements, and other company-produced discourse that were aimed at both clients and care workers. We took a grounded theory approach to coding these materials.[34] Specifically, we identified the ways that care work platforms made workers visible, both in their active encouragement of self-branding and other individualized kinds of visibility, and in their appeals to the legitimacy of formal, institutionally visible work.

This article also draws on in-depth ethnographic interviews that the coauthors conducted with forty-three care workers in New York City, Atlanta, and Washington, DC who regularly seek work through these platforms. Instead of understanding them as research subjects, ethnographic interviewing treats interviewees as informants to their worldviews, cultures, and personal experiences.[35] Drawing on the traditions of several disciplines, including sociology and anthropology, we adopted this approach to not only understand the day-to-day realities of finding work through care work labor platforms, but also the ways that care workers made sense of these otherwise mundane details in relation to the rest of their lives, including their experiences in other kinds of work, or of sharing information and thinking about privacy in other contexts. As Pugh observes, this kind of interviewing can elicit contradictions and paradoxes in interviewees' explanations of their experiences and motivations.[36] For the purposes of examining the conflicting and contradictory ways that visibility is experienced through care work labor platforms, this method's ability to elicit these tensions, as opposed to forced choice surveys or more structured or cognitive approaches to interviewing, made it an appropriate choice for this project.

33 Duffy, Mignon. "Reproducing Labor Inequalities: Challenges for Feminists Conceptualizing Care at the Intersections of Gender, Race, and Class." *Gender & Society* 19, no. 1 (2005): 66–82.

34 Charmaz, Kathy. *Constructing Grounded Theory*. Second edition. SAGE Publications Ltd, 2014.

35 Spradley, James P. *The Ethnographic Interview*. Waveland Press, 2016.

36 Pugh, Allison J. "What Good Are Interviews for Thinking About Culture? Demystifying Interpretive Analysis." *American Journal of Cultural Sociology* 1, no. 1 (2013): 42–68.

In October 2016, we chose the three most widely used platforms among interviewed care workers, including Care.com, UrbanSitter, and SitterCity. Interviewees were recruited through local nanny agencies and worker advocacy groups, Craigslist, neighborhood e-mail lists, and Facebook groups created by nannies for other nannies in the cities we sampled. Interviews were conducted in person and via Skype by the authors and lasted between 45 and 120 minutes. Interviewees received their choice of $20 in cash or an equivalent gift card to Amazon.com. Interviewers followed a semi-structured interview schedule, with questions derived from the content analysis of platforms and company produced discourse as well as general questions about their careers, relationships with clients, and experiences of finding work through labor platforms. From the analysis of platform materials, we identified several themes surrounding the visibility produced by platforms: sign-up and profile creation, the client-view of workers' profiles, communicating with prospective families, and integrating their social media with their care work platform profiles, and asked interviewees questions probing their assumptions and knowledge about the information they were asked to provide, how it might be used, and how they felt about providing personal information though the platform. Within these questions, we asked follow-up questions probing for their expectations and experiences of visibility through platforms. We explicitly asked about their feelings about the privacy of the personal information they provided through the platform, and about their strategies of keeping their information private. We also specifically asked about their strategies of "self-promotion" and ways they might have tried to improve their ranking in platform searches. When interviewees volunteered to show us their profiles or messages they received from platforms, we asked them to send screenshots. At the end of the interview, interviewees also filled out a brief demographic survey. Interviews were recorded, with permission, and transcribed. Transcriptions were coded, in an iterative and interpretive process along with platform materials, according to methods of content analysis.[37] This included a round of open-coding by at least one of the authors, discussion about shared themes emerging across multiple interviews, and the creation of a shared "code-book" that was used to tag sections of interviews. These tags were discussed and synchronized between the two authors, over a series of months, and further refined before deciding on key themes that emerged in an iterative process.

3.5 FINDINGS

3.5.1 *Scaling Intimacy: Creating an Online Market for Informal Care*

The business model of care work platforms, which relies on paid subscriptions from users, depends on scale. As the undersupply of licensed childcare centers throughout the US has led many families to turn to the informal care market, companies like

[37] Corbin, Juliet, Anselm Strauss, and Anselm L. Strauss. *Basics of Qualitative Research*. SAGE Publications Ltd, 2015.

Care.com have framed abundant consumer choice as the key to finding the perfect domestic employee.[38] While the "on-demand" model on labor platforms has emphasized seamlessly connecting consumers with a pool of interchangeable workers, care work platforms advertise the ability to browse and scrutinize a wide range of job candidates. While access to abundant choice is marketed as a selling point for *clients*, the scale of competition – which is framed as a competition for visibility in a sea of search results – is experienced as destabilizing by some care workers. The ability to creatively self-brand and manage one's image online becomes an important skill for leveraging the kinds of visibility that care work platforms have emphasized as important for hiring. In many areas of platform design, online visibility is equated with reputability. In this section, we describe some of the platform design decisions that contribute to these dynamics.

To consumers, Care.com promises to provide "data-driven insights" through customizable search functions that sort care workers based on criteria such as ratings, last log-in, and whether or not the caregiver has a profile picture.[39] The intimate and relational experience of this labor seems to preclude the more abstracted and anonymous characterization of work that crowdwork companies, such as AMT and Crowdflower, have constructed.[40] However, as Irani points out, crowdwork does not only describe the form of labor taking place, but also works as a cultural symbol.[41] In this way, despite the conditions of care work as it is actually executed by careworkers, on-demand care companies use metrics to narrate their workers to potential clients as a caring crowd. Care.com's welcome e-mail for clients encourages them to "browse hundreds of local profiles, post a job . . . then watch the responses roll in." On their client-facing eldercare page, a client's location is pulled from their profile to display numbers for various eldercare options that the site gives immediate access to in her area. This emphasis on the plethora of options, not only in the type of care, but also the number of providers that are available, gives clients the sense of unending options to meet their needs.

But while care work platforms have streamlined access to large pools of candidate profiles, care workers themselves are often felt left with a sense of uncertainty over what it means to build and sustain an online reputation as trustworthy or experienced. Care workers are nudged to check on their accounts with e-mails reminding them, for instance, that a new job is posted every thirteen seconds.[42] But what makes

38 Center for American Progress, "Mapping America's Child Care Deserts," August 2017. www.americanprogress.org/issues/early-childhood/reports/2017/08/30/437988/mapping-americas-child-care-deserts/

39 Care.com, "What We Do," www.care.com/what-we-do.

40 Irani, Lilly. "The Cultural Work of Microwork." *New Media & Society* 17, no. 5 (2015): 720–739; Gray, Mary L., Siddharth Suri, Syed Shoaib Ali, and Deepti Kulkarni. "The Crowd Is a Collaborative Network." In *Proceedings of the 19th ACM conference on computer-supported cooperative work & social computing*, 134–147. ACM, 2016.

41 Irani. "The Cultural Work of Microwork."

42 Care.com, e-mail to authors, October 12, 2019.

a care worker stand out? Hiring for domestic work has typically relied on a third party to vouch for a care worker's reputation, skills, and work experience. Care workers are thus heavily dependent on recommendations from previous employers or on the brokerage provided by nanny agencies. This often includes matching clients with workers, vetting both parties through background checks and interviews, assisting in the negotiation process over terms of employment, and providing ongoing support to clients and workers after hiring. As such, these intermediaries are not only entities that formalize employment but also – like client referrals – act as trusted authorities that vouch for individual workers' reputations.

In the absence of these intermediaries, care workers' individualized profiles serve as proxies for more involved means of brokering trust. As Schoenbaum notes, labor platforms encourage a sense of intimacy in transactions as a strategy for reducing risk: "sharing economy firms rely not on firm reputation or other guarantees by the firm, but rather by making transactions more intimate, that is, by predicating transactions on personal information about buyers and sellers."[43] In our interviews, an oft-repeated refrain from care workers was that looking for work felt a lot like online dating; sending out numerous messages, hopeful conversations with prospective clients through the platform's messaging interface, and the disappointments of being "ghosted" by potential employers.

The responsibilities of care work platforms in their role as employment brokers are often ambiguous to users. While platforms conduct "preliminary screenings" of care workers and provide guidelines, clients are positioned as responsible for soliciting full background checks and otherwise vetting care workers, often by surveilling their online presence. On Care.com, clients are urged to "spend some quality time with our in-depth profiles," to ask and double-check references, and to search a prospective employee's name online for any suspicious information.

Platforms sometimes use proxies for reputability that gesture at the local and socially networked dimensions of worker reputation. For instance, UrbanSitter's website has displayed curated lists of baby-sitters "recommended" by parents affiliated with particular community organizations and schools.

In these ways, care work platforms present themselves as the safe and convenient option, in contrast to a "shadowy" informal market laden with risk. Ultimately, however, the responsibility of safety lies with clients: Care.com urges clients to "pay attention to your first impression – and trust your gut!" Similarly, UrbanSitter advises clients that a "'wrong' feeling is all the justification you need to let someone go (or to not hire them in the first place)." In these ways, care work platforms engage in the project of educating clients on what a quality care worker looks like, and who, by contrast, is risky. Trustworthiness and common sense conceptions of safety are rarely given but emerge through collective shaping of norms, and through prescriptive shaping of expectations. On platforms, as Crawford and Gillespie have pointed

43 Schoenbaum, Naomi. "Gender and the Sharing Economy." *Fordham Urb. LJ* 43 (2016): 1029.

out, the option of "flagging" content as inappropriate is common and serves to "[codify] complaints as a legible regime of feeling."[44] Aside from reputation and rating systems which bring these regimes to bear on an individual level, there are a range of ways in which care work platforms aim to educate clients on discerning the right "fit" among available care workers. More indirectly, how care workers are made visible by the platforms serve in part to communicate and define to clients what qualities, qualifications, and other information should be a part of their judgments about safety and trust. We found that care workers are acutely aware that any slight indication of negative reputation – like a less-than-stellar rating – as this first level of encounter can have a tangible impact on the ability to find work.

For care workers, expectations of online scrutiny often entail making oneself more visible to prove their legitimacy, through self-presentation and biographical narrative in online profiles, site-based credentialing through badges and other markers of employability, and the integration of social media profiles (Facebook, LinkedIn, etc.). It may also mean submitting to formal background checks, or indicating that they are willing to work "above the table" by using proper tax documentation with the IRS. Throughout the process of signing up, building a profile, messaging clients, and using site resources, workers are faced with a range of decisions they must make about what information to put forward about themselves. Sometimes it is not a decision to make: some care work platforms require submitting a Social Security Number to register, from the very start excluding parts of the workforce.

Care workers we spoke to often chose to withhold details they felt uncomfortable sharing, while also acknowledging the trade-offs being made. Visibility can extend beyond the realm of the platform. Workers' profiles on sites like Care.com and SitterCity are publicly visible through search engines like Google, meaning that anyone, even people who aren't members of these platforms, are able to view the personal information posted to individual profiles, including a workers' zip code, age, schools attended, and schedule availability. For some care workers we interviewed, this visibility was a boon to expanding their clientele. For others, it meant walking a delicate balance, at times engaging in strategies to preserve some degree of privacy. In the following sections, we contrast the ways that care workers negotiate different regimes of visibility, and experience the tension between them as strains or pressure points that come with compromises, rejections, frustrations, and struggles to adapt to changing conditions in a digitizing job market.

3.5.2 *Lost in the Crowd*

Karen is a black woman in her early fifties. Born and raised in Georgia, she has been working as a full-time nanny for over thirty years in Atlanta. When the family she was

[44] Crawford, Kate, and Tarleton Gillespie. "What Is a Flag for? Social Media Reporting Tools and the Vocabulary of Complaint." *New Media & Society* 18, no. 3 (March 1, 2016): 3.

working for as a full-time, on-the-books household employee announced their plans to move to another state, Karen began her search to find another family, and was able to rely on severance pay and, following that, unemployment benefits, to support herself during the precarious period between jobs. Hoping to avoid surrendering part of her wages to an agency, she set up accounts on both Care.com and SitterCity and began responding to numerous job listings.[45] She recalled unpleasant memories of the experience, which struck her as impersonal and demoralizing:

> That's why it misses that personal touch because any time you have that human relationship, somebody actual you can see, it just don't give that same value. I tried Care.com, I mean religiously, because I was out of work and then it was a long time before anybody touched bases with me and I felt so generic. I'd get online. I'd tell my story. I'd pour out my heart and it's just like people can get on there because they have the option to go through many, many nannies.

Karen felt alienated when she waded into the broad pool of nannies looking for work on Care.com. After "pouring out her heart" in her profile and messages to families, she found that her years of experience across the childcare industry were devalued by parents who had access to a huge number of potential nannies for hire. In particular, she felt that her status as a professional was not being taken seriously by clients. As Karen explained:

> a lot of the people that was on there . . . they want babysitters . . . It's like, this is my bread and butter! I am not working for no nine, ten dollars an hour . . . Those kind of people want to undermine your faith in your ability . . . I'm telling you, I got years of experience . . . You messing with the wrong person . . . I don't even respond to them because that's a slap in the face to me.

Workers in the caregiving industry have long felt the tensions between societal perceptions of caregiving as a casual form of supplemental employment, and caregiving as a profession deserving of a living wage, benefits, and standards. For individual care workers, employment may nevertheless include both short- and long-term employment, ranging from full-time work with one household to one-off and recurring work with multiple client households. However, the distinction between casual care work and professionalized care has, to an extent, been upheld by the different channels through which hiring takes place. Prior to care work labor platforms, casual care work and full-time nanny positions would not typically have appeared in the same channels. Large traditional household staffing agencies may provide last-minute back-up care and also offer long-term placements, but they would have (and still do) play a large role in the hiring process, including determining appropriate wages for workers with different tiers of professional experience.

[45] Oftentimes, traditional agencies that match nannies with employers will charge a fee that is a percentage of the nanny's salary, charged to the family, on top of the nannies wages. Some nannies feel this may depress their wages, as families are paying fees on top of paying their wages.

Having had this more specialized and limited type of visibility to a select group of prospective client, the broad and indiscriminate visibility of platforms afforded made Karen feel "generic" and the process cold and impersonal.

For older, professional nannies like Karen, care work platforms seemed to blur these distinctions by collapsing diverse workers into a single labor pool. She felt that having her profile displayed alongside casual babysitters flattened distinctions that were important to her professional identity. Although some certification programs exist and some childcare workers obtain degrees in child development, in-home care work lacks institutionalized barriers to entry, meaning that many care workers develop professionalized identities such as "nanny" through building up years of experience. Professional organizations like the International Nanny Association and worker advocacy organizations like the National Domestic Workers Alliance play a significant role in shaping professional identity and advocating for raising standards within the industry. In this case, the visibility Karen was used to through traditional nanny agencies grated against the economics of scale that a platform like Care.com provides to parents, where the factors that determine competitiveness are affected by the ways platforms choose to sort, rank, and make workers visible to clients, and not the more traditional markers of experience such as years in the field, and stable relationships with long-term clients. The visibility regime afforded by the platform, which determined competitiveness by a complex algorithmic logic that was unclear to Karen, was in tension with the kind of visibility she believed she should have as an experienced professional care worker.

To allow job-seekers like Karen to stand out in a vast pool of workers, Care.com offers a number of paid premium services. By paying for extended background checks, they appear higher in search results, receive a special "badge" displayed on their individual profiles, and are promised "more responses to applications." Karen paid for a background check, and membership that allowed her to send more messages to families, but still had little success. Instead, she felt unsettled by the one-sidedness of the platform's visibility regime. She complained that she was often unable to ascertain if the prospective client she was communicating with through the chat feature was male or female because, while she was required to upload a photo to apply for a job, they did not have to in order to post a job. In some instances, she found herself in conversation with a prospective client, only to realize she was being lured into a fake check scam, which she acknowledged she may have fallen for had she been less experienced and cautious. In our fieldwork, we found that care workers frequently encountered scams disguised as ordinary job listings, usually deceiving workers into mailing a check to the scammers.

Jaded, Karen ultimately opted to use a more traditional nanny agency. In most agencies, agency owners have financial incentives to successfully place workers. Care.com may have provided Karen with a ready supply of search results, but the company has no financial incentives to successfully place workers with families. The company relies on a freemium model for revenue, wherein both clients and care workers can use the site for free but must pay a subscription fee to be able to respond to certain job listings or to appear higher in search results. As a result, the company is more strongly incentivized to ensure that a high volume of families and workers stay active and visible on the site, making their premium paid services all the more valuable in order to sort, distinguish, and contact one another.

While Karen's frustration emerged from feeling unable to leverage her extensive experience to stand out in the crowd, others similarly struggled with crafting their image online. Linda, a white care worker in her forties, began searching for work on UrbanSitter after being laid off from her job in 2013, but had difficulty finding a family that would hire her. Although she was eventually able to find three regular families, she felt that as an older woman, she couldn't compete with younger, more savvy and connected care workers. Although UrbanSitter "strongly encourages" workers to upload videos of themselves, Linda was concerned that doing so would hurt her chances, explaining that at her age, a video would not give the positive impression that a "bubbly twenty-something year old" might be able to achieve. Her hunch is supported by research conducted about other platforms. Several studies have found that profile pictures were a primary way people valued and made decisions about where to stay on short-term rental site AirBnB, and while the platform has changed the way it displays its hosts and renters' photos, profile photos remain an important element of platform visibility regimes.[46]

Other women of color relayed frustrating experiences with getting their profiles photos approved in order to start applying for jobs. Laquinta recalled several days of frustrating e-mails rejecting many different profile photos she tried to upload, and finally being successful after she tried a photo where her hair was straight instead of curly. She said that her friend had pointed out that it might have been because she was Black. We asked her if she thought this was true, and Laquinta replied,

> I didn't think about it in that way until she said something about it . . . even then, I'm not going to let my mind go there because I don't like to . . . I would hate for anyone to look at it that way . . . but it was ridiculous. It didn't add up. It didn't make sense to me that they would put so much emphasis on my picture.

Scholars have pointed out the ways that families seeking nannies use stereotypes about a candidate's race and ethnicity to hire care workers, and to the racialized aesthetics of "professional" hairstyles that put unfair burdens on women of color.[47]

[46] Ert, Eyal, Aliza Fleischer, and Nathan Magen. "Trust and Reputation in the Sharing Economy: The Role of Personal Photos on Airbnb." SSRN Scholarly Paper. Rochester, NY: Social Science Research Network, January 1, 2016. https://papers.ssrn.com/abstract=2624181. Edelman, Benjamin, Michael Luca, and Dan Svirsky. "Racial Discrimination in the Sharing Economy: Evidence from a Field Experiment." *American Economic Journal: Applied Economics* 9, no. 2 (April 2017): 1–22. https://doi.org/10.1257/app.20160213.

[47] MacDonald, Cameron Lynne. "Ethnic Logics: Race and Ethnicity in Nanny Employment." In *Caring on the Clock: The Complexities and Contradictions of Paid Care Work*, 153–164. Rutgers University Press, 2015; Rosette, Asleigh Shelby, and Tracy L. Dumas. "The Hair Dilemma: Conform

Linda and Laquinta's experiences highlight the ways that care work platforms construct a visibility regime that rewards self-branding and speedy online communication, despite their irrelevance to the quality of care provided.

Platform visibility regimes placed a premium on workers' abilities to present themselves and their experience through long biographical narratives in their profiles. This created challenges for care workers who did not speak English as their first language, particularly in a context where online communication precedes in-person interactions. Maia, a Mexican woman in her twenties who had come to the US on an au pair program and later found other care work through platforms, reported worrying about her English language skills as she crafted and recrafted the biographical section of her profile with the help of friends. Similarly, Denise, a woman in her fifties who had immigrated from a Francophone West African country, struggled to apply for care work jobs via Care.com's mobile phone app. At the time of our interview, she was employed full-time as a cleaner at a major hotel chain in New York, but because she was getting older, she hoped to find less physically strenuous childcare work that would also give her more free time to take English classes. However, she found that much of the language on care work platforms was confusing, unfamiliar phrases like "date night" or the connotational differences between terms like "nanny" and "babysitter" made it difficult to decide what boxes to tick to describe the work she was looking for. Given the high proportion of care workers who are immigrants, the emphasis on written language in profiles and communication with families prior to getting hired places them at a significant disadvantage.

Despite navigating this visibility regime within significant constraints, workers were not without solutions to some of these problems. In some cases, older care workers recruited the help of relatives to navigate a digitized job market. This was the case for Gloria, a young woman who had recently arrived to the US from Cameroon, and who had begun working in in-home elder care while also working a full-time office job. Besides running her own profile on various care work platforms, she also acted as an online proxy for her mother and aunt who also worked in elder care, managing their profiles, applying to jobs, and responding to messages on their behalf. Although like herself, her mother and aunt were native English speakers, they still found online markets to be difficult to navigate without Gloria's help. Similarly, like Maia above, who enlisted the help of her friends to write her biographical narrative, Kendall, a nanny in Georgia, told us about the ways that she curated and polished her mother's Care.com profile, advising her to add "grandmotherly" touches, and helping her respond to messages from prospective employers. These social workarounds show the limits of the individual address of platforms visibility regimes, and the invisible collective labor that is essential to the

to Mainstream Expectations or Emphasize Racial Identity Makeup, Identity Performance & Discrimination." *Duke Journal of Gender Law & Policy* 14, no. 1 (2007): 407–422.

construction of individual visibility. Despite their appearance as a vast pool of individual profiles, many workers are linked together through invisible networks of mutual aid and support.

The visibility regime of care work platforms emphasizes profile photos, biographical narrative, and rapid response rates to prospective employers in order to remain competitive. This visibility regime also flattens professional distinctions that were meaningful to workers, such as those between casual babysitters and professional care work. The individualized visibility regime of platforms placed older workers, some workers of color, and those for whom English was not their first language at a disadvantage. By highlighting some parts of their identities in ways that were in tension with constraints placed on them by long-standing historical inequities and patterns of labor force discrimination and segregation, platform visibility regimes exacerbate existing inequalities based in race, ethnicity, and age.

3.5.2 *Building a Caring Brand*

While some workers experienced tensions between their identities and platform visibility regimes, others seemed to be in alignment. For some care workers, online marketplaces are a vehicle for building client networks that can be translated into a reputation and sustained income. This has been the experience for Sarah, a Black college student in her early twenties who spoke enthusiastically about her future plans to start her own franchise of childcare centers in Washington, DC. After taking child development classes in high school, she started working part-time at a childcare center while attaining her Bachelors degree. The pay at the center was low, so she began taking on regular babysitting gigs through a variety of platforms, including Care.com, SitterCity, and by staying active and building a presence across different childcare Facebook groups. Sarah kept close attention to platform metrics, and by working for multiple clients she was able to accrue an abundance of five-star ratings on Care.com. In addition to meeting other criteria like responding rapidly to messages, Care.com informed her that she ranked in the top 1 percent of caregivers in her area. The starting point for this success was Sarah's individual profile. Below, she described the ways she constructed her profile according to what potential clients might want:

> a lot of parents like people who go on hikes, [and] speak different languages so I'll put that into my profile. You try to jazz it up as much as you can so that it attracts a lot of families . . . Luckily I always ask people to do a review . . . on Care.com after I sit for them. So far I have 100% for everything . . . A bunch of 5 stars . . . families really like that. They trust that.

Including personal details and hobbies, she blends the personal and professional, presenting herself in the same genre as dating profiles or other online biographical writing on social media. Sarah used her profile as a form of portable professional reputation, in the same way one might use a resume or a LinkedIn profile, to refer clients across the web. Her Care.com profile allowed her to move seamlessly through many different online environments, including Instagram and Facebook where she reported having "3,000 friends," and which provided important sources of future clients and babysitters for her business.

Over time, she found that her network had grown large enough that she could not take on all the job requests she received. Instead, she found a way to turn her reputation into further revenue by running a referral service through the platforms. She now actively recruits care workers and refers families to other sitters she has personally vetted, charging 15 percent of their take-home pay, as well as a $25 fee to set up an initial interview. She also created a codified policy in place for managing her own online reputation, requiring all the care workers in her referral service to sign a written agreement that they "will not maliciously or spitefully try and tarnish [her] business as well if they are fired or let go or if they quit." In this way, she is able to provide a service that is another layer of vetting and brokerage that may have otherwise been provided by a childcare agency. Care.com offers the individualized visibility of care workers' online profiles as a proxy for more involved forms of vetting, but Sarah's interpersonal, human vetting touches upon clients' anxieties in navigating a still informal market.

She described Care.com as a "vessel" for her to promote her own website and businesses. However, despite the ways that her enterprising orientation toward her career resonates with "gig" economy rhetoric encouraging small business development and individual entrepreneurship, Sarah still encountered roadblocks in using certain features of Care.com to build her business. Sarah observed that she didn't think she was "allowed" to put a link to her referral business website on her Care.com profile, and that the platform's CareChat messaging feature automatically censored her phone number and e-mail address. However, she has found other ways to coordinate directly with parents. Although Care.com promotes the individual entrepreneurship of their care workers and small businesses, the platform is only designed to allow for the pursuit of entrepreneurship within the company's own financial interests.

Care.com is a platform where Sarah entrepreneurially made use of the same economies of scale that Karen disliked in order to build her own business. Unlike Karen, she did not feel a tension between her professional identity and the way her profile was displayed and circulated through networked online spaces. Instead, Sarah's entrepreneurial orientation toward her career, as well as the way she pieces together income from several different sources, made individual visibility a natural extension of her own understanding of her career. In this way, Care.com's visibility regime is generally aligned with the entrepreneurial visibility Sarah seeks out to promote herself and her business. Like the gendered labor of social media brand "influencers," Sarah leverages the visibility regimes of social media and care work platforms to brand herself and access job opportunities.

3.6 CONCLUSION

In recent years, various tech companies have set out to construct new avenues for vetting prospective hires, typically by using alternative data such as social media activity. In 2018, the *Washington Post* profiled a company called Predictim that offered to "analyze a person's speech, facial expressions and online history with promises of revealing the hidden aspects of their private lives." The service targeted parents looking to hire child care workers, offering to generate a risk rating by using language-processing algorithms to sift through a care worker's Facebook, Twitter, and Instagram posts. The company claimed to be able to go beyond a conventional background check to assess aspects of a care workers' personality such as "politeness, ability to work with others and 'positivity.'"[48] However, media coverage of the company promptly generated backlash, as critics pointed to the ways in which automated categorization of online speech as inappropriate, obscene, or risky relied on a very skewed understanding of risk and were likely little more than a tool for generating racist judgment of care workers.

While Predictim shuttered after social media platforms cut off its access to their sites, the incident highlights a broader trend in a growing faith in technology to reduce uncertainty in informal economies. Relevant here is that these developments are occurring within workforces that are culturally and legally marginalized, where workers are mostly people of color, who face suspicion as risky and potentially criminal workers.[49] As markets for informal economies, such as domestic work, move online, workers' increased visibility to various actors – clients and companies, but also policy actors and lawmakers – generates uncertain futures over how to govern these new visibilities, and potentially use them in positive ways such as enforcing labor protections. An open question may emerge over whether the work that platforms do, to funnel worker profiles into algorithmic sorting or codify qualifications through on-platform credentials, can be a vehicle toward these ends. For care workers, though, uncertainty abounds over how such systems work, and how workers' own visibility is implicated in their operations. Within this uncertainty, care workers must navigate difficult tensions between making themselves visible in certain ways to potential clients to secure employment, while also navigating competing visibility regimes.

Care work platforms inherit many of the tensions, contradictions, and inequalities that have long existed in domestic work; few labor protections and little enforcement, racial and ethnic disparities in pay and benefits, sexual harassment, as well as job precarity. Moreover, these platforms place the burden of vetting care workers onto clients. In 2019, an article from the *Wall Street Journal* highlighted several

[48] Harwell, Drew. "Wanted: The 'Perfect Babysitter.' Must Pass AI Scan for Respect and Attitude." *Washington Post*, November 23, 2018, sec. The Switch. www.washingtonpost.com/technology/2018/11/16/wanted-perfect-babysitter-must-pass-ai-scan-respect-attitude/.

[49] Pager, Devah. *Marked: Race, Crime, and Finding Work in an Era of Mass Incarceration*. University of Chicago Press, 2008.

incidents involving care workers hired through Care.com, that tragically ended in theft, assault, and murder.[50] A few months later, Care.com removed 46,594 of its daycare center listings after another *Wall Street Journal* article noted that many of its center listings lied about being state-licensed.[51] Following these scandals, Sheila Marcelo – founder and CEO of Care.com – stepped down from her position.[52]

In the aftermath, the company also made a promise to more effectively screen and vet its workforce. It is important to note here that care workers' livelihoods are becoming more closely intertwined with the decisions, design, and policies enacted by platform companies. Reputational scandals that shake consumer faith in care work platforms to properly vet workers can ripple through with consequences for care workers, whose own individual reputations can become suspect. Public concern over care work platforms' laissez-faire regulation of their workforces has led to calls for more involved vetting, leading a competitor to mandate background checks for all care workers using their platform.[53]

But in efforts to recover from reputational harms as well as to protect themselves from liability, care work platform companies may double down on surveillance and scrutiny of workers. But in an industry where invisibility to formal institutions – particularly for immigrants and workers laboring "under the table" for various reasons – are the conditions of possibility for many workers to be able to do their work at all, platform companies must contend with these contradictions. Importantly, as these platforms have grown, there is little clarity over their legal and ethical responsibilities for working against entrenched inequalities within the industry.

Online marketplaces may not be the root cause of new tensions, but their design is not neutral. Policymakers cannot assume that online marketplaces are merely parallel, digitized iterations of offline marketplaces, but have their own dynamics that can shift the experience of finding work. More attention needs to be paid to the ways that care work platforms are designed around a particular archetype of what an "entrepreneurial" domestic worker looks like – one who feels at home in the world of apps, social media, and online self-branding. These new demands for visibility on the part of workers place some workers within conflicting regimes of visibility, in a position in which they must navigate difficult trade-offs between safety, privacy, and employment. These dynamics may ultimately replicate or even exacerbate many of the divisions that

50 Grind, Kirsten, Gregory Zuckerman, and Shane Shifflett. "Care.Com Puts Onus on Families to Check Caregivers' Backgrounds – With Sometimes Tragic Outcomes." *Wall Street Journal*, March 8, 2019, sec. Tech. www.wsj.com/articles/care-com-puts-onus-on-families-to-check-caregivers-backgroundswith-sometimes-tragic-outcomes-11552088138.

51 Shifflett, Shane and Kirsten Grind. "Care.Com Removes Tens of Thousands of Unverified Listings." *Wall Street Journal*, March 31, 2019, sec. Tech. www.wsj.com/articles/care-com-removes-tens-of-thousands-of-unverified-listings-11554040800.

52 Zuckerman, Gregory, and Allison Prang, "Care.com Founder to Step Down as CEO Months After WSJ Report," *Wall Street Journal*, August 6, 2019. www.wsj.com/articles/care-com-founder-to-step-down-as-ceo-months-after-wsj-report-11565089901.

53 UrbanSitter, e-mail sent to author, October 30, 2019.

have defined domestic work in the predigital era. Given these dynamics, an important question is how policymakers can intervene to lessen the conflicts for workers.

BIBLIOGRAPHY

Adler-Bell, Sam and Michelle Miller. "The Datafication of Employment." *The Century Foundation*, December 19, 2018. https://tcf.org/content/report/datafication-employment-surveillance-capitalism-shaping-workers-futures-without-knowledge/.

Ajunwa, Ifeoma, and Daniel Greene. "Platforms at Work: Automated Hiring Platforms and Other New Intermediaries in the Organization of Work." In Vallas, Steven P., and Anne Kovalainen. *Work and Labor in the Digital Age*. Emerald Group Publishing, 2019: 61–91.

Ajunwa, Ifeoma, Kate Crawford, and Jason Schultz. "Limitless Worker Surveillance." *California Law Review* 105, no. 3 (2017): 735–776.

Brown, Kenneth, and Marek Korczynski. "When Caring and Surveillance Technology Meet: Organizational Commitment and Discretionary Effort in Home Care Work." *Work and Occupations* 37, no. 3 (2010): 404–432.

Bureau of Labor Force Statistics (2017) Fastest growing occupations, occupational outlook handbook. www.bls.gov/ooh/fastest-growing.htm.

Burnham, Linda, and Nik Theodore. "Home Economics: The Invisible and Unregulated World of Domestic Work." 2012. www.2016.domesticworkers.org/homeeconomics/.

Care.com, "Care.Com CRCM Investor Presentation." May 2019. https://s22.q4cdn.com/780994659/files/doc_financials/2019/q1/FirstQuarter2019InvestorPresentation_FNL.pdf.

Center for American Progress, "Mapping America's Child Care Deserts," August 2017. www.americanprogress.org/issues/early-childhood/reports/2017/08/30/437988/mapping-americas-child-care-deserts/.

Charmaz, Kathy. *Constructing Grounded Theory*. Second edition. SAGE Publications Ltd, 2014.

Collins, Patricia Hill. "Toward a New Vision: Race, Class, and Gender as Categories of Analysis and Connection." *Race, Sex & Class* 1, no. 1 (1993): 25–45.

Corbin, Juliet, Anselm Strauss, and Anselm L. Strauss. *Basics of Qualitative Research*. SAGE Publications Ltd, 2015.

Citron, Danielle Keats, and Frank Pasquale. "The Scored Society: Due Process for Automated Predictions." *Washington Law Review* 89, no. 1 (2014): 1–33.

Crain, Marion, Winifred Poster, and Miriam Cherry. *Invisible Labor: Hidden Work in the Contemporary World*. University of California Press, 2016.

Crawford, Kate, and Tarleton Gillespie. "What Is a Flag for? Social Media Reporting Tools and the Vocabulary of Complaint." *New Media & Society* 18, no. 3 (March 1, 2016): 410–428.

Daniels, Arlene Kaplan. "Invisible Work." *Social Problems* 34, no. 5 (1987): 403–415. https://doi.org/10.2307/800538.

Duffy, Brooke Erin, and Emily Hund. "Gendered Visibility on Social Media: Navigating Instagram's Authenticity Bind." *International Journal of Communication* 13 (2019): 4983–5002.

Duffy, Mignon. "Reproducing Labor Inequalities: Challenges for Feminists Conceptualizing Care at the Intersections of Gender, Race, and Class." *Gender & Society* 19, no. 1 (2005): 66–82.

Edelman, Benjamin, Michael Luca, and Dan Svirsky. "Racial Discrimination in the Sharing Economy: Evidence from a Field Experiment." *American Economic Journal: Applied Economics* 9, no. 2 (April 2017): 1–22. https://doi.org/10.1257/app.20160213.

Ehrenreich, Barbara, and Arlie Russell Hochschild. *Global Woman: Nannies, Maids, and Sex Workers in the New Economy*. Henry Holt and Company, 2004.

Ert, Eyal, Aliza Fleischer, and Nathan Magen. "Trust and Reputation in the Sharing Economy: The Role of Personal Photos on Airbnb." SSRN Scholarly Paper. Rochester, NY: Social Science Research Network, January 1, 2016. https://papers.ssrn.com/abstract=2624181.

Farrell, Michael. "Care.com, the Big Business of Babysitting." *BostonGlobe.com*, August 14, 2014. www.bostonglobe.com/magazine/2014/08/14/care-com-big-business-babysitting/4Fjpf5q3YUSw3rMn9GraOM/story.html.

Flanagan, Frances. "Theorizing the Gig Economy and Home-Based Service Work." *Journal of Industrial Relations* 61, no. 1 (2019): 57–78.

Flyverbom, Mikkel, Paul M. Leonardi, Cynthia Stohl, and Michael Stohl. "The Management of Visibilities in the Digital Age." *International Journal of Communication* 10 (2016): 98–109.

Foucault, Michel. *Discipline and Punish: The Birth of the Prison*. Vintage Books, 1995.

Gilliom, John. "Struggling with Surveillance: Resistance, Consciousness, and Identity." In *The New Politics of Surveillance and Visibility*, edited by Kevin D. Haggerty and Richard Victor Ericson, 111–129. University of Toronto Press, 2006.

Gilman, Michele, and Rebecca Green. "The Surveillance Gap: The Harms of Extreme Privacy and Data Marginalization." *New York University Review of Law & Social Change* 42 (2018): 253–307.

Glenn, Evelyn Nakano. "From Servitude to Service Work: Historical Continuities in the Racial Division of Paid Reproductive Labor." *Signs* 18, no. 1 (1992): 1–43.

Gray, Mary L., and Siddharth Suri. *Ghost Work: How to Stop Silicon Valley from Building a New Global Underclass*. Eamon Dolan Books, 2019.

Gray, Mary L., Siddharth Suri, Syed Shoaib Ali, and Deepti Kulkarni. "The Crowd Is a Collaborative Network." In *Proceedings of the 19th ACM conference on computer-supported cooperative work & social computing*, 134–147. ACM, 2016.

Grind, Kirsten, Gregory Zuckerman and Shane Shifflett. "Care.Com Puts Onus on Families to Check Caregivers' Backgrounds – With Sometimes Tragic Outcomes." *Wall Street Journal*, March 8, 2019, sec. Tech. www.wsj.com/articles/care-com-puts-onus-on-families-to-check-caregivers-backgroundswith-sometimes-tragic-outcomes-11552088138.

Harwell, Drew. "Wanted: The 'Perfect Babysitter.' Must Pass AI Scan for Respect and Attitude." *Washington Post*, November 23, 2018, sec. The Switch. www.washingtonpost.com/technology/2018/11/16/wanted-perfect-babysitter-must-pass-ai-scan-respect-attitude/.

Hatton, Erin. "Mechanisms of Invisibility: Rethinking the Concept of Invisible Work." *Work, Employment and Society* 31, no. 2 (April 2017): 336–351.

Heller, Nathan. "The Gig Economy Is Especially Susceptible to Sexual Harassment." *The New Yorker*, January 25, 2018. www.newyorker.com/culture/cultural-comment/the-gig-economy-is-especially-susceptible-to-sexual-harassment.

Hochschild, Arlie Russell. *The Managed Heart: Commercialization of Human Feeling*. University of California Press, 2012.

Hunt, Abigail, and Emma Samman. "Gender and the Gig Economy: Critical Steps for Evidence-Based Policy." Working paper. London, UK: Overseas Development Institute, 2019. https://apo.org.au/sites/default/files/resource-files/2019/01/apo-nid217091-1279081.pdf.

Irani, Lilly. "The Cultural Work of Microwork." *New Media & Society* 17, no. 5 (2015): 720–739.

Lair, Craig D., Chad MacLeod, and Ethan Budgar. "Advertising Unreasonable Expectations: Nanny Ads on Craigslist." *Sociological Spectrum* 36, no. 5 (2016): 286–302.

Lyon, David. *Surveillance Society: Monitoring Everyday Life*. First Edition. Open University Press, 2001.

MacDonald, Cameron Lynne. "Ethnic Logics: Race and Ethnicity in Nanny Employment." In *Caring on the Clock: The Complexities and Contradictions of Paid Care Work*, 153–164. Rutgers University Press, 2015.

Otis, Eileen, and Zheng Zhao. "Producing Invisibility: Surveillance, Hunger, and Work in the Produce Aisles of Wal-Mart, China." In *Invisible Labor: Hidden Work in the Contemporary World*, 148–167. University of California Press, 2016.

Pager, Devah. *Marked: Race, Crime, and Finding Work in an Era of Mass Incarceration*. University of Chicago Press, 2008.

Perea, Juan F. "The Echoes of Slavery: Recognizing the Racist Origins of the Agricultural and Domestic Worker Exclusion from the National Labor Relations Act." *Ohio State Law Journal* 72 (2011): 95–138.

Poster, Winifred R. "Emotion Detectors, Answering Machines, and E-Unions: Multi-Surveillances in the Global Interactive Service Industry." *American Behavioral Scientist* 55, no. 7 (July 1, 2011): 868–901.

Pugh, Allison. "What Good Are Interviews for Thinking About Culture?" *American Journal of Cultural Sociology* 1 (2013): 42–68.

Roberts, Sarah T. *Behind the Screen: Content Moderation in the Shadows of Social Media*. Yale University Press, 2019.

Rosette, Asleigh Shelby, and Tracy L. Dumas. "The Hair Dilemma: Conform to Mainstream Expectations or Emphasize Racial Identity Makeup, Identity Performance & Discrimination." *Duke Journal of Gender Law & Policy* 14, no. 1 (2007): 407–422.

Schoenbaum, Naomi. "Gender and the Sharing Economy." *Fordham Urb. LJ* 43 (2016): 1023–1070.

Schulte, Brigid and Alieza Durana. "The Care Report," *New America*, 2016, www.newamerica.org/in-depth/care-report/.

Shifflett, Shane and Kirsten Grind. "Care.Com Removes Tens of Thousands of Unverified Listings." *Wall Street Journal*, March 31, 2019, sec. Tech. www.wsj.com/articles/care-com-removes-tens-of-thousands-of-unverified-listings-11554040800.

Spradley, James P. *The Ethnographic Interview*. Waveland Press, 2016.

Ticona, Julia, and Alexandra Mateescu. "Trusted Strangers: Carework Platforms' Cultural Entrepreneurship in the On-Demand Economy." *New Media & Society* 20, no. 11 (November 2018): 4384–4404. doi:10.1177/1461444818773727.

Van Doorn, Niels. "Platform Labor: On the Gendered and Racialized Exploitation of Low-Income Service Work in the 'On-Demand' Economy." *Information, Communication & Society* 20, no. 6 (2017): 898–914.

Van Oort, Madison. "The Emotional Labor of Surveillance: Digital Control in Fast Fashion Retail." *Critical Sociology*, July 13, 2018, 0896920518778087. https://doi.org/10.1177/0896920518778087.

Wingfield, Adia Harvey and Renee Skeete, "Maintaining Hierarchies in Predominantly White Organizations: A Theory of Racial tasks as Invisible Labor," In Crain, Marion, Winifred Poster, and Miriam Cherry. *Invisible Labor: Hidden Work in the Contemporary World*. University of California Press, 2016.

Zuboff, Shoshana. *In the Age of the Smart Machine: The Future of Work and Power*. Reprint edition. Basic Books, 1989.

Zuboff, Shoshana. *The Age of Surveillance Capitalism: The Fight for a Human Future at the New Frontier of Power*. First Edition. PublicAffairs, 2019.

Zuckerman, Gregory, and Allison Prang, "Care.com Founder to Step Down as CEO Months After WSJ Report," *Wall Street Journal*, August 6, 2019. www.wsj.com/articles/care-com-founder-to-step-down-as-ceo-months-after-wsj-report-11565089901.

4

The Importance of Qualitative Research Approaches to Gig Economy Taxation

Shu-Yi Oei and Diane M. Ring

As the United States tax system continues grappling with how to accurately and appropriately tax workers in the gig economy, it confronts a number of questions. For example, what relationships are included in the gig economy? How many workers and firms are involved, and is the number increasing or decreasing? What particular problems do these workers encounter when engaging with the tax system, and are these meaningfully different from the problems confronted by other taxpayers? Is there a prototypical gig worker, or would gig-specific tax reform or relief have to be tailored to different types of gig workers (e.g., contributors of labor as opposed to contributors of capital)? If there is a prototypical gig worker, what is that worker's profile, and is it shifting? Is independent contractor classification for gig workers appropriate, and is it desired by workers? Is the tax system affecting the labor-supply decisions of gig workers?

Many of these questions have proven difficult to answer due a lack of adequate information. But the answers are important because they will shape how and whether the tax system responds to the gig economy, including how it approaches business deductions, tax withholding, and income definitions, how and whether it utilizes safe harbors and de minimis exceptions, how it designs taxpayer forms and instructions, and how it allocates enforcement and taxpayer education resources. In addition, as we have discussed in previous work, the tax system's evolving responses to the gig sector will affect other legal areas such as employment law, labor law, and antitrust.[1] Thus, the question of how to obtain the data and information necessary to formulate sound tax and related policies for gig work is vital.[2] This chapter discusses

[1] Shu-Yi Oei, *The Trouble with Gig Talk: Choice of Narrative and the Worker Classification Fights*, 81 Law & Contemp. Probs. 107 (2018); Diane M. Ring, *Silos and First Movers in Sharing Economy Debates*, 13(1) Law & Ethics of Hum. Rts. 61 (2019).

[2] *See generally* Emilie Jackson et al., *The Rise of Alternative Work Arrangements: Evidence and Implications for Tax Filing and Benefit Coverage* 10 (Office of Tax Analysis, Working Paper No. 114, 2017), *available at* www.treasury.gov/resource-center/tax-policy/tax-analysis/Documents/WP-114.pdf; Lawrence F. Katz & Alan B. Krueger, *Understanding Trends in Alternative Work Arrangements in the United States* (Nat'l Bureau of Econ. Research, Working Paper No. 25425, 2019), *available at* www.nber.org/papers/w25425.

the limitations of quantitative empirical research on the gig economy and argues that incorporating more qualitative approaches will be essential in attaining a comprehensive understanding of the tax policy issues involved. Specifically, this chapter emphasizes that adoption of a diverse set of research approaches is crucial because the administrative tax return and labor survey data are insufficient and are shaped by prior decisions of gig economy firms and participants. Many questions remain that such quantitative data, by its very nature, cannot answer.

We use the term "gig economy" throughout our discussion to conform with the title of this volume. However, as we have noted in prior work and as we discuss further below, the "gig economy" terminology is contested and has been deliberately wielded to advance particular narratives regarding the sector and to secure favorable regulatory treatment.[3] In this chapter, we largely set the broader question of appropriateness of terminology aside, only flagging those debates where relevant to our analysis.

This chapter proceeds as follows. First, it identifies the key tax issues at stake in the gig economy, including tax administration, worker classification, and impact of taxation on workforce decisions. Second, it discusses two primary ways in which quantitative approaches do not adequately capture the full picture of the tax issues at stake. Quantitative gig data is not neutral, but is instead predetermined by regulatory and compliance decisions made by gig economy firms to date. These strategic decisions – which reflect moves made during the gig economy's infancy combined with strategic shifts over time – have the capacity to affect and frame the design and findings of subsequent empirical research. For example, firms' initial choice to classify workers as independent contractors and to issue Forms 1099-K forced workers receiving those forms to file Internal Revenue Service (IRS) Form 1040 Schedule C (Profit or Loss from Business).[4] This in turn means that tax researchers have to examine Schedule C to detect and to understand the tax behaviors of gig workers and firms. Moreover, firms' decisions to issue Forms 1099-K to only some workers means that the tax return data pool that researchers are studying is likely underinclusive, and may not capture workers earning smaller amounts.[5] In short, threshold choices by firms, workers, and government agencies affect the data we can gather and use, the questions we ask, and the conclusions we reach. In addition, the administrative tax return data and labor survey data upon which much quantitative

[3] Oei, *supra* note 1.

[4] Dep't of the Treasury, Internal Revenue Serv., 2019 Schedule C and Instructions for Schedule C (2018), *available at* www.irs.gov/forms-pubs/about-schedule-c-form-1040.

[5] For studies of taxpayers receiving Forms 1099, see Brett Collins et al., *Is Gig Work Replacing Traditional Employment? Evidence from Two Decades of Tax Returns* (IRS Statistics of Income Division, Working Paper 2019), *available at* www.irs.gov/pub/irs-soi/19rpgigworkreplacingtraditionalemployment.pdf; Katherine Lim et al., *Independent Contractors in the U.S.: New Trends from 15 Years of Administrative Tax Data* (IRS Statistics of Income Division, Working Paper 2019), *available at* www.irs.gov/pub/irs-soi/19rpindcontractorinus.pdf.

research relies are insufficient and limited in scope. Not every important tax policy question can be answered solely by looking at those data sources.

Third, this chapter details how qualitative research methods such as interviews and case studies can flesh out gaps in the quantitative data, can help interpret quantitative data, and can help answer questions that extend beyond the scope of quantitative data. For example, administrative tax return data alone does not reveal how workers grapple with tax compliance issues or how they find information and advice about tax compliance, nor does it tell us about worker attitudes toward tax compliance. As an example of the value that can be added using qualitative research methods, we discuss the findings of a research study we conducted that employed close content analysis of public Internet discussions among ridesharing drivers concerning taxes and tax obligations.[6] That study yielded insights into the key issues confronting forum participants and their behaviors, choices, and attitudes. These types of insights are difficult to glean from tax administrative data.

Of course, qualitative approaches have shortcomings as well. Care must be taken in using and interpreting all types of data regarding the gig economy. But employing a more diverse set of research approaches yields a demonstrably richer account of gig economy tax issues than that provided by quantitative tax administrative and labor survey data alone. This methodological observation regarding the limits of quantitative data extends beyond the study of gig economy taxation; it likely holds true for the study of the larger contingent workforce as well.

4.1 KEY TAX ISSUES IN THE GIG ECONOMY AND THE NEED FOR EMPIRICAL RESEARCH

A decade after the gig economy first emerged, taxpayers and governments continue to face many questions about the appropriate taxation of this sector and how taxation relates to the broader legal and economic issues the sector presents. At present, policymakers confront three major issues in taxing the gig economy: (1) understanding the tax compliance behaviors of gig workers in order to encourage accurate compliance and make sure that compliance burdens are fair; (2) ensuring appropriate classification of gig economy workers (that is, whether they are appropriately classified as independent contractors or as employees); and (3) appreciating how the tax system interacts with workplace law and affects labor decisions in the gig economy. Effective and sensible responses to these issues will rely on a combination of information and policy analysis, hence the need for empirical research.

6 Shu-Yi Oei & Diane M. Ring, *The Tax Lives of Uber Drivers: Evidence from Internet Discussion Forums*, 8 COLUM. J. TAX L. 56 (2017).

4.1.1 *Tax Compliance and Administration*

From the outset, the tax system has grappled with designing tax administration to ensure compliance by gig workers.[7] As a threshold matter, it is clear that, just like other workers, gig workers are subject to income taxation. However, it is not clear whether gig workers fully understand their tax compliance obligations or are preparing their taxes accurately. Recognizing this risk, the National Taxpayer Advocate[8] flagged the need for guidance for sharing economy workers as a Most Serious Problem confronting the tax system and encouraged the IRS to provide such guidance.[9]

The state of compliance among gig workers is intimately linked to compliance choices made by gig economy firms. For example, as we have detailed in previous work, firms such as Uber, Lyft, and Airbnb have taken inconsistent and shifting positions on which tax reporting forms to issue to workers and to whom to issue them. Several firms have chosen to issue a Form 1099-K only to workers engaging in over 200 rides or transactions and earning over $20,000 annually.[10] Such a reporting position risks leaving much gig income unreported to the IRS, which is likely to result in underreporting of income on the worker side.[11] Thus, one outstanding policy question concerns whether the reporting rule should be changed to require more complete reporting of low-dollar transactions by firms to the IRS. Beyond its impact on third-party reporting practices, the reality that much gig work is lower-dollar, more sporadic, and more episodic than traditional work means that it may not make sense for gig workers to invest substantial time and resources in learning

7 Caroline Bruckner , Kogod Tax Pol'y Ctr., American Univ., Shortchanged: The Tax Compliance Challenges of Small Business Operators Driving the On-Demand Platform Economy (2016), *available at* www.american.edu/kogod/research/upload/shortchanged.pdf.

8 The Taxpayer Advocate Service is an independent office inside the IRS tasked with evaluating the impact of tax law, enforcement, and administration on taxpayers, and reporting its findings to Congress. *See* Taxpayer Advocate Service, *National Taxpayer Advocate Reports to Congress and Research*, Internal Revenue Service (June 20, 2019), www.irs.gov/advocate/reports-to-congress.

9 1 Nat'l Taxpayer Advocate, 2017 Annual Report to Congress 165 (2017); *see also* Taxpayer Advocate Service, *National Taxpayer Advocate Blog: Caring about "Sharing" – The IRS Should Do More for Participants in the Gig Economy*, Internal Revenue Service (Nov. 15, 2017), https://taxpayeradvocate .irs.gov/news/nta-blog-caring-about-sharing-the-irs-should-do-more-for-participants-in-the-gig-econ omy?category=Tax%20News; Taxpayer Advocate Service, *National Taxpayer Advocate Blog: Participants in the Sharing Economy Lack Adequate Guidance*, Internal Revenue Service (Jun. 28, 2018), https://taxpayeradvocate.irs.gov/news/nta-blog-participants-in-the-sharing-economy-lack-adequate-guidance-from-the-irs?category=Tax%20News.

10 Oei & Ring, *supra* note 6, at 64–65, 86–87 (discussing the changing positions of gig economy firms regarding Form 1099-K reporting); *see also* Shu-Yi Oei & Diane M. Ring, *Can Sharing Be Taxed?*, 93 Wash U. L. Rev. 989, 1032–41 (2016) (discussing Form 1099-K information reporting rules and their interpretation and the potential effects on firms' information reporting choices).

11 For examples of literature exploring the link between information reporting to the IRS and tax compliance, see James Alm et al., *Do Individuals Comply on Income Not Reported by Their Employer?*, 37 Pub. Fin. Rev. 120 (2009); Leandra Lederman, *Reducing Information Gaps to Reduce the Tax Gap: When Is Information Reporting Warranted?*, 78 Fordham L. Rev. 1733 (2010); Susan Cleary Morse et al., *Cash Businesses and Tax Evasion*, 20 Stan. L. & Pol'y Rev. 37 (2009).

extensive and complicated tax compliance rules.[12] In response, some observers have advocated for the introduction of special regimes applicable to gig workers, such as safe harbors and de minimis rules to alleviate compliance burdens.[13]

Documenting and assessing these tax compliance risks and proposed solutions requires data. For example, discerning the degree of tax compliance among gig workers requires information about the baseline number of gig workers, the income reporting positions of gig economy firms, and the corresponding income reporting positions of the workers. Determining whether reforms or special rules are needed for gig economy participants requires information about the size of the sector and the dollars at stake,[14] but it also requires information about the tax compliance issues confronting gig workers and how these differ from those faced by other populations. Some of this information can be gleaned from analyses of administrative tax return and labor survey data, but as detailed below in Section 4.2, the predetermined state of this data and its corresponding gaps require that additional empirical approaches be employed.

4.1.2 *Worker Classification*

A pervasive gig economy issue confronting tax authorities is that of worker classification. Among gig economy firms, the dominant business model characterizes workers as independent contractors. This reporting choice has been the subject of much litigation by workers, predominantly on labor and employment law grounds.[15]

In the tax system, classification matters because employees and independent contractors (and the firms that engage them) are subject to different federal tax rules. A business that classifies its workers as independent contractors not only avoids labor and employment law obligations to provide assorted protections and benefits to the workers, it avoids responsibility for payroll taxes (Social Security, Medicare,

12 *See, e.g.*, Oei & Ring, *supra* note 6; Oei & Ring, *supra* note 10. For example, gig workers may find themselves only performing work in the sector briefly or sporadically. In contrast, traditional small businesses run by individuals are likely to be longer-lasting.

13 *See, e.g.*, Kathleen D. Thomas, *Taxing the Gig Economy*, 166 U. PA. L. REV. 1415 (2018) (proposing "non-employee withholding" and a "standard business deduction" for gig workers); *see also* NEW GIG Act of 2017, H.R. 4165, 115th Cong. (2017); NEW GIG Act of 2017, S. 1549, 115th Cong. (2017) (proposing a safe harbor for independent contractor treatment; proposing changes to Form 1099-K reporting).

14 *See generally* Andrei Haigiu & Julian Wright, *The Status of Workers and Platforms in the Sharing Economy*, 28 J. ECON. & MGMT. STRATEGY 97 (2019) (deploying a formal economic model to evaluate how worker classification decisions can be detrimental to both businesses and workers).

15 *See, e.g.*, Order Granting Plaintiffs' Motion for Final Approval and Plaintiffs' Motion for Attorneys' Fees, O'Connor et al., v. Uber Technologies, Inc. et al., Case No. 13-cv-03826-EMC, Docket Nos. 945, 935 (N.D. Cal., Sept. 13, 2019) (final settlement approved in two cases against Uber regarding worker classification). In September 2019, Uber was sued in a California class action for violating the state's newly enacted worker classification law set to take effect in 2020. McRay v. Uber, Case No. 4:19-cv-05723-DMR (N.D. Cal., Sept. 11, 2019).

and unemployment)[16] and for tax withholding.[17] On the worker side, those classified as independent contractors report income on Schedule C, are responsible for paying quarterly estimated income taxes and self-employment (Social Security and Medicare) taxes, and (because they are not subject to employer withholding) are responsible for managing their budgets to ensure they can pay these taxes.[18] Collectively, these compliance burdens are generally heavier than those borne by employees. On the flip side, independent contractor/self-employed filers are allowed more generous tax deductions than employees. Furthermore, the 2017 Tax Act arguably introduced some additional tax changes tilting in favor of independent contractor classification, enacting the new Internal Revenue Code (IRC) § 199A 20 percent pass-through deduction and suspending the deduction for employee business expenses in § 67. New § 199A is only available to independent contractors and not employees.

These worker classification issues raise important ongoing questions for the tax system. As an initial matter, are gig workers being appropriately classified under the law? Do existing rules for taxing independent contractors work well when applied to "microbusiness" gig economy workers? Are gig workers aware of new IRC § 199A and if so, has that new provision, together with the suspension of § 67 miscellaneous itemized deductions for employees, affected worker attitudes toward classification and profitability of the work? To the extent tax reform has tilted the balance of tax incentives toward independent contractor classification, it may have introduced a tool by which firms can nudge workers to accept that status, particularly if the costs of being an independent contractor (such as more limited workplace legal protections and benefits at the state and federal level) are not as salient as the more immediately observable tax benefits (e.g., a new 20 percent tax deduction under § 199A).[19] Beyond these impacts, the tax classification of workers may have implications for labor and employment law worker classification outcomes as well.

All these questions require empirical analysis,[20] but only some can be answered by looking at tax administrative data. Nuanced questions such as how workers feel

16 Federal Insurance Contribution Act of 1935, 26 U.S.C. ch. 21, § 3101 et seq; Federal Unemployment Tax Act, 26 U.S.C. ch. 23, § 3301 et seq.; *see also* Shu-Yi Oei & Diane M. Ring, *Tax Law's Workplace Shift*, 100 B.U. L. Rev. 651 (2020).

17 *See* Internal Revenue Code (IRC), 26 U.S.C. §§ 3401, 3402, 3501 et seq.; *id.* §§ 6401, 6050W; *see also* U.S. Dep't of Treasury, Internal Revenue Serv., Publ'n. No. 15, Cat. No. 10000W (Circular E), Employer's Tax Guide (2018) *available at* www.irs.gov/pub/irs-pdf/p15.pdf.

18 I.R.C. § 1401(a), (b); I.R.C. § 164(f)(1). By contrast, for employees, the employer must deposit and report payroll taxes and is nominally responsible for half of Social Security and Medicare taxes. I.R.S. Publ'n No. 15, *supra* note 17. That is, the employer must not only withhold half those taxes from employee wages but must also pay the employer matching portion.

19 *See* Oei & Ring, *supra* note 16.

20 *See, e.g.*, Gad Allon et al., The Impact of Behavioral and Economic Drivers on Gig Economy Workers (Oct. 29, 2018) (unpublished manuscript), *available at* https://papers.ssrn.com/sol3/papers.cfm?abstract_id=3274628 (developing an econometric model of workers' labor decisions by conducting experiments on their financial incentives, in collaboration with a ridesharing firm).

about independent contractor tax issues, how they acquire information necessary to comply with their tax obligations, and how they learn about new laws (and adjust their work and tax compliance behaviors accordingly) are all questions that require different research approaches.

4.1.3 *Tax, Labor Choices, and the Future of Work*

A third set of policy issues concerns how taxation of the gig economy and the independent contractor workforce more generally may drive changes in the nature of work at a micro and macro level. At a micro level, the primary question is how taxation affects decisions to do gig economy work. At a more macro level, the question is how tax policies may affect the shape and future of the workforce, for example, by encouraging the growth of independent contractor or contingent work (either in replacement of traditional employment or as a supplement to it). Empirical studies are important in answering these types of questions. As we have mapped in recent work,[21] tax administrative and labor survey data begin to offer insights into the size and composition of the independent contractor and contingent workforce, and such data is being analyzed by government and academic researchers.[22] The data matters because it might tell us how big the independent contractor/contingent workforce really is, whether and how it is growing or changing, how it relates to traditional employment relationships, and whether we ought to be concerned about the changing nature of work. However, it is not clear that the existing sources of tax administrative and labor survey data are up to the task of delineating how the tax system may be shaping these work choices and trends.

[21] *See* Oei & Ring, *supra* note 16.

[22] Jackson et al., *supra* note 2; Bureau of Labor Statistics, Economic News Release: Contingent and Alternative Employment Arrangements Summary (June 7, 2018), [hereinafter BLS Study] www.bls.gov/news.release/conemp.nro.htm; Lawrence F. Katz & Alan B. Krueger, *The Rise and Nature of Alternative Work Arrangements in the United States, 1995–2015* (Nat'l Bureau of Econ. Research, Working Paper No. 22667, 2016), rev'd in Katz & Krueger, *supra* note 2; U.S. Gov't Accountability Office, Contingent Workforce: Size, Characteristics, Earnings, and Benefits 3 (2015) (size of contingent workforce varies from 5% to 1/3 of total employed labor force depending on definitions and data), www.gao.gov/assets/670/669766.pdf; Anat Bracha & Mary A. Burke, *Who Counts as Employed? Informal Work, Employment Status, and Labor Market Slack* 6 & Figure 2, Panel A (Federal Reserve Bank of Boston, Working Paper No. 16–29, 2016), *available at* www.bostonfed.org/publications/research-department-working-paper/2016/who-counts-as-employed-informal-work-employment-status-and-labor-market-slack.aspx; Katharine G. Abraham et al., *Measuring the Gig Economy: Current Knowledge and Open Issues* (Nat'l Bureau of Econ. Research, Working Paper No, 24950, 2018), *available at* www.nber.org/papers/w24950; Katharine G. Abraham et al., *Driving the Gig Economy* (Nat'l Bureau of Econ. Research, Conf. Paper, 2018), *available at* http://papers.nber.org/conf_papers/f110357/f110357.pdf.

4.2 THE STATE OF DATA ON THE GIG ECONOMY

Recognizing the importance of data and its analysis in addressing key tax issues in the gig economy, academics and government policymakers have begun to conduct empirical research regarding the size and growth of the gig economy and of contingent work more broadly.[23] For example, both the Treasury and the Bureau of Labor Statistics have attempted to measure the size, growth, and composition of the gig economy and independent contractor workforce.[24] Prominent academic economists have also engaged in estimation of the size of gig and contingent work.[25] And private and industry researchers have ventured into the game as well.[26] Thus, the state of learning about the sector is undoubtedly growing.[27]

Yet, researchers have confronted difficulties in gathering and analyzing empirical data about the gig economy and the independent contractor workforce more generally. Even as basic a question as one regarding the sector's size has yielded different answers depending on methodology.[28] Gaining insight into tax compliance concerns and behaviors and the effects of these concerns and behaviors on work is even more challenging. We flag here two limitations of data relevant to gig economy taxation that reveal the need for a more comprehensive approach to empirical research. First, available administrative tax data on the gig economy is determined by prior choices of workers and firms, which may tilt subsequent analysis. Second, available data is insufficient and does not hold the answers to every important policy question posed by the sector.

[23] *See* sources cited *supra* note 22.

[24] Jackson et al., *supra* note 2; BLS Study, *supra* note 22.

[25] Jonathan V. Hall & Alan B. Krueger, *An Analysis of the Labor Market for Uber's Driver-Partners in the United States* (Nat'l Bureau of Econ. Research, Working Paper No. 22843, 2016), *available at* www.nber.org/papers/w22843.

[26] *See, e.g.*, JP MORGAN CHASE INSTITUTE, THE ONLINE PLATFORM ECONOMY IN 2018: DRIVERS, WORKERS, SELLERS, AND LESSORS (2018), www.jpmorganchase.com/corporate/institute/document/institute-ope-2018.pdf; UPWORK & FREELANCERS UNION, FREELANCING IN AMERICA: 2018, at www.upwork.com/i/freelancing-in-america/2018/.

[27] Knowledge about the gig economy will undoubtedly grow further as research opportunities become available in light of big data. *See, e.g.*, Matthew J. Salganik, BIT BY BIT (2018) (guide for conducting social science research in the age of big data).

[28] *See, e.g.*, Abraham et al., *Measuring the Gig Economy*, *supra* note 22; Katz & Krueger, *supra* note 2 (revising 2016 study downwards); Oei & Ring, *supra* note 16 (discussing differences in the literature between Treasury and BLS measurements, and between tax administrative data and survey data); *see generally* Roy Maurer, *Experts Puzzled by New BLS Contingent Workforce Data*, SHRM (June 8, 2018), www.shrm.org/resourcesandtools/hr-topics/talent-acquisition/pages/experts-puzzled-new-bls-contingent-workforce-data.aspx; Anat Bracha & Mary A. Burke, *How Big Is the Gig?* (Nov. 2017) (unpublished manuscript), *available at* www.researchgate.net/publication/321228231_How_Big_is_the_Gig.

4.2.1 *Data is Predetermined and Not Neutral*

First, the data available for study is affected by prior decisions of gig economy firms. In their formative years, firms like Uber and Airbnb used their first-mover advantage to adopt favorable regulatory and tax positions.[29] These positions included classifying workers as independent contractors rather than employees, choosing to issue Forms 1099-K to them, and as noted above in Section 4.1.1, sometimes choosing to issue Forms 1099-K only if dollar and transaction thresholds were met.[30] Firms used the power of words and terminology to buttress these tax and regulatory choices. As one of us has documented, the shift from the "sharing economy" terminology to "gig" terminology may have reflected gig economy firms' eventual concession that work in the sector was (contrary to earlier claims) subject to regulation and taxation, but it also reflected firms' simultaneous interest in ensuring that such work was regarded as contingent and independent "gigging" rather than as constituting an employer-employee relationship.[31]

These threshold worker classification and income-reporting choices by the firms shaped the compliance and tax filing behaviors of workers, and hence shaped the data available to be studied. First, an inevitable effect of the worker classification decision was to push ridesharing drivers and other gig workers into filing IRS Schedule C to report income from gig work. That is, the decision to so classify the workers (and to issue Forms 1099-K) means that many gig workers are filing taxes – reporting income, taking deductions, and bearing self-employment and estimated tax burdens – as independent contractors, not as employees reporting Form W-2

29 Oei & Ring, *supra* note 10 (identifying firms' efforts to employ first-mover advantages to benefit from gaps and ambiguities in the law). Through the early years of 2008 to about 2013, many firms operated as if they were not subject to established regulatory and tax regimes. *See, e.g.*, Jordan Barry & Elizabeth Pollman, *Regulatory Entrepreneurship*, 90 S. CAL. L. REV. 383 (2017) (characterizing firms as regulatory entrepreneurs and detailing new businesses tactics in achieving new legal treatment). Ultimately, however, as the firms grew, continued claims that this sector was not predominantly commercial and was instead "a community of sharers" became untenable. Oei, *supra* note 1. Gradually, the industries saw states and localities impose legal requirements directly on their operations. In some cases, governments simply confirmed that existing regulation applied to the firms. For example, jurisdictions began requiring Airbnb and similar homesharing firms to enter into agreements with governments to collect hotel taxes from guests and remit them to tax authorities. *In What Areas Is Occupancy Tax Collection and Remittance by Airbnb Available?*, AIRBNB, www.airbnb.com/help/article/2509/in-what-areas-is-occupancy-tax-collection-and-remittance-by-airbnb-available (listing jurisdictions in which Airbnb collects and remits occupancy taxes); Oei & Ring, *supra* note 10, at 1023–27 (discussing the increasing number of jurisdictions in which Airbnb collects and remits taxes). In other cases, governments enacted new legislation specifically targeting gig economy businesses, such as state regulation imposing fees and taxes on ridesharing transactions and targeting discriminatory conduct. *See, e.g.*, Mass. Sessions Laws, Acts of 2016, ch. 187 (An Act Regulating Transportation Network Companies) (imposing a new fee and other requirements).

30 *See* Oei & Ring, *supra* note 10.

31 Oei, *supra* note 1, at 107–36, 107 n.1 (noting that in a search of both the NEW YORK TIMES archives and the WALL STREET JOURNAL ONLINE conducted on October 2, 2017, the term "sharing economy" appeared twice as frequently as "gig economy" on the *New York Times* site, and almost four times as frequently on the *Wall Street Journal* site).

income. Accordingly, policymakers and academics looking to parse tax data on gig workers must now garner information about gig workers by examining Schedule C filings, and must tease out gig work from other types of independent contractor or self-employment work being reported on a Schedule C.

Second, the decisions of gig economy firms with respect to information reporting are also material. Having decided to classify workers as independent contractors, firms issued Forms 1099-K to workers rather than Forms W-2 (for reporting employee wages). Under plausible[32] regulatory interpretations, a Form 1099-K need not be issued to payees unless they receive more than $20,000 in payments and engage in more than 200 transactions (e.g., rides).[33] At least some firms adopted this interpretation, and over the years, firms switched back and forth between only issuing Forms 1099-K to payees over these thresholds, issuing Forms 1099-K to payees regardless of how small the amounts, and issuing a different form – Form 1099-MISC – which is subject to a $600 threshold.[34] Firm-level decisions about how to report income (and the instability of these decisions over time) no doubt impact the tax compliance decisions of gig economy workers. The empirical literature shows that information reporting to the IRS by payors of income increases income reporting (and thus tax compliance) by payees.[35] Thus, in years in which firms are not providing workers below the thresholds with a Form 1099-K, those workers are less likely to report their gig income and file Schedule C. Thus, tax return data for those years likely misses some of the workers actually participating in the gig sector.[36]

4.2.2 *Data Is Insufficient*

Administrative tax return data also cannot answer all questions material to tax policymakers. For example, looking only at tax administrative data does not tell us how the taxpayer arrived at the filing positions she took, nor does it provide complete information about whether those filing positions are accurate. While a tax audit may reveal errors in filing positions, it is well known that the audit rate is very low, which means errors may go undetected for an extended period, leading to time lag in policy

[32] Oei & Ring, *supra* note 10 (discussing interpretation of the information reporting regulations and firms' 1099-K reporting positions); Bruckner, *supra* note 7 (same).

[33] I.R.C. § 6050W; Treas. Reg. § 1.6050W-1.

[34] Oei & Ring, *supra* note 10 at 1034–38; Oei & Ring, *supra* note 6, at 64–65. As of 2019, Uber is reporting that it will issue a Form-1099K only to drivers earning more than $20,000 and driving 200 rides or more during the year. *Understanding Your Tax Documents*, UBER, www.uber.com/us/en/drive/tax-information/tax-documents/. Starting in 2018, Lyft similarly announced that despite past practices, it would only be issuing Forms 1099-K to drivers meeting the $20,000/200 rides threshold. *Tax Information for US Drivers*, LYFT, https://help.lyft.com/hc/en-us/articles/115012926967-Tax-information-for-US-drivers. Thus, it would not be surprising if driver confusion over tax reporting forms continues in the face of shifting reporting practices by firms and underlying complexity.

[35] Lederman, *supra* note 11.

[36] *See* sources cited *supra* note 22.

responses.[37] If workers in an industry of first impression are making systematic errors in positions they take, it would be useful to know that quickly in order to either (1) improve compliance upfront (e.g., by providing better guidance) or (2) reform laws that are unfeasible to comply with or are not intuitive.

In particular, with respect to the ridesharing sector, Schedule C filings do not necessarily tell us whether Uber drivers and other gig workers are accurately calculating and deducting the expenses they take on Schedule C (e.g., deductions based on miles driven when working for Uber or Lyft, or depreciation deductions), or what types of legal issues they are confronting. These deductions are not reported on Forms 1099-K or 1099-MISC by payors of income, so they are difficult to corroborate (other than through audit) and their accuracy is not obvious from the face of Schedule C.

Moreover, simply looking at tax return data does not provide information about the *process* by which workers figure out their ultimate tax liability. This process is significant: during the early days of the gig economy, the obligation of ridesharing drivers and homesharers to report their income for tax purposes became quickly apparent, despite early attempts by some to argue for exemption from regulation and taxation more generally.[38] Through a combination of media reporting,[39] some firm guidance to workers,[40] and various tax advising mechanisms,[41] gig economy workers began receiving a clear message that their work was part of a commercial undertaking and subject to taxation. However, the details of how to actually comply were less clear to these workers, some of whom might have been newcomers to gig work.[42]

Thus, an important set of questions – and one not readily answerable by studying only tax return data – concerns how participants in a new sector figure out their tax obligations in the relative absence of clear guidance from the taxing authority,

37 Richard Rubin, *IRS Audit Rate Drops Again as It Examines Fewer High-Income Households*, Wall St. J. (May 20, 2019), www.wsj.com/articles/irs-audit-rate-drops-again-as-it-examines-fewer-high-income-households-11558363990.

38 *See* Oei, *supra* note 1 (describing transition to "gig economy" narrative).

39 *See, e.g.*, Jim Puzzanghera, *Tax Advice for Gig Economy Workers*, L.A. Times (March 24, 2016), www.latimes.com/business/la-fi-qa-tax-gig-economy-20160324-story.html; Mitch Lipka, *How the Sharing Economy Makes Tax Filing Tougher*, Money (Apr. 15, 2015), http://money.com/money/3822148/sharing-economy-taxes-uber-lyft/ (offering tax tips for sharing economy workers); Kathleen Pender, *If You Make Money in the Sharing Economy, the IRS Will Know*, S.F. Gate (Feb. 22, 2014), www.sfgate.com/business/networth/article/If-you-make-money-in-the-sharing-economy-the-IRS-5258941.php.

40 *See, e.g.*, *How Do Taxes Work for Hosts?*, Airbnb, www.airbnb.com/help/article/481/how-do-taxes-work-for-hosts; *Your Tax Questions, Answered*, Uber, www.uber.com/drive/tax-information/; Oei, *supra* note 1 at note 40.

41 *See, e.g.*, Lindsay Van Thoen, *Got a Side Hustle? Here's How to Pay Your Taxes*, Freelancers Union (Feb. 10, 2015), https://blog.freelancersunion.org/2015/02/10/got-side-hustle-heres-how-pay-your-taxes/; Press Release, Intuit, Intuit and Uber Partner to Simplify Filing Taxes for On-Demand Economy Workers (Jan. 28, 2015), *available at* https://investors.intuit.com/news/news-details/2015/Intuit-and-Uber-Partner-to-Simplify-Filing-Taxes-for-On-demand-Economy-Workers/default.aspx.

42 Some might be newcomers because they previously earned W-2 income. Others may be newcomers in the sense that they previously did independent contractor work but on a cash or unreported basis.

whether their attempts are successful, and how their compliance experiences and outcomes might be improved. Thus, there is a strong case for seeking qualitative sources of data to fill the gaps, enrich our knowledge, and help generate more productive tax policy recommendations.

4.3 THE IMPORTANCE OF QUALITATIVE APPROACHES

In light of the limitations of tax return data, the potential for tangible results from a richer methodological approach to tax research in the gig economy is quite real. For example, the researcher might conduct qualitative interviews with gig economy workers and/or tax preparers working with these populations, or might conduct in-depth surveys. Another way to get a sense of how gig workers might be approaching tax questions and finding solutions is to examine spaces in which they congregate, such as online or real-world community spaces.

We now discuss the findings of a study we conducted in the spring of 2015 of public online interactions among ridesharing drivers in three Internet discussion forums – Reddit.com, Uberpeople.net, and Turbotax Intuit AnswerXchange.[43] The study was published in the *Columbia Journal of Tax Law* in 2017 and we only summarize our key findings briefly here.[44] Our study serves as an example of how more in-depth and qualitative approaches can help shed light on tax issues that are difficult to probe using only administrative tax data and high-level survey data.

In our study, we constructed a self-assembled dataset of all Internet discussion threads on three public online discussion forums in which participants discussed tax issues concerning ridesharing drivers – Reddit.com, Uberpeople.net, and the Intuit TurboTax AnswerXchange forum. These online discussions spanned from late 2013 through early-to-mid 2015.[45] Using a combination of descriptive statistics and content analysis, we identified the major substantive tax concerns that occupied forum participants and examined how taxes impacted their driving and profitability decisions. We were also able to gain insight into the tax sophistication and risk attitudes of forum participants as well as their error correction and tax advice dispensing practices. These types of information would be difficult to obtain simply from tax return and aggregated administrative data.

The time periods covered in these Internet forums included some of the first years in which individuals driving for ridesharing companies confronted tax filing and payment obligations. Even at this early stage, Internet forum participants were already actively discussing a range of detailed tax questions, including how to properly determine and document business mileage, which expenses were deductible, and which withholding and estimated tax obligations applied to drivers.[46] This

43 For a more detailed and complete description of our research findings, *see* Oei & Ring, *supra* note 6.
44 Oei & Ring, *supra* note 6.
45 The dates varied by forum. *See id.* at 72, 74, 76.
46 *Id.* at 77.

engagement in learning about their tax obligations belied early claims by some observers that many workers were unaware of their duty to report and pay taxes on earnings from their gig work.[47] What we observed in these forums was that the window of even remotely plausible ignorance of tax obligations[48] had come to an end as waves of media reporting, guidance issued by the firms, and other sources highlighted the existence of tax obligations.[49] Instead, the online discussions showed the degree to which at least some gig economy workers engaged in meaningful attempts at tax compliance and how they struggled to make sense of and conform to the tax system.

4.3.1 *Major Substantive Tax Concerns Occupying Forum Participants*

A significant focus of tax-related discussions on these Internet forums was the question of business expenses and outlays and their deductibility for tax purposes.[50] As noted, because most gig economy firms treat drivers as independent contractors rather than employees, workers have to file IRS Schedule C and are able to deduct costs and outlays associated with driving as "above the line" business expenses. Correspondingly, like other business persons, they are responsible for keeping track of and documenting such costs. We found that forum participants generally understood the value of being able to deduct such costs on their tax returns. However, they were less clear on precisely which expenses could be deducted and how. The degree of attention to deductions among forum participants may reflect the greater complexity and ambiguity regarding this component of the tax system as applied to microbusinesses, especially for those individuals using personal assets (cars or homes) partially for business purposes.

With respect to miles driven in ridesharing specifically, we found that forum participants – many of whom used their personal vehicles in performance of their driving function – needed to determine what portion of the miles driven in their vehicle counted for purposes of deducting business expenses. As we noted in our paper, ridesharing drivers may either use the IRS standard mileage method or may deduct actual expenses spent on driving, but both approaches require them to identify the miles driven for their ridesharing gig.[51] Such a determination includes both a substantive law component and a tax administration one.

47 *See generally* Oei, *supra* note 1 (discussing some of those early claims).
48 Of course, the taxability of income is not dependent on the taxpayer's personal knowledge of the legal system. At best, such factors may influence the application of penalties should they otherwise apply.
49 *See* sources cited *supra* notes 39–41.
50 Oei & Ring, *supra* note 6, at 77.
51 *Id.* at 78-79. I.R.C. § 274(d); Treas. Reg. § 1.274-5(j)(2); I.R.S. Notice 2014-79 (Sec. 3), 2014-2 C.B. 1001; I.R.S. News Release IR-2014-114 (Dec. 10, 2014). Rev. Proc. 2010-51, 2010-2 C.B. 883; U.S. Dep't of Treasury, Internal Revenue Serv., Publ'n. No. 463, Cat. No. 11081L, Travel, Gift, and Car Expenses 14 (2018) *available at* www.irs.gov/pub/irs-pdf/p463.pdf.

On the substantive side, drivers must wrestle with questions such as: Are miles spent driving to passenger "hotspots" deductible, or only miles with a passenger actually in the vehicle? Is having the ridesharing app on and being willing to take passengers sufficient to count mileage as business related, even if no passengers are actually driven (or if personal errands are run at the same time that the app is on)? On the administrative side, questions included: How and when is a taxpayer required to record and document mileage? Are estimates permitted? What forms of proof will be acceptable to the IRS?[52] Despite the significant number of comments on the forums devoted to discussion of what miles "count," a clear consensus on answers to these questions did not truly emerge. However, there was widespread acknowledgment of the duty to report ridesharing proceeds as taxable income and of the fact that only a portion of driving-related expenses – based on a fraction of ridesharing miles driven – were deductible.[53] Drivers devoted some, but notably less forum discussion time to the question of deductibility of non-car-related expenses such as clothing, dry cleaning, water for passengers, and meals for drivers.

As we observed more extensively in our article, forum participants' attention to the deductibility of expenses contrasted with their minimal discussion of income inclusions.[54] By the time we did our study, there seemed to be a general understanding among forum participants that rideshare earnings were clearly income and should be reported on their tax return. This was likely related to the fact that in 2015, Uber issued Forms 1099-K to all drivers, regardless of amounts earned and number of rides given.

It should be noted that the degree of attention focused on business expenses squares with predictions from the economics literature on tax compliance, which anticipates that even if the tax system incorporates features to improve tax compliance in reporting *gross* income (e.g., the introduction of third-party reporting via Form 1099-K), the *net* revenue effect may be less promising than expected because taxpayers may respond by taking excessive deductions, since deductions are not reported to the IRS.[55] But our study offers additional insights not available from the economics literature or from quantitative tax data on the sector, such as how specific features of the formal rules for tax deductibility create ambiguity that could lead to overreporting of drivers' expenses. Additionally, the extensive debates online over deductions revealed the degree to which and the ways in which the driver-taxpayers misunderstood, ignored, complied with, or were intentionally breaching substantive tax law.

52 Oei & Ring, *supra* note 6, at 85–86.

53 Note that our methodology did not allow us to document how gross-basis reporting may have affected expense taking. *See* Joel Slemrod et al., *Does Credit-card Information Reporting Improve Small-business Tax Compliance?* (Nat'l Bureau of Econ. Research, Working Paper No. 21412, 2015), *available at* www.nber.org/papers/w21412.

54 Oei & Ring, *supra* note 6 at 83.

55 Lederman, *supra* note 11; Morse et al., *supra* note 11; Slemrod et al., *supra* note 53.

4.3.2 *Interpretation of Tax Forms Received from Firms*

Our research also found that driver familiarity with information reporting and Form 1099-K was quite variable. This was likely due in part to the timing of our study, which covered Internet forum discussions in 2015 and earlier years.[56] Uber had changed its tax information reporting practices in 2015 and had shifted to reporting *all* driving payments on Form 1099-K, regardless of amounts earned or number of rides given.[57] Lyft, by contrast, was still only issuing Forms 1099-K to those earning above the $20,000/200 transaction threshold.[58] Not surprisingly, drivers posting on all three forums reported confusion about why and when they would receive a Form 1099-K from Uber. Some were puzzled that they received a form at all, while others were confused regarding why they received a form from Uber but not Lyft if they were driving for both.[59]

Forum posters also had questions about the numbers on the Forms 1099-K received. Some correctly understood that the numbers on the forms were gross amounts and that fees (e.g., safe ride fees, tolls, platform fees) had to be deducted by the drivers on IRS Form Schedule C, while others thought the forms contained errors. We saw that more knowledgeable forum participants (including those marketing tax advice and expertise) stepped in to explain how to correctly interpret the forms, though we cannot tell how impactful those interventions were. Again, a qualitative look into ridesharing tax compliance revealed not just that taxpayers might struggle with preparing a tax return based on the Forms 1099-K they received (an observation that might be extracted from tax administrative data) but also illuminated why they found them confusing and how such forms might be better designed or explained to recipients.

4.3.3 *Estimated Taxes and Analyses of Profitability*

Regardless of the forms received, gig workers, like all taxpayers filing as independent contractors in the United States, must meet requirements for quarterly estimated income tax payments during the year.[60] This requires them, in effect, to "withhold" (i.e., set aside) taxes themselves to pay their estimated tax liability on a quarterly basis. Some forum participants seemed unfamiliar with this obligation to pay and withhold.[61] This created two risks for these filers: first, they may owe interest and penalties for estimated tax payments not timely made; and second, they may fail to appreciate the financial impact of taxes (which tend to

[56] Oei & Ring, *supra* note 6, at 72–73, 74–75, 86–87.
[57] *Id.* at 64–65, 85–86.
[58] *Id.*
[59] *Id.* at 86–87.
[60] *See supra* note 18.
[61] Oei & Ring, *supra* note 6, at 91–92.

be due at a future time) when assessing the overall profitability of their current decision to drive.[62]

We were able to observe how taxes factored into posters' assessments of whether it is profitable to drive for ridesharing companies and how to drive profitably.[63] Profitability was among the most frequently discussed topics in the threads we examined, and tax considerations factored into analyses of profitability in a number of different ways. As discussed, taxes obviously were a consideration in determining the overall profitability of the driving decision, though (as noted) forum posters did not always fully appreciate the impact of taxes. In addition, tax numbers also seemed to serve as proxies for analysis of economic losses (e.g., economic wear and tear on the vehicle from driving), though some forum participants appeared to conflate and confuse tax losses (i.e., what is deductible for tax purposes) with economic losses (i.e., true costs of driving).[64] Tax considerations also appeared to frame forum poster computations of profitably more generally: forum posters frequently assessed the profitability of driving on a per mile rather than per hour basis, presumably due to the fact that mileage expenses are computed on a per mile basis.[65] Finally, tax considerations also impacted forum poster analyses of whether it was better to drive on a part-time versus a full-time basis.

Our analysis thus provides valuable texture for understanding how drivers approach and analyze profitability. While quantitative data might be able to link taxpayer characteristics with patterns of ridesharing work and income, it does not illuminate the dynamics underlying that link. For example, quantitative data does not tell us whether taxpayers understood the impact of taxes on profitability but nonetheless chose to trade off current access to cash in exchange for bearing future costs (such as their car wearing out more quickly), or whether they failed to appreciate the impact of taxes in their calculations of profitability at all. Qualitative analysis can be employed here to fill such gaps.

4.3.4 *Worker Classification*

We also saw some discussions about forum participants' understandings of and attitudes toward the worker classification debate.[66] The topic, though not very

62 *Id.* (As we discuss in this 2017 paper, the observations may square with the broader theoretical literature on "tax salience.") *See generally* David Gamage & Darien Shanske, *Three Essays on Tax Salience: Market Salience and Political Salience*, 65 Tax L. Rev. 19 (2011).

63 Oei & Ring, *supra* note 6, at 90–98 (fuller discussion).

64 *Id.* at 94–95.

65 *Id.* at 95–96.

66 Classification as an independent contractor requires that workers bear responsibility for paying and filing all employment-related taxes but increases the likelihood that such taxpayers can meaningfully deduct business expenses. For taxpayers classified as employees, the ability to deduct employee business expenses prior to 2018 was limited by IRC § 67; for taxable years beginning after 2017, the deduction for employee business expenses has been suspended. IRC § 67(g).

prominent on the forums, did arise periodically. To the extent participants commented on worker classification, their views were mixed on whether independent contractor status was desirable. Their responses, however, were relatively uniform in that their preferences were based on reasons other than tax reporting and compliance. Many instead emphasized the positives of not having a boss and expressed concerns about potential liability for back taxes should their classification change.[67]

4.3.5 *Error Correction and Forum Culture*

We were also able to examine broader "cultural" aspects of the discussion forums, including how well forum participants understood tax law, how they approached tax compliance, how knowledge was transmitted and errors corrected in the forums, and the accuracy and content of tax advising taking place in the forums.[68] Reaching beyond the limits of quantitative data, the qualitative picture of how taxpayers identified, interpreted, shared, and reassessed tax knowledge provides valuable clues about knowledge transmission and potentially successful approaches for reaching taxpayers. Notably, although forum participants displayed a range of tax sophistication, and although some forum participants posted erroneous "tax advice" to peers in the Internet forums, those errors were often corrected by other participants on both Reddit and Uberpeople, and often quite rapidly.[69] For example, in one forum, after several participants had noted that they would deduct uniforms and haircuts, other posters joined the conversation to confirm that in fact these were not deductible expenditures.[70] Tax advice dispensed on the forums by posters appearing to be peers (i.e., other drivers) was generally accurate, though there were notable instances of inaccurate or misleading advice as well.[71] Posters often referred to IRS publications in making their statements. Forum posters also discussed the third-party apps, spreadsheets, and other resources they used in documenting and tracking expenses.[72] In addition, we also observed instances of CPAs and others claiming to be experts offering tax advice on the forums, sometimes as a way to market their services.[73]

4.3.6 *Benefits of Qualitative Empirical Study of Internet Forums*

Most labor-focused empirical scholarship on the gig economy and contingent workforce to date has focused on counting the magnitude and changing composition of

67 Oei & Ring, *supra* note 6 at 88.
68 *Id.* at 98–105.
69 *Id.* at 98–99.
70 *Id.* at 99.
71 *Id.* at 102.
72 *Id.* at 101–02.
73 *Id.* at 103–05.

the workforce.[74] This type of research uses tax administrative data and broad survey data to make estimates and predictions. However, as discussed above, tax return data is determined by ex ante choices of taxpayers, which affects the kinds of quantitative data available for study. Independent of this constraint, such tax return data inherently cannot speak to all the important questions relevant to policy formation. Moreover, tax return filing occurs months after the tax year in question, and parsing and analyzing the data takes even longer. More in-depth and qualitative approaches like the one we employed can provide valuable and timely observations and information for tax policymakers.

Most notably, by studying Internet forums, we were able to observe forum participant reactions to tax issues (such as the firms' changing positions on Form 1099 issuance) as they occurred. This can help tax administrators and policymakers flag issues likely to be of concern to taxpayers and tax return filers in real time, which enables them to be more responsive to taxpayer needs. Such intel is valuable from a taxpayer services perspective because it can confirm intuitions about potential problems, signal problems as they occur, and illuminate a path to minimize taxpayer burdens. Interventions based on qualitative data need not be costly, nor irreversible. For example, the IRS established a "Sharing Economy Tax Center" on its website to help gig workers understand their tax obligations better.[75] This type of intervention is arguably low-hanging fruit that, if timely done, may be valuable to many taxpayers.

Moreover, by studying Internet forums, we were able to glean broader insights. For example, we were able to deduce how taxpayers thought about the profitability of their driving decisions and how taxes affected how they assess and frame profitability and the decision to drive. Such profitability assessments may provide more nuanced detail to economic analyses of how taxes impact labor supply decisions. We were also able to gain an appreciation for the degree of accuracy of tax advice on these Internet forums, and the process by which forum participants learned about their tax obligations online. These observations may be useful to taxing authorities in thinking about more or less effective ways to conduct taxpayer education and outreach.

More broadly, we were able to observe how participants in a new economic sector grappled with preexisting tax rules that were not designed with the sector in mind. These findings not only help us understand how well the tax system is working for gig workers, they may also support broader judgments about the adequacy of the tax system in the face of fundamental technological and economic shifts, and about how the system might need to be reformed.

74 *See, e.g.*, Anat Bracha & Mary A. Burke, *The Ups and Downs of the Gig Economy, 2017* (Federal Reserve Bank of Boston Working Paper No. 18–12, 2019), *available at* https://papers.ssrn.com/sol3/papers.cfm?abstract_id=3303101.

75 Internal Rev. Serv., Sharing Economy Tax Center, www.irs.gov/businesses/small-businesses-self-employed/sharing-economy-tax-center.

4.3.7 *Limitations of Our Study*

Our study was, of course, subject to limitations. First, we were not able to determine what percentage of ridesharing drivers posted on the Internet, nor were we able to know how many "lurkers" there were (drivers or interested others who read these public forums but did not post in them). We also do not know how representative forum participants are of ridesharing drivers more generally. We cannot confirm a relationship between what people post on the Internet and what they actually do on their tax returns – for example, just because forum participants seem to understand that income from gig work is reportable does not mean they actually reported that income. We cannot discern whether the accurate tax advice dispensed on the forums drowned out the inaccurate advice, or vice versa.

Finally, our study was only a snapshot: it only dealt with ridesharing drivers, not homesharers. It also does not account for recent changes in the tax law. In particular, the new deduction under IRC § 199A introduced in the 2017 tax reform may impact gig workers. Effective for 2018, independent contractors, but not employees, potentially qualify for a new deduction equal to 20 percent of their qualified business income.[76] Our study does not address how ridesharing drivers may grapple with the intricacies of this complex new deduction, nor does it address how the availability of the deduction may impact driver assessments of (1) the profitability of driving or (2) preferences for independent contractor versus employee classification. The 2017 legislation's suspension of below-the-line miscellaneous itemized deductions may also tilt worker preferences toward independent contractor classification because employee classification would render many expenses below the line and hence unavailable.

Moreover, as noted, our study captured a moment in time when Uber was issuing Forms 1099-K to all drivers while Lyft was only issuing those information reporting forms to drivers earning over the $20,000/200 transactions threshold. In 2016 and 2017, Lyft issued Forms 1099-K to drivers earning over $600.[77] And, as noted, both Uber and Lyft now issue those forms only to drivers earning above the Form 1099-K thresholds. We do not know how drivers may have adjusted their compliance and income reporting behaviors in light of those changes. We also do not know how increases in available guidance (both from the IRS and from other sources) and increasing familiarity among drivers and tax preparers with gig work over time have affected compliance behaviors or forum culture.[78] One notable change over the

[76] Rev. Proc. 2018-57. Although a number of restrictions and limitations apply, few of them apply to workers with qualified business income below $321,400 (married) and $160,725 (single) in 2019. For the many gig economy workers with incomes below statutory thresholds, the more onerous restrictions would not apply and they would likely qualify for the deduction assuming they are independent contractors.

[77] *Tax Information for US Drivers*, Lyft, *supra* note 34.

[78] The guidance now available on the IRS website does spell out the obligation under a bold header entitled "Tax Payments: Those in Sharing Economy May Need to Make Estimated Payments." Internal Rev. Serv., Sharing Economy Tax Center, *supra* note 75. Some firms (Uber and Etsy) also

years has been the increasing level of detail provided to drivers by gig economy firms regarding taxation and tax forms,[79] and the IRS introduction of its "Sharing Economy Tax Center" webpage for gig economy workers.[80]

4.4 CONCLUSION: FUTURE DIRECTIONS

Individually, all research methods have weaknesses. Thus, we have argued the merits of expanding the range of research approaches used to investigate tax in the gig economy to include qualitative techniques such as in-depth interviews and surveys and content-based examinations of public Internet communities. Despite the appeal of quantitative methods that count existing data points (such as those relying on tax return data and answers to high-level surveys), these approaches face two important limitations. First, they simply do not address some of the central tax questions we identified above such as the process by which taxpayers seek to comply with the tax system. Second, the kinds of data available to be counted (including Forms 1099 or Schedule C filings) are not neutral – they are the product of specific choices of firms and workers that dictate what exists to be counted. Approaching tax questions using a richer set of methods offers the greatest likelihood of developing a nuanced understanding of complex tax issues. For example, if researchers were to mine IRS data for evidence of gig worker compliance and noncompliance (including worker demographics and whether they are accurately incorporating new IRC § 199A into their tax filings) and combine this with qualitative interviews regarding how workers approached tax filing, what motivated their work decisions, and how they understood the choices and trade-offs being made, the net empirical results would afford a more robust picture of how gig workers experience the tax law and their compliance obligations. This would in turn inform assessments of the tax system, including how well designed the tax law is and whether particular rules and requirements pose special challenges for small-scale economic transactions. As another example, qualitative interviews regarding how ridesharing drivers understand their relationship to firms for which they drive may provide texture on how they understand and evaluate worker classification issues.

Ultimately, the drive to understand the gig economy and the contingent workforce more broadly takes place in a deeply contested space. Empirical evidence of the existence and shape of the gig and contingent work sectors is often sought by constituencies advancing various positions. Gig economy firms endeavoring to raise capital and appease investors may hope to establish that the sector is large and

provide more guidance. *Do I Owe Quarterly Taxes?*, UBER, https://help.uber.com/partners/article/do-i-owe-quarterly-taxes?nodeId=98a642e5-1123-4895-948a-cb40b6845aa4; *Taxes 101: Understanding the Essentials*, ETSY, www.etsy.com/seller-handbook/article/taxes-101-understanding-the-essentials/22721885775.

79 For example, Uber's website now includes a sample Form 1099-K with an explanation of what the different numbers mean for a driver. *Understanding Your Tax Documents*, UBER, *supra* note 34.

80 INTERNAL REV. SERV., SHARING ECONOMY TAX CENTER, *supra* note 75.

significant. Those concerned about worker protection may aim to demonstrate that traditional work and worker protections are under threat. Constituencies opposed to tax (or other) reforms or special regimes may strive to show that the gig economy is too small to justify even considering reform. The fact that empirical descriptions of the gig economy remain so contested makes it even more imperative that researchers get these descriptions right and that they harness a variety of methodologies to do so.

5

Just a Gig?

Sharing Economy Work and the Implications for Career Trajectory

Alexandrea J. Ravenelle

The gig economy promises short-term, flexible work. Indeed, the temporality of the work is integral to the concept; before the rise of app-based work, "gig" was most commonly used to describe the short-term work of a musician providing a live performance. Yet, as gig work platforms such as Uber, Airbnb, and TaskRabbit enter their second decade, and as "side hustles" are popularized in the media as a solution to stagnant salaries and student loan debt,[1] the question arises: Is gig work intended to be a short-term solution for workers, or an integral component of modern employment? Does gig employment affect a worker's ability to transition into full-time work as an employee outside the gig economy?

Although informal work is hardly a new concept,[2] gig work is unique for its technological component and marketing emphasis on platform-based work as positive alternative to the daily nine-to-five grind. Whereas few would suggest that being a day laborer or house cleaner is an ideal occupation, gig platforms market similar work, done via their apps, as being a desirable and flexible option. Uber, for instance, advertises driving on its platform as offering "No shifts, no boss, no limits," while TaskRabbit, the personal assistant service, has promised workers the opportunity to "Earn money your way," and to "Find jobs you love, at rates you choose, [and to] make a schedule that fits your life."

While individual gigs are rarely sufficient as a single source of income, workers may turn to a platform, or several, as a source of income. For instance, workers often speak holistically about working for TaskRabbit or Uber or another platform and

1 T. J. McCue, "Looking for a Side Hustle or Freelance Gig? Check Out These Sites." *Forbes*, July 28, 2019, www.forbes.com/sites/tjmccue/2019/07/28/looking-for-a-side-hustle-or-freelance-gig-check-out-these-sites/#3676e76b56ad; Amanda Dixon, "Survey: Nearly 1 in 3 Side Hustlers Needs the Income to Stay Afloat." *Bankrate.com*, June 5, 2019, www.bankrate.com/personal-finance/side-hustles-survey-june-2019/.

2 Alejandro Portes, "The Informal Economy and Its Paradoxes." In *Handbook of Economic Sociology*, ed. Neil J. Smelser and Richard Swedberg. Princeton, NJ: Princeton University Press, 1994; Kevin Hart, "Informal Income Opportunities and Urban Employment in Ghana." *The Journal of Modern African Studies*, 11(1) 61–89, 1973, retrieved from www.jstor.org/stable/159873; Kevin Hart, "The Informal Economy." *Cambridge Anthropology*, 10(2), 54–58, 1985, retrieved from www.jstor.org/stable/23816368.

then discuss particular gigs or tasks as aspects of working for said platform, much like an office worker identifies as working for a particular company.[3] At the same time, services generally classify workers as independent contractors, which offers the platforms considerable cost savings over hiring workers as employees, even as it prevents workers from accessing generations of hard-won workplace rights and protections.[4] This lack of protections, partnered with few opportunities for advancement and a lack of fringe benefits, leads gig work to closely resemble the "bad jobs" identified by Kalleberg.[5]

However, platform marketing makes gig work sound similar to a freelance job or consulting arrangement, whereby a worker can exert at least some control over activities and termination, and workplace flexibility is expected – components more commonly found in "good jobs."[6] While gig-based work is marketed by platforms as an attractive opportunity, little attention has been paid to the long-term experience of gig workers. As a result, through longitudinal interviews with eleven gig workers, this chapter seeks to answer the question, what is the impact of gig economy work on a worker's future career trajectory and personal life? To paraphrase Kalleberg, is gig-based work a good or bad job?[7] What distinguishes those workers who move out of gig work from those workers who remain engaged in gig work, whether by choice or circumstance? Do workers think that extensive time spent in gig work as a primary source of income negatively affects their ability to move to stable traditional employment?

In the following section, I connect gig work to the larger discussion of a growing worker reliance on additional sources of income and the impact of underemployment on wages and employment callbacks. I then discuss my research methodology and findings before discussing the implications of gig work in regards to inequality and inefficiency. I argue that the negative career implications of gig work, especially long-term gig work, suggest serious inequities in regards to worker opportunity or experience. These inequities should be cause for concern among labor and employment law scholars, and further support the importance of establishing a social safety net and workplace protections for gig workers.

5.1 LITERATURE REVIEW

The effects of the Great Recession were considerable: a large number of families saw the values of their homes decline; Americans were more pessimistic about their finances and more likely to identify with being in a lower class; and there were

[3] Alexandrea J. Ravenelle, *Hustle and Gig: Struggling and Surviving in the Sharing Economy*. Berkeley: California University Press, 2019.

[4] Ravenelle, *Hustle and Gig*.

[5] Arne Kalleberg, *Good Jobs, Bad Jobs: The Rise of Polarized and Precarious Employment Systems in the United States*. New York, NY: Russell Sage Foundation, 2011.

[6] Kalleberg, *Good Jobs*.

[7] Kalleberg, *Good Jobs*.

numerous negative consequences in terms of physical and mental health outcomes.[8]

Yet, as noted by Kalleberg and von Wachter, "the most unusual and unexpected feature of the Great Recession was the persistence of weak economic conditions in its aftermath."[9] While the number of involuntary part-time workers has dropped, according to the Bureau of Labor Statistics, there were still 1.4 million more involuntary part-time workers in June 2016 than in the months immediately before the beginning of the 2007–2009 recession. In many ways the Great Recession was a perfect storm as generations of technological advances such as the computer, smartphone, and contactless payment systems; the spread of neoliberal policies; the continued expansion of the service sector; the weakening of unions; and the rise of temporary employment were all brought to the forefront.[10] While Kalleberg and von Wachter note that some of the changes began in the 1970s and were masked by the dot-com boom of the early 2000s and the prerecession housing bubble, a decline in market dynamism is thought to contribute to worker difficulties in finding stable employment.[11]

There are two main solutions when one's income doesn't match spending: cut spending or increase income. The sharing economy, which can be described as both a precursor to the gig economy, and an umbrella term that includes on-demand work and the secondhand economy, has offered both solutions.[12] The sharing economy can be defined as a catch-all term for "'peer-to-peer' firms that connect people for the purposes of distributing, sharing, and reusing goods and

8 David B. Grusky, Bruce Western, Christopher Wimer, eds. *The Great Recession*. New York: Russell Sage Foundation, 2011; Michael Hout and Orestes P. Hastings. "The Social Recession: Americans' Subjective Reactions to the Great Recession and Lagging Economy Since 2006." Paper presented at annual meeting of the American Sociological Association, San Francisco (August 16–19, 2014); Diana Frasquilho, Margarida Gaspar Matos, Ferdinand Salonna, Diogo Guerreiro, Cláudia C. Storti, Tânia Gaspar, and José M. Caldas-de-Almeida, "Mental Health Outcomes in Times of Economic Recession: A Systematic Literature Review." *BMC Public Health*, 16, 115, 2016; J. E. Brand, "The Far-Reaching Impact of Job Loss and Unemployment." *Annual Review of Sociology*, 41, 359–375, 2015.

9 Arne Kalleberg and Till von Wachter, "The U.S. Labor Market During and After the Great Recession: Continuities and Transformations." *RSF: The Russell Sage Foundation Journal of the Social Sciences*, 3(3), 1–19, 2017.

10 Kalleberg and von Wachter, "The U.S. Labor Market"; Steven Greenhouse, *The Big Squeeze: Tough Times for the American Worker*. New York: Knopf, 2008; Steven Greenhouse, *Beaten Down, Worked Up: The Past, Present, and Future of American Labor*. New York: Knopf, 2019; Katharine Mieszkowski, "Don't Wanna Be Your (Temp) Slave." Fast Company, August 31, 1998. Retrieved Aug 26, 2017 from www.fastcompany.com/35119/dont-wanna-be-your-temp-slave.

11 Steven J. Davis and John Haltiwanger, "Labor Market Fluidity and Economic Performance." NBER Working Paper No. 20479. Cambridge, Mass.: National Bureau of Economic Research 2014; Jae Song and Till von Wachter. "Long-Term Nonemployment and Job Displacement." Evaluating Labor Market Dynamics, Proceedings from the Jackson Hole Economic Policy Symposium Sponsored by the Federal Reserve Board of Kansas City, Jackson Hole, Wyo. (August 2014). www.kansascityfed.org /publicat/sympos/2014/2014vonWachter.pdf.

12 Koen Frenken, Toon Meelen, Martijn Arets and Pieter van de Glind, "Smarter Regulation for the Sharing Economy," *The Guardian*, May 20, 2015; Ravenelle, *Hustle and Gig*.

services."[13] Supporters of the sharing economy have argued for its ability to reverse economic inequality, stop ecological destruction, counter materialistic tendencies, enhance worker rights, and empower the poor.[14] While Schor and Fitzmaurice have suggested that the sharing economy is simply "an innovation that is capable of re-allocating wealth across the 'value chain,' specifically away from 'middlemen' and towards small producers and consumers," critics have argued that the innovation is less about wealth reallocation and more about wealth concentration, evading regulations, and "sharewashing."[15] As services like Uber and Airbnb continue to grow into multibillion dollar valuations, effectively usurping free services such as Couchsurfing, the so-called sharing economy has become the on-demand or gig economy, garnering complaints of worker exploitation and worse.[16]

Even as incomes have begun to inch upwards after the Great Recession, income volatility, or a swing of more than 25 percent from year to year, remains high. Described as America's "hidden inequality," research by Pew Charitable Trusts found that more than a third of American households experienced large income changes from 2014 to 2015 – roughly five years after the Great Recession ended.[17] While a changing income can be due to increases, such as from a bonus or inheritance, Pew found that the volatility tended to be dramatic, and that while the median household income gain was $20,500, the median income loss was even larger at $25,000.[18] Additionally, families that experience income volatility report reduced financial well-being and lower levels of savings than those with stable income.[19]

[13] Joe Mathews, "The Sharing Economy Boom Is About to Bust." *Time*, June 27, 214. http://time.com/2924778/airbnb-uber-sharing-economy/.

[14] Mathews, "The Sharing Economy Boom"; Rachel Botsman and Roo Rodgers. *What's Mine Is Yours: The Rise of Collaborative Consumption*. New York: Harper Collins, 2010.

[15] Juliet Schor and Connor Fitzmaurice. "Collaborating and Connecting: The Emergence of a Sharing Economy." In *Handbook on Research on Sustainable Consumption*, eds. Lucia Reisch and John Thogersen. Cheltenham, UK: Edward Elgar, 2015, 4; Jon Evans, "Meet the New Serfs, Same as the Old Serfs." *TechCrunch*, Oct. 5, 2013. http://techcrunch.com/2013/10/05/meet-the-new-serfs-same-as-the-old-serfs/; Dean Baker, "Don't Buy the 'Sharing Economy Hype: Airbnb and Uber Are Facilitating Rip-Offs." *The Guardian*, May 27, 2014. www.theguardian.com/commentisfree/2014/may/27/airbnb-uber-taxes-regulation; Anthony Kalamar, "Sharewashing Is the New Greenwashing." *OpEdNews.com*, May 13, 2013. www.opednews.com/articles/Sharewashing-is-the-New-Gr-by-Anthony-Kalamar-130513–834.html.

[16] Ravenelle, *Hustle and Gig*.

[17] Jonathan Morduch and Rachel Schneider, *The Financial Diaries: How American Families Cope in a World of Uncertainty*. Princeton, NJ: Princeton University Press, 2017; Pew Charitable Trusts. "How Income Volatility Interacts with American Families' Financial Security: An Examination of Gains, Losses, and Household Economic Experiences." March 9, 2017. www.pewtrusts.org/en/research-and-analysis/issue-briefs/2017/03/how-income-volatility-interacts-with-american-families-financial-security

[18] Pew, "Income Volatility," 6.

[19] Pew, "Income Volatility."

A 2019 report by the Federal Reserve found that one in ten adults struggled to pay bills in some months due to income volatility.[20] With incomes increasingly volatile, more and more workers are turning to the gig economy. In November 2016, Pew released a study reporting that 8 percent of Americans earned money in the last year by using digital platforms to take on a job or task and nearly a fifth (18 percent) earned money in the last year by selling something online. An additional one percent had rented out property on a home-sharing site. The report notes, "adding up everyone who has performed at least one of these three activities, some 24% of American adults have earned money in the 'platform economy' over the last year."

While some workers are turning to the sharing or gig economy as a supplemental strategy, individuals with lower incomes may find that alternative work is their primary source of income. Work from the Chase Institute found that while workers with incomes in the highest quintile of $84,900 and above had a low level of participation in labor platforms (0.3 percent), individuals with lower incomes ($44,800 and below) had twice as high in such platforms (0.6 percent).[21] A McKinsey Global Work Institute report also noted that lower-income households are more likely to participate in independent work out of a lack of better alternatives.[22] The Federal Reserve further found that financial fragility, such as difficulty handling an emergency expense of $400, was "slightly more common for those engaged in gig work, but markedly higher for those who do so as a main source of income."[23]

Examining deposits into 240,000 anonymized Chase bank accounts, Farrell and Greig found that in one in six sharing economy participants in any given month is new, and more than half of participants exit within twelve months.[24] The researchers found that labor-platform participants (e.g., Uber and TaskRabbit) with more stable mainstream employment and higher incomes, as well as younger participants (thirty-four and under), were more likely to exit within a year. But for those with lower incomes and "who experienced at least one month of non-employment over

20 Federal Reserve Board. "Report on the Economic Well-Being of U.S. Households in 2016." May 2017." Retrieved on August 28, 2017, www.federalreserve.gov/publications/files/2016-report-economic-well-being-us-households-201705.pdf; Pew Research Center. "Shared, Collaborative and On Demand: The New Digital Economy." May 2016.

21 Diana Farrell and Fiona E. Greig. "The Online Platform Economy: Has Growth Peaked?" (November 15, 2017). https://ssrn.com/abstract=2911194.

22 McKinsey Global Work Institute. "Independent Work: Choice, Necessity and the Gig Economy." 2016. www.mckinsey.com/~/media/McKinsey/Global%20Themes/Employment%20and%20Growth/Independent%20work%20Choice%20necessity%20and%20the%20gig%20economy/Independent-Work-Choice-necessity-and-the-gig-economy-Full-report.ashx.

23 Federal Reserve Board. "Report on the Economic Well-Being of U.S. Households in 2018." May 2019. Retrieved on August 28, 2019 www.federalreserve.gov/publications/files/2018-report-economic-well-being-us-households-201905.pdf, 2.

24 Diana Farrell and Fiona E. Greig, "Paychecks, Paydays, and the Online Platform Economy: Big Data on Income Volatility." JPMorgan Chase & Co. Institute, February 2016. https://ssrn.com/abstract=2911293.

this time frame, platforms provide a vital source of additional income."[25] While the additional income provided through gig work may be important for paying the bills, little is known about the long-term implications of gig work for one's career or future life chances.[26]

Research on potentially comparable "bad" jobs, such as in temporary help services or other sectors, suggests that even less-than-ideal work can yield substantial benefits compared to no employment by providing a path to other industries that may offer higher pay or increased stability.[27] However, work by Autor and Houseman found that former welfare recipients who were placed in temporary agency jobs were more likely to remain working within the temporary help sector.[28] Additionally, the short-term nature of the work, combined with more frequent periods of unemployment, "may generate lower earnings and less employment stability over the long-term" compared to direct hire jobs.[29] Work by Ferber and Waldfogel found that having a nontraditional employment history, defined as time spent as a part-time, self-employed, or temporary worker, was associated with lower current wages and benefits for men and women, holding constant for current employment type.[30] For those workers who identified as previously self-employed and incorporated, and women who voluntarily worked part-time in the past, there were no significant effects; suggesting that the effects of long-term self-employment were more positive than a short period of unemployment.[31] However, more recent work by Farber, Silverman, and von Wachter found that "taking an interim job significantly reduces the likelihood of receiving a call-back"[32] while a similar study found that college graduates who were underemployed (i.e., working in retail jobs after completing college) have callback rates that are 30 percent lower than those of applicants who are adequately employed.[33]

25 Farrell and Greig, "Paychecks," 10.

26 Max Weber, *Economy and Society: An Outline of Interpretive Sociology*. trans Ephraim Fischoff et al. eds. Guenther Roth and Claus Wittich. Berkeley: University of California Press, [1922] 1978.

27 Carolyn Heinrich, Peter Mueser and Kenneth Troske, "Welfare to Temporary Work: Implications for Labor Market Outcomes." *The Review of Economics and Statistics*, 87(1), 154–173, 2005.

28 David H. Autor and Susan N. Houseman, "Temporary Agency Employment: A Way Out of Poverty?" in *Working and Poor: How Economic and Policy Changes Are Affecting Low-Wage Workers*, eds. Rebecca M. Blank, Sheldon H. Danziger, and Robert F. Schoeni. New York: Russell Sage Foundation, 2016, 312–337.

29 Autor and Houseman, "Economic," 327.

30 Marianne A. Ferber and Jane Waldfogel, "The Long-Term Consequences of Nontraditional Employment." Columbia University Academic Commons, https://doi.org/10.7916/D8794FDK., *ANNALS of the American Academy of Political and Social Science*, 650(1), 78–97, 1998.

31 Ferber and Waldfogel, "Consequences," 6.

32 Henry S. Farber, Dan Silverman, Till von Wachter, "Factors Determining Callbacks to Job Applications by the Unemployed: An Audit Study." *RSF: The Russell Sage Foundation Journal of the Social Sciences*, 3(3), 2017.

33 John M. Nunley, Adam Pugh, Nicholas Romero, and Richard Alan Seals, Jr., "Unemployment, Underemployment, and Employment Opportunities: Results from a Correspondence Audit Study of the Labor Market for College Graduates." *Industrial and Labor Relations Review*, 70(3), 642–669, 2016.

The gig economy, which has been widely hailed as disrupting established occupations and ways of working, has also been described as allowing for highly educated workers to engage in manual labor for pay. To paraphrase Juliet Schor, the gig economy allows workers with graduate degrees to be hired for housecleaning tasks and manual labor work.[34] Schor has argued that technological novelty, platform branding and the overwhelmingly young, white, and well-educated demographic composition of early adopters, meant that platforms were able to destigmatize certain tasks and present gig work as " technologically advanced, [and] a new, cool thing."[35] As a result, the question arises, is gig economy work simply app-enabled interim work that will reduce the likelihood of gainful stable employment in the future? Or does the technological component of working via an online platform override any sense of it as low-skilled or interim?

5.2 RESEARCH METHODOLOGY

This chapter is based on longitudinal interviews with eleven gig workers for TaskRabbit, a personal assistant gig platform. The eleven workers were among a group of twenty-three TaskRabbit workers who were first interviewed in 2015 while they were actively working via TaskRabbit. In the 2015 interviews, participants were hired for gig work through the services between March and November, and then told about the research project in a face-to-face conversation after rapport had been developed. E-mail and phone numbers were solicited and interviews were scheduled at a later time. Recruiting participants through the platform, over a period of several months, meant relying on the platforms' algorithms to show prospective workers, which ensured that workers were active on the platform and also increased the potential for sample randomness. Three Taskrabbit participants were recruited through snowball sampling, which served to further expand the sample size by providing access to several workers with high hourly rates, and one was recruited through contacts at local colleges.

Participation in the follow-up interviews in 2019 was conducted between February and October 2019, and was limited to workers who were interviewed previously, but no additional selection criteria were employed. As a result, the 2019 interviews include workers who remained active on TaskRabbit; those who had transitioned to a different service (e.g., moving from TaskRabbit to DoorDash delivery service); and those who had left app-based employment entirely, at least temporarily. Efforts were made to follow-up with all twenty-three TaskRabbit workers through a series of e-mail messages and connections via social media networks. Of the twenty-three workers interviewed in 2015, twelve agreed to be interviewed, but only eleven

[34] Juliet B. Schor, "Does the Sharing Economy Increase Inequality within the Eighty Percent?: Findings from a Qualitative Study of Platform Providers." *Cambridge Journal of Regions, Economy and Society*, 10(2), 263–279, 2017, https://doi.org/10.1093/cjres/rsw047.

[35] Schor, "Does the Sharing Economy Increase Inequality," 275.

completed interviews by the time this chapter went to print. It is unclear what, if anything, differentiates those workers who responded to follow-up interview requests and those who did not respond.

In both 2015 and 2019, the research procedures remained the same: participants completed a short demographic survey and participated in a qualitative interview. The survey included questions regarding the worker's age, income, education level, number of hours worked each week, an assessment of their financial situations, and three words describing what attracted them to the sharing economy. The one-on-one interviews focused on open-ended questions: how workers got involved with the gig economy; how involved they remain with the gig economy; reasons for leaving/remaining; experiences finding work in the mainstream economy after/while working in the gig economy; and perceived impact on their life chances and career decisions. While all of the preliminary interviews (except for one) in 2015 were conducted in person, in 2019, three workers had moved out of the area and were interviewed via phone. In the 2019 follow-up interviews, TaskRabbit workers were offered a $25 cash incentive, and those who were interviewed in person were also offered a free meal or snack during the session.

All interviews were recorded before being transcribed, and coded into thematic fields. Survey information was entered into a spreadsheet and analyzed. Broader themes in the data, such as worker views on gig work and experiences after the gig economy, were sorted into topical categories, coded inductively, and analyzed by seeking commonalities. To allow for worker anonymity, all respondents were assigned pseudonyms and potentially identifying details in the narratives were omitted.

Information on the characteristics of the full sample interviewed in 2015 is available in Ravenelle (2019). For those workers who participated in the 2019 follow-up interviews, seven were white, two were Hispanic, one was black/African-American, and one described himself as racially mixed. Workers ranged from 29 to 64 years old, with a median age of 41 and a mean age of 43.5. In 2019, three workers described their incomes as less than $24,999, three earned between $25,000 and 34,999, two earned between $35,000 and 49,999, and one worker each fell into the $50,000–74,999 and $75,000–100,000 ranges. The subset of workers who were interviewed in 2019 was roughly as educated as those originally involved in the study: one had an Associates degree, three had a BA and four had graduate degrees, including one with a doctorate. The remainder had some college.

The 2019 follow-up interviews unearthed two surprising findings. Contrary to the marketing messages of gig platforms, gig work remains highly stigmatized and garners a negative emotional response, even long after workers have left the platforms. And, perhaps even more concerning, many workers who turned to gig work as a stopgap measure remain "stuck" in gig work, which has implications for their personal relationships and career trajectories. In the following section I will provide an overview of these two findings before discussing the larger implications for scholars of work and employment law.

5.3 GIG WORK REMAINS STIGMATIZED WORK

While the platforms market themselves as offering flexibility and the opportunity to be one's own boss, workers rarely identified themselves as small business owners.[36] In the 2015 interview, many workers, especially those on TaskRabbit, laughed outright at the idea that they were entrepreneurs, and instead described themselves as part-time workers or employees without benefits.[37] In addition, many reported that they felt stigmatized by the work, identifying it as a source of embarrassment for themselves or their loved ones. For instance, Richard, a middle-age white male TaskRabbit, began his 2015 interview by sharing that his girlfriend of two years had broken up with him owing to embarrassment over his TaskRabbit work.

Even workers who were ambivalent about gig work, or who couched it in terms of paying higher wages than basic office work in their hometowns still discussed the sense that the work was demeaning in some way. For instance, in 2015, Michael, former college professor, noted,

> I do feel somewhat, not embarrassed ... borderline embarrassed. I do feel peculiar. I mean there is a disconnect between having a PhD and having been a college professor and a famous author. And then suddenly I'm picking up somebody's laundry or whatever. I do wrestle with a feeling that this is somewhat demeaning and I should be embarrassed by this and maybe I am a little bit ...

Likewise, in 2015, Rebecca, a thirty-four-year-old TaskRabbit with an advanced degree, confessed that she often lied to family and friends about her daily work, telling them she was "temping in an office, not tasking in people's homes."[38] Even years after leaving platform-based gig work, participants reported that their sense of gig work as stigmatized remained strong.

> It's like I have a graduate degree. Okay? I'm not an idiot. I can do a lot of things. I choose to do this because it enables me – or should, as I'm told – enable me to pursue creative performance ... And now, I just feel sucky about myself. That sucks, and I don't want to do that anymore ... [The reaction from clients was] "Why are you doing this? Are you really failing your life now? Is this what you have to do?" You have to do, okay. Well, just, you know I get it and it so demeaning. – Will, 41, former TaskRabbit
>
> I guess I was 31 to 35 when I was doing it and that to me just felt so – just desperate, unacceptable, this is not what you should be doing at this point in your life but yet

[36] Alexandrea J. Ravenelle. "Sharing Economy Workers: Selling, Not Sharing." *Cambridge Journal of Regions, Economy and Society*, 10(2), 281–295, 2017; Ravenelle, *Hustle and Gig*.

[37] Ravenelle, "Selling, Not Sharing"; Ravenelle, *Hustle and Gig*.

[38] Ravenelle, *Hustle and Gig*, 161.

> here you are, so yeah, it's just not something that I – and people kind of laugh about it, I feel like there's been jokes about it on SNL, it's like – feels like this stupid hipster thing to do, like a rite of passage that everyone has to do like eating a Tide Pod or it's like shameful. – Rebecca, 38, former TaskRabbit

Even though Rebecca calls gig work "a rite of passage that everyone has to do," she also identifies it as "desperate," "unacceptable," and even "stupid." Rebecca's comparison between TaskRabbit work and eating a Tide Pod, a coated capsule of laundry detergent, is especially noteworthy. The accidental ingestion of the concentrated laundry pods, which resemble gummy candies, but are poisonous and occasionally even lethal, was previously linked to toddlers, but in 2017, the rise of the Tide Pod Challenge led to an increased number of teens and young adults posting viral videos of themselves eating the poisonous packets much to the bafflement of adults.[39]

The idea that gig work has an acceptability timeframe – perhaps during one's early-twenties or before one has a fully developed frontal lobe, as opposed to after one completes a graduate degree – was also mentioned by other gig workers. Will, forty-one, began doing TaskRabbit work when he was in his mid-thirties and stopped when he was in his late-thirties in part due to what he described as a "weird situation in ageism."

> It was so bizarre to me and it got to the point where people were upset by the fact that I was older than them. They didn't want. I mean I'm 41 now. At the time I was you know 37. Yeah. Late 30s and these were like 20-year-old kids that were working for whatever . . . and they're like "Oh yeah. Yeah." And they were kind of sending, it was like a tone in the way they handled me. And in some days, it was like "Oh. Yeah. Take it easy man." I was like "I'm not going to have a heart attack." It's just like, "Come on it's going to be all right." But also, conversely, there were people that were like, "This is embarrassing . . . ."

One potential explanation for the negativity associated with gig work by respondents is that many of the TaskRabbit workers who disparaged gig work in 2015 used it as a primary source of income. Research conducted by Juliet Schor found limited stigma associated with gig work, with one notable exception being a law school graduate who was cleaning houses.[40] In her research on TaskRabbit gig workers, Schor found about half of her respondents were in lucrative professions and roughly a quarter had part-time jobs where gig work was simply part of their repertoire. Even for those who had no other employment, TaskRabbit "seemed to be transitional," due to a recent job loss.[41] But for the workers in my sample, gig work was often viewed as an occupation of last resort.

39 Niraj Chokshi, "Yes, People Really Are Eating Tide Pods. No, It's Not Safe." *The New York Times*, Jan. 20, 2018, www.nytimes.com/2018/01/20/us/tide-pod-challenge.html.

40 Schor, "Does the Sharing Economy Increase Inequality."

41 Schor, "Does the Sharing Economy Increase Inequality," 271.

5.4 A LONGER-TERM LIFESTYLE FOR OLDER WORKERS

Early articles about TaskRabbit and other gig economy services often discussed the opportunity to build a business or create a lucrative career, and profiled gig entrepreneurs who made thousands of dollars each month. Yet, increases in platform commission rates and in the number of workers competing for gigs, partnered with a low unemployment rate, has contributed to the promotion of gig work as a so-called side hustle or supplement to other income sources. The eleven workers who participated in follow-up interviews in 2019 fell into three main categories: four were still active on TaskRabbit or other platforms; four were still involved in gig-based work, although not working via platforms; and three had full-time jobs, but had returned to gig work at times, or were in the process of returning to gig work as an income supplement.

The question arises, what differentiates the workers who transitioned off gig platforms as a primary source of income, compared to those who remain on gig platforms? For one, the three workers who left gig work were young, ranging from twenty-nine to thirty-four years, and tended to have little work experience; for these workers, gig work was transitory, and often recommended by family or friends. For instance, for Emma, thirty, TaskRabbit was seen as a flexible source of income that she turned to between trips overseas to visit her fiancé; once he moved to the US she searched for and accepted a full-time job. In the case of Sarah, thirty-four, a successful dog-walking gig was parlayed into a full-time pet-sitter/personal assistant opportunity. While these workers continued to use gig platforms on occasion, it was seen as supplementary or as a stopgap measure during periods of unemployment. As Jamal, twenty-nine, a former TaskRabbit explained after his second stint on the platform after a period of unemployment, "I'd rather have a real job . . . with a salary and health benefits."

By comparison, the four male workers who remained active on TaskRabbit and other platforms four years after the preliminary interviews were among the older respondents, ranging from thirty-eight to fifty-nine with a mean age of fifty-one in 2019. Unlike the younger workers, who did gig work early in their careers, the older workers turned to gig work after particularly negative experiences in more traditional employment, or when they were desperate after failing to find more stable employment.

Donald, fifty-five, turned to gig work after a traumatic layoff and unsuccessful job search. As Donald explained in 2015, "I got eliminated. I was ambushed after 10, almost 11 years with the company. "I went up to HR for a meeting and I was out the door. I never even got to go downstairs to say goodbye to my coworkers and that was in late 2007 and 2008."

Unable to find another stable full-time job, Donald worked a series of short-term jobs including six to nine-month stints at a bank, educational nonprofit, insurance company, and even for an interior decorator, before turning to gig work selling items for people on eBay. He spent a month on TaskRabbit before being unceremoniously "deactivated" after a negative interaction with the platform's call center staff. In 2015, Donald was quick to explain that the work was an occupation of last resort. "I do think about that, that I have a college degree and I'm cleaning apartments but it's like I can't get a job in my field anymore. I don't know if I've been out too long, I don't know if it's my . . . It's partly my age,". "You know, I've got to make money. I don't really care anymore. I need to get some income coming in."

After leaving TaskRabbit in 2015, Donald moved through a series of gig platforms, including Postmates and Caviar, food delivery services. For a period of time, he worked full-time for a nonprofit before getting laid off, but due to the low wages of the nonprofit position, he continued to do deliveries during lunch and after hours. In 2019, he was piecing together an income from doing deliveries on Shipt, a grocery delivery service, and Caviar, a food delivery service, after a stint doing deliveries via Postmates.

Likewise, Richard, fifty-three, also turned to TaskRabbit in a moment of desperation, in his case after a business venture fell apart and he was unable to find a new job. "I was so destitute . . . running out of money, not getting hired in the beginning of the year that I actually – I'd already had a conversation with my sister who's single and lives [outside New York] to prepare to move in with her. And I didn't care about pride, that's how bad it was. I was out of money," he said, with a laugh.

Likewise, Marcus, thirty-eight, was working via the TaskRabbit app, and doing deliveries for UberEats when we met in 2015. He also turned to gig work as an occupation of last resort after an unpaid internship and seasonal work, explaining,

> I had a very long stretch of unemployment after the Great Recession hit, so at the time I was doing a seasonal temp job. I was working in a shipping office scanning FedEx packages. That began in November and I believe ran through January of 2013. And before that I'd done some kind of an unpaid internship or slave labor over the summer for some kind of a start-up that builds local web pages.

In addition to providing a source of income, app work also served as a respite from active job seeking. As Richard explained, "[my] brother insisted like 'you are not even looking for work'; I said, 'that's right, I'm not.' And in my mind I'm thinking I will when I'm ready – I don't want to tell you I will in two months or I will next week or I will in six months; I don't know."

In the 2015 interviews, gig work was often described as a temporary measure or as a way to make money while determining next steps. For Michael, fifty-three, a former college professor, gig work was also seen as a short-term solution during a period of transition after moving to New York in order to be closer to his significant other. Disenchanted with teaching, and the need to move from place to place as a visiting professor, Michael had hoped to use the platform to find tasks in writing and research, but was mostly hired for errand-running.

"I see this as a temporary thing as I'm moving and I'm still sort of looking around and trying to figure out what I want to do. I am a procrastinator and that's certainly part of this. It's not all high-minded . . . I'm thinking through all of my possibilities and I don't want to rush into things," he said.

> Part of it is just plain procrastination, but I see this as probably a temporary thing while I figure out what I want to do next and as soon as I'm doing the next thing I'm going to stop tasking, but who knows? I mean it's possible that I'll do something else and supplement it with a few tasks here and there. I still envision at some point getting tasks that are more in line with my talents.

The lack of benefits, combined with the general instability of the work, reduced its desirability. For Marcus, considering a return to graduate school, the seasonality of the income was especially problematic. He said:

> I think what motivates me to leave the sharing economy more is a lack of stability, because what I'm seeing is it's pretty slow right now in the summer with deliveries and with events and then it picks up again in the fall and it's steady through the winter. And I would much rather have a steady job that at least has work and is going to pay me the same whether it's July or January, . . . I'd like to go to grad school, but I'm not 100 percent sure how to make that work with the work that I do and even [paying for] things like the GRE or study materials, I think that's out of reach at the moment.

But while gig work was painted as a temporary measure in 2015, except for short stints that Donald and Richard had working off-platform, all four men continued to use gig platforms as their primary source of work and income in 2019. Additionally, all four expected to remain working via app for the foreseeable future. Given their original stance that gig work was temporary, why have these short-term gigs become their primary source of work? The responses from the men point to two primary explanations: the perceived flexibility and variety of gig work; and the difficulties of transitioning from gig-based work to more stable employment.

5.4.1 *Perceived Flexibility and Variety*

One benefit of gig work is the perceived flexibility of the work. For Richard, gig work allows him to spend time with a partner who works in retail management and has a varied schedule. A self-identified member of the "hustle and gig economy," Richard obtains work through roughly half a dozen sources that he prioritizes by income potential.

"I've got TaskRabbit, I've got, you know, word of mouth turned TaskRabbit clients or other people through Yelp and through private clients. I've got Amazon Flex, I've got Door Dash, UberEATS and all the food delivery services," Richard said. "So, my hierarchy is I love to just get private clients without TaskRabbit; secondly,

TaskRabbit; third, Amazon Flex to deliver packages; and fourth – now that I have a truck – I don't want to do food delivery, it's just so much gasoline."

While the income sources are varied, the work itself is fairly static, and generally includes running errands and assembling furniture, or making deliveries. Although he has the flexibility to set his daily schedule, time away from work has a distinct opportunity cost. He explains,

> [It's a] you eat what you kill mentality. And I make a contest, I make a goal, a daily goal, and monthly goal where I need to average X amount of dollars. I'll give you an example. $200 a day, if I can take in $200 a day, let's say a 30-day month is $6,000 a month. So, I take days off, but I'm marking my calendar every day.

Assuming work is forthcoming, Richard has some flexibility to pick his daily source of income and daily schedule, but he doesn't have as much freedom in terms of taking time off. His basic back-of-the-envelope calculation for making $6,000 is to work seven days a week. He can set his daily schedule, but time off comes with the high cost of not making any money.

For Michael, the former professor, the perceived flexibility of the work is addictive. "This is gambling, where I actually have no [risk of] losing, I only win. I mean it doesn't pay very much. But in some ways I prefer it, to something where I would be doing the same thing every day. So it's hard for me to leave with the flexibility and freedom . . .," he said. "I'm sure there are jobs where I could get a real salary, but then I picture myself doing it and I'm like 'huh.' So I think addicted is sort of the right word; I sort of feel it would be hard for me to give this up unless I find a job that I really love."

5.4.2 *Difficulties in Transitioning from Gig Work to Stable Employment*

In addition to the difficulty of finding a job that offered the same perceived level of flexibility, the men noted that it was difficult to transition out of gig work. While Richard says that flexibility is key, he also freely admits that he was looking for full-time employment when he returned to gig work. "I wanted to get back into the industry I used to be in, which was financial markets and selling [data management] software solutions. I didn't get that, but I took the next offer." Unfortunately, Richard's "next offer" was essentially a cold-calling sales job with especially high turnover, a far step down from his days working for a prestigious financial services firm, and he soon left, returning to gig work.

Transitioning to stable employment is also difficult due to the need for a cohesive narrative to tell potential employers. Marcus has worked in gig platform food delivery for more than five years, but would like to get a job in copywriting where he could use his college degree in English; however, he feels he can't compete with newer graduates or those with more experience. Noting that he had started working with a career coach on how to structure his resume and look for work, he explained,

It's hard to explain to an employer no matter what but I would rather say, "hey I'm delivering on my bike and I acquired these skills yadda, yadda, yadda over the last however many years" than have to say, "well, I've been doing so and so but I didn't think I should put it on my resume blah, blah, blah."

In many ways, Marcus' situation isn't that different from the challenges experienced by other workers who try to transition from long-term unemployment or underemployment back into more stable work. Yet, whereas in the past workers may have taken a job in retail or in a temp firm, gig work has been marketed by platforms as an opportunity for economic freedom and entrepreneurship. The possibility that gig work may actually prevent workers from moving forward in their careers, or that it might mire them in short-term, benefit-less work is concerning and at odds with the promise of limitless freedom and income marketed by gig platforms.

Interestingly, rather than viewed as cutting edge, the app-driven component of gig work was also seen as a potential liability. Even when the work was very similar, workers still mentioned experiences where their platform-based work was seen in a negative light. Jose, sixty-four, a former building handyman, turned to TaskRabbit after being laid-off. Dismayed about TaskRabbit's commission rate and problems he had with being reimbursed for expenses, he eventually started doing handyman work on his own, collecting business through word-of-mouth. He later applied for a full-time job with a handyman service that contracted out to local buildings, but paid workers as employees, a service that Jose described as a "glorified TaskRabbit." It was also one of the few times that he talked about TaskRabbit with a full-time employer, and it didn't go over well.

I did mention TaskRabbit to those guys with the handyman service and they were like "yeah, well, this isn't TaskRabbit." There's a weird conception about TaskRabbit . . . A lot of people think that it's a scam and a lot of people think that it's . . . that you're not getting what you should. In other words like these guys they were like "we're professionals and TaskRabbit is a bunch of amateurs trying to make money because they don't know what they're doing." There's a level of professionalism involved where people think well if I want someone who really knows what they're doing I'm not going to call TaskRabbit. But if I need someone to put together a cabinet – an IKEA thing – TaskRabbit is okay. But they're not going to look into TaskRabbit if they want to replace the kitchen sink . . .

Although Jose thought the interview went well, and he "really" wanted to work for the handyman service, as of a year later, he hadn't received a call back. Contrary to the premise that platform-based work might be considered technologically advanced and even appealing, Jose found that the online aspect of TaskRabbit was a negative.

"I don't know what the misconception is [about TaskRabbit]. I guess it seems sort of not unprofessional but I guess I would say . . . I don't know how to describe it. It's like it's not . . . ." he said. "You don't have a lot of recourse. Like if you hire a contractor and this person has a reputation to uphold and they have an office and a place. TaskRabbit is this nebulous thing that exists online and a lot of people don't trust that."

5.5 LONG-TERM CONSEQUENCES OF GIG WORK SUPPORT NEED FOR ADDITIONAL PROTECTIONS

While lots of attention has been paid to the lack of workplace protections and potential for worker exploitation in gig work, little attention has been paid to the implications for worker careers. While platforms argue that the perk of gig work flexibility is so great that it should override the need for standard workplace protections, such as unemployment, workers compensation, and social security contributions, long-term gig work may create path dependencies whereby future options are limited by past decisions. While gig work was seen as a temporary option by all of the workers interviewed in 2015, all eleven of the workers interviewed in 2019 were still working via gig platforms; still using them as supplementary or as transitional options; or were still involved, albeit off-platform, with gig-based work. Even though the unemployment rate was under 4 percent in 2019, none of the workers interviewed in 2015 had permanently transitioned into stable, full-time employment that sufficiently met their financial needs.

While an individual gig may be short-term, the dynamics of engaging in such work, especially for long periods of time, may damage workers' ability to emerge from a transitory gig-based period in their professional lives and secure careers that are more lucrative and satisfying. Although the app-based platforms experience a high level of turnover in terms of workers, this preliminary research suggests that there may be less turnover within gig work as a whole, or from gig work to non-gig work. To date, large-scale quantitative studies have not addressed the movement of gig workers from gig to gig (platform-based or otherwise) versus their movement from gig work into more traditional employment. Although a direct causal relationship between long-term involvement in gig work and a lack of return to stable, full-time employment may be complicated by additional factors such as age, education, and the type of gig work, this study supports the importance of additional research to examine the career outcomes of long-term gig workers, especially older workers who believe – or hope – that their gig work will be short-term.

The lack of movement by long-term gig workers into more stable work also suggests serious inequities in regards to worker opportunity or experience and points to the possibility of a growing precarity among gig workers. Standing has written extensively on the rise of the precariat, workers who have insecure jobs or move uneasily between short-term jobs and spells of unemployment, and who lack any sense of occupational identity or narrative.[42] Such a loss of occupational identity and

[42] Guy Standing, *The Precariat: The New Dangerous Class*. London: Bloomsbury Academic, 2014.

cohesive narrative to one's career may further contribute to the challenges of returning traditional employment. As the experience of Marcus illustrates, several years spent working as a food courier is not a traditional trajectory to the use of one's English degree as a copywriter.

The high level of education among the workers who remain in gig work, whether platform-based or not, should also trouble scholars of labor and employment. The majority of gig workers interviewed for this study have a college education and 36 percent also have at least one graduate degree. While there's nothing inherently wrong with personal assistant work or errand running, these workers are very much underemployed in regards to their education levels, previous work experience and – in many cases – their career aspirations. Even those workers who speak about the positive aspects of gig work, such as the flexibility, relatively fast payment or ease-of-finding work, remained highly ambivalent about the work as a whole, and spoke about continuing to look for stable work or wanting to do something else more in line with their interests and talents.

Finally, this research further supports the importance of establishing a social safety net and workplace protections for gig workers. None of the workers who are engaged in long-term gig work, platform-based or otherwise, are actively saving for retirement. This situation is particularly concerning in the case of the older men (Michael, Donald, and Richard) who are entirely engaged in platform-based gig work. Indeed, both Donald and Richard noted in the 2015 interviews that they had burned through a large portion of their retirement savings by liquidating 401ks and IRAs, and owed extensive tax penalties as a result. While gig workers do contribute to social security – and indeed, are also responsible for the employer's portion of the contribution – they do not receive access to company retirement accounts or contributions. Furthermore, spending months or years at a time with platform-based gig work as one's sole source of income, especially given the lack of matching contributions from gig platforms, further decreases a worker's ability to accrue sufficient retirement savings.

Although workers would be best served by being classified as employees, complete with all of the related workplace benefits and protections, at the very least, workers should have access to a portable benefits program that requires contributions by all gig economy platforms and does not have any waiting periods or vesting limitations. Such a program, which would provide for retirement funds, unemployment, and health insurance, would help to address the movement by gig workers between various platforms. Additional attention should also be paid to removing the multi-year vesting requirement that many 401ks require before workers receive the full company match to their contribution. While vesting policies may be intended to encourage worker longevity and loyalty, they can also hurt workers who move in and out of jobs by reducing their retirement savings. Older workers, who are closer to retirement and have less time available for making contributions, are especially likely to be hurt by draconian vesting requirements.

Much has been made of the gig economy as a source of short-term and flexible work. But as these preliminary findings show, for some workers – especially those who are older – the allegedly short-term promise of gig work may have long-term implications for their career trajectories and ability to return to stable employment, even when the unemployment rate is at record lows. Given the lack of workplace protections or benefits in gig work, the extensive variety of risks experienced by workers, the best advice for gig workers who sell their labor on platforms may be *caveat venditor*: seller beware.

REFERENCES

Autor, D. H., and S. N. Houseman. "Temporary Agency Employment: A Way Out of Poverty?" in *Working and Poor: How Economic and Policy Changes Are Affecting Low-Wage Workers*, eds. Rebecca M. Blank, Sheldon H. Danziger, and Robert F. Schoeni. New York: Russell Sage Foundation, 2016.

Baker, D. "Don't Buy the 'Sharing Economy' Hype: Airbnb and Uber Are Facilitating Rip-Offs." *The Guardian*, May 27, 2014. www.theguardian.com/commentisfree/2014/may/27/airbnb-uber-taxes-regulation.

Bell, D. N. F. and D. G. Blanchflower. "Young People and the Great Recession." Institute for the Study of Labor Discussion Paper Series 5674, 2011. http://ftp.iza.org/dp5674.pdf.

Botsman, Rachel and Roo Rodgers. *What's Mine Is Yours: The Rise of Collaborative Consumption*. New York: Harper Collins, 2010.

Brand, J. E. "The Far-Reaching Impact of Job Loss and Unemployment." *Annual Review of Sociology*, 41, 359–375, 2015.

Bureau of Labor Statistics. U.S. Department of Labor, "The Economics Daily, Number of people working part time for economic reasons falls in June 2016" at www.bls.gov/opub/ted/2016/number-of-people-working-part-time-for-economic-reasons-falls-in-june-2016.htm.

Chokshi, N. "Yes, People Really Are Eating Tide Pods. No, It's Not Safe." *The New York Times*, Jan. 20, 2018, www.nytimes.com/2018/01/20/us/tide-pod-challenge.html.

Davis, S. J., and J. Haltiwanger. "Labor Market Fluidity and Economic Performance." NBER Working Paper No. 20479. Cambridge, Mass.: National Bureau of Economic Research, 2014.

Dixon, A. "Survey: Nearly 1 in 3 Side Hustlers Needs the Income to Stay Afloat." *Bankrate.com*, June 5, 2019, www.bankrate.com/personal-finance/side-hustles-survey-june-2019/.

Dynan, K., D. Elmendorf and D. Sichel. "The Evolution of Household Income Volatility." *The B.E. Journal of Economic Analysis and Policy*, 12(2), 1–42, 2012. Retrieved 18 Aug. 2017, from doi:10.1515/1935-1682.3347.

Evans, J. "Meet the New Serfs, Same as the Old Serfs." *TechCrunch*, Oct 5, 2013. http://techcrunch.com/2013/10/05/meet-the-new-serfs-same-as-the-old-serfs/.

Farber, H. S., D. Silverman, and T. M. von Wachter. "Factors Determining Callbacks to Job Applications by the Unemployed: An Audit Study." *RSF: The Russell Sage Foundation Journal of the Social Sciences*, 3(3), 168–201, 2017.

Farrell, D. and F. E. Greig. "The Online Platform Economy: Has Growth Peaked?" (November 15, 2017). https://ssrn.com/abstract=2911194.

Farrell, D. and F. E. Greig. "Paychecks, Paydays, and the Online Platform Economy: Big Data on Income Volatility." JP Morgan Chase & Co. Institute, February 2016. https://ssrn.com/abstract=2911293.

Federal Reserve Board. "Report on the Economic Well-Being of U.S. Households in 2016." May 2017. www.federalreserve.gov/publications/files/2016-report-economic-well-being-us-households-201705.pdf.

Federal Reserve Board. "Report on the Economic Well-Being of U.S. Households in 2018." May 2019. www.federalreserve.gov/publications/files/2018-report-economic-well-being-us-households-201905.pdf.

Ferber, M. A., and J. Waldfogel. "The Long-Term Consequences of Nontraditional Employment." Columbia University Academic Commons, https://doi.org/10.7916/D8794FDK. *ANNALS of the American Academy of Political and Social Science*, 650 (1), 78–97, 1998.

Frenken, K., Meelen, T., Arets, M. and van de Glind, P. "Smarter Regulation for the Sharing Economy," *The Guardian*, May 20, 2015. www.theguardian.com/science/political-science/2015/may/20/smarter-regulation-for-the-sharing-economy.

Frasquilho, D., M. G. Matos, F. Salonna, D. Guerreiro, C. C. Storti, T. Gaspar, and J. M. Caldas-de-Almeida. "Mental Health Outcomes in Times of Economic Recession: A Systematic Literature Review." *BMC Public Health*, 16, 115, 2016.

Greenhouse, S. *The Big Squeeze: Tough Times for the American Worker*. New York: Knopf, 2008.

Greenhouse, S. *Beaten Down, Worked Up: The Past, Present, and Future of American Labor*. New York: Knopf, 2019.

Grusky, D. B., B. Western, and C. Wimer, eds. *The Great Recession*. New York: Russell Sage Foundation, 2011.

Hart, K. "Informal Income Opportunities and Urban Employment in Ghana." *The Journal of Modern African Studies*, 11(1), 61–89, 1973, retrieved from www.jstor.org/stable/159873.

Hart, K. "The Informal Economy." *Cambridge Anthropology*, 10(2), 54–58, 1985, retrieved from www.jstor.org/stable/23816368.

Heinrich, C., P. R. Mueser and K. R. Troske. "Welfare to Temporary Work: Implications for Labor Market Outcomes." *The Review of Economics and Statistics*, 87(1), 154–173, 2005.

Hout, M., and O. P. Hastings. "The Social Recession: Americans' Subjective Reactions to the Great Recession and Lagging Economy Since 2006." Paper presented at annual meeting of the American Sociological Association. San Francisco (August 16–19, 2014).

Kalamar, A. "Sharewashing Is the New Greenwashing." *OpEdNews.com*, May 13, 2013. www.opednews.com/articles/Sharewashing-is-the-New-Gr-by-Anthony-Kalamar-130513–834.html.

Kalleberg, A. *Good Jobs, Bad Jobs: The Rise of Polarized and Precarious Employment Systems in the United States*. New York: Russell Sage Foundation, 2011.

Kalleberg, A. L. and T. M. von Wachter. "The U.S. Labor Market During and After the Great Recession: Continuities and Transformations." *RSF: The Russell Sage Foundation Journal of the Social Sciences*, 3(3), 1–19, 2017.

Mathews, J. "The Sharing Economy Boom Is About to Bust." *Time*, June 27, 2014. http://time.com/2924778/airbnb-uber-sharing-economy/.

McAfee, A. and E. Brynjolfsson. *Machine, Platform, Crowd: Harnessing Our Digital Future*. New York: Norton, 2017.

McCue, T. J. "Looking for a Side Hustle or Freelance Gig? Check Out These Sites." *Forbes*, July 28, 2019. www.forbes.com/sites/tjmccue/2019/07/28/looking-for-a-side-hustle-or-freelance-gig-check-out-these-sites/#3676e76b56ad.

Mieszkowski, K. "Don't Wanna Be Your (Temp) Slave." *Fast Company*, August 31, 1998. Retrieved Aug 26, 2017. www.fastcompany.com/35119/dont-wanna-be-your-temp-slave.

McKinsey Global Work Institute. Independent Work: Choice, Necessity and the Gig Economy. 2016. www.mckinsey.com/~/media/McKinsey/Global%20Themes/Employment%20and%20Growth/Independent%20work%20Choice%20necessity%20and%20the%20gig%20economy/Independent-Work-Choice-necessity-and-the-gig-economy-Full-report.ashx.

Morduch, J. and R. Schneider. *The Financial Diaries: How American Families Cope in a World of Uncertainty*. Princeton: Princeton University Press, 2017.

Nunley, J. M., A. Pugh, N. Romero, and R. A. Seals, Jr. "Unemployment, Underemployment, and Employment Opportunities: Results from a Correspondence Audit Study of the Labor Market for College Graduates." *Industrial and Labor Relations Review*, 70(3) 642–669, 2016.

Pew Research Center. "Shared, Collaborative and On Demand: The New Digital Economy." May 2016. www.pewresearch.org/internet/2016/05/19/the-new-digital-economy/.

Pew Research Center. "How Income Volatility Interacts with American Families' Financial Security: An Examination of Gains, Losses, and Household Economic Experiences." March 9, 2017. www.pewtrusts.org/en/research-and-analysis/issue-briefs/2017/03/how-income-volatility-interacts-with-american-families-financial-security.

Portes, A. "The Informal Economy and Its Paradoxes," in *Handbook of Economic Sociology*, eds. Neil J. Smelser and Richard Swedberg. Princeton: Princeton University Press, 1994.

Ravenelle, Alexandrea J. "Sharing Economy Workers: Selling, Not Sharing." *Cambridge Journal of Regions, Economy and Society*, 10(2) 281–295, 2017. https://doi.org/10.1093/cjres/rsw043.

Ravenelle, Alexandrea J. *Hustle and Gig: Struggling and Surviving in the Sharing Economy*. Berkeley: University of California Press, 2019.

Schor, Juliet B. "Does the Sharing Economy Increase Inequality Within the Eighty Percent?: Findings from a Qualitative Study of Platform Providers." *Cambridge Journal of Regions, Economy and Society*, 10(2) 263–279 (2017). https://doi.org/10.1093/cjres/rsw047.

Schor, J. B. and C. Fitzmaurice. "Collaborating and Connecting: The Emergence of a Sharing Economy," in *Handbook on Research on Sustainable Consumption*, eds. Lucia Reisch and John Thogersen. Cheltenham: Edward Elgar, 2015.

Schor, J. B. "Debating the Sharing Economy," *Great Transition Initiative* (October 2014), www.greattransition.org/publication/debating-the-sharing-economy.

Schor, J. B. *True Wealth: How and Why Millions of Americans Are Creating a Time-rich, Ecologically-light, Small-scale, High-satisfaction Economy*. New York: The Penguin Press, 2011.

Song, J, and T. von Wachter. "Long-Term Nonemployment and Job Displacement." Evaluating Labor Market Dynamics, Proceedings from the Jackson Hole Economic Policy Symposium Sponsored by the Federal Reserve Board of Kansas City, Jackson Hole, Wyo. (August 2014). www.kansascityfed.org/publicat/sympos/2014/2014vonWachter.pdf.

Standing, G. *The Precariat: The New Dangerous Class*. London: Bloomsbury Academic, 2011.

Weiss, R. S. *Learning from Strangers: The Art and Method of Qualitative Interview Studies*. New York: The Free Press, 1994.

Weber, Max. *Economy and Society: An Outline of Interpretive Sociology*. trans. Ephraim Fischoff et al. eds. Guenther Roth and Claus Wittich. Berkeley: University of California Press, [1922] 1978.

6

Algorithmic Management, Employment, and the Self in Gig Work

Julia Tomassetti

This chapter examines the relationship between algorithmic management and the written agreement that governs the relationship between a gig company and its workers. Algorithmic management is the use of digital algorithms to design, allocate, direct, monitor, correct, evaluate, and compensate work.[1] One of the most pressing regulatory questions confronting the gig economy is whether platform workers are – or should be treated as – employees or independent contractors. I shed light on this question by posing and answering an important sub-question: Should a gig company's partial automation of its managerial authority matter in our consideration of the employee-independent contractor question? I answer this question in the negative: the automation of managerial authority should not matter under current legal standards or when considering how to craft regulations for the gig economy.

To demonstrate, the chapter provides a close reading of an end-user license agreement (EULA) between the on-demand transportation company Uber and its drivers. It reveals that Uber uses the EULA in tandem with algorithmic management to direct its drivers' work and determine the terms of the exchange on an ongoing basis.

I explain the legal and policy import of this finding by drawing on a theory of the "self" implicit in contract law – the agentic self. The *sine qua non* of this self is the capacity to take voluntary action and reflect upon that action and its consequences in a process of self-determination. Because this theoretical lens helps to distinguish enforceable contracts from employment relationships, I use it to analyze the EULA and Uber's management of its drivers' work through digital algorithms. The analysis shows that Uber uses the EULA to conceal contractual infirmities in its relationships with drivers. The EULA masquerades as a contract while giving Uber an open-ended discretion over the main terms of the bargain that is inconsistent with that of an enforceable contract. Uber exercises this discretion through algorithmic

[1] Min Kyung Lee et al., *Working with Machines: The Impact of Algorithmic and Data-driven Management on Human Workers*, *in* Proceedings of the 33rd Annual ACM Conference on Human Factors in Computing Systems 1603–1612 (2015), http://dl.acm.org/citation.cfm?id=2702548.

management to continually recalibrate the bargain in its favor and alter the drivers' obligations.

The chapter illustrates the value of qualitative analysis in gig economy research, even in penetrating what may appear to be an abstruse doctrinal issue. One lesson emerging is that, in trying to navigate the employee/independent contractor dichotomy in the gig economy, judges, regulators, and policy makers should take the independent contractor category more seriously. It is often treated as a default category. The consequence is a failure to subject gig economy EULAs to contractual scrutiny and thereby recognize when the company has assumed trans-contractual discretion to command another's labor. Taking "independent contracting" seriously – as the *contractual* category in the dichotomy – helps to illuminate the nature of the relationship at issue.

Although gig companies are heterogeneous, the findings here are relevant beyond Uber. At a minimum, they are relevant to the many gig companies that claim to be technological intermediaries rather than service producers but are so engaged in the worker-customer transaction as to raise serious questions regarding their workers' employment status.

6.1 CONTRACT AND THE SELF

What is the "self" that the law of private agreements renders and recognizes? This chapter suggests that the preeminent self that contract law picks out as subject and object of regulation is the "agentic self." Its defining feature is the capacity to take voluntary action and to reflect upon its action and its consequences. It is a subject that determines itself through voluntary action – including the making of decisions – and reflection.

Contract law is intimately involved in constructing and bordering this self. For example, the voluntary acts that determine the agentic self have temporal horizons. Contract law determines how far the agentic self can project itself in time from the moment of contractual assent. Thus, when a dispute arises over how long a party's obligations should endure where the contract was for an indefinite duration, courts have found that the contract should last a "reasonable time."[2]

Contract law provides for the state enforcement of certain agreements between private parties. However, the law will not commit taxpayer resources and summon the state's coercive power to assist in the enforcement of all private agreements. The parties must demonstrate both a minimal commitment of, and withholding of, the agentic self in their promises.

For there to be an adequate commitment of the self, the agreement must be the choice of an adequately determined self, not an undetermined self. Courts refuse to

[2] *E.g.*, Haines v. City of New York, 364 N.E.2d 820, 822 (N.Y. 1977) (holding that where contract did not provide a duration term, the court would not presume the parties intended the agreement to last forever).

enforce contractual commitments that are too vague. This is sometimes referred to as the requirement that contractual commitments be "definite."[3] Thus, courts are unwilling to enforce an "agreement to agree," a contract where the parties agree to arrive at a specific agreement in the future.[4] Why require that contracts be "definite"? On the one hand, courts do not want to rewrite a bargain at variance with self-determining acts the parties might have sought to consummate in the contract.[5] On the other hand, a vague bargain suggests an inadequate commitment of the agentic self. The assenting legal subject sought to commit only the hazy fringes of the self rather than an adequately determined self. Failing to form definite interests as to the exchange implies a neglect of the prerequisite voluntary acts of self-determination. Contract law requires evidence that the undertakings of an enforceable agreement reflect a minimal level of self-determination upon assent.

At the same time, the agentic self cannot seek to overcommit – contract law expects that a party's commitment to the other entails only a temporary and discrete abeyance of one's capacity for taking voluntary action. Discreteness is another dimension of definiteness, but here reflects the law's expectation that a party adequately withhold the capacity for self-determination from another's will.[6] So long as obligations are adequately discrete, a party can insist that the other either perform them or provide other satisfaction, even if the other party has changed its mind and does not want to perform. The party seeking enforcement has no right to demand performances of the other *beyond* those specified in the contract, however.

Contract law is comfortable with requiring the breaching party to pay damages where there has been adequate commitment and withholding of the determined self: changing one's mind is an act of self-determination as well, but requiring the breaching party to make some recompense does not trample on that self-determination since the contract required only a temporary and discrete suspension of the capacity for voluntary action. An order that the breaching party actually perform its contractual duties – "specific performance" – is rarer.[7] For personal service contracts, the law appears to recognize that such an agreement requires not just an abeyance of the right of self-determination but a relinquishment of it – albeit measured – to another. Thus, courts will not order specific performance for breaches of personal service contracts.[8]

3 *See* Sun Printing & Publ'g Ass'n v. Remington Paper & Power Co., 139 N.E. 470, 471 (N.Y. 1923). U.C.C. § 2–204(3) provides for cases in which contracts with some open terms need not fail for indefiniteness.

4 *Sun Printing & Publ'g Ass'n*, 139 N.E. at 471.

5 *Id.*

6 *See* Ian R. MacNeil, *Contracts: Adjustment of Long-Term Economic Relations under Classical, Neoclassical, and Relational Contract Law*, 72 Nw. U. L. Rev. 854 (1977) (describing some of the difficulties that contract law has accommodating long-term relationships lacking discrete obligations).

7 *See* Restatement (Second) of Contracts § 359 (1981).

8 *E.g.*, Lumley v Wagner, 42 Eng. Rep. 687 (1852) (noting that court would not compel personal service but granting negative injunction against opera performer).

For contracts to be definite and thus enforceable, they should include the essential terms of the bargain. Although there are exceptions, these tend to include the quantity and price terms, or the terms that answer the question: How much for what? In a sales contract, the price term is generally essential.[9] The importance of the quantity term is evidenced through its narrow exceptions. For example, for an output or requirements contract to be enforceable, it should include an exclusive dealing provision.[10]

This chapter does not presume that there is a consensus on precisely what "self" contract law recognizes and constructs, or that contract law comprises a coherent set of doctrines and decisions. Nonetheless, some genus of the agentic self appears to be the omphalos of several major theories offering philosophical justifications for contract law, including the consent, bargain, and will theories.[11] The agentic self that contract law limns also resembles the "unencumbered self" in some liberal theories of political philosophy.[12] It has the capacity to act voluntarily in choosing commitments, whether they be social, moral, or material. And it is reflexive in determining itself through reflections upon its choices and their consequences.

6.2 EMPLOYMENT VERSUS CONTRACT

What happens where one party seeks to overcommit the self? How does the law deal with a situation where one party places too much of its capacity for voluntary action at the disposal of another? The law reacts in several ways. The law outlaws this agreement in its most extreme form: the Thirteenth Amendment prohibits slavery. The law's understanding of the agentic self, its boundaries, and their impregnability has also changed over the years. In colonial America, indentured servitude was generally not thought to be "involuntary" so long as the servant entered the arrangement voluntarily. An 1821 case, however, held that once the servant no longer wanted to be indentured, the agreement became involuntary, regardless of whether it was entered voluntarily.[13]

In forms less extreme than slavery and indentured servitude, the law permits these arrangements to exist today as employment relationships: where an agreement not only seeks to commit the undetermined self but to allow another to determine the self, the agreement is an employment relationship.

9 U.C.C. § 2–305 recognizes a contract for the sale of goods with an open price term but provides for implied terms.

10 *E.g.*, Mid-S. Packers, Inc. v. Shoney's, Inc., 761 F.2d 1117, 1121–22 (5th Cir. 1985).

11 *See* Randy E. Barnett, *A Consent Theory of Contract*, 86 Colum. L. Rev. 269 (1986) (describing different theories of contract).

12 Michael J. Sandel, *The Procedural Republic and the Unencumbered Self*, 12 Pol. Theory 81 (1984).

13 *See* Robert J. Steinfeld , The Invention of Free Labor: The Employment Relation in English and American Law and Culture, 1350–1870, at 144–45 (1991) (quoting *In re* Clark, 1 Blackf. 122, 123–25 [Ind. 1821]); Robert J. Steinfeld , Coercion, Contract, and Free Labor in the Nineteenth Century 29–30 (2001) (discussing the decline of indentured servitude in the US).

While legal actors and lay persons often refer to employment as a "contract,"[14] doctrinally it is not.[15] Its origins are in the preindustrial master-servant relationship, where the master had a property right to the labor of the servant. Treatise writers and judges moved the master-servant relationship from the shelf of property to that of contract, but it retained its authoritarian vintage.[16]

The common law defines employment as an agreement to work for another under the other's right of control in exchange for remuneration.[17] But what is work? It is the use of one's voluntary faculties. From the *Umwelt* of contract, employment appears as an unenforceable, indefinite "agreement to agree." But more than this, it is an agreement in which one party says, "I choose to allow you to choose for me": employment is an agreement to *obey*. Employment entails placing one's capacity for voluntary action at the disposal of another, or subjugating one's energetic and cognitive capabilities to another's command. An employee agrees to alienate what she cannot under contract law and still be capable of contractual assent, of adequately withholding the agentic self.

Employment gives one party a right to determine the critical terms of the agreement during the course of the relationship, the terms that describe, "*what* for *how much*?" When an employee is paid an hourly wage, for example, the agreement is missing a quantity term: the employee agrees to provide an indefinite amount of labor – whatever the employer can extract for an hour – in return for a definite amount of pay.[18] The employer determines the quantity term by commanding the employee as to the nature, pace, and intensity of the work. The relationship is open-ended on one side, and the employer determines essential aspects of the bargain in the course of the relationship, *after* the purported contractual assent. This indefiniteness is not incidental. Ronald Coase, the founder of transaction cost economics, intimated that the whole purpose of employment was to provide one side a degree of flexibility unrecognized by contract law.[19] Sections 6.3 and 6.4 show that this anti-contractual and one-sided discretion also characterizes Uber's relationship with its

14 Franklin G. Snyder, *The Pernicious Effect of Employment Relationships on the Law of Contracts Symposium: The Role of Contract in the Modern Employment Relationship*, 10 Tex. Wesleyan L. Rev. 33 (2003) (discussing how courts sought to resolve employment disputes under contract law before the advent of employment legislation); Stephen Nayak-Young, *Revising the Roles of Master and Servant: A Theory of Work Law*, 17 U. Pa. J. Bus. L. 1223 (2014) (critiquing the "freedom of contract" view of employment due to the status-like elements of employment).

15 For a more detailed discussion of the doctrinal contrast between a contract and employment relationship see Julia Tomassetti, *From Hierarchies to Markets: FedEx Drivers and the Work Contract as Institutional Marker*, 19 Lewis & Clark L. Rev. 1083–152, 1101–06 (2015).

16 *See generally* Christopher L. Tomlins, Law, Labor, and Ideology in the Early American Republic 268–78 (1993).

17 Restatement (Second) of Agency § 220(1) (1958).

18 This phenomenon is apparent at the macro level in the widening gap between worker pay and productivity. *The Productivity–Pay Gap*, Economic Policy Institute (July 2019), www.epi.org/productivity-pay-gap/.

19 Ronald H. Coase, *The Nature of the Firm*, 4 Economica 386, 391–92 (1937).

drivers. However, it is mainly the price term that the agreement leaves subject to Uber's ongoing determination.

A related anti-contractual feature of employment is that it leaves interpretative authority over the agreement largely to the employer's discretion. Parties to commercial contracts often grant discretion to one party to fill in certain gaps and resolve ambiguities in the terms. However, the common law imposes a duty of "good faith" on the parties, authorizing courts to police opportunistic behavior and abuses of discretion.[20] Most states either do not recognize a duty of good faith in employment agreements or recognize only a weaker version of the duty in employment.[21] Likewise, in contracts, courts assume authority to supply missing terms according to default rules, like industry custom or a course of dealing.[22] However, they permit employers to dictate these terms in employment relationships.[23] Some have observed that, if employment is a contract, it would be a strange one in giving one party a right to determine the rules of the relationship and whether the other party was complying with them.[24]

Instead of outlawing employment, the law deals with the problem of the over-committed self primarily through two measures: the first is to make employment an at-will relationship by default. In all but one state, and subject to certain common law and statutory exceptions, either party can terminate an employment relationship without notice, and for a good reason, a bad reason, or no reason.[25] Recall that, the problem employment poses for contract law is that one party commits her very faculty of contractual assent to the commands of another. Making employment at-will deals with this problem by removing, formally, the commitment.[26] This does

20 *E.g.*, Centronics Corp. v. Genicom Corp., 562 A.2d 187 (N.H. 1989). Also, where the contract gives one side considerable discretion, the court may question whether the parties actually intended to contract. *Id.*

21 *See* Tomassetti, *From Hierarchies to Markets*, *supra* note 15, at 1083, 1105 n.107 (2015); Lea VanderVelde, *Where Is the Concept of Good Faith in the Restatement of Employment?*, 21 EMP. RTS. & EMP. POL'Y J. 335 (2017) (noting the common law's incomplete recognition of the good faith duty in employment).

22 *E.g.*, U.C.C. § 1–303 (providing for the use of course of performance, course of dealing, and usage of trade as contractual defaults).

23 *E.g.*, Asmus v. Pac. Bell, 999 P.2d 71, 81 (Cal. 2000); Karl E. Klare, *The Labor-Management Cooperation Debate: A Workplace Democracy Perspective*, 23 HARV. C.R.-C.L. L. REV. 39 (1988) (discussing the assumption that employers had authority over anything not in the collective bargaining contract).

24 *See* ALAN FOX, BEYOND CONTRACT: WORK, POWER AND TRUST RELATIONS 183–84, 187–88 (1974).

25 *See* Tomassetti, *From Hierarchies to Markets*, *supra* note 15, at 1101–02 (discussing at-will employment); Vandervelde, *supra* note 21(critiquing at-will employment).

26 At-will employment is a textbook case of a contract that should fail for want of consideration: The employer says, "I agree to provide you work if and for so long as I feel like it," and the employee says, "I agree to work for you if and for so long as I feel like it"; JOHN R. COMMONS, LEGAL FOUNDATIONS OF CAPITALISM 285 (Univ. of Wisc. Press 1959) (1924) ("The labor contract is therefore not a contract, it is a continuing implied renewal of contracts at every minute and every hour, based on the continuance of what is deemed, on the employer's side, to be satisfactory service, and, on the laborer's side, what is deemed to be satisfactory conditions and compensation.").

little to address the inequality that compels individuals into these relationships instead of real contracts.

The second response, legislation, does address this problem. Several state and federal statutes restrict the employer's abuse of its open-ended discretion, for instance, by requiring the employer to pay a minimum wage or prohibiting sexual harassment. The National Labor Relations Act helps employees contest the employer's discretion through organizing and bargaining collectively. These efforts counter the law's sanctioning of a relationship that authorizes one party, nominally through contract but without the usual contractual safeguards, to command another's use of her physical, cognitive, and emotional faculties, and to determine critical terms of the exchange as it goes along. Most who agree to such imbalanced relationships lack other means of earning a living in a system that largely conditions access to the material and social necessaries of life on money.

This chapter is not an endorsement of the agentic self of contract law. So long as minimal requisites for enforcement are satisfied, the agentic self of contract law is quite impervious to breach. Many contracts may honor this notion of the agentic self but are hardly testaments to fair bargaining or free choice, like a contract of adhesion for an important consumer product.[27] The point of this chapter is to demonstrate that agreements between gig workers and gig companies sometimes fail to abide by even this anemic notion of agency.

6.3 EMPLOYMENT STATUS IN THE GIG ECONOMY

While not a new question or confined to gig work, one of the most pressing questions confronting the gig economy is whether gig workers are, or should be deemed to be, employees or independent contractors. The statutes mentioned above usually restrict access to their protections to "employees" and oblige only "employers" to comply.[28] This chapter cannot review all of the regulatory and judicial activity regarding the issue of employment status in the gig economy, but a few developments warrant mention: Successful lobbying by gig companies has led several states to pass legislation deeming platform workers to be "independent contractors" under state legislation.[29] Several states have also passed "ABC laws."[30] The latter should foreclose the ability of many gig companies to classify their workers as independent contractors, because to do so the hirer must demonstrate that the workers provide

[27] *See* Margaret Jane Radin, Boilerplate: The Fine Print, Vanishing Rights, and the Rule of Law (2013).

[28] Maya Pinto , Rebecca Smith & Irene Tung, Nat'l Emp't Law Project, Rights at Risk: Gig Companies' Campaign to Upend Employment as We Know It 2 (2019).

[29] *Id.*

[30] Anna Deknatel & Lauren Hoff-Downing, *ABC on the Books and in the Courts: An Analysis of Recent Independent Contractor and Misclassification Statutes*, 18 U.Pa. J.L. & Soc. Change 53 (2015). California recently passed an ABC law. Stats. 2019, ch. 296, § 1.

services outside the regular course of its business.[31] Gig workers in the US and abroad have brought many lawsuits alleging that their companies misclassified them as independent contractors. In the US, courts have been enforcing the companies' arbitration agreements, depriving workers of judicial consideration of the employment status question.[32] However, we have had some opportunity to see how adjudicators are thinking about this issue in hearings over worker compensation benefits and a few court decisions. In *O'Connor v. Uber Technologies* and *Cotter v. Lyft*, two federal courts denied motions by Uber and its competitor Lyft, respectively, to rule that drivers were independent contractors without a trial.[33] In *Lawson v. Grubhub*, however, the court ruled that food couriers for a delivery platform were independent contractors.[34]

Recently, *Razak v. Uber Technologies* became the first US court decision to rule on the status of drivers for an on-demand ride company.[35] It held that Uber limousine drivers were independent contractors.[36] Uber's position in *Razak* was that its contracts defined the parties' obligations to one another and specifically prohibited Uber from controlling drivers' work in many ways. The *Razak* court agreed and even reproduced eleven block quotes from Uber's contracts with drivers.[37] The court found significant that the agreements "specifically detail the many ways that Uber is *not* entitled to control … drivers."[38]

6.4 THE EULA

This chapter examines the EULAs from *Razak*.[39] Most of the terms and App features from *Razak* are the same today, but I note where there are relevant changes.

In *Razak*, Uber entered into a "Technology Services Agreement" ("EULA") governing the relationship between Uber and a "Customer," meaning an "independent company in the business of providing transportation services."[40] The EULA

31 Deknatel & Hoff-Downing, *supra* note 30. While ruling that the drivers were independent contractors, even the *Razak* court rejected Uber's argument that the drivers were not integral to its business. Razak v. Uber Techs., Inc., No. CV 16–573, 2018 WL 1744467, at 19 (E.D. Pa. Apr. 11, 2018).

32 Rebecca Smith, *Gig Companies Are Facing Dozens of Lawsuits Over Workplace Violations*, National Employment Law Project (Aug. 8, 2019), www.nelp.org/publication/gig-companies-facing-dozens-lawsuits-workplace-violations/.

33 O'Connor v. Uber Techs., Inc., 82 F. Supp. 3d 1133, 1153 (N.D. Cal. 2015); Cotter v. Lyft, Inc., 60 F. Supp. 3d 1067, 1082 (N.D. Cal. 2015).

34 Lawson v. Grubhub, Inc., 302 F. Supp. 3d 1071, 1093 (N.D. Cal. 2018).

35 *Razak*, 2018 WL 1744467, at 19, *vacated and remanded*, 951 F.3d 137 (3d Cir. 2020).

36 *Id.* Since writing this chapter, the decision has been reversed, 951 F.3d 137 (3d Cir. 2020).

37 *Id.* at 5–6.

38 *Id.* at 14 (emphasis in original).

39 Defendants' Statement of Undisputed Material Facts in Support of Motion for Summary Judgment at Ex. 11 (Technology Services Agreement, December 11, 2015), *Razak*, No. CV 16–573, 2018 WL 1744467 [hereinafter *EULA*]; *Id.* at Ex. 12 (Driver Addendum to Technology Services Agreement, December 11, 2015) [hereinafter Driver EULA].

40 EULA, pmbl.

obligates the Customer to enter into a similar "Driver Addendum" ("Driver EULA") with any drivers the Customer "hired" as a condition of Uber granting them access to the Driver App. The EULA requires the Customer to enforce the Driver EULA against its drivers and grants Uber a right to enforce the Driver EULA as a third-party beneficiary. Despite Uber only agreeing to contract with a business entity, in most cases, the driver and business entity are one individual.

The EULA is drafted as a software license granting Customers rights to use the software in the form of the Driver App.[41] Uber claims to provide "on-demand lead generation and related services that enable transportation providers to seek, receive and fulfil on-demand requests for transportation services by Users seeking transportation services," which includes "access to the Driver App and Uber's software, websites, payment services . . . ."[42] In return, the Customer pays Uber a "Service Fee" for each completed ride as a commission for the "lead."[43]

Uber claims it is not a party to the agreement between the Customer and passenger for transportation: "Customer's provision of Transportation Services to Users creates a direct business relationship between Customer and the User . . . ."[44]

6.5 THE APP

Drivers had to log onto the App once a month to avoid deactivation. Otherwise, a driver could choose whether and when to log on, and could log off without penalty at any time other than during a trip or upon receiving a ride request.[45] When someone requested a ride through the App, the App sent the request to one driver, according to a formula in part based on a driver's distance from the pickup location. A driver had fifteen seconds to accept the request before Uber sent it to another driver.[46] The App did not require the passenger to indicate a destination until the driver arrived.[47] After the ride, the App directed the passenger and driver to rate one another on a scale of one to five stars.[48] Via the App, Uber charged the passenger's credit card on file with Uber. It paid the driver any sums owed after making

41 I discuss the significance of drafting the agreement as a software license in Julia Tomassetti, *Rebalancing Worker Rights and Property Rights in Digitalised Work in* Labour Law and the Gig Economy: Challenges Posed by the Digitalisation of Labour Processes (Jo Carby-Hall and Lourdes Mella Méndez eds., Routledge forthcoming).

42 EULA, cl. 1.7.

43 *Id.*, cl. 2.4; *Razak*, 2018 WL 1744467, at 6.

44 *Id.*, cl. 2.3.

45 *Id.*, cl. 2.1.

46 *Razak*, 2018 WL 1744467, at 2.

47 *Id.* Uber has since introduced a feature enabling a driver, twice a day, to only receive ride assignments when the passenger wants to travel in the general direction of a destination selected by the driver. *How Does Uber's Destination Filter Work?*, THE RIDESHARE GUY BLOG AND PODCAST (2016), https://therideshareguy.com/how-does-ubers-destination-filter-work/.

48 Plaintiffs' Statement of Disputed or Undisputed Facts at Ex. D (Driver Deactivation Policy), Razak v. Uber Techs., Inc., No. CV 16–573 (E.D. Pa. Sept. 13, 2017), 2017 WL 4052417 [hereinafter Deactivation Policy].

deductions for expenses, such as for vehicle financing.[49] Uber paid a driver only for the time she was transporting a passenger, and not for waiting to receive a ride request from Uber or driving to the passenger's pickup location on behalf of Uber.

6.6 THE OSTENSIBLE ABSENCE OF EMPLOYER DISCRETION

The EULAs include several recitations regarding the identity of the parties and nature of their relationship. For instance, the EULA provides that, with the exception of Uber acting as the Customer's "agent" for purposes of collecting the passenger fare,

> the relationship between the parties under this Agreement is solely that of independent contracting parties. The parties expressly agree that: (a) this Agreement is not an employment agreement, nor does it create an employment relationship, between Uber and Customer or Uber and any Driver; and (b) no joint venture, partnership, or agency relationship exists between Uber and Customer or Uber and any Driver.[50]

And, "Uber does not, and shall not be deemed to, direct or control Customer or its Drivers generally or in their performance under this Agreement specifically, including in connection with the operation of Customer's business, the provision of Transportation Services, the acts or omissions of Drivers, or the operation and maintenance of any Vehicles."[51] As to the price term, the EULA provides: "In consideration of Uber's provision of the Driver App and the Uber Services for the use and benefit of Customer and its Drivers hereunder, Customer agrees to pay Uber a service fee on a per Transportation Services transaction basis calculated as a percentage of the Fare determined by the Fare Calculation . . . ."[52] The Preamble provides, "Customer acknowledges and agrees that Uber is a technology services provider that does not provide transportation services, function as a transportation carrier, nor operate as a broker for the transportation of passengers."[53]

The EULA describes at length the particular ways in which Uber purportedly has no right to control the Customers/Drivers:

> As between Uber and Customer, Customer acknowledges and agrees that: (a) Customer and its Drivers are solely responsible for determining the most effective, efficient and safe manner to perform each instance of Transportation Services.[54]
>
> Customer and its Drivers retain the *sole right to determine when, where, and for how long* each of them will utilize the Driver App or the Uber Services. Customer and its Drivers retain the option, via the Driver App, *to attempt to accept or to decline*

49 *Razak*, 2018 WL 1744467, at 18.
50 EULA, cl. 13.1.
51 *Id.* at cl. 2.4.
52 *Id.* at cl. 4.4.
53 *Id.* at pmbl.
54 *Id.* at cl. 2.2; *see also* Driver EULA, cl. 2.4.

> *or ignore a User's request for Transportation Services* via the Uber Services, *or to cancel an accepted request* for Transportation Services via the Driver App, subject to Uber's then-current cancellation policies. With the exception of any signage required by local law or permit/license requirements, *Uber shall have no right to require Customer or any Driver to: (a) display Uber's or any of its Affiliates' names, logos or colors* on any Vehicle(s); or (b) *wear a uniform or any other clothing* displaying Uber's or any of its Affiliates' names, logos or colors . . . .[55]

Likewise, the EULA implies that the Customer charges the passenger for the fare and states that Uber merely "recommend[s]" a fare, via its App:

> *Customer is entitled to charge a fare* for each instance of completed Transportation Services provided to a User that are obtained via the Uber Services ("Fare"), where such Fare is calculated based upon a base fare amount plus distance (as determined by Uber using location-based services enabled through the Device) and/or time amounts, as detailed at www.uber.com/cities for the applicable Territory (" Fare Calculation") . . . . In addition, the parties acknowledge and agree that as between Customer and Uber, *the Fare is a recommended amount, and the primary purpose of the pre-arranged Fare is to act as the default amount in the event Customer does not negotiate a different amount.* Customer shall always have the right to: (i) charge a fare that is less than the pre-arranged Fare; or (ii) negotiate, at Customer's request, a Fare that is lower than the pre-arranged Fare (each of (i) and (ii) herein, a "Negotiated Fare"). Uber shall consider all such requests from Customer in good faith.[56]

6.7 UBER'S DISCRETION

The excerpts above might seem to constrain Uber's discretionary authority over drivers. The EULA simulates that key terms have been decided upon contractually in advance, allowing each party to rationally plan, and limiting the authority of each over the other. A closer reading of the EULA, however, together with documents it incorporates, shows that Uber reserves a right to control how drivers perform their work, and to determine drivers' performance obligations and the essential terms of the bargain during the course of the relationship.

6.8 AUTHORITY TO ESTABLISH AND ENFORCE (UNDISCLOSED) RULES

The *O'Connor* EULA appeared to give Uber at-will authority to terminate ("deactivate" drivers).[57]

[55] EULA, cl. 2.4 (emphasis added).
[56] *Id.* at cl. 4.1 (emphasis added).
[57] Defendants' Notice of Motion and Motion to Dismiss at Ex. 1, cl. 4.1.1 (Software License and Online Services Agreement, July 2013), O'Connor v. Uber Techs., Inc., 82 F. Supp. 3d. 1133 (N.D. Cal. 2015) (No. 13–03826-EMC).

The court took note of this language as evidence that might indicate the drivers were employees,[58] and the revised EULA from *Razak* ostensibly denies Uber at-will authority:

> Customer acknowledges and agrees that Uber reserves the right, at any time in Uber's sole discretion, to deactivate or otherwise restrict a Driver from accessing or using the Driver App or the Uber Services if such Driver fails to meet the requirements set forth in this Agreement or the Driver Addendum.[59]
>
> Termination. Either party may terminate this Agreement: (a) without cause at any time upon seven (7) days prior written notice to the other party; (b) immediately, without notice, for the other party's material breach of this Agreement . . . . In addition, Uber may terminate this Agreement or deactivate Customer or a particular Driver immediately, without notice, with respect to the Customer and/or any Driver in the event Customer and/or any Driver, as applicable, no longer qualifies, under applicable law or the standards and policies of Uber, to provide Transportation Services or to operate the Vehicle, or as otherwise set forth in this Agreement.[60]

The EULA appears to give Uber a right to terminate drivers without notice only where the Customer/Driver has breached the agreement's "requirements" or "standards and policies of Uber." What are these "requirements," "standards and policies"?

6.9 UNKNOWN PERFORMANCE STANDARDS

While the excerpts suggest Uber may not control how drivers perform their work, Uber uses performance metrics to evaluate how drivers provide transportation services through the App. These include star ratings, and acceptance and cancellation rates. However, the EULA does not specify these standards, and only even mentions the ratings. The only time Uber discloses these supposed "contractual" obligations to a driver is when the driver is approaching their breach.

For example, the EULA requires a Customer/Driver to meet a "Minimum Average Rating" to avoid deactivation:

> Ratings. Customer acknowledges that Uber desires that Users have access to high-quality services via Uber's mobile application. In order to continue to receive access to the Driver App and the Uber Services, each Driver must maintain an average rating by Users that exceeds the minimum average acceptable rating established by Uber for the Territory, as may be updated from time to time by Uber in its sole discretion ("Minimum Average Rating"). . . . In the event a Driver's average rating falls below the Minimum Average Rating, Uber will notify Customer and may

58 *O'Connor*, 82 F. Supp. 3d at 1149.
59 EULA, cl. 3.1.
60 *Id.* at cl. 12.2.

> provide the Driver, in Uber's discretion, a limited period of time to raise his or her average rating above the Minimum Average Rating. If such Driver does not increase his or her average rating above the Minimum Average Rating within the time period allowed (if any), Uber reserves the right to deactivate such Driver's access to the Driver App and the Uber Services.[61]

Hiding in plain sight in a provision otherwise detailing what Uber is not allowed to do is also Uber's right to establish cancellation policies: "Customer and its Drivers retain the option, via the Driver App, to attempt to accept or to decline or ignore a User's request for Transportation Services via the Uber Services, or to cancel an accepted request for Transportation Services via the Driver App, *subject to Uber's then-current cancellation policies* . . . ."[62] And the EULA expects that drivers not decline ride requests for a "period of time," and "strive to accept a substantial portion" of requests:

> Customer acknowledges and agreed that repeated failure by a Driver to accept User requests for Transportation Services while such Driver is logged in to the Driver App creates a negative experience for Users of Uber's mobile application. Accordingly, Customer agrees and shall ensure that if a Driver does not wish to accept User requests for Transportation Services for a period of time, such Driver will log off of the Driver App.[63]
>
> Driver agrees that if they are logged in to the Driver App, they will strive to accept a substantial portion of User requests for Transportation Services, and that if they do not wish to accept User requests for Transportation Services for a period of time, they will log off of the Driver App.[64]

Upon assenting to the EULAs, where do Customers/Drivers find the "Average Minimum Rating," Uber's "current cancellation policies," or the required acceptance rate?

The EULA also incorporates "supplemental terms,"[65] including a "Driver Deactivation Policy."[66] The Policy provides: "Riders or Drivers who break this code [of conduct] may be barred from using Uber, either temporarily or permanently."[67] In the next section, entitled "Quality," Uber provides, "There are several ways we measure driver quality, with the most important being Star Ratings and Cancellation Rates."[68] The Policy does not disclose the star rating or cancellation rate needed to avoid deactivation, but instead discusses a warning system and training: "*What leads to deactivation?* There is a minimum average rating in each

61 *Id.* at cl. 2.6.
62 *Id.* at cl. 2.4.
63 *Id.* at cl. 2.6.
64 Driver EULA, cl. 2.4.1.
65 EULA, cl. 14.2.
66 Deactivation Policy.
67 *Id.*
68 *Id.*

city. This is because there are cultural differences in the way people in different cities rate each other. We will alert you over time if your rating is approaching this limit and you'll also get information about quality improvement courses that may help you improve."[69] As to cancellation rates, the Policy provides:

> High-quality drivers typically have a low cancellation rate less than 5%. *What leads to deactivation?* Each city has a maximum cancellation rate, based on the average cancellation rate of drivers in the area. We will alert you multiple times if your cancellation rate is much higher than other drivers in your city, after which you may not be able to go online for a short period of time. If your cancellation rate continues to exceed the maximum limit, you may be deactivated.[70]

The Deactivation Policy also includes "Acceptance Rates" as a way Uber measures "driver quality." It provides that "not accepting trip requests does not lead to permanent deactivation."[71] However, "If you are consistently not accepting trip requests, we will notify you that your ability to remain online may be at risk. If your acceptance rate does not improve, you may temporarily be logged out of the app for a limited period of time."[72] The EULA provision below alludes to Uber's right to penalize drivers through fare adjustments for other aspects of their performance, including the route drivers take and any behavior prompting a passenger complaint. Uber does, however, qualify this control by promising to act in a "reasonable manner":

> Uber reserves the right to: (i) adjust the Fare for a particular instance of Transportation Services (e.g., *Driver took an inefficient route*, Driver failed to properly end a particular instance of Transportation Services in the Driver App, technical error in the Uber Services, etc.); or (ii) cancel the Fare for a particular instance of Transportation Services in (e.g., a User is charged for Transportation Services that were not provided, *in the event of a User complaint*, fraud, etc.). *Uber's decision to reduce or cancel the Fare in any such manner shall be exercised in a reasonable manner.*[73]

In sum, the EULA requires that drivers meet Uber's performance criteria to avoid penalty. However, these requirements are unavailable to Customers/Drivers when they click assent to the EULA. The Deactivation Policy that the EULA incorporates instead indicates that Uber will disclose these requirements only when giving

69 *Id.* (emphasis in original). It is still the case that Uber does not disclose the required minimum star rating to drivers, except for those who drive for some of Uber's more expensive service tiers. *See* Vehicle Requirements in Los Angeles, UBER, www.uber.com/drive/los-angeles/vehicle-requirements/.

70 Deactivation Policy (emphasis in original).

71 *Id.*

72 *Id.*

73 EULA, cl. 4.3 (emphasis added). Uber also reserved the right to determine and vary vehicle requirements. EULA section, "Vehicle Standards," requires that Customers/Drivers meet "any additional standards or requirements in the applicable Territory . . . ." *Id.* at cl. 3.2.

warnings or taking disciplinary measures. It appears that the drivers' supposed contractual obligations *never existed* in a form definite enough to constitute contractual obligations. Rather, Uber assumed the hallmark of employer discretion – to determine the rules of the relationship as it went along and whether drivers were complying with them.

6.10 DETERMINING ESSENTIAL TERMS OF THE EXCHANGE AT ITS DISCRETION

The EULA permits Uber to determine an essential term of the exchange as the relationship proceeds – the price. A driver's earnings were based on the fare and portion of the fare that Uber took, the "Service Fee."[74]

The EULA's Fare restrictions belie Uber's simulated reality that drivers enter a contractual relationship with passengers, and, like other independent contractors, negotiate the contract price with their own customers. Uber controlled the Fare's upper limit by prohibiting the driver from charging less. Since it required the driver to charge the rider through the App and reserved a right to reject the driver's request in "negotiations" with Uber to charge a lower fare, Uber also exercised substantial control over the lower limit.[75]

The fiction that Uber does not sell ride services or determine the fare has become even more implausible since Uber began providing the potential rider with a fare upfront without the pretense of the driver's involvement.[76] Also, Uber has now decoupled driver pay from passenger fares, using different algorithmic formulas to determine them.[77] This renders even less tenable the claim that the Service Fee is a "commission" for Uber's "lead."

While Uber made some aspects of the formula for calculating the fare available on its website, it also reserves a right to change the fare calculation unilaterally:

> Uber reserves the right to change the Fare Calculation at any time in Uber's discretion based upon local market factors, and Uber will provide notice to Customer in the event of changes to the base fare, per mile, and/or per minute amounts that would result in a change in the recommended Fare for each instance of completed Transportation Services. Continued use of the Uber Services after any such change in the Fare Calculation shall constitute your consent to such change.[78]

74 *Id* at cl. 4.4.

75 *Id.* at cl. 4.1. *See supra* text accompanying note 56.

76 Aaron Gordon & Dhruv Mehrotra, *Uber and Lyft Take a Lot More from Drivers Than They Say*, JALOPNIK (Aug. 26, 2019), https://jalopnik.com/uber-and-lyft-take-a-lot-more-from-drivers-than-they-sa-1837450373.

77 *See* New Addendum Redefines Service Fee, UBER DRIVERS FORUM, https://uberpeople.net/threads/new-addendum-redefines-service-fee.167531/; Gordon & Mehrotra, *supra* note 76.

78 EULA, cl. 4.2.

Uber also reserves a right to unilaterally modify the Service Fee: "Uber reserves the right to change the Service Fee at any time in Uber's discretion based upon local market factors, and Company will provide you with notice in the event of such change. Continued use of the Uber Services after any such change in the Service Fee calculation shall constitute Customer's consent to such change."[79] The Service Fee and Fare Calculation are the price terms of the EULA. Why is Uber permitted to deny Customers/Drivers access to the App even when they have not violated the EULAs, but simply object to Uber's unilateral modification of the price term? The authority Uber claims is *not* consistent with the usual requirements imposed by contract law for modifying contracts.[80] However, Uber's approach precisely tracks how courts treat unilateral modifications of *at-will employment* relationships: the employer may modify the contract to the employee's disadvantage without providing consideration except in the form of not terminating the employee right away. The employee "accepts" the modification by not quitting.[81] Here, Uber has claimed a unilateral right, based on case law regarding *employment* relationships, to modify an essential term of the bargain.

The EULA reserves Uber's right to determine performance standards for drivers that are disclosed only in the proximity of breach, determine whether drivers have met these standards, unilaterally modify these standards, and terminate drivers for not meeting them. It also permits Uber to determine an essential term of the agreement – the price term – during the course of the relationship. Together, these provisions depict a relationship much closer to one of employment than one of contract.

6.11 DISCRETION CARRIED OUT AND REFINED THROUGH ALGORITHMIC MANAGEMENT

Uber embeds its reserved discretion over drivers' work not only in the EULA but also in the App. It uses algorithmic management to direct, surveil, correct, and compensate drivers' production of ride services in ways not defined in the EULA, and to continually adjust the main terms of the exchange to its advantage.[82] This

79 *Id.* at cl. 4.4. Another clause provides Uber a broad right to modify the agreement unilaterally, including the fares, also without adhering to the requirements of contract law. *See Id.* at cl. 14.1.

80 Uber has not offered additional consideration or limited its right of unilateral modification to cases of unanticipated circumstances. *See* Angel v. Murray, 322 A.2d 630, 637 (R.I. 1974) (modifications without additional consideration must be voluntary and due to unanticipated circumstances). Nor does its broad authority apply only to cases where the provisions are ambiguous. *See* ConFold Pac., Inc. v. Polaris Indus., 433 F.3d 952, 955–56 (7th Cir. 2006).

81 *See* Lake Land Emp. Grp. of Akron, LLC v. Columber, 804 N.E.2d 27, 31–32 (Ohio 2014) (ruling that employer who refrained from terminating at-will employees provided sufficient consideration for modifying agreement to employees' disadvantage).

82 *See* Lilly Irani, *Difference and Dependence among Digital Workers: The Case of Amazon Mechanical Turk*, 114 S. ATLANTIC Q. 225, 228 (2015) ("The work of management itself is semiautomated; labor relations play out in large part through routine acts of programming.").

algorithmic management introduces additional uncertainty for the drivers as to the nature of their bargain. The "selves" presupposed by Uber's algorithmic management are not the agentic selves recognized by contract law.

6.12 DIRECTING AND MONITORING THE INTENSITY AND PACE OF THE WORK

Uber uses the algorithm to direct the intensity and pace of drivers' work. To provide just one example, Uber gives a driver fifteen seconds to respond to a request and logs her out of the App if she declines three in a row. Uber also uses its technology to monitor drivers' work closely, including acceptances, rejections, cancellations, and passenger ratings. According to Uber's website, the App can now monitor drivers' acceleration and braking in some locations. Uber colonizes the driver's space for voluntary action through a fine-grained imposition of time and task discipline. This is hard to reconcile with the space for self-determination imagined and rendered by contract law in its requirements for an adequate withholding of the self.

6.13 ADJUSTING THE TERMS OF THE EXCHANGE

Through algorithmic management, Uber continually adjusted the quantity-to-price ratio, or the terms that answer the question: How much work for how much pay? Under a conventional view of employment in which the employee is paid by the hour, the quantity term is left open and subject to the employer's determination: the employer seeks to extract what valuable labor it can from the employee by the hour. The gig company tends to leave the price term open instead. The bargain is that, in exchange for a definite amount of time the driver chooses to be logged into the App, Uber will pay an indefinite amount of money. Unlike the conventional employee, the driver generally controls how long it works; however, she does not know whether or how much Uber will pay her for her services. In both cases, the employer determines the work/pay rate of exchange.

Uber manipulates this rate (the price term) through algorithmic management:

(1) While a driver can decline the occasional ride request without risking deactivation, Uber deprives the driver of information needed to calculate the "profitability" of a ride in deciding whether to accept a request. The passenger is not required to provide her destination until the driver arrives at the pickup location.[83] Uber pays drivers only for the time spend transporting a passenger, and not for waiting to receive a ride request or driving to the

[83] Razak v. Uber Techs., Inc., No. CV 16–573, 2018 WL 1744467, at 3 (E.D. Pa. Apr. 11, 2018); EULA cl. 2.2.

passenger's pickup location.[84] Thus, the driver may have to drive a long way to the pickup location, only to find that the passenger is travelling a short distance.[85]

(2) Uber implements "surges," meaning it raises passenger fares in a certain area for a certain period.[86] The purpose is to increase the number of drivers in an area and dampen the number of ride requests. The App shows drivers a surge map and the fare increase for different areas.[87] Uber and the *Razak* court contended that this information provides drivers with entrepreneurial opportunities.[88] However, Uber withholds from drivers information they need to rationally evaluate the work/pay exchange. For example, Uber does not disclose how many other drivers are online or information about passenger demand.[89] Drivers have expressed frustration with driving to a surge zone only to arrive and find the surge is over.[90]

(3) Uber adjusts fare and payment formulas often. A study of Uber's DC drivers reported:

> Uber drivers struggle to make sense of the company's constantly changing rules and opaque management practices. In the four years it has been operating in Washington, D.C., Uber has reduced its base rate for drivers several times, added a rider safety fee (and then increased it, calling it a booking fee), and raised the commission it takes from new drivers. The rules and details of work for Uber change, sometimes hourly. . . . One driver commented that "They're really playing games with [the rates], and . . . I don't like that."[91]

Workers do not know how much they earn largely because of the fluctuating algorithms on which pay is based and the numerous expenses they must deduct. Of

[84] Being available to accept ride requests is an essential part of the process of producing on demand rides. *See* Julia Tomassetti, *Digital Platform Work as Interactive Service Work*, 22 Emp. Rts. & Emp. Pol'y J. 1 (2018).

[85] *Razak*, 2018 WL 1744467, at 3.

[86] *Id.* at 16.

[87] Uber recently changed its surge pricing so that drivers now receive an extra flat amount. How surge pricing works, Uber, www.uber.com/us/en/drive/partner-app/how-surge-works/.

[88] *Razak*, 2018 WL 1744467, at 16.

[89] *Id.* at 5. Other developers have stepped up in creating Apps that provide drivers some of the information gig companies withhold. Julie Weed, *These Apps Are an Uber Driver's Co-Pilot*, N.Y. Times, October 17, 2019, www.nytimes.com/2019/10/17/business/apps-uber-lyft-drivers.html.

[90] Noam Scheiber, *How Uber Uses Psychological Tricks to Push Its Drivers' Buttons*, N.Y. Times, April 2, 2017, www.nytimes.com/interactive/2017/04/02/technology/uber-drivers-psychological-tricks.html. Uber says that surges last longer under its new model. Uber Under the Hood, *What Moves Us: Shedding More Light on New Driver Surge*, Medium (2019), https://medium.com/uber-under-the-hood/what-moves-us-shedding-more-light-on-new-driver-surge-d580488a6761.

[91] Katie Wells, Kafui Attoh & Declan Cullen, *The Work Lives of Uber Drivers: Worse Than You Think*, Working-Class Perspectives (July 10, 2017), https://workingclassstudies.wordpress.com/2017/07/10/the-work-lives-of-uber-drivers-worse-than-you-think/.

the 40 drivers we interviewed and surveyed, only a handful knew what percentage of their fares Uber takes.[92]

The above evidence of Uber's manipulation of the main terms of the exchange belies Uber's and the *Razak* court's arguments that Uber offers drivers entrepreneurial opportunity. The EULA does not fix discrete obligations upfront in a way that enables the driver to evaluate expected gains and losses rationally. Likewise, the App hides information that would help drivers estimate the time and resources they need to commit to earn a living.

The flipside of the uncertainty that algorithmic management creates for drivers regarding the terms of the bargain is an advantage for Uber. It bears emphasizing that the uncertainty drivers face is not simply an example of the "market mediation" of work – the phenomenon whereby companies transfer market risks to workers or expose workers to the vagaries of the market.[93] The "risk" drivers face is imposed by Uber's calculated choices regarding its App design, what data to collect, how to use it, and what information to provide drivers. For example, the information that Uber withholds from drivers in determining surge zones it uses to manipulate drivers to its advantage.[94] For example, the more drivers on the road, the less time customers have to wait, but the less likely it is that a driver will receive a request.[95] If Uber has a contractual relationship with its "Customers," this opportunistic behavior would seem to breach its duty of good faith. Algorithmic management and the data Uber collects through this management enables Uber to continuously refine key parameters of the bargain to its benefit. These refinements are reflected in changes to its programming, EULAs, and policies. For example, evidence suggests that over the past few years Uber (and its competitor Lyft) has been decreasing the portion of the fare it pays drivers.[96]

6.14 AUGMENTING THE INDEFINITENESS OF THE EULA

In addition to making the terms of the bargain uncertain, algorithmic management augments the uncertainty inscribed in the EULA regarding the supposedly contractual standards that drivers must meet to avoid termination. Uber uses algorithmic management to make ongoing adjustments to the performance standards that it expects of drivers. An ethnography of Uber drivers highlights the uncertainty this creates with regard to the customer service Uber expects of drivers:

> Uber controls how drivers behave through weekly performance metrics . . . delivered after the fact of their work. . . . Even though drivers know ratings are averaged

[92] *Id.*

[93] Arne Kalleberg, Good Jobs, Bad Jobs: The Rise of Polarized and Precarious Employment Systems in the United States, 1970s to 2000s (2011).

[94] Scheiber, *supra* note 90.

[95] *Id.*

[96] Gordon & Mehrotra, *supra* note 76.

> and that one rating should not make a difference, drivers express much care and dissatisfaction anytime their rating goes down. A typical comment is, "What's the formula to get these results??!"[97]

The report on DC drivers found:

> Drivers reported that Uber was not transparent about its policies on both minor issues, like how much a driver would be compensated when a passenger vomits, and major ones, like "time-outs" (penalties for not accepting the right number of rides in a certain time period) and de-activation (permanent suspension). It's a system of "smoke and mirrors," in the words of one driver.[98]

Uber's use of algorithmic management indicates that Uber does not simply fail to *disclose* to drivers their contractual obligations. The materialization of these standards in the form of warnings or decisions to penalize or terminate drivers suggests that Uber never *established* these contractual standards ex ante. The star rating needed to avoid deactivation, for example, depends on drivers' performance relative to other drivers.[99] The judge in *O'Connor* also cited evidence of Uber's ex post invention of contractual requirements, including an "email terminating underperforming Uber driver because business was 'slower than normal and we have too many drivers ... [so] we have to look for accounts to deactivate.'"[100]

6.15 REQUIRING TRANS-CONTRACTUAL PERFORMANCES

Research suggests that the imposition of unknown performance standards produces obsequiousness.[101] As noted above in Section 6.12, Uber determines on an ongoing basis the point at which a driver's performance metrics trigger a warning or termination. In effect, this means that the best means a driver has of ensuring compliance with her contractual duties and thus avoiding deactivation is to engage in *trans*-contractual performances. Deepa Das Acevedo illustrates this phenomenon in an excerpt about driving under similar conditions for Uber's competitor Lyft:

> even though Alex may not be given a specific order to "pick up Joe Smith," she might know that if she does not pick up a large enough percentage of Joe, Jack, and John, she will be terminated from the app. The trouble is that Alex is not quite sure what that magic percentage is or whether she and Lyft will agree on when she's met it, so Alex is not really free to reject any of those passengers.[102]

97 Alex Rosenblat & Luke Stark, *Algorithmic Labor and Information Asymmetries: A Case Study of Uber's Drivers*, 10 INT'L J. OF COMM. 3758, 3772, 3775 (2016).
98 Wells, *et al.*, *supra* note 91.
99 Rosenblat & Stark, *supra* note 97, at 3772.
100 O'Connor v. Uber Techs., Inc., 82 F. Supp. 3d 1133, 1143 (N.D. Cal. 2015).
101 Deepa Das Acevedo, *Unbundling Freedom in the Sharing Economy*, 91 S. CAL. L. REV. 793 (2017).
102 *Id.* at 825–26.

The findings from the DC study illustrate that the production of servility extends even to drivers' formal freedom to determine their schedules: "A majority of the drivers we interviewed reported that their wages have dropped so much that they will only drive during hours when there is likely to be surge pricing or in areas where other incentives give them a better chance of earning decent wages."[103]

6.16 ANALYSIS: DOES THE AUTOMATION OF MANAGERIAL AUTHORITY MATTER?

Instructions from an App to a gig worker often appear to differ little from those delivered by a human supervisor to an employee. Uber's App, for example, directs a driver, personally, to undertake a ride assignment that the driver ignores at her peril.

A difference between the human manager and Uber is that many of Uber's managerial decisions are partially automated through its App. Uber's position appears to be that this should make a legal difference. First, it has suggested that its programming decisions represent the terminal point of its own agency.[104] Like a contract, the parameters of the algorithm are fixed upfront. And, since algorithms cannot exercise discretion in producing outputs, Uber cannot be held responsible for these outputs as an employer, even if the algorithmic outputs look like managerial commands or changes to the bargain. For instance, in its brief to the court in *Razak*, Uber argued: "Defendants do not control the number of trip requests that are generated by riders or the number of requests Plaintiffs will receive . . . .Instead, trip requests are determined by the number of riders searching for rides, the number of other drivers who are available, and the location of the rider and driver."[105]

Second, Uber's stance appears to be that programming decisions are technical decisions that cannot be managerial decisions. For instance, below Uber refers to a disciplinary practice as a "system integrity measure," disregarding that Uber decided that a ride request would go to only one driver at a time, a managerial choice about its division of labor: "it is undisputed that if a transportation provider ignores three trip requests, the Uber App may automatically move the transportation provider offline as a system integrity protection and in an effort to avoid extended wait times for riders who are waiting for a transportation provider to accept the trip request."[106]

[103] Wells, *et al.*, *supra* note 91.

[104] *See* Tarleton Gillespie, *The Relevance of Algorithms*, *in* Media Technologies: Essays on Communication, Materiality, and Society 167–193 (Tarleton Gillespie, Pablo J. Boczkowski, & Kirsten A. Foot eds., 2014) ("Whatever choices are made are presented both as distant from the intervention of human hands, and as submerged inside of the cold workings of the machine.").

[105] Memorandum of Law in Support of Defendants' Motion for Summary Judgment at 34–35, Razak v. Uber Techs., Inc., No. CV 16–573 (E.D. Pa. Apr. 11, 2018), 2018 WL 1744467.

[106] Defendants' Revised Reply to Plaintiffs' Statement of Facts Opposing Defendants' Motion for Summary Judgment at 77, *Razak*, No. CV 16–573, 2018 WL 1744467.

A close reading of the EULA and interrogation of Uber's use of algorithmic management through the lens of the agentic self counsels that we reject Uber's distinctions: Uber uses the EULA and algorithmic management to usurp the driver's contractual agency. The EULA and App require that the driver relinquish her capacity for voluntary action to the direction of another.

The theory of the agentic self entreats us to take independent contracting more seriously as a *contractual* category if we want to better understand how to regulate the gig economy. The EULA to which the driver clicks assent has the trappings of an enforceable contract, an agreement in which the parties have fixed the essential terms of a bargain upfront. A close reading shows, however, that the EULA describes something much closer to an employment relationship than an enforceable contract.

First, while the EULA references certain performance standards, like Minimum Average Ratings or those contained in its "policies," Uber fails to disclose these contractual duties in more than phantasmal form upon drivers' assent. That these duties materialize only when Uber sends warnings or takes disciplinary action suggests that the drivers never committed to definite duties in the first place, because Uber devised them ex post in directing, monitoring, correcting, and penalizing drivers' work.

Second, Uber reserves the authority in the EULA to determine the main terms of the exchange during the course of the relationship. And, using algorithmic management, Uber continually recalibrates these terms to its benefit. The drivers' assent to the EULA entails complying with software that continually changes the price term and interjects new obligations and demands for trans-contractual performances into the relationship. Algorithmic management stretches the driver's self across un-assented to commands and changing terms, far past the borders of self-withholding that contract law recognizes and patrols.

6.17 CONCLUSION

The chapter sought to demonstrate why the partial automation of managerial authority in gig work does not, as a regulatory matter, warrant treating gig workers like Uber drivers differently than workers subject to nonautomated authority. If nonautomated managerial authority is evidence of an employment relationship, automating this authority should not change the legal analysis and conclusion.

The chapter reached this conclusion using a very modest understanding of the agentic self from contract law, a body of law that routinely sanctions economic coercion. Even under this etiolated version of self-determination, Uber drivers look much more like employees than independent contractors.

The partial automation of managerial authority should also not change the policy prescription. Regulators should take special notice of "contracts" that permit someone to purchase the use of another's capacity for voluntary action and pretend this can be done without purchasing the person. Legislation protecting worker rights is essential to routing modern relationships of servitude. Those who agree to these unbalanced relationships rather than contractual ones often do so because they lack the power to demand the latter.

We have reason to be particularly concerned that gig workers enjoy statutory rights, especially the right to organize. As others have recognized, digital technology offers unmatched abilities to direct, surveil, and correct the labor process.[107] And algorithmic management permits a fine-grained colonization of the worker's energies through time and task discipline.[108] Further, the data collection and computation abilities of this technology enable companies to continually recalibrate the bargain to their favor.

This analysis does not aspire to any claims about how workers experience this form of management. However, while many gig companies design their work relationships to read to judges and the pubic as "independent contracting," ethnographic studies suggest that workers experience them more ambiguously.[109] My analysis shows that this ambivalence is not out of line with how the self interpellated through contract law would grapple with these relationships.

[107] *E.g.*, O'Connor v. Uber Techs., Inc., 82 F. Supp. 3d 1133, 1152 (N.D. Cal. 2015) ("This level of monitoring, where drivers are potentially observable at all times, arguably gives Uber a tremendous amount of control.").

[108] *E.g.*, New App Features and Data Show How Uber Can Improve Safety on the Road, UBER NEWSROOM (2016), www.uber.com/newsroom/safety-on-the-road-july-2016/ (discussing App's ability to monitor drivers' speed).

[109] *E.g.*, Emmanuel Josserand & Sarah Kaine, *Different Directions or the Same Route? The Varied Identities of Ride-Share Drivers*, J. INDUS. REL. 1 (2019).

7

Regulating Transportation Systems without Authority (or Data)

Plugging an Uber- and Lyft-Sized Hole in City Transportation Planning and Policy

Zak Accuardi

Two organizations share a commercial building on San Francisco's Market Street. On one floor you have the San Francisco County Transportation Authority (SFCTA), which employs approximately forty staff to administer several local transportation funding sources and monitor and manage local congestion. SFCTA allocated approximately $100 million in sales and other tax revenue to fund transportation investments in San Francisco in 2018.[1] On another floor sits the headquarters of a publicly traded company called Uber, which in the first quarter of 2019 brought in more than $3 billion in revenue ($1 billion in net losses) and at the end of 2018 employed more than 22,000 staff,[2] not including millions of estimated "driver-partners" who have driven for the service globally.[3]

The SFCTA is tasked with leading long-term transportation planning for San Francisco and understanding the impact of more people and jobs on the city/county's and region's transportation system, in which Uber plays an increasingly prominent role. Yet while Uber has been picking up and dropping off passengers in San Francisco since its launch in 2009, SFCTA did not have detailed data about the company's operations or scale until 2016, and the agency had to work for it.

That SFCTA, during those seven years, had such a significant blind spot made the agency typical among its peers in local government. That SFCTA now has even a snapshot of Uber and Lyft's operations in San Francisco – increasingly outdated, as the data were collected in 2016 – make it an exception.

1 San Francisco County Transportation Authority, "Annual Report," 2018, www.sfcta.org/sites/default/files/2019–03/AR%202018%20190205.pdf.

2 Uber Technologies, Inc., "Form S-1 Registration Statement" (Securities and Exchange Commission, April 11, 2019), www.sec.gov/Archives/edgar/data/1543151/000119312519103850/d647752ds1.htm.

3 Melissa Berry, "How Many Uber Drivers Are There?," *The Rideshare Guy* (blog), June 1, 2019, https://therideshareguy.com/how-many-uber-drivers-are-there/.

The pervasive lack of data on Uber and Lyft's operations is largely due to cities' and other local governments' lack of regulatory authority over transportation network companies (TNCs). US cities' authority to set rules for TNCs has been systematically preempted by state laws following Uber and Lyft's successful lobbying efforts, and despite a precedent of municipal regulation of the for-hire vehicle industry.[4]

Relevant preemptive state laws tie local governments' hands in a variety of ways. These laws prevent municipalities from regulating their labor market (e.g., by setting a minimum wage for Uber and Lyft drivers) or from implementing consumer protections (e.g., by strengthening background check laws for Uber and Lyft drivers). Municipalities are also commonly unable to incentivize desirable travel behaviors (e.g., by levying taxes or fees on Uber and Lyft trips), and unable to mandate data reporting from Uber and Lyft that would inform transportation planning decisions and facilitate regulatory oversight of labor rules and local business taxes, for example.

These restrictions make it harder for cities to do their jobs. Still, cities retain powerful tools at their disposal to increase the alignment between municipal goals and Uber and Lyft operations. In this chapter I will refer to these tools as examples of "implicit regulation" – means by which cities can effectively "regulate" Uber and Lyft in the transportation sphere without explicitly setting out requirements for TNCs per se. In doing so, cities can align these implicit regulatory actions with urgent safety, equity, and environmental sustainability goals.

This chapter will first provide a framework for the implicit regulation of Uber and Lyft, featuring brief examples from recent practice. Tools in the implicit regulation toolbox include street design, traffic enforcement, and pilot projects developed in partnership with Uber and Lyft, among others – depending on local regulatory structures. These implicit regulatory approaches can and should be aligned with broader transportation policy goals, including improving street safety, improving transportation access, and reducing driving. Implicit regulatory approaches are poorly equipped, however, to address TNCs' labor or consumer protection implications.

Implicit regulation is likely to be most effective in accomplishing city goals when those tools can be targeted to solve specific transportation problems, for example a specific safety problem in a specific geographic area. This kind of targeting requires access to data on TNC operations, which, as already

[4] Joy Borkholder et al., "Uber State Interference: How Transportation Network Companies Buy, Bully, and Bamboozle Their Way to Deregulation" (Washington, DC: National Employment Law Project and Partnership for Working Families, January 2018); Olivia Solon, "How Uber Conquers a City in Seven Steps," *The Guardian*, April 12, 2017, sec. Technology, www.theguardian.com/technology/2017/apr/12/why-everyone-hates-uber-seven-step-playbook.

discussed, are in short supply at the local government level. While cities can act in the absence of these data, they do so with one hand tied behind their back.

The chapter continues with a more detailed case study focused on one agency's approach to creatively securing the data its leadership felt was necessary to inform planning and policy. Specifically, the SFCTA partnered with computer scientists at Northeastern University to collect data on TNC travel in San Francisco. This data collection required seeking alignment on goals and identifying opportunities for mutual benefit between researchers and agency staff. The collaboration was facilitated by the agency's technical expertise and required the development of a sophisticated technical methodology that involved scraping twelve terabytes of data from the Uber and Lyft application programming interfaces (APIs).

This story offers both hopeful and cautionary conclusions. First, it highlights a creative and partnership-driven problem-solving approach on the part of a public agency in the face of an information asymmetry that inhibits effective policy-making. Second, it lays bare the burden that TNCs place on local governments by way of successful State lobbying efforts, an unwillingness to share data needed to inform policy, and the development of an effective communications machine.

The SFCTA case study was informed by a series of semi-structured interviews with involved stakeholders including SFCTA staff and Northeastern researchers. Interviews were conducted over the phone in May and June 2019.

7.1 UBER AND LYFT CREATE AND CONTRIBUTE TO PROBLEMS THAT REQUIRE POLICY SOLUTIONS

TNCs' rapid growth has affirmed that consumers value on-demand transportation services and revealed previously unmet demand in the for-hire vehicle market, which previously consisted almost exclusively of taxis. At the same time, Uber and Lyft's meteoric rise has both created new local transportation policy challenges and highlighted existing transportation policy shortcomings.

The demonstrated and potential benefits of TNCs to their users and to society at large are significant. TNCs' "pooled" rides offer the potential to move more people in fewer vehicles, allowing cities to make more efficient use of scarce road space. Millions of people have earned money driving for Uber and Lyft in the US and beyond. Access to Uber and Lyft provides people who can afford to use TNCs with one more transportation option, even in areas without reliable walking, biking, or public transit access.

At the same time, TNCs' growth has created or contributed to an array of outcomes that specifically challenge local government goals, including with respect to safety, equity, transportation access, and sustainability.

7.1.1 *Safety*

TNCs' adverse street safety impacts are concentrated around passenger pick-up and drop-offs, particularly when drivers stop on streets dense with pedestrian, bicycle, and automotive activity, or in crosswalks or bike lanes. TNC trips' concentration in densely populated, transit-rich areas also increases car traffic, potentially exacerbating both crash risks and air quality hazards. One recent analysis associates a significant increase in road fatalities with the entry of TNCs into new transportation markets,[5] though that study does not show causation.[6]

7.1.2 *Equity*

Income is positively correlated with TNC use,[7] creating an imbalance likely to grow as TNC prices increase over time. Absent significant investments in more affordable alternatives, this imbalance risks entrenching a two-tier transportation system that perpetuates a gap in transportation access between the relatively poor and relatively wealthy. Transportation access is among the strongest predictors of intergenerational economic mobility,[8] suggesting potential long-term implications for income inequality more broadly.

Labor market implications are not this chapter's focus, but similarly present substantial equity concerns regarding wage transparency, fair wages, and employee classification. Driver wages can be low once maintenance and other costs are accounted for,[9] drivers take on significant liability risk, and Uber and Lyft have carefully structured their business in order to avoid affording drivers the rights of employees.[10] TNCs' implications for taxi workers are also substantial given the rapid decline in taxi trips,[11] creating a need for policy-makers' attention in terms of mitigating harm to taxi drivers and preserving competition and fairness in the for-hire vehicle market more broadly.

5 John M. Barrios, Yael V. Hochberg, and Livia Hanyi Yi, "The Cost of Convenience: Ridesharing and Traffic Fatalities." New Working Paper Series (Chicago, IL: Stigler Center for the Study of the Economy and the State, October 2018).

6 Joe Cortright, "Unsafe Uber? Lethal Lyft? We're Still Skeptical," *City Observatory* (blog), April 3, 2020, www.cityobservatory.org/unsafe-uber-lethal-lyft-still_skeptical-2/.

7 Bruce Schaller, "The New Automobility: Lyft, Uber, and the Future of American Cities" (New York, NY: Schaller Consulting, July 25, 2018), www.schallerconsult.com/rideservices/automobility.pdf; Aaron Smith, "Who in America Uses Ride-Hailing Apps Like Uber or Lyft," *Pew Research Center: Internet, Science & Tech* (blog), May 19, 2016, www.pewinternet.org/2016/05/19/on-demand-ride-hailing-apps/.

8 Raj Chetty et al., "Where Is the Land of Opportunity? The Geography of Intergenerational Mobility in the United States," *The Quarterly Journal of Economics* 129, no. 4 (2014): 1553–1623.

9 Andrew J. Hawkins, "How Much Do Lyft Drivers Earn an Hour? It's Complicated," *The Verge*, April 12, 2018, www.theverge.com/2018/4/12/17230500/lyft-driver-pay-earnings-hourly-expenses.

10 Alexia Fernández Campbell, "Uber and Lyft Have Launched a Campaign to Avoid Government Regulation in California," *Vox*, October 29, 2019, www.vox.com/identities/2019/10/29/20938109/ab5-uber-lyft-ballot-initiative-referendum.

11 Schaller, "The New Automobility: Lyft, Uber, and the Future of American Cities."

7.1.3 *Transportation Access*

TNCs' negative traffic congestion effects have been most systematically documented by the TNCs themselves, whose recently published analysis reinforces the findings of several previous studies at the local and national level.[12] SFCTA showed that TNC trips are heavily concentrated in San Francisco's most densely populated neighborhoods and job centers, areas strongly correlated with growth in on-street traffic.[13] Similar trip patterns have been shown in New York City, Toronto, and Chicago, with varying traffic implications.[14]

7.1.4 *Sustainability*

A UC Davis summary of literature on the likely impact of TNCs on vehicle miles traveled (VMT) and greenhouse gas emissions shows that TNCs are likely to contribute to increases in both VMT and emissions due to induced travel, impacts on mode choice, and zero-passenger vehicle miles; undesirable emissions impacts could to some degree be mitigated via TNC fleet electrification requirements and incentives.[15] Pooled rides – at the center of TNC claims regarding potential environmental benefits – have limited availability outside of the densest cities in the US and would need to reach unprecedented penetration levels in order to achieve desired outcomes.[16]

Survey data collected independently by UC Davis[17] and San Francisco Municipal Transportation Agency (SFMTA)[18] show that TNCs are likely to reduce

12 Laura Bliss, "How Much Traffic Do Uber and Lyft Cause?," *CityLab* (blog), August 5, 2019, www.citylab.com/transportation/2019/08/uber-lyft-traffic-congestion-ride-hailing-cities-drivers-vmt/595393/.

13 San Francisco County Transportation Authority, "TNCs & Congestion" (San Francisco, CA: San Francisco County Transportation Authority, October 2018).

14 Bruce Schaller, "Unsustainable? The Growth of App-Based Ride Services and Traffic, Travel and the Future of New York City" (New York, NY: Schaller Consulting, February 27, 2017), www.schallerconsult.com/rideservices/unsustainable.pdf; Big Data Innovation Team, City of Toronto and University of Toronto Transportation Research Institute (UTTRI), "The Transportation Impacts of Vehicle for Hire in the City of Toronto," June 2019, www.toronto.ca/wp-content/uploads/2019/06/96c7-Report_v1.0_2019–06-21.pdf; Mary Wisniewski and Jennifer Smith Richards, "Uber and Lyft Said Ride-Sharing Would Cut Traffic Congestion and Supplement Public Transit. But Has It Worked?," *Chicago Tribune*, June 7, 2019, www.chicagotribune.com/news/breaking/ct-biz-ride-share-congestion-loop-20190520-story.html.

15 Caroline Rodier, "The Effects of Ride Hailing Services on Travel and Associated Greenhouse Gas Emissions" (Davis, CA: National Center for Sustainable Transportation, April 2018), https://escholarship.org/uc/item/2rv570tt.

16 Schaller, "The New Automobility: Lyft, Uber, and the Future of American Cities."

17 Regina Clewlow and Gouri Shankar Mishra, "Disruptive Transportation: The Adoption, Utilization, and Impacts of Ride-Hailing in the United States." Research Report (UC Davis Institute of Transportation Studies, October 2017).

18 Jason Lee, William Tyner, and Nealay Vasavda, "Moving Minds: The Next Generation of Real-Time Transit Information in San Francisco," *Transportation Research Record* 2672, no. 8 (2018): 523–535.

transit ridership. A recent study by Graehler, Jr. et al. reinforces this finding.[19] This tendency undermines financial support for public transit via fare revenues, forcing agencies to consider funding cuts that risk sending public transit into a downward spiral of reduced service, reduced ridership, reduced funding, more cuts, and so on.

7.2 SOME LOCAL GOVERNMENTS CAN REGULATE TNCS DIRECTLY

In order to avoid local regulation, Uber and Lyft successfully pursued a legislative strategy focused on state preemption, taking a page from the tobacco and gun lobbies. As a result, as of January 2018 forty-one of fifty state governments preempted direct local regulation of TNCs.[20] Among local jurisdictions that do retain regulatory authority, that authority is typically limited to the regulation of TNCs as businesses within the for-hire vehicle industry, restricting those governments' influence over or oversight of the labor or consumer protection aspects of TNCs' operations.

A handful of major US cities have retained direct regulatory authority over the for-hire vehicle industry, with New York City, Chicago, and Washington, DC the most prominent. These three cities alone play a significant role in the national TNC landscape, together comprising roughly one in ten TNC trips in the US in 2017.[21]

The New York City Taxi and Limousine Commission (TLC) requires Uber and Lyft drivers to acquire a TLC license, and the City is carved out of the State's regulatory jurisdiction in the relevant State legislation. The TLC uses a combination of data collection, pricing, and fleet management tools to inform policy and regulate TNCs. The TLC has been collecting per-trip TNC data since 2015. The agency has also introduced per-trip fees and Americans with Disabilities Act (ADA) accessibility requirements, set a minimum requirement for net driver earnings, and capped the number of for-hire vehicles allowed in New York City.[22]

Peer agencies in Chicago and Washington, DC, are among the others with authority to set rules for the local for-hire vehicle industry. The City of Chicago Business Affairs and Consumer Protection department is charged with regulating for-hire vehicles,[23] and opted to release a partial dataset of Chicago TNC operations in early 2019. In Washington, DC, the Department of For-Hire Vehicles has similar authority.[24]

19 Michael Graehler, Jr., Richard Alexander Mucci, and Gregory D. Erhardt, "Understanding the Recent Transit Ridership Decline in Major US Cities: Service Cuts or Emerging Modes?" (2019), https://usa.streetsblog.org/wp-content/uploads/sites/5/2019/01/19–04931-Transit-Trends.pdf.

20 Borkholder et al., "Uber State Interference: How Transportation Network Companies Buy, Bully, and Bamboozle Their Way to Deregulation."

21 Schaller, "The New Automobility: Lyft, Uber, and the Future of American Cities."

22 City of New York, "TLC Initiatives," NYC Taxi & Limousine Commission, 2019, www1.nyc.gov/site/tlc/about/tlc-initiatives.page.

23 City of Chicago, "Public Vehicles," Business Affairs and Consumer Protection, 2019, www.chicago.gov/content/city/en/depts/bacp/supp_info/bacppublicvehicles.html.

24 Washington, District of Columbia, "Department of For-Hire Vehicles," Department of For-Hire Vehicles, 2019, https://dfhv.dc.gov/.

Other cities have been granted limited regulatory authority via specific state legislation. San Francisco, for example, secured authority from the State of California to levy per-trip fees to TNC trips (subject to voter approval).[25] New York, Chicago, and Washington, DC each levy fees on TNCs using their existing regulatory authority.

In addition to the cities with full or partial regulatory authority, many airports or airport authorities have retained the authority to levy fees on TNC pick-up and drop-offs. This has been prudent in large part because TNCs have already begun to significantly impact airport parking revenue, which can provide a significant percentage of overall airport operating revenues.[26] TNC industry growth is also impacting parking revenues for parking operators more broadly, including local governments.

7.3 ALL LOCAL GOVERNMENTS CAN REGULATE TNCS *IMPLICITLY*

Local governments' authority remains substantial in the realm of regulating the transportation system at large, both via physical and institutional infrastructure. Local governments have effectively used the design and planning of physical infrastructure to achieve social or policy goals, often including discriminatory goals like racial segregation. For example, Robert Moses infamously demonstrated the power of infrastructure design as de facto policy by building low-clearance bridges across the access roads to Jones Beach – that clearance being low enough to prevent people from accessing the New York beach by public bus.

Similar tools can be and are increasingly used to effect positive change in cities around the country, allowing local governments to use existing regulatory authority to address urban transportation challenges that Uber and Lyft highlight, contribute to, or create. This section will propose a framework for this "implicit" regulatory toolbox, citing a handful of examples from recent practice.

7.3.1 *Street Design*

Freight, for-hire and personal vehicles, and even electric scooter companies compete for access to some of the most valuable real estate in modern cities. By providing more, less, or exclusive access to for-hire vehicles picking up or dropping off passengers, cities can concentrate curbside activity to reduce on-street safety conflicts and minimize congestion caused by mid-block stops.

[25] Phil Ting, "Ting Bill Helping San Francisco Raise Revenues from TNCs to Fund Transportation Infrastructure Heads to the Governor," Official Website – Assemblymember Phil Ting, September 4, 2018, https://a19.asmdc.org/press-releases/20180831-ting-bill-helping-san-francisco-raise-revenues-tncs-fund-transportation.

[26] Peter Mandle and Stephanie Box, "Transportation Network Companies: Challenges and Opportunities for Airport Operators" (Washington, D.C.: Transportation Research Board, August 28, 2017), https://doi.org/10.17226/24867.

Early pilots like Washington, DC's late night TNC pick-up and drop-off zones – in which curbside parking spaces in a neighborhood with several bars are used exclusively for TNC pick-up and drop-off during late night hours on weekends – have shown early promise. Washington has added pilots throughout the city as part of a broader effort to make the curbside more efficient in the delivery of both people and goods.[27]

Access to traffic lanes could provide cities with another tool to use, for example to incentivize high-occupancy vehicle occupancy. With high-occupancy vehicle or carpool lanes already commonplace on highways, cities could theoretically implement a similar requirement on city streets. For example, the SFMTA provides taxis with access to some bus lanes – a luxury that could be afforded to pooled rides with appropriate enforcement mechanisms in place.

7.3.2 *Traffic Enforcement*

Enforcement of existing rules can incentivize behavior change, for example in areas with high concentrations of TNC pick-ups and drop-offs in pedestrian crossings or bike lanes. This strategy has been used in San Francisco, supported by digital "geo-fencing" technology that allows the City to define specific areas where pick-ups and drop-offs are not allowed (in this case, in partnership with Uber and Lyft).[28] Enforcement is easier in environments like airports where pick-up and drop-off rules and expectations are clear and consistent.

Enforcement programs have limitations. Traffic enforcement is a relatively high-cost intervention, requiring staff time and program oversight, though fees can help recover those costs. Enforcement requires ongoing effort and as such is not easily scaled-up. Enforcement also carries potential adverse equity implications given the potential for racial profiling and discrimination.

7.3.3 *Pilot Programs*

Pursuing and negotiating pilots can create opportunities to steer TNC operations, negotiate increased access to data, and leverage TNC strengths to improve transportation system performance. Given that pilot projects tend to be voluntary or involve relatively low-cost contracts, their efficacy in achieving local government goals is limited to the strength of alignment in TNC and public sector interests.

[27] Washington, District of Columbia, "Mayor Bowser and DDOT Announce Pick-Up/Drop-Off Zone Pilot Program Expansion," October 26, 2018, https://ddot.dc.gov/release/mayor-bowser-and-ddot-announce-pick-updrop-zone-pilot-program-expansion.

[28] Mariella Moon, "Uber and Lyft Will Test Dedicated Pick-up Spots in San Francisco," *Engadget* (blog), November 9, 2017, www.engadget.com/2017/11/09/uber-lyft-pick-up-dropoff-spots-san-francisco/.

A diverse array of studies have reviewed relevant pilots and "partnerships," and emphasized the importance of setting clear goals and aligning the interests of public agencies with private companies (including but not limited to TNCs) in service of identified goals.[29]

Particularly in the case of pilot projects, it is essential to collect data that allows a public agency to measure its own and its partners' success in achieving pilots' goals. In TNC-related pilot projects, this has proved challenging, with local governments frequently unable to evaluate projects' efficacy in the absence of appropriate data.[30]

7.4 GOOD TRANSPORTATION POLICY REQUIRES GOOD TNC DATA

Without good data, local governments are likely to make suboptimal decisions about transportation policy and infrastructure investments. Absent data local governments may also lack the ability to effectively measure the efficacy of their decisions, creating a self-reinforcing cycle that involves lacking data, setting suboptimal policy, failing to understand the impact of that policy due to the lack of data, and so forth.[31]

In the absence of good data,[32] local governments can either set policy based on theory and anecdote or they can seek out creative, alternative means of securing some minimum amount of data that allows for informed decision-making. Such creative approaches have included driving for Uber and Lyft[33] or setting up Bluetooth beacons throughout Seattle's downtown.[34]

In transportation policy-making, data on TNC operations serves several purposes that could influence short- and long-range planning and street design. Local

[29] Shin-pei Tsay, Zak Accuardi, and Bruce Schaller, "Private Mobility, Public Interest" (New York, NY: TransitCenter, 2016); Philippe Crist, "Shaping the Relationship Between Public Transport and Innovative Mobility" (International Transport Forum, 2017), www.itf-oecd.org/sites/default/files/docs/shaping-relationship-public-transport-innovative-mobility.pdf.; Terra Curtis et al., "Partnerships Between Transit Agencies and Transportation Network Companies" (Washington, DC: Transportation Research Board, April 16, 2019), https://doi.org/10.17226/25425.

[30] Deepa Das Acevedo, "Data Deficits in Municipal Rideshare Collaborations," *Saint Louis University Law Journal* 63 (2019): 24.

[31] Washington Metropolitan Area Transit Authority, "Transportation Network Companies (TNCs) in the Washington Region" (April 6, 2018), www.mwcog.org/assets/1/28/04062018_-_Item_2_-_Transportation_Network_Companies_(TNCs)_in_the_Region.pdf.

[32] While a full discussion of what constitutes "good data" is both context-specific and beyond the scope of this chapter, see, for example: National Association of City Transportation Officials and International Municipal Lawyers Association, "Managing Mobility Data" (Washington, DC: National Association of City Transportation Officials and International Municipal Lawyers Association, April 2019), www.nacto.org/wp-content/uploads/2019/05/NACTO_IMLA_Managing-Mobility-Data.pdf.

[33] Laura Bliss, "Cities Have to Get Creative When Uber and Lyft Won't Release Trip Data," *The Atlantic*, January 13, 2018, www.citylab.com/transportation/2018/01/to-measure-the-uber-effect-cities-get-creative/550295/.

[34] Seattle Department of Transportation, "New Mobility Playbook" (Seattle, WA: City of Seattle, September 2017), https://newmobilityseattle.info/storage/app/media/Documents/newmobilityplaybookfurtheractionsappendices.pdf.

governments use information on how streets are used, when, and by whom to plan transportation networks and design streets that improve safety, reduce pollution, create more desirable public spaces, enable freight and people to move more efficiently, and more. TNC trips have grown to be an increasing percentage of overall travel demand – 0.5 percent nationally, with 10 percent of Americans using TNCs at least monthly on average, as of 2017.[35]

Some data relevant to TNC-related transportation policy-making will not come from TNCs themselves and are better furnished by survey tools, for example – though TNCs could be helpful in facilitating such surveys. These data include user demographics, insights on why people use TNCs, or what transportation options TNC users might have chosen in the absence of TNCs' availability, among others.

TNCs' data – particularly on trip volume, time, vehicle occupancy, and spatial travel patterns – are among their most closely guarded assets. Uber was embroiled in scandal in 2017 when the use of their internally developed "Greyball" tool – designed to avoid oversight in part by excluding regulators from using the company's app to collect data – was published by the *New York Times*.[36]

Uber and Lyft have historically refused nonregulatory city requests for data, though public agencies with clearly articulated goals and negotiating leverage have found some success.[37] Uber shared data with the Pinellas Suncoast Transit Authority related to the agency's Direct Connect pilot, but only after that data was provided to third-party researchers.[38] Lyft withdrew from a federal pilot program after it could not come to terms on data-sharing (among other conflicts) with two transit agencies.[39]

In response to calls for data-sharing, TNCs often express concerns regarding user privacy and interfirm competitiveness (i.e., exposing "trade secrets"). With respect to privacy, TNCs have the technical ability to appropriately anonymize data while providing useful planning insight. In terms of competitiveness, it is unclear whether or to what extent the publication of origin-destination of Uber and Lyft trip data in New York City has affected either company's operations in the largest US market.

35 Matthew Wigginton Conway, Deborah Salon, and David A. King, "Trends in Taxi Use and the Advent of Ridehailing, 1995–2017: Evidence from the US National Household Travel Survey," *Urban Science* 2, no. 3 (2018).

36 Mike Isaac, "How Uber Deceives the Authorities Worldwide," *The New York Times*, March 3, 2017, sec. Technology, www.nytimes.com/2017/03/03/technology/uber-greyball-program-evade-authorities.html.

37 Acevedo, "Data Deficits in Municipal Rideshare Collaborations."

38 Colin Murphy, Kevin Karner, and Zak Accuardi, "When Uber Replaces the Bus: Learning from the Pinellas Suncoast Transit Authority's 'Direct Connect' Pilot" (Chicago, IL: Shared-Use Mobility Center, June 2019).

39 Allison Grossman and Paul Lewis, "Contracting for Mobility: A Case Study in the Los Angeles and Puget Sound Regions" (Washington, DC: Eno Center for Transportation, October 30, 2019), www.enotrans.org/wp-content/uploads/2019/10/MOD_Contracting_Final_10-29-19.pdf.

Uber and Lyft have each taken tentative steps toward voluntarily sharing more data, though the practice remains inconsistent. Uber's "Movement" platform, for example, publishes data in a limited number of cities (including both travel times and roadway speeds) without disclosing trip volume or travel patterns.[40] Uber and Lyft are both partners on the SharedStreets project, which provides multiple North American cities with access to data on the relative concentration of TNC pick-up and drop-offs by curbside street segment.[41] This implicit regulatory approach in effect provides TNCs with dedicated physical infrastructure in exchange for data. Additional, evolving data standards like the Mobility Data Specification – which is currently used for shared bikes and electric scooters (not for TNCs) – offer additional prospects for standardizing the collection and sharing of data from private mobility companies, possibly including TNCs.[42]

7.5 THE SFCTA CREATIVELY SECURED TNC DATA TO INFORM LOCAL TRANSPORTATION POLICY

In the face of state preemption, the SFCTA found a way to collect enough baseline data to start answering some of the policy questions raised by TNCs' growth in the county. The following case study is informed by interviews with agency staff and academic researchers who were involved in the development of the *TNCs Today* report that resulted from their work.

SFCTA's work showcases the value of applying creative problem-solving to collect the data necessary to answer pressing policy and planning questions. The agency's experience also provides concrete examples of several direct and indirect burdens that TNCs place on public agencies in the form of demanding significant staff time and attention. Finally, this story provides insight into some of the challenges, opportunities, and institutional conditions necessary for a public agency to conduct technical research on public policy in collaboration with an independent third-party.

By 2015, TNCs had become a frequent topic of conversation and public debate in San Francisco. Following sustained public controversy around Google's employee shuttle service and the death of six-year-old Sophia Liu after she was struck by an off-duty Uber driver,[43] private transportation services were firmly in the public eye. Heading into 2016, senior officials at SFCTA were getting more and more questions from their board and from members of the public about how TNCs were impacting

40 Uber, "Uber Movement: Let's Find Smarter Ways Forward, Together." 2019, https://movement.uber.com/cities?lang=en-US.

41 SharedStreets, "Taxi and TNC Activity." SharedStreets, 2019, https:/sharedstreets.io/taxi-tnc-activity/.

42 LA Department of Transportation, "Mobility Data Specification: Information Briefing" (City of Los Angeles, October 31, 2018), https://ladot.io/wp-content/uploads/2018/12/What-is-MDS-Cities.pdf.

43 Evan Sernoffsky, "Ex-Uber Driver Guilty of Manslaughter for Killing Girl in SF Crosswalk," *SFChronicle.com*, August 2, 2018, www.sfchronicle.com/bayarea/article/Uber-driver-guilty-of-manslaughter-for-killing-13127623.php

the city and region. Those same officials tried and failed to get Uber and Lyft to share local TNC trip data, and they sought information from wherever else they could find it, including among other start-ups and third-party data vendors.

SFCTA was unsatisfied with what they found. They lacked access to any data on TNC operations because the California Public Utilities Commission (CPUC) had assumed responsibility for TNC regulation in 2013, preempting local governments across the state.[44]

This preemption has created regulatory challenges for the City and County of San Francisco, among other local governments in California. The CPUC requires TNCs to submit annual reports summarizing hours and miles driven, and service provided by zip code throughout the state,[45] but these data are not made available to local government agencies within the State.[46] At the same time, the City of San Francisco is suing the State of California, on the grounds that state law effectively exempts TNCs from local taxes.[47] Lyft responded to the threat of a separate lawsuit by agreeing to share historical trip data with relevant City staff – a lawsuit that Uber fought and ultimately lost.[48]

As of 2016, San Francisco policy-makers had tried and failed to make progress in understanding the increasingly prominent role of TNCs on city streets. These policy-makers were left with a growing list of unanswered questions about the implications of the companies' operations.

7.5.1 *SFCTA Identifies and Pursues an Opportunity for Collaboration*

Against this regulatory backdrop, a SFCTA staffer's interest was piqued after seeing an article that had been released in late 2015 in which researchers had scraped data from the Uber app in order to "audit" the company's surge pricing algorithm.[49] Led by Christo Wilson and Alan Mislove of Northeastern University, the researchers were interested in understanding whether the surge pricing algorithm worked, more

44 San Francisco County Transportation Authority, "The TNC Regulatory Landscape: An Overview of Current TNC Regulation in California and Across the Country" (San Francisco, CA: San Francisco County Transportation Authority, December 2017).

45 California Public Utilities Commission, "Required Reports TNCs Must Provide the CPUC," State of California, 2019, www.cpuc.ca.gov/General.aspx?id=3989.

46 An ongoing "Phase III" rulemaking process will revisit this policy and seven other relevant regulatory questions: San Francisco County Transportation Authority, "The TNC Regulatory Landscape: An Overview of Current TNC Regulation in California and Across the Country."

47 Adam Brinklow, "SF Sues California over Law That Shelters Lyft, Uber Drivers," *Curbed SF* (blog), February 9, 2018, https://sf.curbed.com/2018/2/9/16995402/sf-lawsuit-california-lyft-uber-drivers-licenses.

48 For references to these and other past and ongoing cases and investigations pursued by the City of San Francisco in relation to Uber and Lyft, see: City Attorney of San Francisco, "Uber and Lyft Archives," City Attorney of San Francisco, 2019, www.sfcityattorney.org/category/news/uber-and-lyft/.

49 Le Chen, Alan Mislove, and Christo Wilson, "Peeking Beneath the Hood of Uber," in *Proceedings of the 2015 Internet Measurement Conference* Tokyo, Japan: Association for Computing Machinery, 2015), 495–508.

or less, as intended. Their analysis examined Uber activity in parts of New York City and San Francisco.

Without understanding the potential implications for transportation planning and policy, Wilson and Mislove had developed a research methodology that provided an unprecedented view into Uber's operations. Joe Castiglione – SFCTA's Deputy Director for Technology, Data, and Analysis – reached out to Mislove and Wilson, described the potential value of their analysis to his employer's work, and asked if they could replicate their analysis for the entirety of San Francisco. For the study to present a comprehensive view of TNC activity, it would also need to include Lyft.

Mislove and Wilson would be able to make all of this happen, they said – and they were willing, especially when the agency committed to providing access to another dataset that the researchers could not scrape from TNCs' apps: data on taxi trips in San Francisco.[50] Having identified clear opportunities for mutual benefit, researchers and agency staff built a collaboration that could leverage their respective skills and expertise to better understand for-hire vehicle travel in San Francisco.

The agency would secure data on a previously opaque policy issue, and researchers would have robust new datasets ripe for future work. SFCTA's transportation expertise and unusually deep data analysis savvy gave the researchers confidence that they could rely on the agency as a research collaborator, fostering trust that facilitated the working relationship. Northeastern researchers were impressed, for example, that their SFCTA counterparts were able to work with twelve terabytes of data shared on a physical hard drive.[51]

Castiglione and Drew Cooper, a Senior Transportation Modeler in Castiglione's group, worked with Mislove and Wilson to identify a relatively modest scope focused on merely understanding what was happening: How many TNC vehicles are there on the road at any given time? How many trips do they complete? When and where do those trips take place? How much driving do TNCs do in San Francisco, in aggregate, every day?

SFCTA and Northeastern were committed to the project and worked quickly together – agency staff and academic researchers noted in interviews that they

50 San Francisco's taxi trip data may have been a public record under relevant freedom of information laws – but at a minimum, providing researchers with direct access to these data saves those researchers the headache of filing a public records request. These data would inform a follow-up paper comparing service and accessibility in TNC and taxi markets in San Francisco and New York. See: Shan Jiang et al., "On Ridesharing Competition and Accessibility: Evidence from Uber, Lyft, and Taxi," in *Proceedings of the 2018 World Wide Web Conference*, WWW '18 (Republic and Canton of Geneva, Switzerland: International World Wide Web Conferences Steering Committee, 2018), 863–872, https://doi.org/10.1145/3178876.3186134.

51 As a point of contrast, as of 2018 Uber's engineering team was working with databases on the scale of hundreds of petabytes – or roughly 10,000 times more data. See: Reza Shiftehfar, "Uber's Big Data Platform: 100+ Petabytes with Minute Latency," *Uber Engineering Blog* October 17, 2018, https://eng.uber.com/uber-big-data-platform/.

believed they could rely on their counterparts to make deadlines when necessary. The project took roughly six months to complete.

This project's approval and success grew from a culture and agency leadership that valued this work, supported its completion, and allowed staff the flexibility to experiment with new modes of working. Castiglione and Cooper sought and received approval to move forward from the agency's Executive Director, with consultation from the agency's legal counsel, who did not believe the agency was taking on meaningful legal risk.[52] With a relatively small staff and a broad mandate, SFCTA leadership see research as an essential part of the agency's mission and empower staff to pursue opportunities as they arise, especially timely data analysis designed to inform pressing public policy questions. This project was also delivered on a compressed time scale relative to some of the agency's multiyear research and planning processes.

7.5.2 *Processing and Packaging the Results*

The SFCTA and Northeastern teams collaborated to stitch together data from 200 digital "sensors" deployed to blanket San Francisco, storing Uber and Lyft vehicle locations – as displayed on the home screens of both apps – for almost six weeks in late 2016. Each "sensor" was a temporary user account digitally positioned on an evenly spaced grid that cut across the city in order to maximize the likelihood that the sensor network would be able to observe all the Uber and Lyft vehicles driving at a given time. The researchers had applied a similar approach to audit surge pricing in their 2015 paper, but at a much smaller scale.

The collaborators' strong shared baseline of technical expertise enabled the academics and agency staff to more easily solve this and other technical challenges. Perhaps chief among them was the task of converting disparate, duplicative records from the digital sensor network across two companies into a unified dataset summarizing all TNC trips in San Francisco during a two-

[52] In large part, this reflected the agency's assessment that any legal risk would be borne by the Northeastern team, since the researchers were collecting the data – in potential violation of Uber's and Lyft's terms of service. While there can be ethical concerns regarding the collection of "personally identifiable information," none appear to have been collected in this project, and Northeastern researchers aggregated the data to avoid sharing vehicle-specific GPS locations before sharing it with SFCTA. For a critique of SFCTA's approach – published by a think tank that has received funding from both Uber and Lyft – see: Joseph Jerome, "Ethically Scraping and Accessing Data: Governments Desperately Seeking Data," *Center for Democracy & Technology* (blog), May 3, 2018, https://cdt.org/blog/ethically-scraping-and-accessing-data-governments-desperately-seeking-data/.

The researchers were also aware of the risk involved, and for their part have raised ethical concerns regarding the opacity of "black box" algorithms that operate on a ubiquitous societal scale – for more, see: Christo Wilson and Alan Mislove, "We're Suing the Federal Government to Be Free to Do Our Research," *The Conversation* (blog), March 27, 2017, http://theconversation.com/were-suing-the-federal-government-to-be-free-to-do-our-research-74676.

week period.[53] It is hard to imagine an agency in a smaller city pulling this off without significant support from consultants, adding cost and institutional complexity to the undertaking.

SFCTA and Northeastern researchers agree that the dataset they generated is not ideal, and SFCTA felt data directly from Uber or Lyft would be more representative of the companies' operations. While validation efforts undertaken by both the SFCTA and Northeastern teams gave them confidence in the findings, it is hard to assess the degree of accuracy in the researchers' analysis – though subsequent studies have affirmed their results. For example, Uber and Lyft's own analysis suggests that, if anything, SFCTA significantly underestimated TNCs' overall share of vehicle miles traveled in the County.[54]

The agency tried to be careful in framing its assertions, and to be clear about what the joint analysis with Northeastern could and could not tell readers with any confidence. Researchers and SFCTA communications staff explicitly identified examples of data and analyses that were *not* included in the report. These "omissions" included vehicle occupancy, trip purpose, and traveler demographics (since the methods used only tracked *vehicle* locations). The agency's decision to message their findings conservatively was in part designed to anticipate pushback from the TNCs themselves.

Until the final report's publication, the agency chose not to discuss the project except with those who were directly involved in the project or needed to know about it. The agency applied this relatively secretive approach due to both uncertainty regarding whether they would succeed and due to concerns about how the potentially controversial project would be viewed by both other agency staff and the TNCs themselves. Staff feared that if Uber or Lyft got wind of what the researchers were doing, the companies might attempt to pressure SFCTA into shutting down the project. While senior SFCTA leaders had some discomfort about the project's lack of procedural transparency prior to publication, those leaders trusted their staff – and the potential value of the data seemed to outweigh any potential risks.

7.5.3 TNCs Today's *Public Reception and Impact*

The final report, dubbed *TNCs Today*, gave the agency a powerful new tool to combat misinformation, helped address questions coming from agency leadership and the local public, and provided timely analysis to inform SFCTA's near-term research agenda and long-term planning efforts.[55] A lack of detailed TNC research globally also contributed to international interest in *TNCs Today*.

53 The analytical methodology is reviewed in detail in: Drew Cooper et al., "Profiling Transport Network Company Activity Using Big Data," *Transportation Research Record* 2672, no. 42 (2018): 192–202.

54 Bliss, "How Much Traffic Do Uber and Lyft Cause?"

55 San Francisco County Transportation Authority, "TNCs Today: A Profile of San Francisco Transportation Network Company Activity" (San Francisco, CA: San Francisco County Transportation Authority, June 2017).

SFCTA's study also challenged pervasive public narratives about TNCs' role in the transportation system – in part promulgated by TNCs themselves – that TNCs complement public transit services by providing first- and last-mile connections. While *TNCs Today* findings do not contradict that narrative per se, the high relative concentration of TNC travel in San Francisco's most transit-rich areas cast doubt on visions of TNCs' contributions to a multimodal transportation utopia. As of summer 2019 and according to SFCTA's website analytics, *TNCs Today* remained the agency's highest-download report.

The SFCTA Board of Directors was pleased to have new data to shed light on a growing and high-profile transportation challenge. Furthermore, via conference presentations, academic publications,[56] and substantial media coverage, SFCTA raised its profile and gained credibility, including among academic researchers and other possible collaborators. Numerous transportation agencies and regulators have reached out to the SFCTA and Northeastern researchers in hopes of replicating the analysis. To the interviewees' knowledge, no other agencies have done so.

Uber and Lyft largely refrained from commenting publicly on the analysis after its publication. Still, the fact that agencies must proactively consider and plan for TNCs' strategic communications efforts lays bare the companies' success in building influence and power that indirectly hampers government's work simply by consuming their attention.

Representatives from Uber did, however, have a private phone call with SFCTA and Northeastern researchers to discuss the *TNCs Today* report's findings – a phone call that interviewees described as tense, particularly in contrast to Uber's reaction to the Northeastern researchers' first study. Following the publication of *Peeking Beneath the Hood of Uber*, Uber spoke with Northeastern researchers on the phone and made a point to correct a software bug in the Uber app's surge pricing code that the researchers' work had highlighted. Lyft did not comment on *TNCs Today* to SFCTA staff.

SFCTA and partner agency SFMTA have built on the success of *TNCs Today* and other early efforts. In 2017, the agencies released a set of "Emerging Mobility Principles" developed through a public engagement process and intended to inform ongoing policy efforts and a joint research and planning agenda.[57] Multiple follow-up reports have already been released, one of which – *TNCs and Congestion* – builds directly on the dataset developed through the *TNCs Today* research process.[58]

[56] Cooper et al., "Profiling Transport Network Company Activity Using Big Data"; Gregory D. Erhardt et al., "Do Transportation Network Companies Decrease or Increase Congestion?," *Science Advances* 5 (2019): eaau2670.

[57] San Francisco County Transportation Authority, "Emerging Mobility," SFCTA, 2019, www.sfcta.org/policies/emerging-mobility.

[58] San Francisco County Transportation Authority, "TNCs & Congestion"; Erhardt et al., "Do Transportation Network Companies Decrease or Increase Congestion?"

Others include *The TNC Regulatory Landscape*[59] and *Emerging Mobility Evaluation Report*.[60]

7.5.4 *Lessons from SFCTA's Experience*

When public agencies face a policy-relevant knowledge gap and lack the authority or independent ability to fill it, they can give up or get creative. Agencies in this position often benefit from working in partnership with individuals and organizations that bring complementary expertise and experience to the table – including, when feasible, TNCs themselves.

Agency leaders who are able to foster a culture of evidence-based planning and policy-making and who empower their staff to take risks and exercise creativity in their work are more likely to reap the benefits of innovative research approaches like that employed by SFCTA and Northeastern. At SFCTA, this strategy has also informed subsequent academic collaborations.

Still, developing the staff ethos and the capacity to deliver on ambitious projects is no small task. Across the board, interviewees felt that the technical expertise of SFCTA staff was and remains exceptional, which calls into question how realistic it would be for other agencies to pursue similarly technical research without hiring consultants.

Finally, this case study highlights the breadth of the impact that Uber and Lyft's state lobbying machine can have on local government. First, SFCTA must go out of its way to invest time in collecting basic data necessary to do its job. Second, the agency must proactively plan to counteract TNCs' possibly reactionary communications strategies. Third, the agency must engage in long-term lobbying efforts to attempt to at least partially overturn the pre-emptive State regulations that constrain SFCTA's authority. And as this story plays out in cities across the country, the vast majority of Uber's staff can still focus on improving and marketing the company's core product – since the company's lobbying efforts require but a small fraction of its multibillion-dollar budget.

7.6 CONCLUSION

Urban transportation systems are changing rapidly, are still far too dangerous for people who choose to walk and bike,[61] and remain a particularly challenging sector

59 San Francisco County Transportation Authority, "The TNC Regulatory Landscape: An Overview of Current TNC Regulation in California and Across the Country."

60 San Francisco County Transportation Authority, "Emerging Mobility Evaluation Report" (San Francisco, CA: San Francisco County Transportation Authority, July 2018), www.sfcta.org/sites/default/files/2019–02/Emerging%20Mobility%20Studies_11.pdf.

61 Heather Zaccaro, "Dangerous by Design 2019" (Washington, DC: Smart Growth America, 2019), https://smartgrowthamerica.org/app/uploads/2019/01/Dangerous-by-Design-2019-FINAL.pdf.

to decarbonize.[62] Local governments face an ongoing imperative to mitigate shortcomings in urban transportation policy that Uber and Lyft's operations place in stark relief, and which legal structures advanced by Uber and Lyft reinforce by preempting local regulatory authority.

Local governments rarely have the time, resources, or patience to collect the data needed to carefully design policy and planning solutions to address these challenges. In retrospect, it borders on the absurd that SFCTA had to work with academics to scrape TNCs' APIs to figure out how many TNCs used to drive in San Francisco every day. At the same time, local governments must grow more comfortable acting under uncertainty in an increasingly diverse and complex urban transportation environment.

While it would be convenient for cities if TNCs shared data more liberally, cities cannot count on TNCs to do so freely. In the absence of relevant data, the negative impacts of TNC operations highlight a need for some degree of policy and regulatory action in a few key areas.

First, agencies should find ways to collect the data they need when they genuinely need it. Agencies have a growing menu of technology and survey-based tools at their disposal to evaluate projects. Local governments must often make decisions in the face of significant uncertainty, and creative problem-solving approaches like SFCTA's *TNCs Today* can help agencies mitigate and act under that uncertainty.

Second, urgent concerns like street safety and climate change create imperatives to reduce vehicle speeds and to reduce the share of people traveling alone in cars. Rising to this occasion will require agencies to develop a stronger bias toward action in both direct and implicit regulatory approaches – regardless of the quality of data available. It would be well-justified for local governments to grow more comfortable redesigning streets and enforcing traffic violations based on theory and educated guesses, even when marginally more targeted and effective solutions might be enabled by access to improved data. Access to high-quality data cannot be a precondition for local governments to act in the face of crises in street safety, inequality, and climate change.

Third, in cases where states are willing to revisit existing regulations, it would be beneficial to devolve certain regulatory authorities to local government. Most important among these would be authority to levy fees, collect data, and set wage and consumer protection requirements (e.g., including for ADA accessibility). Fees and data collection are more important to addressing transportation system challenges like safety and greenhouse gas emissions, while wage and consumer protection requirements apply to broader labor and social challenges. Looming worker classification questions remain more appropriately dealt with at the state and federal levels.

[62] Umair Irfan, "After Years of Decline, US Carbon Emissions Are Rising Again." *Vox*, January 8, 2019, www.vox.com/2019/1/8/18174082/us-carbon-emissions-2018.

Finally, SFCTA's experience highlights the value of building more sophisticated technical expertise into government, whether directly, via contracts, or through external partnerships. The existing lack of technical savvy creates a self-reinforcing chicken and egg problem: staff often do not have access to the right data, and companies hesitate to provide data due to agencies' perceived lack of technical savvy, in particular with respect to protecting user privacy.

Uber and Lyft are gaming a transportation system that has been designed both legally and physically for cars, and their successes highlight the imperative not merely for for-hire vehicle regulatory reform but for the accelerated redesign of our streets.[63] Both formal and "implicit" regulatory approaches are necessary to overcome the unhealthy path dependencies in urban infrastructure laid bare by TNC operations.

OTHERS

Barrios, John M, Yael V. Hochberg, and Livia Hanyi Yi. "The Cost of Convenience: Ridesharing and Traffic Fatalities." New Working Paper Series. Chicago, IL: Stigler Center for the Study of the Economy and the State, October 2018.

Berry, Melissa. "How Many Uber Drivers Are There?" *The Rideshare Guy* (blog), June 1, 2019. https://therideshareguy.com/how-many-uber-drivers-are-there/.

Big Data Innovation Team, City of Toronto, and University of Toronto Transportation Research Institute (UTTRI). "The Transportation Impacts of Vehicle for Hire in the City of Toronto." June 2019. www.toronto.ca/wp-content/uploads/2019/06/96c7-Report_v1.0_2019–06-21.pdf.

Bliss, Laura. "Cities Have to Get Creative When Uber and Lyft Won't Release Trip Data." *The Atlantic*, January 13, 2018. www.citylab.com/transportation/2018/01/to-measure-the-uber-effect-cities-get-creative/550295/.

"How Much Traffic Do Uber and Lyft Cause?" *CityLab* (blog), August 5, 2019. www.citylab.com/transportation/2019/08/uber-lyft-traffic-congestion-ride-hailing-cities-drivers-vmt/595393/.

Borkholder, Joy, Mariah Montgomery, Miya Saika Chen, and Rebecca Smith. "Uber State Interference: How Transportation Network Companies Buy, Bully, and Bamboozle Their Way to Deregulation." Washington, DC: National Employment Law Project and Partnership for Working Families, January 2018.

Brinklow, Adam. "SF Sues California over Law That Shelters Lyft, Uber Drivers." *Curbed SF* (blog), February 9, 2018. https://sf.curbed.com/2018/2/9/16995402/sf-lawsuit-california-lyft-uber-drivers-licenses.

California Public Utilities Commission. "Required Reports TNCs Must Provide the CPUC." State of California, 2019. www.cpuc.ca.gov/General.aspx?id=3989.

Campbell, Alexia Fernández. "Uber and Lyft Have Launched a Campaign to Avoid Government Regulation in California." *Vox*, October 29, 2019. www.vox.com/identities/2019/10/29/20938109/ab5-uber-lyft-ballot-initiative-referendum.

63 Gregory H. Shill, "Should Law Subsidize Driving?," *NYU Law Review* 95 (2020).

Chen, Le, Alan Mislove, and Christo Wilson. "Peeking Beneath the Hood of Uber." In *Proceedings of the 2015 Internet Measurement Conference*, 495–508. Tokyo, Japan: Association for Computing Machinery, 2015.

Chetty, Raj, Nathaniel Hendren, Patrick Kline, and Emmanuel Saez. "Where Is the Land of Opportunity? The Geography of Intergenerational Mobility in the United States." *The Quarterly Journal of Economics* 129, no. 4 (2014): 1553–1623.

City Attorney of San Francisco. "Uber and Lyft Archives." City Attorney of San Francisco, 2019. www.sfcityattorney.org/category/news/uber-and-lyft/.

City of Chicago. "Public Vehicles." Business Affairs and Consumer Protection, 2019. www.chicago.gov/content/city/en/depts/bacp/supp_info/bacppublicvehicles.html.

City of New York. "TLC Initiatives." NYC Taxi & Limousine Commission, 2019. www1.nyc.gov/site/tlc/about/tlc-initiatives.page.

Clewlow, Regina, and Gouri Shankar Mishra. "Disruptive Transportation: The Adoption, Utilization, and Impacts of Ride-Hailing in the United States." Research Report. UC Davis Institute of Transportation Studies, October 2017.

Conway, Matthew Wigginton, Deborah Salon, and David A. King. "Trends in Taxi Use and the Advent of Ridehailing, 1995–2017: Evidence from the US National Household Travel Survey." *Urban Science* 2, no. 3 (2018).

Cooper, Drew, Joe Castiglione, Alan Mislove, and Christo Wilson. "Profiling Transport Network Company Activity Using Big Data." *Transportation Research Record* 2672, no. 42 (2018): 192–202.

Cortright, Joe. "Unsafe Uber? Lethal Lyft? We're Still Skeptical," *City Observatory* (blog), April 3, 2020, www.cityobservatory.org/unsafe-uber-lethal-lyft-still_skeptical-2/.

Crist, Philippe. "Shaping the Relationship Between Public Transport and Innovative Mobility." International Transport Forum, 2017. www.itf-oecd.org/sites/default/files/docs/shaping-relationship-public-transport-innovative-mobility.pdf.

Curtis, Terra, Meg Merritt, Carmen Chen, David Perlmutter, Dan Berez, and Buffy Ellis. "Partnerships Between Transit Agencies and Transportation Network Companies." Washington, D.C.: Transportation Research Board, April 16, 2019. https://doi.org/10.17226/25425.

Das Acevedo, Deepa. "Data Deficits in Municipal Rideshare Collaborations." *Saint Louis University Law Journal* 63 (2019).

Erhardt, Gregory D., Sneha Roy, Drew Cooper, Bhargava Sana, Mei Chen, and Joe Castiglione. "Do Transportation Network Companies Decrease or Increase Congestion?" *Science Advances* 5, (2019): eaau2670.

Graehler, Jr., Michael, Richard Alexander Mucci, and Gregory D. Erhardt. "Understanding the Recent Transit Ridership Decline in Major US Cities: Service Cuts or Emerging Modes?" presented at the 98th Annual Meeting of the Transportation Research Board, Washington, D.C., 2019. https://usa.streetsblog.org/wp-content/uploads/sites/5/2019/01/19–04931-Transit-Trends.pdf.

Grossman, Allison, and Paul Lewis. "Contracting for Mobility: A Case Study in the Los Angeles and Puget Sound Regions." Washington, DC: Eno Center for Transportation, October 30, 2019. www.enotrans.org/wp-content/uploads/2019/10/MOD_Contracting_Final_10–29-19.pdf.

Hawkins, Andrew J. "How Much Do Lyft Drivers Earn an Hour? It's Complicated." *The Verge*, April 12, 2018. www.theverge.com/2018/4/12/17230500/lyft-driver-pay-earnings-hourly-expenses.

Irfan, Umair. "After Years of Decline, US Carbon Emissions Are Rising Again." *Vox*, January 8, 2019. www.vox.com/2019/1/8/18174082/us-carbon-emissions-2018.

Isaac, Mike. "How Uber Deceives the Authorities Worldwide." *The New York Times*, March 3, 2017, sec. Technology. www.nytimes.com/2017/03/03/technology/uber-greyball-program-evade-authorities.html.

Jerome, Joseph. "Ethically Scraping and Accessing Data: Governments Desperately Seeking Data." *Center for Democracy & Technology* (blog), May 3, 2018. https://cdt.org/blog/ethically-scraping-and-accessing-data-governments-desperately-seeking-data/.

Jiang, Shan, Le Chen, Alan Mislove, and Christo Wilson. "On Ridesharing Competition and Accessibility: Evidence from Uber, Lyft, and Taxi." In *Proceedings of the 2018 World Wide Web Conference*, 863–872. WWW '18. Republic and Canton of Geneva, Switzerland: International World Wide Web Conferences Steering Committee, 2018. https://doi.org/10.1145/3178876.3186134.

LA Department of Transportation. "Mobility Data Specification: Information Briefing." City of Los Angeles, October 31, 2018. https://ladot.io/wp-content/uploads/2018/12/What-is-MDS-Cities.pdf.

Lee, Jason, William Tyner, and Nealay Vasavda. "Moving Minds: The Next Generation of Real-Time Transit Information in San Francisco." *Transportation Research Record* 2672, no. 8 (2018): 523–535.

Mandle, Peter, and Stephanie Box. "Transportation Network Companies: Challenges and Opportunities for Airport Operators." Washington, DC: Transportation Research Board, August 28, 2017. https://doi.org/10.17226/24867.

Moon, Mariella. "Uber and Lyft Will Test Dedicated Pick-up Spots in San Francisco." *Engadget* (blog), November 9, 2017. www.engadget.com/2017/11/09/uber-lyft-pick-up-dropoff-spots-san-francisco/.

Murphy, Colin, Kevin Karner, and Zak Accuardi. "When Uber Replaces the Bus: Learning from the Pinellas Suncoast Transit Authority's 'Direct Connect' Pilot." Chicago, IL: Shared-Use Mobility Center, June 2019.

National Association of City Transportation Officials and International Municipal Lawyers Association, "Managing Mobility Data" (Washington, DC: National Association of City Transportation Officials and International Municipal Lawyers Association, April 2019), www.nacto.org/wp-content/uploads/2019/05/NACTO_IMLA_Managing-Mobility-Data.pdf

Rodier, Caroline. "The Effects of Ride Hailing Services on Travel and Associated Greenhouse Gas Emissions." Davis, CA: National Center for Sustainable Transportation, April 2018. https://escholarship.org/uc/item/2rv570tt.

San Francisco County Transportation Authority. "Annual Report," 2018. www.sfcta.org/sites/default/files/2019-03/AR%202018%20190205.pdf.

"Emerging Mobility." SFCTA, 2019. www.sfcta.org/policies/emerging-mobility.

"Emerging Mobility Evaluation Report." San Francisco, CA: San Francisco County Transportation Authority, July 2018. www.sfcta.org/sites/default/files/2019-02/Emerging%20Mobility%20Studies_11.pdf.

"The TNC Regulatory Landscape: An Overview of Current TNC Regulation in California and Across the Country." San Francisco, CA: San Francisco County Transportation Authority, December 2017.

"TNCs & Congestion." San Francisco, CA: San Francisco County Transportation Authority, October 2018.

"TNCs Today: A Profile of San Francisco Transportation Network Company Activity." San Francisco, CA: San Francisco County Transportation Authority, June 2017.

Schaller, Bruce. "The New Automobility: Lyft, Uber, and the Future of American Cities." New York, NY: Schaller Consulting, July 25, 2018. www.schallerconsult.com/rideservices/automobility.pdf.

"Unsustainable? The Growth of App-Based Ride Services and Traffic, Travel and the Future of New York City." New York, NY: Schaller Consulting, February 27, 2017. www.schallerconsult.com/rideservices/unsustainable.pdf.

Seattle Department of Transportation. "New Mobility Playbook." Seattle, WA: City of Seattle, September 2017. https://newmobilityseattle.info/storage/app/media/Documents/newmobilityplaybookfurtheractionsappendices.pdf.

Sernoffsky, Evan. "Ex-Uber Driver Guilty of Manslaughter for Killing Girl in SF Crosswalk." *SFChronicle.com*, August 2, 2018. www.sfchronicle.com/bayarea/article/Uber-driver-guilty-of-manslaughter-for-killing-13127623.php.

SharedStreets. "Taxi and TNC Activity." *SharedStreets*, 2019. https:/sharedstreets.io/taxi-tnc-activity/.

Shiftehfar, Reza. "Uber's Big Data Platform: 100+ Petabytes with Minute Latency." *Uber Engineering Blog* October 17, 2018. https://eng.uber.com/uber-big-data-platform/.

Shill, Gregory H. "Should Law Subsidize Driving?" *NYU Law Review* 95 (2020).

Smith, Aaron. "Who in America Uses Ride-Hailing Apps Like Uber or Lyft." *Pew Research Center: Internet, Science & Tech* (blog), May 19, 2016. www.pewinternet.org/2016/05/19/on-demand-ride-hailing-apps/.

Solon, Olivia. "How Uber Conquers a City in Seven Steps." *The Guardian*, April 12, 2017, sec. Technology. www.theguardian.com/technology/2017/apr/12/why-everyone-hates-uber-seven-step-playbook.

Ting, Phil. "Ting Bill Helping San Francisco Raise Revenues from TNCs to Fund Transportation Infrastructure Heads to the Governor." Official Website – Assemblymember Phil Ting, September 4, 2018. https://a19.asmdc.org/press-releases/20180831-ting-bill-helping-san-francisco-raise-revenues-tncs-fund-transportation.

Tsay, Shin-pei, Zak Accuardi, and Bruce Schaller. "Private Mobility, Public Interest." New York, NY: TransitCenter, 2016.

Uber. "Uber Movement: Let's Find Smarter Ways Forward, Together." 2019. https://movement.uber.com/cities?lang=en-US.

Uber Technologies, Inc. "Form S-1 Registration Statement." Securities and Exchange Commission, April 11, 2019. www.sec.gov/Archives/edgar/data/1543151/000119312519103850/d647752ds1.htm.

Washington, District of Columbia. "Department of For-Hire Vehicles." Department of For-Hire Vehicles, 2019. https://dfhv.dc.gov/.

"Mayor Bowser and DDOT Announce Pick-Up/Drop-Off Zone Pilot Program Expansion," October 26, 2018. https://ddot.dc.gov/release/mayor-bowser-and-ddot-announce-pick-updrop-zone-pilot-program-expansion.

Washington Metropolitan Area Transit Authority. "Transportation Network Companies (TNCs) in the Washington Region." presented at the Transportation Planning Board, Washington, DC, April 6, 2018. www.mwcog.org/assets/1/28/04062018_-_Item_2_-_Transportation_Network_Companies_(TNCs)_in_the_Region.pdf.

Wilson, Christo, and Alan Mislove. "We're Suing the Federal Government to Be Free to Do Our Research." *The Conversation* (blog), March 27, 2017. http://theconversation.com/were-suing-the-federal-government-to-be-free-to-do-our-research-74676.

Wisniewski, Mary, and Jennifer Smith Richards. "Uber and Lyft Said Ride-Sharing Would Cut Traffic Congestion and Supplement Public Transit. But Has It Worked?" *Chicago Tribune*, June 7, 2019. www.chicagotribune.com/news/breaking/ct-biz-ride-share-congestion-loop-20190520-story.html.

Zaccaro, Heather. "Dangerous by Design 2019." Washington, DC: Smart Growth America, 2019. https://smartgrowthamerica.org/app/uploads/2019/01/Dangerous-by-Design-2019-FINAL.pdf.

8

Words Matter

How Tech Media Helped Write Gig Companies into Existence

Sam Harnett

In 2010, Farhad Manjoo received a PR email from an employee at a company called UberCab. At the time, Manjoo was trying to carve out a name for himself as a technology columnist at *Slate*. "What our tiny company is doing for San Francisco right now is huge," the email said. Manjoo read on about a new "startup" connecting drivers to riders through a phone app. The employee sounded "ecstatic," and the "joy was contagious." Manjoo was intrigued, particularly by the prospect that UberCab could reduce car use and ownership. In a *New York Times* column years later, Manjoo recalled his naïveté. "Here was a company that could credibly claim to be changing the world. It might unpave paradise and tear down the parking lots," Manjoo wrote, "The more I learned about UberCab's bold idea, the more deeply I swooned."[1] He wasn't the only one intrigued.

Manjoo was part of a collective media swoon over companies like Uber and TaskRabbit. It lasted for years and helped pave the way for a handful of companies that represent a tiny fraction of the economy to have an outsized impact on law, mainstream corporate practices, and the way we think about work. The content generated by swooning pundits and journalists made it seem like these companies were ushering in not only an inevitable future, but a desirable one. They helped convince the public and regulators that these businesses were different from existing corporations – that they were startups with innovative technology platforms designed to disrupt established firms by efficiently connecting consumers to independent, empowered gig workers. This was not only false, it was the exact rhetorical cover these companies needed to succeed.

Journalists and pundits both normalized and at times generated this rhetoric and framing. It was then repeated by politicians, amplified by academics, and finally enshrined in laws that legalized the business models of these app-based service-delivery companies. It would be years before some media organizations began taking a more nuanced and critical approach to the companies in the "sharing economy"

[1] Farhad Manjoo, "The Uber I.P.O. Is a Moral Stain on Silicon Valley." *New York Times*, May 1, 2019, www.nytimes.com/2019/05/01/opinion/uber-ipo.html.

that they helped write into existence. By then, it was too late. Venture capital had been gained. Consumers were habituated. Lobbyists were at work. New laws were on the books and IPOs were on the way. The force that fueled this media swoon was a relatively new and journalistically problematic trend in media: "tech" reporting.

In this chapter, I describe how the conventions of tech journalism helped paint these companies and their gig work as disruptive, liberating, and futuristic in a way that guided the actions of politicians, judges, and legislators, all of whom remain unaware of just how much they were influenced by tech reporters. First, drawing on my own reporting, I call into question the designation of app-based service delivery companies like Lyft and Fiverr as "tech companies" and expose flaws in how media outlets covered them. Second, I trace how tech reporting evolved, developed its bad habits, and negatively changed practices in mainstream journalism. Third, I outline the main archetypes of problematic media approaches to app-based service-delivery companies. Finally, I show how the rhetoric and ideology in the flawed content influenced academics, politicians, regulators, and lawmakers.

8.1 MISTAKEN IDENTITIES

I have covered companies like Lyft and Fiverr for seven years, and my reporting made one thing evident early on: tech journalism's primary way of approaching these businesses did not get at the heart of the story. Worse, it was misleading. The conventions of the "tech beat" primed reporters to pump up these apps as disruptive and innovative advancements for consumers. This framing distorted the real, common business model of these companies, which was to use the banner of "tech" to avoid regulations, drive down labor costs, and undercut competition. The innovation-disruption lens dehistoricized these app-based service-delivery companies, clouding how they fit into decades-long trends like the erosion of worker earnings or the increase in compulsive consumption. This not only benefited app-based service-delivery companies, but was factually inaccurate. As a reporter I gathered two kinds of evidence that showed this: interviews with workers for these apps and a close look at the actual technology behind them.

8.2 WORKER PERSPECTIVE

The innovation-disruption narrative may make a convenient through line in a story, but it does not match the experiences and perspectives of the "gig" workers I interviewed. Lyft driver Dan Carrigan, interviewed in 2014, is a prime example of both this disconnect and why it was easy for so many reporters to misrepresent workers like him.[2] At first Carrigan told me he drove Lyft because he wanted

2 Sam Harnett, "What the 'Sharing Economy' Costs Workers." KQED, December 18, 2014, www.kqed.org/news/10374498/workers-in-the-sharing-economy-struggle-to-be-heard.

flexibility while trying to start his own business. This story would easily slide into the innovation-disruption framework, but it's far from the full picture of who Carrigan is, why he was doing this job, and what he really thought about it.

By spending a day with Carrigan, I found out his real motivation for driving Lyft: he'd been laid off from his job, and like many other drivers, couldn't find a better option. He wanted protections like workers compensation and overtime, but believed he had to choose between that and flexibility. He was unaware that more privileged workers often get both. What Carrigan did fully understand though is the illusion that driving Lyft made him free because he could work when he wanted. In reality Carrigan said he felt helpless as Uber and Lyft put more cars on the road and slashed his rates. Declining income forced him to drive more often and change his schedule to drive at peak times. Carrigan also felt if anything went wrong – if he got into an accident or hit a pedestrian – he would be totally on his own, and that did not make him feel very free at all. Carrigan did not believe he was part of "the sharing economy," "operating his own business as a 'driver-partner,'" or "disrupting" much of anything.[3] He was just a guy trying to earn some extra money with a part-time job while he dreamed of some way to free himself from the grind of capitalism that brought him no joy and limited autonomy. This is not an innovative or disruptive story at all, but it's one I heard again and again from the Uber drivers, "Taskers," Instacart shoppers, and all other manner of workers for these app companies.

8.3 WORDS MATTER

"Why can't we just call Uber and TaskRabbit and all the rest of them startups or at least tech companies?" A somewhat exasperated editor asked me that back in 2014. We were trying to finish a story, and every time she sent the draft back with "startup" and "tech company" in it, I took them out and sent it back. Those two words were at the top of a list of problematic terms I had begun to collect, and this time around I was refusing to let them into the story.

Whenever news breaks there is a critical time frame where terms are established to describe what is happening. This language develops into a sticky shorthand that is repeated again and again. In the process the terms become so normalized it's difficult to detect the subtext and assumptions packed into them. They start to seem neutral and natural. Eventually both reporters and the public no longer think about what it means to call pay increases "wage hikes," mass murderers "shooters," or Ann Coulter a "provocateur." This kind of charged shorthand is rampant in the world of tech journalism, which traffics in new companies and services.

[3] "Driver-partners" is how Uber describes its workers.

When I started covering companies like Uber, I found myself increasingly encountering these problematic terms.[4] These included Silicon Valley-speak like "pivot," "friction," "innovate," "disrupt," "platform," and "startup," but also big, baggy words like "freedom" and "efficiency." Companies like Uber and Lyft got their own section on my list with terms like "transportation network company," "gig," "rideshare," "sharing economy," and "collaborative consumption." I fought to cut these terms, but I was sometimes overruled or had to settle for scare quotes because editors thought these words were essential and benign. Eventually, the editor I was working with came to understand that a word like "startup" was editorializing because it was endowed with positive associations (new, fresh, not your typical corporation!) yet provided no concrete definition (how old can a startup be? How many employees can it have? How much revenue?).

The presence of these words subtly change the way readers and listeners think about the companies in question. Being deemed a "tech" company is a massive brand boost. "Tech" corporations have traditionally had high consumer favorability ratings and have not been scrutinized like firms in other industries. The tech label is particularly important for companies like Uber which, to avoid regulations, rely on the premise that they are merely "tech platforms" connecting "independent businesses" with consumers. (Incidentally, companies like Facebook and Google spent years honing a similar "platform" argument to avoid regulation as media entities.) In the 2010s, app-based service-delivery companies depended on eschewing regulations, or at least evading them until their services had become too entrenched to be shut down. To do that they needed people to think of them as totally new, "innovative" businesses. Lucky for them, there were a growing number of tech journalists, and their livelihood depended on finding and pumping up companies into the next big thing, even if those companies weren't developing any new technology.

8.4 WHAT TECHNOLOGY, REALLY?

Here's a question: If Uber or Instacart or Fiverr are really tech companies, what technology have they created? It's not the GPS or smartphones they rely on to connect workers and consumers: GPS got started back in 1973 and the iPhone appeared in 2007 (and that, itself, was preceded by the internet-connected BlackBerry). App-based service-delivery companies aren't developing silicon chips like Intel or AMD, creating consumer software like Adobe, or making networking switches like Cisco. They don't get money from inventing new tech, but from venture capital and by taking a slice of every transaction made by their contingent labor force. If tech was the key to the business, then you would think a company like

[4] For example, I did a piece about how "sharing economy" had been coopted from true digital sharing initiatives like freecycle and couch-surfing: "The Movement to Kill the Phrase Sharing Economy." KQED, February 4, 2016, www.kqed.org/news/10851717/the-movement-to-kill-the-phrase-sharing-economy.

Lyft or Uber would have been worried about Flywheel. The San Francisco taxi industry developed the Flywheel app to exactly mimic Uber and Lyft, but these companies weren't scared at all. That's because the reason they were able to offer rides more conveniently and cheaper than taxi companies had nothing to do with technology. They were able to put as many cars on the road as they wanted and pay drivers as little as possible because they were using the guise of technological innovation to avoid transportation regulations and labor laws.

It is true that once a company like Uber achieves scale, it requires computer engineers to adapt or create new tools that potentially push the boundaries of digital technology. The true tech stories at these companies are about managing server traffic and crunching data quickly. These are the tasks most of the employees with PhDs in computer science are working on at the company. But this kind of tech story doesn't make a catchy "tech" journalism headline. When Uber posted a detailed article on its blog about the work involved in managing over 100 petabytes of data, the post made few media ripples, which isn't surprising.[5] It's difficult to find any article about the actual computer science and technological advances happening at companies branded as "tech." That's because the modern tech media ecosystem has evolved to have a particular set of conventions.

8.5 THE ORIGIN OF TECH JOURNALISM

Today there is a well-established ecosystem of tech media, including "tech" sections on most major news publications, tech-dedicated outlets like *TechCrunch* and *Venturebeat*, and a whole host of blogs and podcasts. Similar to other long-standing areas of reporting like "Arts," "Science," and "Business," "Tech" has conventions that determine what stories get told and how. These particularities of the "tech" beat are what led to the problematic swoon over companies like Uber and TaskRabbit. To better understand why the habits and rules of the modern tech ecosystem were so beneficial to app-based service companies, we have to take a step back and look at how it originated.

Modern tech journalism has some of its earliest roots in niche publications like *Byte*, *Creative Computing*, and *InfoWorld* – magazines geared toward electronics hobbyists. *Popular Electronics* was prototypical to the format. It was filled with reviews on the latest hardware and software, and written in a digital-positive tone that reveled in all things "nerd."[6] On the heels of these magazines came publications like *Macworld* and *PC Magazine* which carried over the product review format and techno-awe, but expanded the audience to everyday electronics consumers.

[5] Reza Shiftehfar, "Uber's Big Data Platform: 100+ Petabytes with Minute Latency." Uber Blog, October 17, 2018, https://eng.uber.com/uber-big-data-platform/.

[6] A 1975 cover story on the MITS Altair microcomputer kit reportedly stoked the imaginations of Bill Gates and Paul Allen; Wall Text, "We Have a Basic." New Mexico Museum of Natural History and Science, Albuquerque, NM.

Still, these had limited reach: as recently as the early 1990s you didn't see "tech" sections in most media publications, nor did you encounter "tech reporters." Then, at the annual Macworld conference on January 2nd, 1993, *Wired* magazine made its debut.

Wired was not just a magazine about hardware, software, and video games, but a publication that looked at the whole world through a digital lens. The digital revolution was happening, and *Wired* was going to be the first to tell you about it. Establishing this editorial viewpoint was one of the three major ways *Wired* laid the groundwork for today's modern tech ecosystem. The second was injecting traditional magazine formats with the techno-utopian, digital-positive tone and the opinionated, first-person, review style of earlier tech publications. The third and biggest impact was simply proving the existence of a broader general audience for tech news. That encouraged a slew of new tech media ventures. By the mid-2000s there were dozens of blogs like *VentureBeat*, *Gizmodo*, and *TechCrunch*. Mainstream publications soon followed suit: *The New York Times* launched its *Bits Blog*, CBS bought *CNet*, and NPR began *All Tech Considered*. Tech sections appeared on websites, journalists became tech reporters, and tech pundits appeared on TV.

There are many characteristics of the modern tech media ecosystem that result in misleading journalism, especially in the case of app-based service-delivery companies. First is the format problem: that wide-eyed, first-person review-style inherited from older tech publications. This sets reporters up to approach apps like Uber and TaskRabbit not as journalists digging into how the companies that make these apps operate, but as consumers interested in the experience of using the apps. A second major problem is that modern tech reporting lost almost all interest in covering *actual* technology. In the tech sections of media organizations like *The New York Times* or on websites like *TechCrunch*, you're not going to get advice about building your own computer or the ins and outs of a new programming language. Instead you're going to find stories about the services and products of corporations that leverage the internet and digital devices to make money. This tendency made it easy for reporters to gloss over the lack of real tech innovation behind apps like Uber and Instacart and to fetishize them as new technologies. The third major problem is the imperative to break the story. This is always a pressure in journalism, but it's ramped up even more for tech reporters, whose reputation is staked on being the first to know about the latest new thing. This encourages reporters to create and repeat jargon which furthers the case that what they're writing about is truly new. There's not much of a tech story if you approach Uber like a cab company or DoorDash as a food delivery service. Altogether, these conventions generated recurring content which spread misinformation and positive bias about these companies to everyone from consumers to legal actors like judges, regulators, and politicians.

8.6 FIVE ARCHETYPES OF MISINFORMATION

The first major editorial mistake, and the one that paved the way for all the rest, was the decision media organizations made to treat app-based service delivery corporations as "tech companies," and thus the sole province of the tech beat. Companies like Uber and Lyft would have gotten far more scrutiny from transportation reporters; similarly, TaskRabbit and Fiverr would have been characterized more accurately by labor reporters. Media organizations did not make this decision with intent to mislead, but as a result of financial pressure. The internet and its effect on the advertising model of journalism has increased the need for media organizations to get clicks and get them cheap. The first-person, product-review-style conventions of tech journalism described above lead to catchy content about new products consumers want to get their hands on. Even better for efficiency's sake, a tech reporter can do most of these stories without leaving her desk or interviewing anyone. Once media organizations deemed these corporations "tech companies," each new entrant followed a predictable path through the tech media ecosystem.

Most of the problematic content generated about app-based service-delivery companies as they moved through that ecosystem falls into five archetypes: the introductory review, the first-person experiential story, the outlier worker profile, the techno-utopian think piece, and finally the founder interview. First, whenever a new service or company appears, reporters rush to write the introductory review ("There's this new thing, I tried using it, and here's how it works"). These pieces are consumer-focused and usually little more than rewrites of company press releases with no outside sources. After this, comes the first-person, experiential stories ("I signed up to work for these apps myself, and this is what it's like"). This injects the biases of the reporter's privileged experience and fails to capture the reality of the work. Third, is the outlier worker profile ("You can make it if you hustle"). These are longer feature stories that rely on anecdotes and eye-grabbing outliers instead of thorough ethnographic journalism. Then follows a slew of techno-utopian think pieces ("These apps are part of a new trend that will save us"). These are usually op-eds and more concerned with speculating about the future rather than situating in history. Fifth, there's the founder interview ("These people changed the world, and here's how they did it"). In this final step, media organizations give a CEO or early employee a platform to spool out their story with little or no pushback. By doing a close reading of content from each of these different archetypes, we can pinpoint the emergence of the rhetoric and factoids that influenced the thought of the general public, academics, lawmakers, and regulators.

8.6.1 *The Introductory Review*

In 2010, UberCab's public relations emails to reporters like Farhad Manjoo started to bear fruit. In July of that year, *TechCrunch* published an article titled, "UberCab

Takes The Hassle Out Of Booking a Car Service."[7] The article opens by lamenting how "frustrating" it is to find a cab, and then pivots to a solution: "Enter UberCab, a new service that offers an on-demand car service." (This phrasing, "Enter this" or "Enter that," is a common trope in this kind of article.) The rest of the piece is essentially an excited how-to guide for using the app. "If UberCab were in the city that I live in," the author concludes, "I'd probably use it." At the bottom of the article is a link to a promotional demo on Uber's website.

This is the Ur-narrative of tech journalism: there's a problem, a new digital solution, the personal experience of trying it out, and finally speculation about how it will positively change the world. App-based service-delivery companies could usually count on one of these introductory articles, particularly from *TechCrunch*. In March of 2009, the blog delivered for Airbnb, even throwing in a discount: "AirBnB is offering $50 off any trip that is booked from now until Monday, March 9th. All you have to do is type in 'TECHCRUNCH' when booking."[8] Procrastinating for a party in 2013? *TechCrunch* brings you "Whisky As A Service with Instacart and Lasso."[9] Dreading the "pain point" of walking your dog in 2015? *TechCrunch* posits the new Wag! service can reduce the cost.[10] These articles established the innovation-disruption rhetoric that more broadly focused media organizations would emulate. By the middle of 2013, CNN wondered if we were at "the end of consumerism" in its own introductory piece about the new "sharing economy."[11] Later that year, *All Things Considered* dedicated a week to "exploring the sharing economy," during which reporters questioned whether we were switching away from "ownership to access."[12] The problematic rhetoric used in these introductory articles established the shorthand, or the terms, which would cast positive light on these companies and shape public discourse and perception for years.

8.6.2 *The First-Person Experience*

After these introductory articles, journalists from more established media organizations wrote longer, more involved first-person pieces about working for the "apps." In

7 Leena Rao, "UberCab Takes the Hassle out of Booking a Car Service." *TechCrunch*, July 5, 2010, https://techcrunch.com/2010/07/05/ubercab-takes-the-hassle-out-of-booking-a-car-service.

8 Leena Rao, "Y Combinator's Airbed and Breakfast Casts a Wider Net for Housing Rentals as AirBnB." *TechCrunch*, March 4, 2009, https://techcrunch.com/2009/03/04/y-combinators-airbed-and-breakfast-casts-a-wider-net-for-housing-rentals-as-airbnb.

9 Alex Wilhelm, "Whisky as a Service in San Francisco: Instacart v. Lasso." *TechCrunch*, December 12, 2013, https://techcrunch.com/2013/12/12/whiskey-as-a-service-in-san-francisco-instacart-v-lasso.

10 Alex Wilhelm, "Wag Launches Its On-Demand Dog Walking App in San Francisco." *TechCrunch*, April 5, 2014, https://techcrunch.com/2015/04/05/wag-launches-its-on-demand-dog-walking-app-in-san-francisco.

11 Madeleine Acey, "What Is the Sharing Economy?" CNN, June, 2013. http://edition.cnn.com/interactive/2013/06/world/sharing-economy/.

12 NPR, "Share and Share Alike, A Time of Collaborative Consumption." November 11, 2013. www.npr.org/sections/alltechconsidered/2013/11/11/244570695/q-a-a-time-of-collaborative-consumption.

January 2015, Joel Stein produced an emblematic feature of this archetype for *Time* magazine titled "Baby, You Can Drive My Car and Do My Errands and Rent My Stuff."[13] This story set off a series of similar articles, and Stein was interviewed about the piece on NPR. (This, incidentally, is a common feature of the tech-media ecosystem: a journalist who reports on something new instantly becomes a topic-expert.[14]) In his article, Stein relates a series of adventures in the "sharing economy." He rents his car out to a slightly sweaty French guy through RelayRides, lives out his "lifelong fantasy of collecting people's stories" by driving for Lyft, satisfies his wonder if he could be a chef on EatWith, and then tries to rent his family's stuff out on Yerdel. The *Time* URL headline is: "Joel Stein's Wild Ride Through the Sharing Economy."

This is exactly what articles of this ilk are: a wild ride. They do not show us what it's like to be a worker on these apps, but instead what it's like to be a journalist trying them out to write an article. We don't know if Stein could make a decent living on any of these apps, what it's like to drive sixty hours a week for Lyft or Uber to make ends meet, why someone would actually do these jobs, who these people are, or what their lives are really like. There are some setbacks for Stein, like when an Italian woman damages his car, but mostly we hear about all the fun he had meeting people, what it's like to try different jobs, and why people, like the founder of Lyft, believe these apps are the future. Then Stein moves on to his next assignment. Of course in this context, the app work comes across as freeing and fulfilling, which is exactly what companies like Lyft and Fiverr wanted to project. Even in stories of this kind that provided a more critical look at this job or the earnings, the sheer choice of the first-person format alone suggests you could get to the truth about these apps not by thoroughly documenting the lives of actual workers, but by just testing the app yourself and describing how it makes you feel.

8.6.3 *The Outlier Worker Profile*

Starting in 2013, a whole slew of similar articles popped up about Uber and Lyft drivers who were trying to appeal to customers by offering karaoke in their cars or outfitting them with neon lights and high-quality sound systems. These stories are part of a category of content portraying app labor as not truly work, but a potentially fun side-hustle. In a similar vein, there were a spate of stories about celebrities like Shaq or DJ DeadMau5 driving Lyft and Uber, and famous people like Conan O'Brien and Ice Cube getting rides. If driving Uber or Lyft was really hard work, why would a celebrity like Shaq do it and seem to be having so much fun? These

[13] Joel Stein, "Baby, You Can Drive My Car, and Do My Errands, and Rent My Stuff ... " *Time*, January 29, 2015, www.time.com/3687305/testing-the-sharing-economy.

[14] Emma Bowman, "When The Sharing Economy Brings Unexpected Experiences," NPR, April 27, 2015, www.npr.org/sections/alltechconsidered/2015/04/27/402563555/when-the-sharing-economy-brings-unexpected-experiences.

stories are subgenres of the "You Can Make It If You Hustle" archetype, which portrays gig work as something fun and flexible that anyone could succeed at if they were just entrepreneurial enough, had the right attitude, and maybe some neon lights.

These stories were especially pernicious when they used a single outlier to create a false impression of how much money a person could potentially earn working for these companies. This was the case of a profile of David Feldman on CNBC. He reportedly said he "would not be happy if I just worked for 10 years in a gray cubicle. That is not what I would want on my tombstone." So Feldman quit the "rat race" of finance, took a long trip to Europe, and then "cracked the code to successful freelancing." According to CNBC, he was making six figures copywriting and marketing through the website Fiverr. Feldman was hustling.[15] It was hard, but he had found a way to "make it," which was the title of the CNBC series in which Feldman appeared.

Outlier profile stories like this were often single-sourced and the earnings were not confirmed. The worker's word was taken as truth. Even more problematically, the *company's* word was taken as truth regarding earnings. In 2014, Uber reported that the median earnings for drivers working forty hours a week in New York was 90,000 dollars, a figure reprinted by *Business Insider*, *Entrepreneur*, and CNBC.[16] A *Washington Post* headline proclaimed: "Uber's Remarkable Growth Could End the Era of Poorly Paid Cab Drivers."[17] *Business Insider* posted an article with a list of the best cities to make 100,000 dollars a year driving for Uber.[18]

The drivers were perplexed. On a forum, one asked the group, "so who of you are actually making six figures?"[19] Pushback did emerge against the six-figure claims, as some journalists tried to get a clearer picture of what workers actually made by looking at ride receipts and spending time driving for the apps themselves.[20] The

15 Sarah Berger, "This 38-Year-Old Quit His Finance Job – Here's How He's Making 6 Figures Freelancing on Fiverr." CNBC, December 20, 2018, www.cnbc.com/2018/12/18/how-this-38-year-old-is-making-6-figures-freelancing-on-fiverr.

16 Jillian D'Onfro, "Uber Says Its Drivers Are Making $75,000–$90,000 a Year." *Business Insider*, May 27, 2014, www.businessinsider.com/uber-drivers-salary-90000–2014-5; Geoff Weiss, "The Median Income of an Uber Driver in NYC Is Nearly $100,000." *Entrepreneur*, May 28, 2014, www.entrepreneur.com/article/234289; CNBC, "Uber's $90K salary could Disrupt the Taxi Business." May 28, 2014, www.cnbc.com/2014/05/28/uber-may-be-tripling-cab-driver-salaries.

17 Matt McFarland, "Uber's Remarkable Growth Could End the Era of Poorly Paid Cab Drivers." *The Washington Post*, May 27, 2014, www.washingtonpost.com/news/innovations/wp/2014/05/27/ubers-remarkable-growth-could-end-the-era-of-poorly-paid-cab-drivers.

18 Maya Kosoff, "How Much You Have to Work to Make $100,000 Driving for Uber, Lyft, and Sidecar." *Business Insider*, January 13, 2015, www.businessinsider.com/where-to-work-to-to-make-100000-driving-for-uber-lyft-and-sidecar-2015-1.

19 UberPeople.Net, "So which one of you is making over $100k?" September 19, 2014, www.uberpeople.net/threads/so-which-one-of-you-is-making-over-100k.3875.

20 Dan Kedmey, "Do UberX Drivers Really Take Home $90K a Year on Average? Not Exactly." *Time*, May 27, 2014, www.time.com/119587/do-uberx-drivers-really-take-home-90k-a-year-on-average-not-exactly.

truth of course was that on average drivers were making far less than six figures. It is not even proven that they always make over minimum wage. In 2017, Uber agreed to pay 20 million dollars to settle accusations that it lied to drivers about their potential earnings, but the damage had already been done.[21] It would take years of reporting to shake loose the idea that it was common to make a good living or at least have a fulfilling job hustling through these apps.

8.6.4 *The Techno-Utopian Think Piece*

In the summer of 2013 Thomas Friedman wrote, "It all started with an air mattress." That's how he opened a *New York Times* opinion piece titled "Welcome to the Sharing Economy."[22] The piece is part Silicon Valley mythology story, part user guide to Airbnb, and it's all strung together with quotations from the company's CEO, Brian Chesky, along with boosterish exclamations from Friedman. At one point he writes: "Turns out there is an innkeeper residing in all of us!" The not-too-subtle subtext of these kinds of opinion pieces is that this "technology" (which again is just a mobile app and a company with venture capital to pursue regulatory arbitrage) can save us from the ills of modern-day capitalism – things such as feelings of alienation, growing income inequality, and evaporating sense of purpose. The piece fails to root Airbnb in any historical context and is rife in speculation about a better future. In order to sell the utopia Friedman breathes life into the gravely misleading idea that Airbnb and these other apps are part of some imagined trend called the "sharing economy."

The sharing economy myth was one of the most damaging and egregious mistakes in the content generated about these companies. Not only was it indefensibly wrong and cloaked their business operations in altruism, it created a confusing category that conflated things as different as Lyft, Airbnb, TaskRabbit, RelayRides, and Freecycle. Friedman's opinion piece jump started this trend-beast. Soon after it was published, writers began proclaiming the futuristic, "sharing economy" utopia was already upon us. In a *Wired* article titled, "How Airbnb and Lyft Finally Got Americans to Trust Each Other," Jason Tanz wrote that "we are entering a new era of Internet-enabled intimacy."[23] In a *New York Times* article titled "How Technology Could Help Fight Income Inequality," Tyler Cowen considered the utopia more speculatively, "perhaps the sharing economy can make it easier to live in much

[21] Federal Trade Commission, "Uber Agrees to Pay $20 Million to Settle FTC Charges That It Recruited Prospective Drivers with Exaggerated Earnings Claims." January 19, 2017, www.ftc.gov /news-events/press-releases/2017/01/uber-agrees-pay-20-million-settle-ftc-charges-it-recruited.

[22] Thomas Friedman, "Welcome to the 'Sharing Economy.'" *New York Times*, July 21, 2013, www .nytimes.com/2013/07/21/opinion/sunday/friedman-welcome-to-the-sharing-economy.

[23] Jason Tanz, "How Airbnb and Lyft Finally Got Americans to Trust Each Other." *Wired*, April 23, 2014, www.wired.com/2014/04/trust-in-the-share-economy/.

smaller spaces and rent needed items," he wrote.[24] The utopian possibilities posited by pundits like Friedman filtered back to reporters like Farhad Manjoo, whose first instinct was to wonder if Uber could decrease car ownership, rather than to look into things like the company's funding sources, business model, or real-world impacts.

When it became clear that those utopian predictions weren't coming true, that there was very little sharing going on but instead a whole lot of labor, the narrative shifted to how these apps were the future of work. In 2013, *Wired* published a piece by the CEO of Fiverr who posited that the gig economy could save the American worker by allowing them to brand and market themselves in the inevitable future of freelancing.[25] "[The sharing economy] will improve your career," Alexandre Douzet wrote for *Mashable* in 2014.[26] A *Forbes* opinion piece in 2014 gave five reasons why "half of us would be freelancers by 2020."[27] The volume of this kind of content legitimized a trend when there was no conclusive data to show that freelancing and part-time work was on the rise. In fact, data would soon come out showing otherwise.[28] Regardless, reporters and pundits were pumping out articles suggesting app work was not only desirable but the inevitable "future of work." What regulator or lawmaker would want to stand in the path of the future?

8.6.5 *The "Founder" Interview*

Do you know why Lyft is spelled with a "y" instead of an "i"? This is the teaser for an interview with Lyft CEO John Zimmer on Guy Raz's NPR program, *How I Built This*, "a show about innovators, entrepreneurs, idealists, and the stories behind the movements they built."[29] On the program Raz actively avoids hard questions, and instead peppers the interview with "wows," and a few "that's crazy"s. He embraces the innovation-disruption rhetoric wholeheartedly. He refers to Lyft as a "rideshare," a term that had been long dropped for its inaccuracy; calls them "indispensable;" and says that "the state of California almost killed Zimmer's company" by attempting to regulate it. In other episodes, Raz speaks with Apoorva Mehta of Instacart and Joe Gebbia of Airbnb, both of whom he approaches in a similar fashion.

24 Tyler Cowen, "How Technology Could Help Fight Income Inequality." *New York Times*, December 6, 2014, www.nytimes.com/2014/12/07/upshot/how-technology-could-help-fight-income-inequality.

25 Micha Kaufman, "The Gig Economy: The Force That Could Save the American Worker?" *Wired*, September, 2013, www.wired.com/insights/2013/09/the-gig-economy-the-force-that-could-save-the-american-worker/.

26 Alexandre Douzet, "How the Sharing Economy and Instant Gratification Will Shape Your Career." *Mashable*, September 7, 2014, www.mashable.com/2014/09/07/sharing-economy-job-search/.

27 Micha Kaufman, "Five Reasons Half of You Will Be Freelancers in 2020," *Forbes*, February 28, 2014, www.forbes.com/sites/michakaufman/2014/02/28/five-reasons-half-of-you-will-be-freelancers-in-2020/.

28 Ben Casselman, "Maybe the Gig Economy Isn't Reshaping Work After All." *New York Times*, June 7, 2018, www.nytimes.com/2018/06/07/business/economy/work-gig-economy.html.

29 Guy Raz, "Lyft: John Zimmer." NPR, June 25, 2018, www.npr.org/2018/06/22/622601114/lyft-john-zimmer.

Raz isn't the only one handing the microphone to those in power, but he is emblematic of the approach.[30] In the case of Mehta, Gebbia, and Zimmer, Raz was late to the party. The origin mythologies of the companies these men had founded had been memorialized dozens of times already. Raz interviewed John Zimmer in February 2018, by which point Lyft and the entire on-demand service sector had not only become well-established but embroiled in numerous legal battles and scandals, none of which he brings up in his interview. Raz's show, and others like it, is structured to be a safe space for powerful people to unspool their origin stories and establish their rhetoric with no real pushback. This is the final stage in the tech media ecosystem, where the mythologies about these companies are threaded into Silicon Valley's much heralded and unassailable history of innovation.

8.7 THE DROWNED OUT CRITICAL VOICE

From the onset of app-based service-delivery companies, some pundits and reporters like Noam Schieber and Evgeny Morozov were trying to present a clearer picture of what was actually going on.[31] This was an uphill battle for two big reasons. First, speculative and boosterish content about digital services fit far better into the conventions of tech media – namely, awe over all things digital and a first-person consumer-centric approach. Second, the terms of the debate had been so quickly and firmly established by the tech media ecosystem that even those writing nuanced pieces had to work very hard to avoid words like "rideshare," "platform," and "the sharing economy," which were subtly injecting positive spin into the way people thought about app-based service-delivery companies. For years, these more critical articles were drowned out in the more general media swoon.

[30] For similar founder-interviews, see Adam Bryant, "Bryan Chesky of AirBnB, on Scratching the Itch to Create." *New York Times*, October 12, 2014, www.nytimes.com/2014/10/12/business/brian-chesky-of-airbnb-on-scratching-the-itch-to-create; *Marketplace*, "Brian Chesky of AirBnB on 'the worst idea ever.'" August 27, 2015, marketplace.org/shows/corner-office-from-marketplace/brian-chesky-airbnb-worst-idea-ever/; Derek Thompson, "AirBnB CEO Brian Chesky on Building a Company and Starting a 'Sharing' Revolution." *The Atlantic*, August 13, 2013, theatlantic.com/business/archive/2013/08/airbnb-ceo-brian-chesky-on-building-a-company-and-starting-a-sharing-revolution/278635/.

[31] For examples of critical reporting and opinion pieces see Noam Scheiber, "Silicon Valley Is Ruining 'Sharing' for Everybody," *The New Republic*, August 13, 2014, https://newrepublic.com/article/119072/silicon-valleys-sharing-economy-airbnb-lyft-are-selling-big-lie; Alexandra Le Tellier, "Opinion: The Sharing Economy Isn't 'Collaborative Consumption,' It's 'Disaster Capitalism.'" *Los Angeles Times*, June 5, 2014, www.latimes.com/opinion/opinion-la/la-ol-sharing-economy-collaborative-consumption-disaster-capitalism-20140604-story.html; Evgeny Morozov, "The 'Sharing Economy,' Undermines Workers' Rights." *Financial Times*, October 14, 2013, www.ft.com/content/92c3021c-34c2-11e3-8148-00144feab7de.

8.8 THE NARRATIVE SPREADS

If it is your job to make laws or determine how they are applied, you might not want to admit your decisions and thought could be influenced by an outside force like media created for popular consumption. It's true that overt bias in the news is easy to spot: the op-ed from a tech CEO or the promotional introduction article in *TechCrunch*. Still, there are all sorts of ways this content can influence one's thinking. First, there is the subtle effect of charged rhetoric like "innovate," "disrupt," and "platform," that gets picked up and repeated so often it is accepted as natural and neutral. Second, there is the challenge of disregarding the implications when trusted sources like *NPR* or *The New York Times* decide to cover corporations like Uber and TaskRabbit primarily as tech companies. This adds weight to the argument that these corporations represent a novel technology. Lastly, even if you do not interact directly with the content of the tech media ecosystem, it reaches you through everyone around you who has been impacted by it. The following sections explore how the rhetoric and ideology of tech journalism permeated the discourse and ideas of academics, politicians, and regulators. Although this section largely focuses on San Francisco and California, you will find the kind of influence it describes is in no way limited to these areas.

8.8.1 *Academics*

For academics, as with journalists, there is increasing professional pressure to find a cutting-edge topic of which to be the expert. It is a perverse incentive that causes two major problems: first, academics can aggrandize and distort the truth of something just by writing and talking about it; second, the pressure to say something new encourages them to go one step farther and see trends and results that don't exist.

Ivy League economists Lawrence Katz and Alan Krueger offer a clear example of academics who, influenced by this drive and the media atmosphere, produced flawed scholarship that had major repercussions. In 2016, they wrongly concluded that the number of people with some kind of independent work arrangement had increased 5 percent in a decade – a fact they attributed in part to apps like Uber. Their report drew a large amount of media attention and was quoted widely. Two years later, a federal report determined that their findings were false and the number of independent workers had actually *fallen* by around half a percent. To their credit, Katz and Krueger admitted their mistake, but it was too late. Their original report had already influenced reporters and helped fuel the speculation that gigs were the future of work.

Even when academics have taken a more critical or nuanced approach, they still often fall into the trap of adopting the pro-innovation language developed by tech media. There are countless published papers that refer to these companies as "disruptive" and "innovative" "platforms" that are part of the "sharing economy."[32] It is easy to trace this language back to the tech media ecosystem, although sometimes the authors of these papers make it even clearer by actually citing news articles.[33] There was not a concerted effort in academia to develop new, less ideologically charged ways to describe these apps, the work done on them, or the companies behind them.

8.8.2 *Politicians*

Politicians quickly began to repeat the innovation-disruption rhetoric honed by tech media, and doing so offered an easy way to both burnish their own brands as cutting-edge lawmakers and to connect with constituents who appreciated the new services. In San Francisco, former Mayor Ed Lee declared July 15, 2013, Lyft Day, and the city's Deputy Innovation Officer (itself a title informed by the innovation-disruption rhetoric) presented the proclamation to Lyft. It reads like a Lyft press release, describing the company as a "ridesharing" "technology platform," connecting people to "shared rides with community drivers."[34] Other local politicians parroted the same language. In 2014, David Chiu, a member of the San Francisco Board of Supervisors, said "I believe we are becoming the capital of the Sharing Economy. We've been a city of innovation since the Gold Rush." He made the statement at the "Share Conference," cosponsored by Lyft and Airbnb.[35] On the national level, Democratic Senator Mark Warner from Virginia was one of the first to adopt the "sharing economy" as a talking point. He gave a TedX Talk titled "How the government can work for – not against – companies like Uber," spoke at MIT's On-Demand Economy Conference, appeared at a roundtable at an app-based labor contracting firm called Moonlighting, and is quoted saying things like, "I'm not afraid of disruptive change," and "We're not going to slow this disaggregation

32 See generally: Julia Ticona, et al., "Trusted Strangers: Carework Platforms' Cultural Entrepreneurship in the On-Demand Economy." *Sage Journals*, May 15, 2018, https://journals.sagepub.com/doi/abs/10.1177/1461444818773727?journalCode=nmsa; Nestor M. Davidson., et al., "The Sharing Economy as an Urban Phenomenon." *Yale Law & Policy Review*, Volume 34, Issue 2, 2016, https://ylpr.yale.edu/sharing-economy-urban-phenomenon.

33 In an abstract for a paper in the *Fordham Urban Law Journal*, Abbey Stemler quotes both a *TIME* article declaring the sharing economy as one of "ten ideas that will change the world," and projections from *Forbes* that she argues prove the sharing economy "is moving beyond a fringe movement and becoming a disruptive economic force;" Abby Stemler, "Betwixt and Between: Regulating the Sharing Economy." *Fordham Urban Law Journal*, December 8, 2014, https://papers.ssrn.com/sol3/papers.cfm?abstract_id=2535656.

34 Lyft Blog, "Lyft Day in San Francisco." July 15, 2013, https://blog.lyft.com/posts/2013/7/15/lyft-day-in-san-/.

35 Steven Jones, "Renting Isn't Sharing." *San Francisco Bay Guardian*, Volume 48, Number 34, 2014, http://sfbgarchive.48hills.org/sfbgarchive/2014/05/20/renting-isnt-sharing/.

between employer and employee down."[36] Warner became increasingly critical of app-based service-delivery and vocal about the need for worker protections, but his framing that these apps were innovative, disruptive, and the inevitable future of work came right out of the tech media ecosystem.

Innovation rhetoric also appears in numerous state laws that preemptively legalize the labor model of companies like Uber, Lyft, and Handy. CS/HB 7087, passed by the Florida State Senate, describes the apps as "a marketplace platform's technology application."[37] The same language appears in laws passed in Arizona and Indiana, among others. Having politicians repeat and sign this language into law was a coup for Lyft and Uber, particularly in the early years when local authorities were fining their drivers and municipalities were issuing cease-and-desist letters. What had begun as a catchy story told by journalists had gained traction with politicians. The next step was getting state-level regulators to buy the innovation-disruption framing, which they often did.

8.8.3 *Regulators*

In 2013 the California Public Utilities Commission (CPUC) decided to not regulate Uber and Lyft as taxi companies, but instead to create a new regulatory category called "Transportation Network Companies," or TNCs. The decision hinged on the determination that these companies were built on new technology, a position in line with the rhetoric formulated by tech media, echoed by academics, and repeated by politicians. Michael Peevey, the head of the CPUC, chose to view these companies as something wholly new. He recalled in his book how his daughter introduced him to Uber and how he thought it was "wonderful." "My god," he wrote, "here we have an application of a new yet modest technology . . .."[38] Peevey did not want his agency to stand in the way, and it didn't. It turned the rhetoric into reality by deeming Ubers and Lyfts a new kind of transportation, TNCs.

8.9 THE CRITICAL APPROACH HAPPENS . . . TOO LATE

Media organizations took years to set aside the rose-colored, innovation-disruption glasses through which they had been viewing companies like DoorDash and Lyft. In 2015, the Associated Press took a step toward fixing the misleading rhetoric by advising reporters to drop the term *rideshare*, although it is still widely used today. Even a veteran and skeptical journalist like *New York Times* reporter Mike Isaac has

[36] Mark Warner's Website, "Senator Warner Addresses the Opportunities and Challenges of the 'Sharing Economy.'" www.warner.senate.gov/public/index.cfm/on-demand-economy.

[37] Bill No. CS/HB 7087, Sess. of 2018, www.flsenate.gov/Session/Bill/2018/7087/Amendment/648194/PDF.

[38] Michael Peevey, Diane Wittenberg, *California Goes Green: A Roadmap to Climate Leadership*. CreateSpace Independent Publishing Platform, September 13, 2017.

not been able to escape using this problematic word. However, the real shift in coverage emerged as a side effect of the 2016 election and the ensuing discussion about how Facebook and other technology companies facilitated electoral manipulation. Tech suddenly lost some of its positive veneer and protection from scrutiny: there was far less appetite for a story about some cool new app that could make the world a better place, and far more hunger for stories about what tech companies were really up to. Some tech reporters who had built their careers boosting the latest app were now starting to take a critical look, and at the same time it became easier for non-tech reporters to pitch stories that examined gig companies in the context of labor laws, local governance issues, and transportation regulations.

In most cases, though, it was too late. Companies like Uber and Lyft had used the years-long media swoon to break into markets all over the world, rake in billions in venture capital, and legalize their business practices. This brings us back to Farhad Manjoo, who is one of the few tech reporters to have publicly admitted a mistake in the way they approached companies like Uber. In 2010, Manjoo had been an enthusiastic reporter at *Slate*, pumping out almost an article a day on things like the latest iPhone and which were the best drones for sale around Christmas time. His work at *Slate* eventually landed Manjoo a columnist position at *The New York Times*. With more time to write his articles and the professional security that came with reaching a peak in the journalism world, Manjoo became far more critical of app-based service-delivery companies and ashamed of his earlier reporting on them.

"Back then," Manjoo wrote,

> as a naïve, baby tech pundit, I was prone to spinning out elaborate visions of tech-abetted progress. Boy, was I a dope ... Nearly a decade later ... I'm sickened and saddened by my naïveté ... Because of where it came from and how it was cheered on, Uber felt little cultural pressure to divvy up its gains more equitably.[39]

Manjoo's realization and public regret are admirable, but in the meantime the companies that benefited from tech journalism's coverage have established insurmountable advantages. They set the terms of debate and the language with which to engage in that debate; they managed to influence academics, politicians, and regulatory actors in ways that most of these individuals *would not themselves recognize*; and they didn't even have to do most of the work: they just had to rely on swooning tech journalists whose careers depended on finding and pumping up whatever gadget or app that seemed like it could become the next big thing.

39 Farhad Manjoo, "The Uber I.P.O. Is a Moral Stain on Silicon Valley." *New York Times*, May 1, 2019, www.nytimes.com/2019/05/01/opinion/uber-ipo.html.

BIBLIOGRAPHY

Acey, Madeleine. "What Is the Sharing Economy?" CNN, June, 2013. http://edition.cnn.com/interactive/2013/06/world/sharing-economy/

Berger, Sarah. "This 38-Year-Old Quit His Finance Job – Here's How He's Making 6 Figures Freelancing on Fiverr." CNBC, December 20, 2018. cnbc.com/2018/12/18/how-this-38-year-old-is-making-6-figures-freelancing-on-fiverr.

Bowman, Emma. "When the Sharing Economy Brings Unexpected Experiences." NPR, April 27, 2015. npr.org/sections/alltechconsidered/2015/04/27/402563555/when-the-sharing-economy-brings-unexpected-experiences.

Brustein, Joshua. "In App Land, Lots of Ways to Get a Ride." *New York Times*, December 2, 2012. https://bits.blogs.nytimes.com/2012/12/02/get-a-ride-apps

Bryant, Adam. "Bryan Chesky of AirBnB, on Scratching the Itch to Create." *New York Times*, October 12, 2014. www.nytimes.com/2014/10/12/business/brian-chesky-of-airbnb-on-scratching-the-itch-to-create.

Casselman, Ben. "Maybe the Gig Economy Isn't Reshaping Work After All." *New York Times*, June 7, 2018. www.nytimes.com/2018/06/07/business/economy/work-gig-economy.html.

Chen, Brian. "Uber Maker of Summon-a-Car App, Adds Fare Splitting." *New York Times*, July 15, 2013. https://bits.blogs.nytimes.com/2013/07/15/uber-maker-of-summon-a-car-app-adds-fare-splitting.

CNBC. "Uber's $90 K salary could disrupt the taxi business." May 28, 2014. cnbc.com/2014/05/28/uber-may-be-tripling-cab-driver-salaries.

CNN Business. "What Is the Shared Economy?", November 28, 2014. www.youtube.com/watch?v=ElJnFgpPATA.

Cowen, Tyler. "How Technology Could Help Fight Income Inequality." *New York Times*, December 6, 2014. www.nytimes.com/2014/12/07/upshot/how-technology-could-help-fight-income-inequality.

Davidson Nestor M., Infranca John J. "The Sharing Economy as an Urban Phenomenon." *Yale Law & Policy Review*, Volume 34, Issue 2, 2016. https://digitalcommons.law.yale.edu/cgi/viewcontent.cgi?referer=www.google.com/&httpsredir=1&article=1697&context=ylpr.

D'Onfro, Jillian. "Uber Says Its Drivers Are Making $75,000–$90,000 a Year." *Business Insider*, May 27, 2014. businessinsider.com/uber-drivers-salary-90000–2014-5.

Douzet, Alexandre. "How the Sharing Economy and Instant Gratification Will Shape Your Career." *Mashable*, September 7, 2014. mashable.com/2014/09/07/sharing-economy-job-search/.

Federal Trade Commission. "Uber Agrees to Pay $20 Million to Settle FTC Charges That It Recruited Prospective Drivers with Exaggerated Earnings Claims." January 19, 2017. ftc.gov/news-events/press-releases/2017/01/uber-agrees-pay-20-million-settle-ftc-charges-it-recruited.

Friedman, Thomas. "Welcome to the 'Sharing Economy.'" *New York Times*, July 21, 2013. www.nytimes.com/2013/07/21/opinion/sunday/friedman-welcome-to-the-sharing-economy.

Harnett, Sam. "The Movement to Kill the Sharing Economy." KQED, February 4, 2016. www.kqed.org/news/10851717/the-movement-to-kill-the-phrase-sharing-economy.

Harnett, Sam. "What the 'Sharing Economy' Costs Workers." KQED, December 18, 2014. www.kqed.org/news/10374498/workers-in-the-sharing-economy-struggle-to-be-heard.

Jones, Steven. "Renting Isn't Sharing." *San Francisco Bay Guardian*, Volume 48, Number 34. 2014. http://sfbgarchive.48hills.org/sfbgarchive/2014/05/20/renting-isnt-sharing/.

Kaufman, Micha. “Five Reasons Half of You Will Be Freelancers in 2020.” *Forbes*, February 28, 2014. forbes.com/sites/michakaufman/2014/02/28/five-reasons-half-of-you-will-be-freelancers-in-2020/.

Kaufman, Micha. “The Gig Economy: The Force That Could Save the American Worker?” *Wired*, September, 2013. wired.com/insights/2013/09/the-gig-economy-the-force-that-could-save-the-american-worker/.

Kedmey, Dan. “Do UberX Drivers Really Take Home $90K a Year on Average? Not Exactly.” *Time*, May 27, 2014. time.com/119587/do-uberx-drivers-really-take-home-90k-a-year-on-average-not-exactly.

Kosoff, Maya. “How Much You Have to Work to Make $100,000 Driving for Uber, Lyft, and Sidecar.” *Business Insider*, January 13, 2015. businessinsider.com/where-to-work-to-to-make-100000-driving-for-uber-lyft-and-sidecar-2015–1 uberpeople.net/threads/so-which-one-of-you-is-making-over-100 k.3875.

Le Tellier, Alexandra. “Opinion: The Sharing Economy Isn't ‘Collaborative Consumption,’ It's ‘Disaster Capitalism.’” *Los Angeles Times*, June 5, 2014, www.latimes.com/opinion/opinion-la/la-ol-sharing-economy-collaborative-consumption-disaster-capitalism-20140604-story.html.

Manjoo, Farhad. “The Uber I.P.O. Is a Moral Stain on Silicon Valley. *New York Times*, May 1, 2019. www.nytimes.com/2019/05/01/opinion/uber-ipo.html.

McFarland, Matt. “Uber's Remarkable Growth Could End the Era of Poorly Paid Cab Drivers.” *The Washington Post*, May 27, 2014. washingtonpost.com/news/innovations/wp/2014/05/27/ubers-remarkable-growth-could-end-the-era-of-poorly-paid-cab-drivers.

Meece, Mickey. “Car-Pooling Makes a Surge on Apps and Social Media.” *New York Times*, July 4, 2012. www.nytimes.com/2012/07/05/technology/technology-makes-car-pooling-safer-and-easier.

Morgan, Jacob. “Why the CEO of Fiverr Thinks the Future of Work Is About the Gig Economy.” *Forbes*, November 30, 2015. forbes.com/sites/jacobmorgan/2015/11/30/why-the-ceo-of-fiverr-thinks-the-future-of-work-is-about-the-gig-economy/.

NPR. “For Ridesharing Apps Like Lyft, Commerce Is a Community.” October 14, 2013. www.npr.org/sections/alltechconsidered/2013/11/14/245242805/for-ridesharing-apps-like-lyft-commerce-is-a-community.

NPR. “Share and Share Alike, A Time of Collaborative Consumption.” November 11, 2013. www.npr.org/sections/alltechconsidered/2013/11/11/244570695/q-a-a-time-of-collaborative-consumption.

Peevey, Michael, Wittenberg, Diane. *California Goes Green: A Roadmap to Climate Leadership*. CreateSpace Independent Publishing Platform. September 13, 2017.

Rao, Leena. “UberCab Takes the Hassle out of Booking a Car Service.” *TechCrunch*, July 5, 2010. https://techcrunch.com/2010/07/05/ubercab-takes-the-hassle-out-of-booking-a-car-service.

Rao, Leena. “Y Combinator's Airbed and Breakfast Casts a Wider Net for Housing Rentals as AirBnB.” *TechCrunch*, March 4, 2009. https://techcrunch.com/2009/03/04/y-combinators-airbed-and-breakfast-casts-a-wider-net-for-housing-rentals-as-airbnb.

Raz, Guy. “Lyft: John Zimmer.” NPR, June 25, 2018.

Rosenberg, Tina. “It's Not Just Nice to Share, It's the Future.” *New York Times*, June 5, 2013. https://opinionator.blogs.nytimes.com/2013/06/05/its-not-just-nice-to-share-its-the-future/.

Scheiber, Noam. “Silicon Valley Is Ruining ‘Sharing’ for Everybody.” *The New Republic*, August 13, 2014, https://newrepublic.com/article/119072/silicon-valleys-sharing-economy-airbnb-lyft-are-selling-big-lie.

Shiftehfar, Reza. "Uber's Big Data Platform: 100+ Petabytes with Minute Latency." Uber Blog, October 17, 2018. https://eng.uber.com/uber-big-data-platform/.

Silver, James. "The Sharing Economy, a Whole New Way of Living." *The Guardian*, August 4, 2013. www.theguardian.com/technology/2013/aug/04/internet-technology-fon-taskrabbit-blablacar.

Stein, Joel. "Baby, You Can Drive My Car, and Do My Errands, and Rent My Stuff . . . " *Time*, January 29, 2015. time.com/3687305/testing-the-sharing-economy.

Stemler, Abby. "Betwixt and Between: Regulating the Sharing Economy." *Fordham Urban Law Journal*, December 8, 2014. https://papers.ssrn.com/sol3/papers.cfm?abstract_id=2535656.

Tanz, Jason. "How Airbnb and Lyft Finally Got Americans to Trust Each Other." *Wired*, April 23, 2014. www.wired.com/2014/04/trust-in-the-share-economy/.

Thompson, Derek. "AirBnB CEO Brian Chesky on Building a Company and Starting a 'Sharing' Revolution." *The Atlantic*, August 13, 2013. theatlantic.com/business/archive/2013/08/airbnb-ceo-brian-chesky-on-building-a-company-and-starting-a-sharing-revolution/278635/.

Ticona Julia, Mateescu Alexandra. "Trusted Strangers: Carework Platforms' Cultural Entrepreneurship in the On-Demand Economy." *Sage Journals*, May 15, 2018. https://journals.sagepub.com/doi/abs/10.1177/1461444818773727?journalCode=nmsa.

WBUR. "Trust in the Age of the Sharing Economy." July 9, 2014. www.wbur.org/hereandnow/2014/07/09/trust-sharing-economy.

Weiss, Geoff. "The Median Income of an Uber Driver in NYC Is Nearly $100,000." *Entrepreneur*, May 28, 2014. entrepreneur.com/article/234289.

Wilhelm, Alex. "Wag Launches Its On-Demand Dog Walking App in San Francisco." *TechCrunch*, April 5, 2014. https://techcrunch.com/2015/04/05/wag-launches-its-on-demand-dog-walking-app-in-san-francisco.

Wilhelm, Alex. "Whisky as a Service in San Francisco: Instacart v. Lasso." *TechCrunch*, December 12, 2013. https://techcrunch.com/2013/12/12/whiskey-as-a-service-in-san-francisco-instacart-v-lasso.

9

Rewriting the Rules

Gig Companies' Drive for Labor Deregulation

Rebecca Smith and Maya Pinto

They call us partners, [but] they make the rules, set the price ... Uber kept dropping prices every season to gain more ridership to satisfy their growth, and it didn't matter to Uber if the driver is not even making minimum wage.

– Fawzi Kamel, Uber driver, San Francisco, March 2017[1]

Late on a Sunday night in February 2017, erstwhile Uber CEO Travis Kalanick used his personal Uber app to hire a driver to shuttle himself and a couple of friends through San Francisco. When Kalanick's driver, Fawzi Kamel, a six-year Uber veteran, realized whom he was transporting, he seized the opportunity to confront the executive on the company's unilateral rate cuts that had left him in financial ruin. Kamel told Kalanick, "I lost $97,000 because of you. I'm bankrupt because of you." While reports have backed up Kamel's claims,[2] Kalanick denied that significant rate cuts had been made on the Uber Black service for which Kamel drove, describing any such assertions as "bullshit." As Kalanick exited the car, he vented his exasperation about Kamel's supposed lack of personal responsibility: "Some people don't like to take responsibility for their own shit. They blame everything in their life on somebody else."[3]

Kamel's dashboard-camera video of the interaction surfaced on Bloomberg's news website two days later, and within hours, Kalanick shot off a seven-sentence all-staff email message (also posted to Uber's website), subject line "A profound apology," in which he declared that he had "treated an Uber driver disrespectfully," was

[1] Rima Abdelkader and Alexander Smith, "Uber Driver Fawzi Kamel Explains Why He Argued with CEO Kalanick," *NBC News*, March 1, 2017, www.nbcnews.com/news/us-news/uber-driver-fawzi-kamel-explains-why-he-argued-firm-s-n727496.

[2] Jim Edwards and Hannah Roberts, "Uber Drivers Tell Us Travis Kalanick Is Wrong: Uber *Has* Paid Them Less Over Time," *Business Insider*, March 4, 2017, www.businessinsider.com/uber-travis-kalanick-drivers-paid-less-2017–3.

[3] Julie Carrie Wong, "Uber CEO Travis Kalanick Caught on Video Arguing with Driver About Fares," *The Guardian*, March 1, 2017, www.theguardian.com/technology/2017/feb/28/uber-ceo-travis-kalanick-driver-argument-video-fare-prices.

"ashamed," and concluded that the incident pointed to a need for him to "change as a leader and grow up."[4] Kalanick's apology boiled the problem down to his deficient leadership skills rather than acknowledging and making plans to fix the structural problems in Uber's business model that leave drivers like Kamel vulnerable to exploitation and without channels for recourse. Kamel's analysis, as suggested by the quote that opens this chapter, draws a very clear line between his financial trouble and Uber's control-without-responsibility business model. In fact, at the time of the incident, Kamel was a plaintiff in a pending misclassification and wage theft lawsuit against Uber.

Soon after issuing the public statement, Kalanick decided to apologize privately to Kamel. What was reportedly meant to be a five-minute meeting turned into an hour-long rehashing of the argument in the car days before, with Kamel again making his case and Kalanick this time offering a $200,000 (of his personal funds) *mea culpa* – a tacit, although one-off, acknowledgment of the negative material effect his company's policies had on one of its drivers.

The Kamel-Kalanick exchange, its backstory, and its aftermath are instructive of the way gig companies like Uber characterize their relationship with workers connected to their apps, the effects of that characterization on workers, and of some of the ways in which workers challenge it.

The exchange occurred just as Kalanick, working with lobbyist-investor Bradley Tusk and Lyft, was leading a well-funded campaign to ensure that transportation network companies (TNCs) would be written out of any obligations state law imposed on them as employers. By the end of 2017, they had convinced a majority of US states to enact special laws designating TNC drivers as independent contractors.[5] Uber's TNC carveout efforts were just beginning to be scaled up by the aspiring "Uber of home services" gig company Handy; under Tusk's wing, the first carveout of gig companies across multiple sectors – a so-called "marketplace contractor" carveout policy – passed in Arizona in 2016.[6]

In the last decade, numerous companies that straddle the high-wage technology and low-wage service sectors have emerged. These so-called "gig" companies use internet-based technology platforms to coordinate and manage on-demand piecework in a growing number of sectors, including taxi, food delivery, domestic work,

4 "A Profound Apology," Uber Newsroom, March 1, 2017, www.uber.com/newsroom/a-profound-apology.

5 Joy Borkholder, Mariah Montgomery, Miya Saika Chen, and Rebecca Smith, *Uber State Interference: How Transportation Network Companies Buy, Bully, and Bamboozle Their Way to Deregulation*, 10, 12–13 (New York: National Employment Law Project and Partnership for Working Families 2018), www.nelp.org/publication/uber-state-interference/.

6 Maya Pinto, Rebecca Smith, and Irene Tung, *Rights at Risk, Gig Companies' Campaign to Upend Employment as We Know It*, 4–5 (New York: National Employment Law Project, 2019), www.nelp.org/publication/rights-at-risk-gig-companies-campaign-to-upend-employment-as-we-know-it/.

nursing, and education.[7] Technology-facilitated gig work is only the latest iteration of a fifty-year-old pattern of workplace fissuring – the rise of "nonstandard" or "contingent" work that is subcontracted, franchised, temporary, freelance, or on-demand.[8] Gig companies are using new methods of labor mediation to control work remotely without accepting responsibility for its quality, to extract rents from workers, and to shift risks and costs of service provision onto workers, consumers, and the general public. Their practices leave workers vulnerable to economic insecurity, discrimination, and harassment.

This chapter describes the ways in which gig companies, flush with investor cash, are shaping regulation that favors their independent contractor business model and preempts challenges to their employment practices. We provide an account of the strategies and tactics that companies are using to maintain an independent contractor workforce in the face of contestations from workers, consumers, and regulators. And we suggest that the expanding set of business interests joining ranks with gig companies to rewrite employment standards threatens a recalibration of what workers in the US expect in exchange for their labor.

For decades, our organization, the National Employment Law Project (NELP), has collaborated with worker organizations and community groups to combat the misclassification of employees as independent contractors. NELP was founded fifty years ago as a legal services organization and today works with various partners on legal, policy, and media advocacy to expand access to good jobs and strengthen supports for unemployed workers. In the last decade, as gig companies have taken misclassification to a new level and have sought to spread lack of accountability across many industries, NELP has intensified its research, litigation, and policy work in this area. This chapter draws on that work.

9.1 GIG COMPANIES' LABOR PRACTICES AND POLICY EFFORTS TO SANCTION THEM

Through their labor and employment practices and public policy efforts, gig companies exert significant control over the on-the-job conditions of gig workers. Firms design compensation and evaluation systems often opaque, semi- or fully-automated, and using inputs that can be biased – that leave workers prone to economic insecurity. Companies devise employment contracts with nonemployee and forced arbitration provisions that erect barriers to workers seeking recourse for

7 Sarah A. Donovan, David H. Bradley, and Jon O. Shimabukuro, "What Does the Gig Economy Mean for Workers?" Congressional Research Service, CRS Report R44365, February 5, 2016, 2, https://fas.org/sgp/crs/misc/R44365.pdf.

8 David Weil, *The Fissured Workplace: Why Work Became So Bad for So Many and What Can Be Done to Improve It* (Boston: Harvard College, 2014).

mistreatment. To the same effect, they have lobbied for administrative and legislative policies that lock gig workers into independent contractor status.

9.1.1 *Gig Companies Offer Jobs Fraught with Quality Issues*

9.1.1.1 Low Wages

Academic studies have found TNCs to be paying subminimum wage rates. A study by economists at the New School for Social Research and the University of California at Berkeley on app driver pay in New York City, utilizing company-supplied earnings data for over three million trips during the week of October 15, 2017, found that 73 percent of drivers in the city were earning less than a $15-equivalent ($17.22 before expenses) hourly wage.[9] Many drivers had incomes so low they qualified for Medicaid and federal supplemental nutrition assistance. A Massachusetts Institute of Technology-funded study by economists at Stanford, utilizing January 2017 earnings data collected via a survey of 1,121 drivers across the US, found that average net pay was between $8.44 and $10 per hour.[10]

A study of delivery worker wages by Seattle-based worker center Working Washington analyzed over 1,400 pay records from February and March 2019, supplied by Instacart delivery workers from across the US, and found that average net hourly pay was $7.66.[11] At a September 2019 Seattle City Council hearing on the gig economy, Instacart worker Mia Kelly displayed recent pay records revealing hourly pay of $3.76.[12]

9.1.1.2 Changing Terms of Service

Fare cuts are a perennial issue raised by TNC drivers.[13] In March 2019, just before it released its initial public offering (IPO), Uber reduced per-mile pay by 25 percent,

9 James Parrott and Michael Reich, *An Earnings Standard for New York City's App-based Drivers* (New York: The New School Center for New York City Affairs; Center on Wage and Employment Dynamics, University of California, Berkeley, 2018) 5–6, www.centernyc.org/an-earnings-standard/.

10 Stephen Zoepf, "The Economics of Ride-Hailing, Revisited," Author's Statement, March 5, 2018, http://ceepr.mit.edu/files/papers/2018–005%20Authors%20Statement.pdf.

11 *Delivering Inequality, What Instacart Really Pays, and How the Company Shifts Costs to Workers* (Seattle, WA: Working Washington, April 17, 2019), https://payup.wtf/instacart/delivering-inequality.

12 Seattle City Council, Housing, Health, Energy, and Workers' Rights Committee Lunch & Learn, "Discussion with National Academic Experts and Gig Economy Workers," September 3, 2019, Testimony of Mia Kelly, www.seattlechannel.org/mayor-and-council/city-council/city-council-all-videos-index/?videoid=x106801.

13 Sage Lazzaro, "Uber Drivers Plan Boycott After Fare Cuts Slash Their Earnings to Below Minimum Wage," *Observer*, January 19, 2016, https://observer.com/2016/01/uber-drivers-plan-boycott-after-fare-cuts-slash-their-earnings-to-below-minimum-wage/; Rebecca Burns, "The Sharing Economy's 'First Strike': Uber Drivers Turn Off the App," *In These Times*, October 22, 2014.

from $.80 to $.60 cents per mile.[14] In late 2018, Instacart unveiled a new pay structure, and workers began to notice as much as a 40 percent drop in earnings.[15] In 2017, an Amazon Flex driver told a news outlet that his pay went from $300 to $200 per week after Amazon switched its pay formula of base wage plus tips to incorporating tips into base wage.[16]

Companies also change other terms of service without notice. According to Zubin Soleimany, attorney for the New York Taxi Workers Alliance, a new contract can pop up while a driver is in app, with a rider in the car, but the app will freeze until the driver hits "accept."[17] The changes mean, for example, that while Uber's commission was 20 percent in 2015, a recent survey of drivers in Seattle found that its commission is now 31 to 38 percent of fares.[18] Not only Uber, but other platforms whose terms of service we reviewed, including Postmates,[19] Handy,[20] Grubhub,[21] and DoorDash,[22] indicated that the platform could change any standard at any time.

9.1.1.3 Tip-Stealing

In early 2019, workers at Instacart started sharing screenshots of their pay records on a social media platform and found that the company was routinely stealing workers' tips, and using them to subsidize wages.[23]

9.1.1.4 Cancellation Fees

Cancellation fees can penalize workers for making safe choices. Handy charges workers fees for cancelling appointments, making workers less likely to leave unsafe situations. Mariana Viturro, deputy director of the National Domestic Workers Alliance, which represents Handy workers, explains that when a Handy worker is

[14] Sarah Holder, "Why L.A.'s Ride-Hail Drivers Went on Strike," *CITYLAB*, March 26, 2019, www.citylab.com/transportation/2019/03/uber-lyft-nyc-la-driver-wage-strike/585715/.

[15] Kevin Roose, "After Uproar, Instacart Backs Off Controversial Tipping Policy," *New York Times*, February 6, 2019, www.nytimes.com/2019/02/06/technology/instacart-DoorDash-tipping-deliveries.html?auth=login-email&login=email.

[16] Jacob Ward, "The Dark Side of Amazon: Drivers Complain of Pay Cuts," *Al Jazeera*, November 26, 2017, www.youtube.com/watch?v=aaKzXcq4gpo.

[17] Zubin Soleimany, telephone conversation with author, July 8, 2019.

[18] O'Connor v. Uber Technologies, Inc., 82 F.Supp.3d 1133, 1142 (N.D. Cal. 2015); *Uber and Lyft Take More, Pay Drivers Less* (Seattle: App-Based Drivers Association, May 2019), https://d3n8a8pro7vhmx.cloudfront.net/teamsters117/pages/4359/attachments/original/1557327859/Uber_and_Lyft_ Take_More__pay_drivers_less_-_ABDA_Report.pdf?1557327859.

[19] Postmates Fleet Agreement Effective May 11, 2019, https://fleet.postmates.com/legal/agreement.

[20] Handy Service Agreement, www.handy.com/pro_terms.

[21] Grubhub Terms of Use and Privacy Policy, Updated December 7, 2017, https://driver.grubhub.com/terms-of-use/.

[22] DoorDash Independent Contractor Agreement, www.DoorDash.com/dasher/us/ica/.

[23] "We've Got Receipts, Instacart," Working Washington (post), February 6, 2019, www.workingwa.org/instacart/receipts.

confronted with a job that is much more distasteful or dangerous than advertised, Handy standards dictate that a worker cannot leave without permission and cannot cancel the job without paying a fee, even though they may feel unsafe or need to spend far more hours on a job than was advertised. Because pay premiums are tied to ratings, they feel intense pressure to work for free or in situations where they feel unsafe.[24]

9.1.1.5 Lack of Access to Benefits and Social Insurance

When they label their workers "independent contractors," gig companies contribute nothing to Social Security, workers' compensation, unemployment insurance, or paid family leave. Some of the companies have said that they are interested in providing benefits to workers as independent contractors, but that they are unable to do so until worker classification questions are settled. Most recently, perhaps in response to a court decision in California (described in Section 9.2.4), the CEO of Uber and cofounder and CEO of Lyft penned an op-ed saying that they want to provide benefits to workers, as well as comply with a pay standard and negotiate with a workers' organization, but only if they can also be released from other obligations as employers.[25]

9.1.1.6 Discrimination

Gig companies' service satisfaction ratings systems outsource performance evaluation to consumers and are a "potential backdoor to employment discrimination." Discriminatory customer ratings systems can have material impacts on workers. For example, Zubin Soleimany told NELP that a New York Taxi Workers Alliance member was kicked off the platform because a passenger reported that he was drunk, when in reality he was suffering from allergies. The driver is a devout Muslim who has never taken a drink of alcohol in his life.[26] According to a case study of Uber's customer ratings system, potentially biased customer ratings determine drivers' access to special higher-fare work and factor into decisions about deactivation, and drivers need to maintain a certain average customer rating to remain active drivers.[27]

24 Mariana Viturro, telephone conversation with author, July 8, 2019.

25 Dara Khosrowshahi, Logan Green and John Zimmer, "Uber, Lyft Read to Do Our part for Drivers," *San Francisco Chronicle*, June 12, 2019, www.sfchronicle.com/opinion/openforum/article/Open-Forum-Uber-Lyft-ready-to-do-our-part-for-13969843.php?psid=9zHuu.

26 Zubin Soleimany, telephone conversation with author, July 8, 2019.

27 Alex Rosenblat, Karen Levy, Solon Barocas, and Tim Hwang, *Discriminating Tastes, Customer Ratings as Vehicles for Bias* (New York: Data and Society, October 2016) 7, https://datasociety.net/output/discriminating-tastes-customer-ratings-as-vehicles-for-bias/.

9.1.2 *Forced Arbitration Bars Workers Access to Justice*

One way in which gig companies have attempted to cement a regulation-free environment is by blocking workers from filing claims in courts. They have long made it a practice to require workers to sign forced arbitration agreements, which require workers to litigate their claims individually in closed-door, non-court settings. Legal scholar Charlotte Garden has analyzed their use and effects by companies including Uber, Lyft, Instacart, Grubhub, Postmates, Caviar, DoorDash, Handy, TaskRabbit, and Amazon Mechanical Turk, concluding that the provisions reduce the costs and risks to employers of misclassifying workers.[28] Gig companies have defended virtually every worker challenge by sending workers to arbitration. Uber's IPO filing indicates that it is currently facing 60,000 arbitration claims.[29] Lyft is currently facing over 3,400 arbitration claims.[30]

9.1.3 *Rewriting Employment Standards*

Gig companies have sought to ensure that they can operate in a state-sanctioned regulation-free environment. Since 2014, online labor platform companies like Uber and Handy, backed by powerful corporate allies and lobbyists, have worked to rewrite employment standards to carve themselves out of responsibility and lock their workers into independent contractor status. Employee status confers a host of labor rights and protections that independent contractor status does not. (See Table 9.1.)

The major impetus behind company-funded carveout policy campaigns is an onslaught of gig worker statutory and regulatory claims that began in 2013 (discussed below in Section 9.2.1). Indeed, a 2015 headline in a leading business journal read, "The Gig Economy Won't Last Because It's Being Sued to Death."[31] In 2016, Handy CEO Oisin Hanrahan admitted that the "marketplace platform company" carveout policies his company has taken a lead in pushing "would definitely help with some of the litigation that's in play."[32] Bradley Tusk summed up the strategy: "What is ultimately

[28] Charlotte Garden, "Disrupting Work Law: Arbitration in the Gig Economy." *U. Chi. Legal F.*, 2017, 205, 234, https://digitalcommons.law.seattleu.edu/cgi/viewcontent.cgi?article=1794&context=faculty.

[29] Uber Technologies, Inc., Form S-1 Registration Statement under the Securities Act of 1933, Filed with the U.S. Securities and Exchange Comm'n, Apr 11, 2019, www.sec.gov/Archives/edgar/data/1543151/000119312519103850/d647752ds1.htm; Alexia Fernández Campbell, "California Is Cracking Down on the Gig Economy," *Vox*, May 30, 2019, www.vox.com/policy-and-politics/2019/5/30/18642535/california-ab5-misclassify-employees-contractors.

[30] Alison Frankel, "3,420 Lyft Drivers Claim the Company Won't Pay Arbitration Fees to Launch Their Cases," *Reuters*, December 14, 2018, www.reuters.com/article/legal-us-otc-lyft/3420-lyft-drivers-claim-the-company-wont-pay-arbitration-fees-to-launch-their-cases-idUSKBN1OD2KC.

[31] Sarah Kessler, "The Gig Economy Won't Last Because It's Being Sued to Death," *Fast Company*, February 17, 2015, www.fastcompany.com/3042248/the-gig-economy-wont-last-because-its-being-sued-to-death.

[32] Josh Eidelson, "U.S. Labor Board Complaint Says On-Demand Cleaners Are Employees," *Bloomberg*, August 30, 2017, www.bloomberg.com/news/articles/2017-08-31/u-s-labor-board-complaint-says-on-demand-cleaners-are-employees.

TABLE 9.1 *Labor standards for employees versus independent contractors*

Labor Right or Protection	Employee	Independent Contractor
Right to organize and bargain collectively	Yes	No
Minimum wage and overtime protections	Yes	No
Access to unemployment insurance	Yes	No
Access to workers' compensation, paid sick days, paid family leave (where available)	Yes	No
Employer contributions to Social Security	Yes	No
Anti-harassment, discrimination protections	Yes	No

TABLE 9.2 *Three phases of carveout policies*

Phase	Timeframe	Scope
Phase I: "transportation network company" carveout policies	2014 to 2017	"Transportation network driver" providing service via "transportation network company"
Phase II: "marketplace contractor" carveout polices	2016 to present	"Qualified marketplace contractor" providing service via "qualified marketplace platform"
Phase III: "uniform worker classification" policies	2019 to present	Any "person" who signs a contract with stipulated provisions

a better business decision? To try to change the law in a way that you think works for your platform, or to make sure your platform fits into the existing law?"[33]

The carveout policy campaigns have proceeded in a few phases. (See Table 9.2.) In the first phase, between 2014 and 2017, TNCs carved themselves out of state labor standards in over twenty-five US states. The TNC carveout campaigns emerged soon after the first publicly disclosed state agency decision finding an Uber driver to be an employee was issued in 2013.[34] In a second phase of carveouts, "marketplace platform companies" including companies offering services beyond transportation convinced legislators to carve them out of labor standards in eight states – in seven states (Arizona, Florida, Indiana, Iowa, Kentucky, Tennessee, and Utah) via the legislature and in one state (Texas) administratively.[35] A third phase of carveouts, led by the

33 Lydia DePillis, "For Gig Economy Workers in These States, Rights Are at Risk," *CNN Money*, March 14, 2018, https://money.cnn.com/2018/03/14/news/economy/handy-gig-economy-workers/index.html.

34 Berwick v. Uber Technologies, Inc., No. 11-46739, 2015 WL 4153765 (CA Labor Commissioner, Department of Industrial Relations, Division of Labor Standards Enforcement, June 4, 2015); Uber, No, 4371509 (California Unemployment Appeals Board, Jun. 1, 2015).

35 Maya Pinto, Rebecca Smith and Irene Tung, *Rights at Risk, Gig Companies' Campaign to Upend Employment as We Know It*, 4–5 (New York: National Employment Law Project, 2019), www.nelp.org/publication/rights-at-risk-gig-companies-campaign-to-upend-employment-as-we-know-it/.

most powerful business lobby group in the US, the American Legislative Exchange Council (ALEC), would rewrite employment standards so that companies operating in any sector can designate their employees to be independent contractors.[36] ALEC's ambitions seem to match those of the gig companies – to create a new paradigm of what work means, relieving many employers of duties to pay payroll taxes or comply with minimum standards. While the model "uniform worker classification" policy acknowledges the growth of the "gig economy" in its preamble, it applies across the board to all workers in every occupation. Bills closely resembling the ALEC model were introduced but did not advance in Missouri and West Virginia in 2019.[37]

9.1.4 *Misleading and Manipulative Messaging*

Tens of millions in venture capital investment dollars have allowed gig companies to pour resources into message development and media outreach supporting their carveout campaigns.[38] Gig companies set up false choices for workers, policymakers, and regulators between employee status and access to benefits and flexible work schedules. And to exert pressure on lawmakers to support carveout policies, Bradley Tusk advises gig companies to raise the specter that their opposition to the policies will label them Luddites thwarting economic progress:[39] "[M]ost politicians don't want to be branded as anti-tech and anti-innovation, so if giving you a win helps them achieve that, you may be in luck."[40]

The founder of gig company Managed by Q, which provides on-demand office management services using employees, explained, "There's a false choice between flexibility and good jobs." Managed by Q employees control their own schedules and receive training and benefits. Employee delivery drivers at gig company Enjoy can select which days of the week they wish to work.[41] Indeed, employee status is compatible with flexible work arrangements. Employee benefits like paid time off – for example, paid family leave, sick time, and vacation - allow workers to balance

36 "Uniform Worker Classification Act," American Legislative Exchange Council (cached webpage August 25, 2018), https://web.archive.org/web/20180825021800/https:/www.alec.org/model-policy/uniform-worker-classification-act/.

37 "An ACT to repeal section 285.500, RSMo, and to enact in lieu thereof two new sections relating to the misclassification of workers," Missouri SB 313, https://legiscan.com/MO/text/SB313/id/1879711; "Uniform Worker Classification Act." West Virginia HB 2786, www.wvlegislature.gov/Bill_Status/bills_text.cfm?billdoc=hb2786%20intr.htm&yr=2019&sesstype=RS&i=2786.

38 Maya Pinto, Rebecca Smith and Irene Tung, *Rights at Risk, Gig Companies' Campaign to Upend Employment as We Know It*, 4–5 (New York: National Employment Law Project, 2019) www.nelp.org/publication/rights-at-risk-gig-companies-campaign-to-upend-employment-as-we-know-it/.

39 Bradley Tusk, *The Fixer: Saving Startups from Death by Politics* (New York: Penguin/Portfolio, 2018).

40 Id.

41 Alana Semuels, "What Happens When Gig-Economy Workers Become Employees," *Atlantic*, September 14, 2018, www.theatlantic.com/technology/archive/2018/09/gig-economy-independent-contractors/570307/.

work and family responsibilities without foregoing pay or putting in overtime. And, employer-funded training and loan support programs facilitate workers' pursuit of education and training.

In states like California, Alabama, and New York, gig companies have sought to deflect attention from the labor standards losses incarveout proposals by including or informally offering lawmakers a small "portable benefits" contribution for gig workers.[42] These private systems would offer workers meager benefits compared to existing social insurance systems that cover employees.[43]

9.2 GIG WORKERS CLAIMING RIGHTS

> I appreciate having the job. I don't begrudge any of these CEOs who have these companies. I don't begrudge you your homes or your cars that you've purchased. But what I do not appreciate is that you are stealing from me. Not only are you taking the food off my plate but you are taking the fork out of my mouth.
>
> – Mia Kelly, Instacart Shopper, Seattle[44]

Through litigation, organizing, and policy advocacy, gig company workers have challenged the labor and employment practices, and public policy efforts of gig companies.

9.2.1 *Worker Claims Challenge Company Practices*

A review of litigation filed in the last several years by workers against just eight gig companies – Uber, Lyft, Handy, DoorDash, Instacart, Postmates, Grubhub, and Amazon – finds that these companies have been sued at least seventy times by workers claiming employee status and state and federal wage violations, tip-stealing, discrimina-

[42] Sarah Kessler, "The Uber of Home-Cleaning Proposed a Law That Would Retroactively Solve Its Legal Issues," *Quartz*, January 13, 2017, https://qz.com/882656/the-uber-of-home-cleaning-proposed-a-law-that-would-retroactively-solve-its-legal-issues/; CA AB-2765, "Employment Benefits: Digital Marketplace: Contractor Benefits," https://leginfo.legislature.ca.gov/faces/billTextClient.xhtml?bill_id=201720180AB2765; AL SB 363, "Portable Benefit Plans Established for Contractors of Market Place Platforms," https://legiscan.com/AL/text/SB363/id/1753340.

[43] Sarah Kessler, "Handy Is Quietly Lobbying State Lawmakers to Declare Its Workers Aren't Employees," *Quartz at Work*, March 30, 2018, https://work.qz.com/1240997/handy-is-tryingto-change-labor-law-in-eight-states/. See, Alabama SB 363, CA AB 2765, Rebecca Smith and Nell Abernathy, "Little Financial Security if 'Gig Economy' Benefits Plan," *Albany Times-Union*, February 27, 2017.

[44] Seattle City Council, Housing, Health, Energy, and Workers' Rights Committee Lunch & Learn, "Discussion with National Academic Experts and Gig Economy Workers," September 3, 2019, Testimony of Mia Kelly, www.seattlechannel.org/mayor-and-council/city-council/city-council-all-videos-index/?videoid=x106801.

tion, and unfair shifting of business costs onto workers.[45] These legal claims filed by workers at online labor platforms operating in multiple sectors allege that the companies wield various forms of control that indicate an employer-employee relationship. Uber alone has been sued in at least thirty-eight instances for improperly classifying its drivers as independent contractors, including two cases pending in federal courts of appeals. Lyft's IPO disclosures to the Securities and Exchange Commission list nine misclassification worker lawsuits, and our review located three additional cases. Handy workers in California, Massachusetts, and Georgia have claimed in five class-action lawsuits that Handy misclassifies them, underpays wages (e.g., off-the-clock, minimum wage, and overtime violations), makes unlawful pay deductions, and fails to offer rest and meal breaks. Grubhub has been sued four times, DoorDash and Instacart three times, Postmates once. Amazon's app-based delivery drivers have also sued the giant at least four times. As noted above, the companies have ensured that no legal precedent can be established by subjecting workers to forced arbitration.

Perhaps because forced arbitration does not bind governmental agency action, workers have seen more successful outcomes by submitting claims to state regulatory agencies. Several state agencies have ruled in workers' favor in matters from unemployment insurance to workers' compensation and wage claims.[46] In Oregon, a Bureau of Labor and Industries policy concluded that Uber drivers are employees for purposes of state workers' compensation and unemployment insurance laws.[47] The Alaska workers' compensation Board entered into a settlement with Uber in 2015 in which Uber agreed not to operate in that state without paying its workers' compensation premiums.[48] In 2017, the Board was overridden by a TNC carveout bill.[49] As noted, Lyft indicated in its IPO filing with the Securities and Exchange Commission that it was under investigation in five states for its failure to pay into social insurance.[50] Uber's filing disclosed that it, too, is being audited in California.[51]

45 Rebecca Smith, *Gig Companies Are Facing Dozens of Lawsuits over Workplace Violations* (New York: National Employment Law Project, 2019), www.nelp.org/publication/gig-companies-facing-dozens-lawsuits-workplace-violations/.

46 *See, e.g.*, Berwick v. Uber Technologies, Inc., No. 11-46739, 2015 WL 4153765 (CA Labor Commissioner, Department of Industrial Relations, Division of Labor Standards Enforcement, Jun. 4, 2015); Uber, No. 4371509 (California Unemployment Appeals Board, Jun. 1, 2015); In the Matter of Uber Technologies Inc., N.Y. Unemployment Ins. Appeal Bd., No. 596722, July 12, 2018. Two additional unfavorable decisions are currently on appeal. In the Matter of Uber Technologies Inc., N.Y. Unemployment Ins. Appeal Bd., No. 596722, July 12, 2018; Lowman v. Unemployment Compensation Board of Review, 178 A.3d 896 (Pa. Commonwealth Ct. 2018).

47 Advisory Opinion on the Employment Status of Uber Drivers, Oregon Bureau of Labor and Industry, October 14, 2015, http://uberlawsuit.com/Oregon.pdf.

48 In the Matter of the Petition for a Finding of the Failure to Insure Workers' Compensation Liability, and Assessment of a Civil Penalty Against, Uber Technologies, Inc. and Raiseri, LLC, Respondents, Alaska Work. Comp.Bd., 2015, 2015 WL 4699265.

49 Alaska AK Stat. 9.65.350 (2017).

50 Lyft, Inc., Form S-1 Registration Statement Under the Securities Act of 1933, filed with the United States Securities and Exchange Commission, March 1, 2019, www.sec.gov/Archives/edgar/data/1759509/000119312519059849/d633517ds1.htm.

51 Uber Technologies, Inc., Form S-1 Registration Statement.

Recently, the New York Court of Appeals found that a Postmates courier, and all those similarly situated, were employees under that state's unemployment insurance law.[52]

9.2.2 *Organizing in the Gig Economy: a Potent Counterweight to Company Claims*

The companies have been doing the organizing work for us, because they see drivers as profit centers, not as people.

– Leonard Smith, Lead Organizer, Teamsters App-Based Driver Association, Seattle[53]

On May 8, 2019, drivers in eight US locations turned off their apps to protest the Uber IPO.[54] Across the country, workers have made similar demands: pressuring gig companies for greater job security, a livable income, more transparency in the ride-hailing companies' fare systems, and a limit on the companies' commissions to guarantee that drivers receive 80 to 85 percent of a fare.[55]

The New York Taxi Workers Alliance (NYTWA) is perhaps the oldest and most effective group bringing attention to the practices of TNCs and the "race to the bottom" that those practices engender for taxi and TNC drivers alike. Since at least 2016, NYTWA has periodically staged strikes to protest the frequent rate cuts that the two major rideshare companies unilaterally impose on drivers.[56] In a telephone interview, Zubin Soleimany told us that the May 2019 strikes, in which NYTWA took a lead role, served two purposes: They disrupted the companies' narrative, and showed that drivers know the work is not economically sustainable. Second, the strikes proved to the companies that workers have the power to coordinate nationally and internationally despite differences in workforces and cities.[57] In Seattle, Leonard Smith agrees that while it is impossible to have a strike in the traditional sense because of turnover, the strikes serve to bring the issue before the public.[58]

52 Matter of Vega, __ NY3d __, 2020 Slip Op 02094 [NY Ct App 2020] www.nycourts.gov/ctapps/Decisions/2020/Mar20/13opn20-Decision.pdf.

53 Leonard Smith, telephone conversation with author, August 1, 2019.

54 Shirin Ghaffary, "The Uber Strike Shows How Drivers Remain One of the Company's Biggest Liabilities," *Vox*, May 7, 2019, www.vox.com/recode/2019/5/7/18528512/uber-driver-strike-gig-economy-labor-dilemma.

55 Faiz Siddiqui, "Uber and Lyft Drivers Strike for Pay Transparency – After Algorithms Made It Harder to Understand," *The Washington Post*, May 8, 2019, www.washingtonpost.com/technology/2019/05/08/uber-lyft-drivers-strike-pay-transparency-after-algorithms-made-it-harder-understand/?utm_term=.fe7109170d70.

56 Sage Lazzaro, "Uber Drivers Plan Boycott After Fare Cuts Slash Their Earnings to Below Minimum Wage," *Observer*, January 19, 2016, https://observer.com/2016/01/uber-drivers-plan-boycott-after-fare-cuts-slash-their-earnings-to-below-minimum-wage/; Rebecca Burns, "The Sharing Economy's 'First Strike': Uber Drivers Turn Off the App," *In These Times*, October 22, 2014, http://inthesetimes.com/working/entry/17279/the_sharing_economy_first_strike_uber_drivers_turn_off_the_app.

57 Zubin Soleimany, telephone conversation with author, July 8, 2019.

58 Leonard Smith, telephone conversation with author, August 1, 2019.

Membership of the National Domestic Workers Alliance (NDWA) includes workers who do app-based home service work,[59] whom the organization has mobilized along with its internal legal and policy expertise to play a key role in defeating marketplace platform bills in California, Colorado, Georgia, and North Carolina. NDWA, which has led ten successful campaigns for domestic workers bills of rights in states and cities around the US, describes the carveout bills as a "low blow for domestic workers: [the] legislation does the very thing NDWA has been fighting against – and repairing – for a decade: stripping workers [of] rights and protections."[60] To complement its policy efforts, NDWA has also created a platform-based application to facilitate voluntary benefits contributions by employers. Their app is called Alia, and it allows employers to contribute to a worker's account, to be used for paid time off or other benefits that a worker might need. According to Mariana Viturro, NDWA's Deputy Director, the organization views Alia as a platform to more widely distribute a system of portable benefits to domestic workers.[61]

In Washington State, the worker center Working Washington has been organizing app-based delivery workers, principally at Instacart, Postmates, and DoorDash, and has garnered 10,000 members in just a few short months.[62] The group has developed an online wage calculator through which workers can piece together pay rates and check them against company promises and labor standards, and it has set up online forums where workers can discuss and share evidence of job quality issues, like screenshots of their pay records, with each other and with delivery-app customers.[63] In an Instacart forum, screenshots showing tip-stealing fomented a worker-consumer campaign that won a company policy change: Instacart no longer deducts tips from promised base pay, and has agreed to repay all workers whose wages had been affected.[64] The group is now leading a Postmates $15 minimum hourly wage campaign.[65] In describing what has made the Working Washington organizing so successful in such a short period of time,

59 National Domestic Worker Alliance, www.domesticworkers.org/jobs.

60 Rocio Avila, Letter to Assemblyman Tony Thurmond regarding CA AB 2765, April 10, 2018.

61 Mariana Viturro, e-mail correspondence with author, October 11, 2019.

62 Seattle City Council Housing, Health, Energy, and Workers' Rights Committee, Testimony of Rachel Lauter.

63 Sean Captain, "Drive for Instacart and You Could Make $29.05 for an Hour's Work – or $2.74," *Fast Company*, February 22, 2019, www.fastcompany.com/90309043/instacart-drivers-say-this-data-proves-theyre-still-being-underpaid.

64 Kevin Roose, "After Uproar, Instacart Backs Off Controversial Tipping Policy," *New York Times*, February 6, 2019, www.nytimes.com/2019/02/06/technology/instacart-DoorDash-tipping-deliveries.html; "Earn Eighty Cents an Hour by Delivering Groceries with Instacart!" Working Washington (post) February 6, 2019, www.workingwa.org/instacart-eighty-cents; Andrew J. Hawkins, "Instacart Revises Controversial Pay Policy After Accusations of Tip Stealing," *The Verge*, February 6, 2019, www.theverge.com/2019/2/6/18214335/instacart-reverse-controversial-pay-policy-tip-stealing; Caroline O'Donovan, "Delivery Startups Are Using Tips to Fulfill Pay Promises, and Customers Are Mad, *BuzzFeed News*, February 5, 2019, www.buzzfeednews.com/article/carolineodonovan/delivery-startups-Are-using-tips-to-fulfill-pay-promises.

65 Megan Rose Dickey, "Postmates Workers Want Minimum Delivery Guarantees and at Least $15 per Hour," *TechCrunch*, May 5, 2019, https://techcrunch.com/2019/05/20/postmates-workers-want-minimum-delivery-guarantees-and-at-least-15-per-hour/.

Executive Director Rachel Lauter credited customer solidarity with workers, a robust media campaign, and online organizing strategies that have facilitated worker information-sharing and public engagement.[66]

9.2.3 *Sectoral Policy Campaigns Deliver Workers' Rights*

9.2.3.1 New York TNCs

New York City has a unique body, the New York City Taxi and Limousine Commission (TLC), established in 1971, with standards-setting jurisdiction over medallion (yellow) taxicabs and other for-hire vehicles and companies including TNCs.[67] In 2018, thanks primarily to organizing and advocacy work by NYTWA (the TLC heard six hours of testimony, largely from its members, on job quality issues like low driver income), New York became the first city in the country to impose minimum pay standards – a $15-equivalent minimum hourly wage of $17.22 – and a cap on the number of licenses issued to TNCs operating in the city.[68]

9.2.3.2 Seattle TNCs

In 2015, the years-long effort of Teamsters Local 117 to organize taxi and TNC drivers in Seattle culminated in an ordinance that afforded these workers the right to collectively bargain with the companies that employ them.[69] Their campaign took place in the context of intense political pressure on the City Council, led by Uber and Lyft, which had forced the Council to back away from an earlier ordinance capping the number of TNC drivers on the road at any time.[70] The ordinance was significant because it rested in part on a theory that TNC drivers are, in fact, independent contractors. Thus, workers argued that they were exempt from the National Labor Relations Act, which covers only "employees," and the city's power to regulate was not preempted by the NLRA. The ordinance was challenged and litigation is ongoing.

At the same time, Mayor Jenny Durkan has announced a new effort, backed by the Teamsters. Her proposal would establish a $0.51 per-ride surcharge on riders, to be used to fund public transit, housing, and a benefit for drivers. It will establish a minimum pay standard for drivers, a Drivers' Resolution Center with a process

66 Rachel Lauter, telephone conversation with author, July 15, 2019.

67 "About TLC," New York Taxi and Limousine Commission, www1.nyc.gov/site/tlc/about/about-tlc.page.

68 Winnie Hu, "Taxi Medallions, Once a Safe Investment, Now Drag Owners into Debt," *New York Times*, September 10, 2017, www.nytimes.com/2017/09/10/nyregion/new-york-taxi-medallions-uber.html?module=inline.

69 Seattle, Wash., SMC 6.31.100, 6.31.735 (2015).

70 Seattle, Wash., Ordinance 124441 (Mar. 19,2014), http://clerk.seattle.gov/~public/meetingrecords/2014/fullcouncil20140707_1.pdf.

for arbitrating deactivations, and, importantly, will not prohibit drivers from claiming employee status under state law.[71]

9.2.3.3 Domestic Work in Multiple Jurisdictions

As the National Domestic Workers Alliance was organizing workers and passing domestic worker bills of rights in several jurisdictions, gig companies were creeping into what had been an off-line business. That meant that NDWA had to consider how the gig company incursion would impact both its organizing strategy and its policy proposals, and it responded with a new twist. In July 2018, NDWA, its local affiliate Casa Latina, and SEIU 775 led a campaign for a Seattle Domestic Worker Bill of Rights. The law covers all domestic workers within the city, including nannies, housekeepers, caregivers, gardeners, and others working in and around a home. The bill of rights extended the city's $15 minimum wage to domestic workers, protects them from discrimination and retaliation, and guarantees them meal and rest breaks. It covers domestic workers whether or not they are technically the "employees" of a householder or other entity, by simply defining "domestic worker" and "hiring entity" and assigning certain responsibilities to the hiring entity. It makes no distinction between platform and other workers.

NDWA plans to build on these successes with a comprehensive national effort. Senator Kirsten Gillibrand (NY) and Representative Pramila Jayapal (WA) have introduced a federal domestic worker bill of rights that will cover both on- and off-line domestic workers: nannies, caregivers, and cleaners.[72]

9.2.4 *Codifying the ABC Test for Employment Status*

In April 2018, the struggle over the classification of all workers, including those in the gig economy, came to a crucial turning point in California. The California Supreme Court decided a case called *Dynamex Operations West, Inc. v. Superior Court of Los Angeles*, Cal.5th 903, 416 P.3d 1 (2018), noted above in Section 9.1.1.5. In that case, involving workers at a package delivery company, the court clarified that the simple and straightforward three-factor "ABC" test should be used to determine whether someone is an employee or independent contractor. The worker is presumed to be an employee, unless the company can prove the worker is (1) free from employer control, (2) performing work outside the regular scope of the business, and (3) independently established in that trade. California Assembly Bill 5, legislation that

[71] City of Seattle, "Mayor Announces Fare Share Plan Including Fair Wages, New Housing Near Transit," September 19, 2019, www.youtube.com/watch?v=aZEw10dSwwM.

[72] Domestic Workers Bill of Rights Act H.R.3760 (116th Cong., 2019), www.congress.gov/bill/116th-congress/house-bill/3760; S. 2112 (116th Cong., 2019), www.congress.gov/bill/116th-congress/senate-bill/2112.

codified the ABC test for wage and hour law in California in 2019, was the most powerful rejoinder yet to the carveout effort that had been sweeping the nation.

The ABC test is a commonly used test for establishing employee status around the country. In addition to California, there are currently three states that use an ABC test to determine employment relationships for all wage and hour laws: Massachusetts, New Jersey, and Vermont. Nine more states use the test for some sectors, typically construction, and more than half of US states use the test in their unemployment insurance laws.[73]

The decision, in the birthplace of the "gig economy," set off an epic battle about worker classification and the labor standards that should apply to app-based work. When the AB 5 legislation was introduced in December 2018, the opposition campaign kicked into high gear. It featured a rash of opinion pieces about the end of entrepreneurship, and a Chamber of Commerce funded "I'm Independent" campaign.[74] In a tactic similar to that used by the TNCs in past efforts, the TNCs used their apps to conscript drivers into lobbying against the bill. Uber's text messages are titled "Protect Drivers' Flexibility,"[75] and "Fight for Driver Flexibility in California." Uber's text includes the following: "Unless lawmakers take action now to modernize the law, you could lose your ability to work with multiple apps and control when and where you drive." Lyft's warns drivers that "Legislators are considering changes that could cause Lyft to limit your hours and flexibility." DoorDash, too, e-mailed its employees to ask them to lobby against the bill.[76]

[73] Del. Code § 3501 (2009); Ill. Compiled. Stat. § 185:10 (2008); 39-A Me. Stat. § 1043 (2011); Md. Code, Labor and Employment § 3-903 (2009); Minn. Stat. § 181.723 (2009); N.J. Stat. § 34:20-4 (2008); Neb. Rev. Stat. § 48-2903 (2010); N.Y. Labor Law § 861-c (2010); 43 Pa. Stat. § 933.3 (2011). States using some form of the ABC test for unemployment insurance are Alaska, AK Stat. 23.20.525(8)(2019); Arkansas, A. C.A §11-10-210(2019); California, Cal. Lab. Code § 2750.3(2019); Colorado, C.R.S.A. §8-70-115(b) (2016); Connecticut, C.G.S.A §31-222(a)(1)(B)(2016); Delaware, 19 Del.C. §3302(10)(K)(2019); Georgia, Ga. Code Ann. §34-8-35(f)(2012); Hawaii, HRS §383-6(2019);); Idaho, I.C. §72-1316(2019); Illinois, 820 I.L.C.S. 405/212((2019); Indiana, Ind. Code §22-4-8-1(2019); Louisiana, LSA-RS §23:1472(12)(E)((2018); Massachusetts, M.G.L.A. 151A §2(2018); Maryland, MD Code, Labor and Employment §3- 903(c)(1)(ii)(2012); Maine, 26 M.R.S.A. § 1043(11)(E)((2019); Montana, MCA 39-51-204(2020); Nebraska, Neb.Rev.St. § 48.604(5)(2017); New Hampshire, N.H. Rev. Stat. § 282-A:9(3)(a)-(c); New Jersey, N.J.S.A § 43:21-19(6)((2019); New Mexico, N.M.S.A. § 51-1-42(F)(5)(2015); Nevada, NRS 612.085(2019); Ohio, RC § 4141.01(2019); Oklahoma, 40 Ok.Stat.Ann § 201(14)(2014); Oregon, ORS 670.600(2017), ORS 657.040(2020); Pennsylvania, 43 PS § 753(l)(B)(2013); Utah, Utah Code Ann. § 35A-4-204(3)(2006); Vermont, 21 V.S.A. § 1301(6)(B); Washington, RCW 50.04.145(2008); and West Virginia. W. Va. Code § 21A.1A.16(7)(1997).

[74] The "I'm Independent" Coalition webpage indicates it is a project of the California Chamber of Commerce, "I'm Independent Coalition," https://imindependent.co.

[75] Melissa Caen, "Uber, Lyft Use Apps to Get Drivers to Oppose Employee Status," *KPIX CBS*, June 16, 2019, https://sanfrancisco.cbslocal.com/2019/06/16/uber-lyft-try-to-stop-proposed-law-that-defines-drivers-as-employees/.

[76] Josh Eidelson, "Gig Firms Ask California to Rescue Them from Court Ruling," *Bloomberg*, August 5, 2018, www.bloomberg.com/news/articles/2018-08-05/gig-firms-ask-california-dems-to-rescue-them-from-court-ruling.

In the end, the companies' tried-and-true method for fighting worker organizing did not deliver for them. AB 5 was approved by California lawmakers on September 11 and signed by Governor Gavin Newsom shortly thereafter.[77]

9.3 GIG COMPANIES' ONGOING ATTEMPTS TO BLOCK WORKERS FROM ASSERTING THEIR RIGHTS

9.3.1 *Litigating to Defend Deregulation*

In many cases where workers have won baseline labor rights, the companies have sued to block them from taking effect. After Seattle passed a collective bargaining ordinance covering transportation workers, including taxis and platform-based drivers, the ordinance was challenged in court in three separate lawsuits, by Uber, Lyft, members of the Uber-financed "Drive Forward" drivers' organization, and the Chamber of Commerce.[78] Eventually, the Ninth Circuit Court of Appeals decided, in 2018, that it violated the federal Sherman Anti-trust Act, and litigation continued.[79] After New York adopted a temporary cap on new TNC vehicles, Uber sued to challenge the cap.[80] After the city passed the minimum driver payment standard mentioned above in Section 9.2.3.1, Juno and Lyft challenged it in court.[81] Their lawsuit was dismissed in May 2019.[82] Less than twenty-four hours after California lawmakers approved AB 5, Uber announced that it would litigate the question of its coverage.[83]

9.3.2 *Policy Efforts to Roll Back AB 5*

On October 29, 2019, Uber, Lyft, and other gig companies filed an initiative to roll back AB 5 and exempt themselves from the law.[84] Uber, Lyft, and DoorDash had

77 CA AB-5 (2019), https://legiscan.com/CA/votes/AB5/2019.

78 Charlotte Garden, "The Seattle Solution: Collective Bargaining by For-Hire Drivers and Prospects for Pro-Labor Federalism," *Harv. Law & Pol'y Review*, 2018, 9, https://harvardlpr.com/wp-content/uploads/sites/20/2018/01/Garden-SeattleSolution.pdf.

79 US Chamber of Commerce of the United States v. Seattle, 890 F.3d 790 (9th Cir. 2018).

80 Andrew J. Hawkins, "Uber Sues to Overturn New York City's Cap on New Ride-hail Drivers, *The Verge*, February 15, 2019, www.theverge.com/2019/2/15/18226599/uber-nyc-driver-cap-lawsuit-de-blasio.

81 Janet Burns, "Lyft, Juno Sue NYC to Block Minimum Pay Rule for Drivers," *Forbes*, January 30, 2019, www.forbes.com/sites/janetwburns/2019/01/30/lyft-and-juno-sue-nyc-to-block-minimum-pay-rules-for-drivers/&146602b857b7.

82 Janet Burns, "Judge Blocks Lyft's Lawsuit Against NYC Ride-hail Rules, *Forbes*, May 7, 2019, www.forbes.com/sites/janetwburns/2019/05/07/nyc-judge-denies-lyft-lawsuit-against-new-ride-hail-rules/&79d952b74150.

83 Carolyn Said, "Uber: We'll Fight in Court to Keep Drivers as Independent Contractors," *San Francisco Chronicle*, September 11, 2019, www.sfchronicle.com/business/article/Uber-We-ll-fight-in-court-to-keep-drivers-as-14432241.php.

84 "Protect App-Based Drivers and Services Act" 19-0026, filed with Attorney General of California October 29, 2019, https://oag.ca.gov/system/files/initiatives/pdfs/19-0026%20%28App-Based%20Drivers%29.pdf.

previously indicated that each had pledged $30 million for the ballot initiative to overturn the law.[85] The initiative represents a continuation of the same strategies the companies have relied on in the past: overcome opposition with a huge campaign war chest and continue to claim that this work is different than other work. Later that day, workers responded: "After working 80-hour weeks, sleeping in our cars and surviving on poverty wages, drivers organized and won support for AB 5 from both the public and lawmakers. Now, instead of obeying the law, Uber, Lyft, and DoorDash want to spend $90 million to avoid accountability—all while claiming it will 'protect' drivers," said Lyft driver Edan Alva.[86] The policy and organizing battle between those who would rewrite the rules and those who resist them is continuing.

9.3.3 *Companies That Use Nonstandard and Contingent Work Arrangements Are Uniting*

In 2019, a new business coalition called the Coalition for Workforce Innovation emerged.[87] This coalition includes many gig, temp and staffing, retail, and other businesses. This new threat illustrates the breadth and depth of the project to rewrite the rules of employment in the country. Its mission is to "modernize" workplace laws and make "independent work" applicable "across all positions, platforms and industries."

9.4 CONCLUSION

In the online labor platform sector, workers and the organizations that represent them are struggling against a well-funded effort by gig companies to rewrite employment standards and prevent worke frrsom accessing employee rights and protections. Efforts to build platform employer accountability are gaining traction across the country, most especially in coastal states like California, New York, and Washington. The policy and organizing battles taking shape in these states will who gets to rewrite the rules of employment in the US.

85 Carolyn Said, "Uber, Lyft, DoorDash May Ask Voters to Keep Drivers as Gig Workers," *San Francisco Chronicle*, August 29, 2019, www.sfchronicle.com/business/article/Uber-Lyft-DoorDash-may-ask-voters-to-keep-14400521.php.

86 Alexia Fernandez Campbell, "Uber and Lyft Have Launched a Campaign to Avoid Government Regulation in California," *Vox*, October 29, 2019, www.vox.com/identities/2019/10/29/20938109/ab5-uber-lyft-ballot-initiative-referendum.

87 Coalition for Workforce Innovation website, https://workforceinnovation.net.

BIBLIOGRAPHY

App-Based Drivers Association. "Uber and Lyft Take More, Pay Drivers Less." Seattle, WA: May 2019, https://d3n8a8pro7vhmx.cloudfront.net/teamsters117/pages/4359/attachments/original/1557327859/Uber_and_Lyft_Take_More__pay_drivers_less_-_ABDA_Report.pdf?1557327859.

Borkholder, Joy, Mariah Montgomery, Miya Saika Chen, and Rebecca Smith, "Uber State Interference: How Transportation Network Companies Buy, Bully, and Bamboozle Their Way to Deregulation." New York: National Employment Law Project and Partnership for Working Families, 2018, 13. www.nelp.org/publication/uber-state-interference/.

Donovan, Sarah A., David H. Bradley, and Jon O. Shimabukuro. "What Does the Gig Economy Mean for Workers?" Washington DC: Congressional Research Service Report R44365, February 5, 2016, 2. https://fas.org/sgp/crs/misc/R44365.pdf.

Garden, C. "Disrupting Work Law: Arbitration in the Gig Economy." *U. Chi. Legal F.*, 2017, 205, https://digitalcommons.law.seattleu.edu/cgi/viewcontent.cgi?article=1794&context=faculty.

Garden, C. (2018). "The Seattle Solution: Collective Bargaining by For-Hire Drivers and Prospects for Pro-Labor Federalism." *Harv. Law & Pol'y Review*, 2018. https://harvardlpr.com/wp-content/uploads/sites/20/2018/01/Garden-SeattleSolution.pdf.

Parrott, James and Michael Reich. "An Earnings Standard for New York City's App-based Drivers." New York: The New School Center for New York City Affairs; Center on Wage and Employment Dynamics, University of California, Berkeley, 2018. www.centernyc.org/an-earnings-standard/.

Pinto, Maya, Rebecca Smith and Irene Tung. "Rights at Risk: Gig Companies' Campaign to Upend Employment as we Know It." New York: National Employment Law Project, 2019. https://s27147.pcdn.co/wp-content/uploads/Rights-at-Risk-4–2-19.pdf.

Rosenblat, Alex, Karen Levy, Solon Barocas and Tim Hwang. "Discriminating Tastes, Customer Ratings as Vehicles for Bias." New York: Data and Society, October 2016. https://datasociety.net/output/discriminating-tastes-customer-ratings-as-vehicles-for-bias/.

Tusk, Bradley. *The Fixer: Saving Startups from Death by Politics*. New York: Penguin/Portfolio, 2018.

Weil, David. *The Fissured Workplace: Why Work Became So Bad for So Many and What Can Be Done to Improve It*. Boston: Harvard College, 2014.

Working Washington. "Delivering Inequality, What Instacart Really Pays, and How the Company Shifts Costs to Workers." Seattle, WA: April 2019. https://payup.wtf/instacart/delivering-inequality.

10

What Regulators Could Gain by Listening to Rideshare Drivers

Harry Campbell

Uber and Lyft have worked hard the past couple years to listen to drivers and improve the experience but they still have a way to go. Regulators on the other hand, are just getting started, but the good news is that they know they need to act. This chapter will lay out exactly why it is so important for regulators to listen to, and understand the lives of the rideshare drivers they are trying to regulate.

When regulators don't listen to drivers, there's a lot that can go wrong. Even a simple policy like enforcing that drivers get their business licenses can have ill-intended effects because although drivers are technically business owners, few drivers treat this like an actual business. The transient nature of the job also means that a driver could cross city lines multiple times in a single day and be required to get business licenses in multiple cities just in order to operate. If drivers were to truly follow the letter of the law, it would be a costly proposition that could prohibit many from signing up and limit work opportunities for the constituents that need this gig the most.

Another misperception happens when regulators look at drivers and the companies they work for like they are playing on the same team. It turns out that could not be further from the truth. Uber may think of themselves as a technology company and call its drivers "partners" but I have never heard a driver refer to themselves as a partner. Uber and Lyft have spent millions of dollars on lobbying while drivers have hardly had a seat at the table. I saw this first hand when I traveled to Austin after Uber and Lyft pulled out of the city over an ordinance that required rideshare drivers to be fingerprinted. There was a fierce battle over this issue but drivers were the ones who suffered the brunt of the damage. Within days of the ordinance passing, Uber and Lyft abruptly stopped services, leaving passengers stranded and drivers without a job. Again, regulators failed to listen to drivers, but if they had, they would have found out that most drivers were actually for fingerprinting since it made them seem safer, but more importantly, it limited competition. This example will highlight that while it's important to consider driver's viewpoints, they are just one piece of the puzzle.

Uber and Lyft have run into issues with insurance over the years because they have always looked to provide the bare minimum coverage to their drivers. In almost every state, regulators have failed to close the Period 1 gap, which allows Uber to provide no collision coverage when a driver is online but without a fare. Even though Uber provides coverage once a trip is accepted and a driver is with a passenger, this gap means that drivers have to purchase a special type of insurance called rideshare insurance in order to be fully covered. And as you might imagine, most drivers don't – either because they're unaware or the cost is too expensive. Uber and Lyft are well aware of this but they know that they can save some money by not providing full coverage during Period 1 and letting drivers handle or not handle this cost. If regulators were to talk to drivers, they would quickly learn that many drivers don't have rideshare insurance because they either don't know they need it or they know they need it, but just can't afford it. It would be much better and smoother for all to require Uber and Lyft to extend coverage during this period so drivers are fully protected.

Finally, I will touch on the most important issue for drivers – low wages. This is something that comes up time and time again in my conversations with drivers and it is a big reason for Uber and Lyft's abysmal retention rate. Two-thirds of all drivers quit within six months and for almost all of them, it's because the pay just isn't enough.[1] When drivers are treated as independent contractors, there's no minimum wage or worker protections like an employee would get and there are some drivers who end up earning less than minimum wage through no fault of their own. But this is an issue where regulators can have a real impact and in fact, we are already seeing movement from cities like New York that have instituted a minimum pay for rideshare drivers and states like California that have passed Assembly Bill 5 which aims to codify law that would require Uber and Lyft to classify their drivers as employees.[2]

10.1 BACKGROUND

I started driving for Uber and Lyft in 2014 part-time and like many rideshare drivers, what attracted me early on was the flexibility and earnings potential. At the time, I was working full-time as an aerospace engineer for Boeing but on nights and weekends, I hit the road as an Uber and Lyft driver. It was nerve-racking the first time I tapped the accept button and ferried my first passenger from the library at a local college to the dorms nearby but it was also an exhilarating experience, and frankly one that never gets old.

1 "Wage Gap Study Reveals a Lot About Driving for Uber," *The Rideshare Guy*, last modified February 21, 2018, https://therideshareguy.com/wage-gap-study-reveals-a-lot-about-driving-for-uber/.

2 "New York Sets Nation's First Minimum Wage for Uber, Lyft Drivers," *Bloomberg*, last modified December 4, 2018, www.bloomberg.com/news/articles/2018-12-04/new-york-sets-nation-s-first-minimum-wage-for-uber-lyft-drivers.

I quickly learned that driving for Uber and Lyft was not rocket science, but it also was not as easy as it seemed. Driving for hire is the ultimate combination of customer service, safe driving and navigation, and running a business. Most people figure out the first two pretty easily but it is the "running the business" part that seems to trip a lot of drivers up.

During my first few months as a driver, I had a lot of questions but unlike my day job in a cubicle, there was no one whom I could turn to for help. Uber and Lyft's customer support was comically poor and their responses often made you wonder whether there was a real human on the other end or just a robot sending canned responses. My "coworkers" were aplenty but they were scattered all over the city in their own vehicles. So I started looking online for drivers to chat with and began to document my experience as a driver on my blog called *The Rideshare Guy*. I wrote about everything from getting signed up and started with these services to finding ways to maximize profits and do your taxes as an independent contractor. And of course, I talked about all the crazy stuff that happens in-between midnight and 3 am on a Saturday night in Newport Beach.

Over the years, that blog has grown into a multimedia business that now reaches hundreds of thousands of drivers a month and offers videos, podcasts, an online course and even a book to aspiring drivers and other workers in the gig economy.[3] I estimate that I've personally had the pleasure of speaking with over 50,000 drivers over the years via e-mail, in person, on the phone, and over social media.

After a couple years of driving part-time, I quit my day job to work on my blog full-time. I've never been a full-time driver and these days I consider myself more of a blogger than an active driver but I have personally tried out gigs ranging from driving for Uber and Lyft to delivering food with Postmates and DoorDash and even charging scooters for Bird. This first-hand experience has taught me a lot about these services but it's not the same as what you would get from actually driving, day in and day out. So instead of relying on just personal experience, I'm also able to listen and collate the experience of tens of thousands of drivers on various issues.

One of the unique things about the rideshare industry is that there is no typical driver. Depending on who you are talking to, there is a ton of variability when it comes to age, background, and even pay. A part-time driver may love driving for Uber since they can work whenever and wherever they want and don't rely on the income. But a full-time driver is putting in forty to fifty hours a week and does not get to enjoy the same type of scheduling flexibility. So the latter is effectively working like a full-time employee but without any of the worker protections. Is it any wonder that these types of drivers want to be classified as employees for Uber and Lyft?

The best way to describe my role though is as that of a middle man. My business is catered toward supporting and providing resources for drivers but the blog has also

[3] Harry Campbell, *The Rideshare Guide: Everything You Need to Know About Driving for Uber, Lyft, and Other Ridesharing Companies* (Skyhorse, 2018), www.amazon.com/Rideshare-Guide-Everything-Ridesharing-Companies/dp/1510735313.

given me access to many of the people working at the actual rideshare companies, investors, regulators, and companies looking to develop new products and services for drivers. In fact, I may be the only person who's ever driven for Uber and also had the opportunity to interview their CEO, as I did at a driver event in Los Angeles in early 2018.[4]

So I've been able to develop an institutional knowledge of how these services work through participation and observation. Getting into this industry at the ground floor may have been due to luck but it also puts me in the unique position of historian since I have studied the industry full-time for nearly its entire existence. During that time:

- Uber and Lyft have garnered a tremendous amount of media attention and I've been a trusted media source for thousands of stories.[5]
- The products, rules, and regulations have changed immensely since the companies were founded and we've covered that evolution and its impact on the industry.
- I've covered the industry from the driver's and worker's perspective which gives me unique insight into how these companies operate.

Through most of Uber and Lyft's history, rideshare drivers have not had a voice in the regulatory process and it's led to bad policies and outcomes. Unlike Uber and Lyft, who are massive multibillion dollar companies with hundreds of public policy employees and lobbyists at the ready, drivers are relatively underpaid and just don't have the time to go lobby for their causes. Regulators have failed to understand this most basic dynamic and may be missing out on a key perspective.

Over the past couple of years, we have seen a wave of organizing efforts in the driver community take place. Starting with the Independent Drivers Guild (IDG) in New York City and now in California, there are groups like Rideshare Drivers United and Gig Workers Rising who lead the effort in favor of AB5. So if regulators won't come to drivers, you can bet these groups will start to make drivers' demands be heard.

10.2 WHAT CAN GO WRONG WHEN REGULATORS DON'T LISTEN TO DRIVERS

In 2016, the city of San Francisco started enforcing a business license requirement on the city's 37,000 Uber and Lyft drivers.[6] The license would cost drivers $91 a year

4 "Recap of My Live Q&A with Uber CEO Dara Khosrowshahi," *The Rideshare Guy*, last modified April 13, 2018, https://therideshareguy.com/recap-of-my-live-qa-with-uber-ceo-dara-khosrowshahi/.

5 "The Rideshare Guy in The Media," *The Rideshare Guy*, accessed October 16, 2019, https://therideshareguy.com/rideshare-guy-around-the-web/.

6 "SF to require Lyft, Uber drivers to obtain business licenses," *SFGATE*, last modified April 15, 2016, www.sfgate.com/bayarea/article/SF-to-require-Lyft-Uber-drivers-to-obtain-7250137.php.

if they earned $100,000 or less in gross receipts. The requirements seems reasonable in theory but in reality, a Bay Area rideshare driver could pick-up and drop-off passengers in San Francisco, Oakland, and San Jose, and that's all in just one day!

Not to mention the privacy issues related to this business license requirement since all registered businesses are searchable on the city's website. That means that for every transportation network company (TNC) driver who operates a business out of their car, their home address would have to be listed as the business' address on the government website even though they're not operating their business out of their home.

This shouldn't be a debate over whether a business license is a reasonable requirement or not though. Let's assume that we all agree, business owners should all have business licenses. The problem is that most Uber and Lyft drivers may not even realize they are running a business. You are allowed to sign up and drive for Uber without registering for a business license so a lot of drivers reasonably assume that one is not necessary.

In this situation, regulators are punishing the symptom but failing to address or even understand the root cause. Uber likes to shift a lot of the risk and liability onto their contractors by using marketing slogans like, "Uber partners with entrepreneurial drivers and as independent contractors, they are responsible for following appropriate local requirements."[7] In reality, drivers have no idea of the local requirements until they get hit in the mail with a huge bill from the city for three years of unpaid business license fees and penalties.

If regulators would have talked to even one Bay Area driver about this issue, they would have quickly learned that they were imposing a ridiculous requirement on drivers. Fortunately though, in California at least, SB-182 was eventually passed in 2017 which stated that, "Any local jurisdiction that requires a driver to obtain a business license to operate as a driver for a transportation network company may only require that driver to obtain a single business license, regardless of the number of local jurisdictions in which the driver operates."[8]

Drivers in California can now operate freely and are only required to get a single business license in the city in which they operate even if they're driving across multiple cities. This type of regulation makes sense but most drivers are still left unaware that they need a business license in the first place because it's not part of the Uber and Lyft application process. In 2016, I heard from dozens of drivers who were receiving bills in the mail for hundreds of dollars in owed fees and penalties because

7 "Uber, Lyft Drivers Need Business Licenses to Operate in San Francisco," *The Wall Street Journal*, last modified April 15, 2016, www.wsj.com/articles/uber-lyft-drivers-need-business-licenses-to-operate-in-san-francisco-1460762952.

8 "SB-182 Transportation network company: participating drivers: single business license," California Legislative Information, accessed October 16, 2019, https://leginfo.legislature.ca.gov/faces/billTextClient.xhtml?bill_id=201720180SB182.

they never paid for a business license. But almost all of them had no idea it was even required.

Cities are punishing drivers but if they were serious about enforcing this issue, they should look to the California Public Utilities Commission (CPUC) which regulates TNCs and ask them to make it a part of Uber and Lyft's application process. That shifts the onus on to the companies to fight with regulators and decide whether a certain fee is fair or not instead of levying fees and fines onto drivers who just don't know any better.

10.3 WHY REGULATORS NEED TO UNDERSTAND THE DYNAMIC BETWEEN DRIVERS AND RIDESHARE COMPANIES

It is pretty easy to get signed up as an Uber or Lyft driver and I often joke that all you need is an eligible vehicle and a pulse. But there is a reason why it is so easy and that stems from the fact that drivers are the limiting factor to growth in the rideshare business. Since retention is so poor, the easier it is to sign up drivers and get them approved, the more these companies can grow and keep their marketplace of riders and drivers in balance.

Uber and Lyft currently run an online background check on prospective drivers but there are no fingerprint-based background checks like there are with taxi drivers (except in NYC). There has been a lot of debate over the years whether fingerprint background checks are indeed safer but many new drivers like the current process since there's a low barrier to entry which makes it easy to "try it out." When I first signed up to drive with Lyft all the way back in 2014, I did it from the comfort of my couch. But I do not know if I would have signed up if I had to go into some DMV-like government office and submit a fingerprint or pee into a cup. Now for me, it was just some extra income but for others, it could be the difference between putting food on the table or having enough money for rent.

In 2016, Austin, Texas became one of the first cities in the US to pass legislation that required all rideshare drivers in the city to be fingerprinted.[9] But Uber and Lyft were so opposed to this outcome that rather than comply, they actually pulled out of the city with almost no notice and thousands of drivers were without a job and a way to earn income for their families overnight.

I traveled to Austin in the weeks after the pull-out to meet with drivers, regulators, and folks in the industry to learn more about the situation.[10] It turned out that a lot of the drivers I talked to were actually in favor of fingerprinting, but not for all the

9 "What's next for Uber, Lyft and Austin's fingerprint check ordinance?," *Statesman*, accessed October 16, 2019, www.statesman.com/news/20160904/whats-next-for-uber-lyft-and-austins-fingerprint-check-ordinance.

10 "RSG Special Report: How's Austin Doing Without Uber and Lyft?," *The Rideshare Guy*, last modified June 8, 2016, https://therideshareguy.com/rsg-special-report-hows-austin-doing-without-uber-and-lyft/.

reasons you might think. Drivers liked the idea because it would show to the public and to their passengers that rideshare was safe. But they also liked the law because it would limit competition and make it tougher for new drivers to sign up. Since drivers are only paid when they have a passenger in the car, they want as many trips as possible in a given shift. From a driver's perspective, if there are less new drivers signing up, that means more rides for them. The marketplace is nowhere near this simplistic but many drivers see it this way. So while fingerprinting may have been good for their pocketbook, it may not have been the best thing for all constituents.

In Austin, the regulators opposing Uber and Lyft were solely focused on safety or at least their perception that fingerprint-based background checks were safer than online name-based background checks. But there was also a concerted push for fingerprint-based checks by local taxi owners and operators. And while Uber and Lyft publicly stated they felt online checks were just as safe, their real motivation was to keep the sign-up process as burden-free as possible for new drivers.

So while all sides had ulterior motives, this issue highlights the inherent tension between TNCs and its drivers – drivers want as few drivers on the road as possible and TNCs want as many drivers on the road as possible. In this case, if regulators would have listened to drivers, they may have realized that drivers supported their cause but mainly for the wrong reasons.

Uber and Lyft ended up going around the local Austin city regulations and getting statewide TNC-friendly legislation passed that allowed them to continue using online-based background checks. But the input of drivers was never even taken into consideration and to this day, many drivers complain of oversaturation since the companies have no disincentives to flood a market with drivers. When Uber and Lyft pulled out of Austin, drivers lost a lot of money and turned to Facebook Groups like "Arcade City" to facilitate thousands of illegal rides for cash and booked directly with drivers. It turns out that you can't just shut demand off like a faucet.

As we will see throughout this chapter, drivers have all too often been ignored when it comes to policy decisions but just like Uber and Lyft, when given free reign, their motivations can be quite self-serving too. It's important to balance the input of each party: Uber/Lyft, regulators, passengers, and drivers, in order to come up with the best policy.

In this case, it doesn't have to be one or the other though. In fact, around the same time, Austin's neighbor to the south, San Antonio, had gotten into a similar tussle with Uber and the two parties eventually agreed on a compromise that would give drivers the option to get fingerprinted which would earn them a special certification from the San Antonio Police Department on their driver profiles.[11] So brand new drivers wouldn't be stifled by archaic fingerprinting requirements and passengers could see whether their driver had gone through additional screening or not.

[11] "Uber's Siege on San Antonio," *Slate*, last modified October 16, 2015, https://slate.com/business/2015/10/uber-returns-to-san-antonio-after-throwing-a-massive-tantrum-over-regulations.html.

This solution never ended up gaining much traction but I think it makes a lot of sense. If passengers prefer riding with a driver who has been fingerprinted, and don't mind the potential extra wait time, they could have that option. The city of San Antonio didn't require Uber and Lyft to give passengers an option to only get rides from drivers who had been fingerprinted but I think that would have been smart.

What regulators in Austin missed in this case was that drivers were divided on this issue. New and potential drivers valued being able to get signed up and started without the hassle of getting fingerprinted but experienced drivers liked the idea of fingerprint-based checks because they were already in and it would lock out new drivers.

These days, Uber even lets passengers select whether the driver can talk to them or not with UberQuiet mode, so why not give them the option to select a driver who has been fingerprinted? And who knows – maybe they will even charge riders more for this feature and share the love with their drivers . . . I mean, partners.

10.4 WHAT ELSE CAN GO WRONG? SHIFTING OF RISK AND LIABILITY

As I dove head first into the gig economy and started talking to drivers, I realized just how many were treating this casually instead of understanding and accepting the reality that they were now running a business. As mentioned, Uber and Lyft only require new drivers to pass an online background check and a vehicle inspection (in most states) but rideshare insurance is a product that really should also be required.

TNCs and regulators will allow drivers to sign up with personal insurance but almost every insurance carrier has had a livery exclusion on their policy from day one. So if personal insurance carriers were to find out that you were driving for rideshare, you would be dropped from your insurance plan or worse, if you got into an accident and they found out, you could have your coverage denied. Insurance companies take this matter so seriously, many of them now ask this as part of their standard screening process when reviewing an accident claim for all of their customers.

The rideshare insurance issue doesn't come up often since Uber and Lyft provide commercial insurance when you're en route to pick up a rider (Period 2) or on a trip (Period 3). But when you're parked on the side of the road or driving around looking for a fare (Period 1), TNCs actually provide no collision coverage and state minimum liability limits.

Rideshare insurance is a separate personal insurance policy now offered by most of the major carriers in almost every state but since it is not required, most drivers sign up without it and it is not until they get into an accident during Period 1 that they realize they need it.[13]

[13] "Rideshare Insurance – Best Options for Uber & Lyft (By State)," *The Rideshare Guy*, last modified October 8, 2019, https://therideshareguy.com/rideshare-insurance-options-for-drivers/.

I would not have a problem with this setup if it were not for the fact that so many drivers have no idea they are not covered until it is too late. I can recall conversations with drivers where they were shocked to find out that companies worth tens of billions of dollars did not provide adequate insurance, and I don't blame them. It should be a safe assumption that you are covered at all times but since regulators don't understand the different periods, they don't require it from Uber and Lyft.

As you might imagine, Uber and Lyft don't exactly make drivers aware of this at any point in the onboarding process either. In fact, they take it one step further with their $1,000 and $2,500, respectively, collision deductibles. Drivers who get into accidents during Periods 2 and 3 are often shocked to find out how high these deductibles are, and Lyft's is especially alarming. A full-time driver would be lucky to earn $15–20 per hour so a $2,500 deductible means that a driver would have to work 143 hours at $17.50 per hour in order to cover a single deductible, whether they're at fault for the accident or not.

All too often, it seems like Uber and Lyft are able to satisfy regulators' policies but at the expense of shifting added risk or liability onto drivers. You can bet that Uber and Lyft are well aware of the local regulator's insurance requirements but drivers not so much. An entire industry and product line had to be created simply because regulators never closed this Period 1 loophole. If they simply required Uber to extend the same commercial insurance during Periods 2 and 3 to Period 1, these problems would all go away. If Uber and Lyft required companies to have no more than a $500 or $1,000 deductible (or to match their personal deductibles), then drivers would not be financially ruined should they get into an accident.

What is interesting though is that when Uber and Lyft sign up new drivers for one of their vehicle leasing or rental programs, they do require them to get rideshare insurance. So when the TNCs own the cars, they want to make sure they are fully covered. But when it comes to drivers, they are on their own.

What regulators are missing here is that TNCs are perfectly happy to enforce rules or grant benefits to drivers when it works to the companies' advantage, but argue that it would destroy their business models to do exactly the same thing when the government asks them to.

10.5 WHAT DO DRIVERS CARE MOST ABOUT AND WHAT CAN THE GOVERNMENT DO TO HELP?

The complaint of low wages is not unique to rideshare drivers. Everybody wants to make more money but at a macro-level, the trend we have seen in the rideshare industry is that Uber and Lyft have continually lowered rates over the years, and thus driver pay, and made driving less flexible. It is now cheaper than ever to hail a ride which also means that drivers are getting paid less than ever. And while both companies may need to raise prices eventually to improve their profitability, there's no guarantee that they'll share that extra revenue with drivers. In fact, they're already doing the opposite as the company's take rate has steadily been increasing over the years.

With Uber and Lyft at the helm and in charge of pricing, drivers have become vastly underpaid. But the solution doesn't entail giving drivers free reign over setting prices, that could lead to them pricing themselves out of the market and less transportation options for everyone. Uber is a marketplace after all and an elastic one at that. When you increase prices and keep the number of drivers constant, there will be less rides to go around.

Many drivers end up quitting because of the low pay but there are others who may not have the option. Both companies tout the flexibility of rideshare driving but when you're driving thirty to fifty hours a week, there are only so many hours in the day to work. Drivers have no say when it comes to setting rates and companies often cut rates without any notice.[14] Over the years, I've seen this happen countless times and unfortunately there's not a lot that drivers can do. As a result of rate cuts, many drivers put in less hours or quit altogether but Uber and Lyft know that for every driver who quits, they can replace them with another.

As rates have come down, Uber and Lyft have also instituted a series of weekly driver incentives which aim to boost pay but allow the companies to have more control over when and where drivers drive. In short, the pay has gotten much worse for drivers over the years and the job has gotten less flexible. Since there is also a lot of variability in earnings, some drivers on the left side of the curve even report earning less than minimum wage.

This is an issue where cities are starting to take notice, but mainly because of driver organizations like the IDG that are making them pay attention. In early 2019, New York City passed the nation's first minimum wage for ridesharing drivers, guaranteeing a minimum wage of at least $17.22 per hour after expenses. Because Uber and Lyft care first and foremost about low request times for their passengers, they have been incentivized over the years to flood the market with drivers. The NYC legislation aimed to curb that by capping the number of drivers and requiring pay based on the utilization of drivers. So drivers will be guaranteed the pay rate even during slow periods, incentivizing companies to keep drivers busy.

Whenever I talk to drivers about pay, their solution to the issue is often to just raise rates. But if you gave drivers free reign to set prices, they might just price themselves out of the market. The problem is that up until now, Uber and Lyft have been given the keys to pricing and they've gone too far in the other

[14] "Los Angeles Uber Driver Pay Cuts: Why Are Drivers Striking?," *The Rideshare Guy*, last modified March 27, 2019, https://therideshareguy.com/ubers-new-rates-la-strike/.

direction. Regulators have adeptly stepped in in this case and listened to the issues of drivers: oversaturation of drivers and low pay. The solution they came up with is the perfect compromise since it allows them to maintain a minimum wage but also one that is based on utilization. NYC is the leading transportation market in the world and we are already starting to see other cities follow in their footsteps and consider similar legislation.

But we know that Uber and Lyft won't go down without a fight. Regulators need to understand that Uber and Lyft rarely back down from a fight and when they think they're right, they rarely stop unless they've won, as we saw in Austin for example. In New York City, Uber and Lyft have already retaliated against the minimum wage rules by no longer allowing drivers to go online in less busy areas. This makes sense from the company's perspective since they don't want to have to pay drivers who are sitting there not working. In this case, the city listened to driver's demands but they need to understand that there are trade-offs. You can force these companies to pay drivers more, but you need to be ready to counter their changes or accept the trade-offs.

In California, regulators have worked with driver organizing groups to push forward AB5, which would codify into law an existing ruling making rideshare drivers employees. But a majority of drivers I have spoken with don't want to be employees, since for all of Uber and Lyft's faults, they value the flexibility that rideshare affords them. If Uber and Lyft are already imposing certain restrictions because of minimum wage rules in New York City, you can bet that they will push back hard on full-blown employees.

This may be the toughest issue of all for regulators to sort out but it starts with talking to drivers and understanding the things that all drivers have in common. All drivers want to make more but not all want to become employees to do so.

10.6 CONCLUSION

We all know how to drive so I don't blame regulators for thinking that they understand what it's like to be an Uber or Lyft driver. But as I've shown in this chapter, driving for hire is a lot tougher than it seems.

There are a number of steps that regulators can take to fix erroneous regulations and prevent future errors. Talking to drivers and just understanding the reality of the lives they face on a daily basis could easily solve issues like what we saw with the business licenses in San Francisco. The relationship between TNCs and their drivers is more complex but understanding that the two sides are not on the same team, like we saw in Austin, helps regulators to weigh input from all sides.

Often, regulators have good intentions, like with insurance and protecting the public, but they don't go far enough. Requiring Uber and Lyft to extend their commercial insurance coverage to Period 1 would solve a lot of problems for drivers. Finally, regulators can have a big impact on pay but it's important to understand if their actions are helping all drivers or just some. New York City's legislation for minimum pay was well received by all but not every driver in California wants to become an employee. Only time will tell if regulators have made the right decision.

Index

Lightning Source UK Ltd.
Milton Keynes UK
UKHW022151061120
372964UK00002B/37

9 781108 487764